Modern Hatreds

Cornell Studies in Security Affairs

edited by

Robert J. Art

Robert Jervis

Stephen M. Walt

A list of titles in this series is available at www.cornellpress.cornell.edu.

Modern Hatreds

The Symbolic Politics of Ethnic War

Stuart J. Kaufman

Cornell University Press

Ithaca and London

First published 2001 by Cornell University Press
First printing, Cornell Paperbacks, 2001

Printed in the United States of America

Library of Congress Cataloging-in-Publication Data

Kaufman, Stuart J.
Modern hatreds : the symbolic politics of ethnic war / Stuart J. Kaufman.
p. cm. — (Cornell studies in security affairs)
Includes bibliographical references and index.
ISBN 978-0-8014-8736-1 (pbk. : alk. paper)
1. Europe, Eastern—Ethnic relations—Political aspects. 2. Europe, Eastern—Politics and government—1989–. 3. Caucasus—Ethnic relations. 4. Caucasus—Politics and government. 5. Atrocities—Europe, Eastern. I. Title. II. Series.
DJK51 .K38 2001
947'.0009'049—dc21 2001001668

Cornell University Press strives to use environmentally responsible suppliers and materials to the fullest extent possible in the publishing of its books. Such materials include vegetable-based, low-VOC inks and acid-free papers that are recycled, totally chlorine-free, or partly composed of nonwood fibers. For further information, visit our website at www.cornellpress.cornell.edu.

Paperback printing 10 9 8 7 6 5 4 3

The Seven Rules of Nationalism:

A Beginner's Guide to Ethnic Politics

1. *If an area was ours for 500 years and yours for 50 years, it should belong to us—you are merely occupiers.*
2. *If an area was yours for 500 years and ours for 50 years, it should belong to us—borders must not be changed.*
3. *If an area belonged to us 500 years ago but never since then, it should belong to us—it is the Cradle of our Nation.*
4. *If a majority of our people live there, it must belong to us—they must enjoy the right of self-determination.*
5. *If a minority of our people live there, it must belong to us—they must be protected against your oppression.*
6. *All of the above rules apply to us but not to you.*
7. *Our dream of greatness is Historical Necessity, yours is Fascism.*

—*Unknown*

Contents

Acknowledgments

I thank the United States Institute of Peace and the Smith Richardson Foundation for the generous funding that made this project possible. I also received additional, much-appreciated financial support from the University of Kentucky, the International Research and Exchanges Board (IREX), the Kennan Institute, and the Council on Foreign Relations. Earlier versions of Chapters 5 and 6 were published, respectively, as "Spiraling to Ethnic War: Elites, Masses, and Moscow in Moldova's Civil War," *International Security* 21, no. 2 (Fall 1996): 108–38; and "The Irresistible Force and the Imperceptible Object: The Yugoslav Breakup and Western Policy," *Security Studies* 4, no. 2 (Winter 1994/95): 281–329.

My intellectual debts are too many to be fully acknowledged, but I particularly thank Matthew Evangelista, Patrick James, Robert Jervis, Karen Mingst, Stephen Saideman, and Jack Snyder, who read all or most of the manuscript and gave valuable comments. I also owe thanks to Catherine Dale, David Darchiashvili, Stephen Jones, George Khutsishvili, Ghia Nodia, and Ronald Suny, from whom I learned so much about the Caucasus; to the personnel of UNOMIG, who helped me reach Abkhazia; to Liana Kvarchelia and Paula Garb, who also helped with my Abkhazia trip; and to Guram Svanidze, who helped me reach South Ossetia. I am also grateful to Stephen Bowers, Jeff Chinn, William Crowther, Nicholas Dima, Charles King, Pal Kolsto, Vasile Nedelciuc, and Steven Roper, valuable and valued colleagues in the study of Moldova; and Benjamin Frankel, Sean Lynn-Jones, Obrad Kesic, Dennison Rusinow, Howard Warshawsky, and William Zimmerman for their ideas and suggestions on the Yugoslavia chapter. Much-appreciated help also came from Airat Aklaev, Roy Allison, Douglas Blum, Charles Davis, Renee De Nevers, Michael Desch, Leokadia Drobizheva,

[1]

Stories about Ethnic War

Beginning in the spring of 1992, Bosnia experienced an ethnic slaughter whose savagery replayed some of the worst horrors of the Nazi era. Serbian paramilitary forces swept into defenseless towns, murdering indiscriminately in order to terrorize the Bosnian Muslim population into fleeing. In some cases, the killers set up ambushes and machine-gunned their victims in flight. In other cases, they rounded up the population, singled out educated men for murder, shipped the remaining men to concentration camps, and expelled the women and children. Women were often gang-raped; the men typically beaten and tortured before being killed or imprisoned. While the perpetrators of these acts were usually outsiders, local Serbs also participated, shipping their neighbors to concentration camps and identifying their acquaintances on the executioners' lists.

In the concentration camps, the horrors were even worse. According to one account:

> Humiliation, terror and mental cruelty were almost universally deployed. Captured men would be told that they were to be executed the following day. At dawn they would be taken out, convinced that they were to be killed, only to be thrown into a new detention camp. They were forced to sing Serb nationalist songs to entertain their jeering tormentors, and to avoid being beaten. They were told that their wives had been raped and then killed, that their children were dead. They were forced, on pain of death, to perform atrocities against each other—mutilation, physical and sexual, and, even, mutual killing. They were forced to dig mass graves and collect and bury the bodies of their families and neighbors. Sometimes, those on grave detail would themselves be killed and thrown on top of the bodies they had just delivered.[1]

In other cases, it was the guards who mutilated and tortured prisoners to death.[2]

Such events cry out for explanation. What could motivate the leaders of a nation to organize the expulsion, torture, rape, and murder of a large portion of their country's inhabitants? What could motivate their followers to sink to such savagery, often aimed against their own lifelong neighbors? The purpose of this book is to answer that question—to develop a theory to explain why ethnic wars occur and how they might be prevented.

Bosnia is, of course, an extreme case, but it is not unique. Three of the four ethnic wars examined in this book also featured ethnic cleansing, atrocities, and massacres of civilians, albeit on a smaller scale. I open this book with a reminder of Bosnia's horrors to make the point that no account of ethnic war is adequate which does not explain how such things can happen. How do leaders capable of ordering such savagery come to power? What makes them decide to give such orders? What motivates their followers to carry them out? And most difficult of all, how can we devise an explanation that accords with the facts not only in Bosnia but in other ethnic wars as well?

A number of explanations or stories about ethnic war have been offered. Many of them can be summed up in a simple phrase: ancient hatreds; manipulative leaders; economic rivalry; and so on. The argument of this book is that an adequate theory of ethnic war must combine the insights from all of these approaches to explain why ethnic war happens when it does and—just as important—to explain why it usually does not happen. A saying has it that to every complicated question there is at least one simple, direct, easy-to-understand wrong answer: the simple stories about ethnic war are, individually, wrong answers of this overly simplified type. The mistakes are important because, even though the stories are insightful, they too frequently lead to mistaken policy conclusions about how ethnic wars might be stopped. The second purpose of this book, therefore, is to show how an enhanced understanding of the driving forces behind ethnic wars can lead to better ideas about how to avoid or stop them.

I begin by surveying the stories analysts have told about the conflict in Yugoslavia, since these stories span the gamut of explanations of ethnic war generally. The narratives differ in fundamental ways: in their accounts of the nature of ethnic groups, in their contentions about what spurs the groups to fight, and in their evaluations of who is to blame and what can be done about such conflicts. Understanding the different assumptions is the first step toward combining the insights conveyed by each story into a more comprehensive explanation.

Stories about Ethnic War

ancient hatreds

One of the stories most favored by journalists to explain ethnic wars is that they are the result of "ancient hatreds" or long-standing bitterness. Journalist Robert Kaplan is the most prominent teller of this story, writing of the Balkans: "This was a time-capsule world: a dim stage upon which people raged, spilled blood, experienced visions and ecstasies. Yet their expressions remained fixed and distant, like dusty statuary. 'Here, we are completely submerged under our own histories,' Luben Gotzev, Bulgaria's former Foreign Minister, told me."[3] On Bosnia, specifically, Kaplan adds: "Bosnia is rural, isolated, and full of suspicions and hatreds to a degree that the sophisticated Croats of Zagreb could barely imagine.... Bosnia did have one sophisticated urban center, however; Sarajevo, where Croats, Serbs, Muslims and Jews had traditionally lived together in reasonable harmony. But the villages all around were full of savage hatreds, leavened by poverty and alcoholism. The fact that the most horrifying violence—during both World War II and the 1990s—occurred in Bosnia was no accident."[4]

There is much here that is insightful. The attention to rage, suspicion, and hatred is necessary to understand the ethnic cleansing, mass murders, and other atrocities that visited the region in the 1990s. Although the bloodless conventions of social science make it simpler for academics to sweep such messy emotions aside when building their theories, those who visit the region find it impossible to explain what they find without reference to emotions.

The most discerning of the journalists also note the curious defensive justifications participants use to rationalize their brutality. Thus Reuters correspondent Andrej Gustincic, on the start of war in Bosnia:

> "Do you see that field?" asks a Serbian woman, pointing to a sloping meadow by the Drina river. "The jihad (Moslem Holy War) was supposed to begin there. Foca was going to be the new Mecca. There were lists of Serbs who were marked down for death," the woman says, repeating a belief held by townspeople and gunmen. "My two sons were down on the list to be slaughtered like pigs. I was listed under rape." None of them have seen the lists but this does not prevent anyone from believing in them unquestioningly.[5]

The fear expressed by this woman is manifest, but even taking that fear into account, such ridiculous accusations—a town in Bosnia to be the new Mecca?—can only be believed by someone already deeply prejudiced.

Kaplan is right also to point to the historical origins of these attitudes. The hatreds actually do have "ancient" roots, tracing back to the legends surrounding the 1389 Battle of Kosovo Field, at which the Serbs were defeated by the Ottomans, ushering in five centuries of Muslim Turkish rule. Strictly speaking, resentment of such events cannot be "ancient," but must be renewed in each generation. Here Kaplan points to the role of culture, especially the epic poems about Kosovo that glorified the Serbian defeat there as a necessary sacrifice for building a "heavenly kingdom." It was through these poems that generation after generation of Serbs passed down hatred of Muslim Turks, even after Turkish rule was overthrown in the nineteenth century.

On closer inspection, however, the story Kaplan tells is misleading. First of all, Kaplan seems to be portraying a hatred which is not only "ancient" but continuous. In his telling, the Balkans is a blood-drenched region whose inhabitants have always been killing each other: bloody Bosnia was the scene of savage warfare not only in the 1990s, but also repeatedly in the past, most recently during World War II. The trouble with this picture is that Bosnia was also the locale for some of the most openly pluralistic attitudes in the Balkans, where intermarriage among ethnic groups was high before the war, and where Sarajevo celebrated its religious diversity with significant populations of four great religions—Islam, Eastern Orthodoxy, Catholicism, and Judaism. The hatred may have had deep roots, but it increased dramatically in the years before the war, while tolerance decreased equally. Why?

Second, myths of Kosovo notwithstanding, the disputes that generated the wars in the Balkans—and the South Caucasus—are invariably modern, the product in every case of twentieth-century conflicts, not medieval or "ancient" ones. Serbs and Croats had a tradition of conflict but not of war against each other until World War II, and the dispute that caused them to fight then traced back only to the founding of the "first Yugoslavia" in 1918. Kaplan's account of the Serb-Croat dispute actually supports this point, as the historical disputes that get most of his attention are the ones concerning the events of World War II. The same is true regarding the Bosnian Muslims: although the Muslims were involved in the World War II bloodshed, it is only by the most egregious historical sleight of hand that Serbs conflate the secularized, Serbo-Croatian speaking Bosnian Muslims with the Turkish-speaking holy warriors of the Ottoman Empire.

A third problem concerns the assumptions about ethnic identity that underlie this story. In ethno-nationalist mythology, the ethnic group has existed for millennia, and has always yearned for a country of its own: this is the "primordialist" theory of ethnicity. The fact that people believe their ethnic groups to be primordial does not, however, mean that they are. Ethnic nationalism is a modern ideology which, for most of the eastern half of Europe, has been current for little over a century. Before that time, the peasants of the Balkans and the South Caucasus did not usually identify themselves as, say, "Croats" or "Georgians" or "Azerbaijanis" at all: it is only in the twentieth century that they were convinced to adopt these identities on the basis of shared language, religion, and historical mythology. Before that, identities were typically much more local. Ethnic groups are not necessarily "primordial" at all.

A final problem with this story is the implication for policymakers. President Bill Clinton is reported to have concluded, after reading Kaplan's book, that any sort of external intervention in the Balkans was doomed to failure, since the conflict was driven by uncontrollable "ancient hatreds." Journalist Misha Glenny offers the opposite prescription based on essentially the same analysis, writing: "Historically, the only way to keep these people apart once fighting begins has been for an outside power to intervene and offer its protection to all citizens, in particular, from the imperial urges of Croatia and Serbia."[6] But this is not true: the only previous time Croatia and Serbia fought each other, during World War II, their conflict was started by outside intervention—the Nazi invasion—and stopped by Tito's indigenous communist Partisans. In the 1990s, reestablishing peace depended primarily on establishing a new balance of power, which the parties were quite rational enough to respect. Balkan violence is indeed driven in part by violent emotions, but those emotions rise and fall; studying how and why they do so, and in connection with what other sorts of events, is required to understand how the passions can be calmed.

MANIPULATIVE LEADERS

An alternative account of Yugoslavia's ethnic wars focuses on the role of the leaders of Yugoslavia's constituent nations in starting the war. Scholar Bogdan Denitch puts it this way: "Rather than being caused by a popular upsurge of national hate from below, the civil war was the result of policy decisions from the top combined with an all-too-effective use of the mass media, especially television."[7] V. P. Gagnon generalized this conclusion into an overarching theory of ethnic war, stating: "I argue that violent conflict along ethnic cleavages is provoked by elites in order to create a domestic political context in which ethnicity is the only politically relevant identity.... [B]y constructing individual interest in terms of threat to the group, endangered elites can fend off domestic challengers who seek to mobilize the population against the status quo, and can better position themselves to deal with future challenges."[8] In other words, leaders of ethnic communities provoke ethnic war in order to keep (or, perhaps, grab) power for themselves.

When this story is told about Yugoslavia, the central character is Slobodan Milosevic, President of Serbia and, according to former U.S. Ambassador Warren Zimmerman, "the slickest con man in the Balkans." Milosevic first came to power by provoking an ethnic riot in the Kosovo region, and then exploiting the political fallout to betray—and replace—his erstwhile patron Ivan Stambolic as president of Serbia. His ruling strategy centered around using the media to drum up Serbian nationalist passions, exaggerating the plight of ethnic Serbs in the mostly Muslim Albanian region of Kosovo, denouncing Croats as equivalent to World War II-era Ustasha fascists, blaming other nationalities for the economic problems facing Serbs, and so on. Milosevic then harnessed the passions he had aroused, mobilizing crowds for demonstrations that led to the overthrow of independent regional leaders. When regional leaders in Slovenia and Croatia began to resist, Milosevic began to mobilize for war.

Milosevic's partners in crime, according to this story, were his adversaries Franjo Tudjman, avatar of Croatian chauvinism, and Alija Izetbegovic, courtly proponent of Bosnian Muslim self-assertion. While Milosevic was doing everything in his power to provoke conflict, these two leaders played into his hands by justifying many of his charges of ethnic chauvinism. Thus Milosevic's charges that Croatia was "Ustasha" seemed justified when Tudjman was filmed kissing the traditional Croatian flag, which had also been the banner of the Ustasha fascists. Tudjman's determined attempts to relegate ethnic Serbs to the status of second-class citizens similarly helped Milosevic's argument. Then, when they approached the brink of war, the leaders of Slovenia, Croatia, and Serbia pushed the situation over the edge by negotiating in such unconscionable bad faith that they delegitimized the very idea of holding talks. The fires of war, according this story, were thus the result not of spontaneous combustion but of the efforts of leaders to fuel and ignite them.

While this story captures part of the truth about Yugoslavia, it too has its limitations. First, if there was an "absence of gut hate among the broad layers of the population" in Yugoslavia, as Denitch claims,[9] how did the leaders manage to arouse such violent passions against other groups? While the media campaigns sponsored by Milosevic and neighboring leaderships undoubtedly deserve much of the blame, such campaigns can work only by playing on hostile attitudes or prejudices that already exist.

Second, even if the leaders of Yugoslavia did play an important role in provoking ethnic violence, it is misleading to overgeneralize from that fact. In other ethnic conflicts, including most of those in the Caucasus region, hostility and violence bubbled up from below rather than being provoked by top-down manipulation. Stories of ethnic war need the flexibility to consider that different conflicts are dissimilar in this regard: a one-size-fits-all theory of manipulative leaders simply is not adequate.

Third, too much of a focus on the role of leaders encourages analysts to gloss over the role of historical and situational effects, which are important in explaining why manipulative leaders succeed in some times and places but not others. Thus Denitch spends so much effort distancing the Croatian people from the atrocities perpetrated on their behalf by the Ustasha fascists that he underplays the deep scars those events left on the Serbian psyche. Focus on the leaders may also lead one to gloss over the reality of the grievances on which the leaders play: Milosevic was plausible because it was uncomfortable for the Serbs in Kosovo to live as a minority among the culturally different Albanians, and Serbs were suffering from the effects of a decade of economic stagnation.

One strength of the "manipulative leaders" story is that it has room for leaders who manipulate not only the interests of their ethnic group but also the group's identity. The "constructivist" theory of ethnicity starts from the fact that most ethnic identities are new, and points out that new group identities can be "constructed" when the situation is favorable. This will turn out to be important in explaining the case of Moldova, where ethnic Russian leaders increased their political leverage by creating a "Russophone" identity that embraced not only ethnic Russians but also the Ukrainian minority and committed communist ideologues from other groups. This story helps explain one of the mysteries of ethnic conflict: how the identity of the groups themselves can be changed in the course of such conflicts. Still, by itself, the "manipulative leader" story is insufficient for a full understanding of ethnic war.

ECONOMIC RIVALRY

The basic question of politics is "who gets what?" The "who" usually refers to groups with a shared interest in getting a particular "what." Theorists applying this perspective to ethnic conflict come to the conclusion that ethnic groups are simply another sort of interest group, competing with each other for economic and political goods just as other groups do. The story they tell is that the choice of mobilizing one's ethnic group instead, say, of a social class, is a purely "instrumental" one: people organize as an ethnic group when it seems the most practical way to get what they want, and they organize on different lines when *that* seems more likely to work.

While no one tells the story of Yugoslavia's fall as purely a case of economic rivalry, the work of Brookings Institution scholar Susan Woodward comes fairly close.[10] Woodward emphasizes what the other stories overlook—the decade-long economic stagnation which, as is typical in such cases, made all other conflicts including ethno-nationalist ones more tense. Although Yugoslavs increasingly agreed that economic reform was necessary, they disagreed over the sort of reform they should adopt because of regional differences across the Yugoslav economy. Croatia and Slovenia, with the most economically developed and internationally competitive regions of the country, favored economic decentralization that would take power—and their tax money—away from the notoriously inefficient federal government. Serbia, leading the other, less-developed parts of the country, argued in favor of recentralization and especially a strengthening of Yugoslavia's central bank to tame the country's equally notorious inflation problem. This conflict was also a tug-of-war over political power, with each side wishing to concentrate power where they would have the most access to it.

The trouble with this story is that it does not explain why people might resort to war. Surely if the root of Yugoslavia's problem was economic, no one could have considered that a rational solution was a war that would sever economic ties between different parts of the country, provoke international economic sanctions against some areas while other areas were bombed to rubble, promote massive looting, and destroy the rule of law that made normal economic life possible. If different regions could not agree on an economic policy, they could have amicably split, as the Czech Republic and Slovakia did. All would have been better off economically had they done so.

Another problem with this story is that it is even less true of other ethnic wars than it is of Yugoslavia's. The outbreak of the ethnic wars in Palestine and India in 1947, for example, occurred not because of economic problems but because the withdrawal of British colonial troops created an opportunity for long-standing hostility to be expressed by leaders and followers. Similarly, while the collapse of the Soviet Union was in large part the result of Soviet economic weakness, the pattern of ethnic violence cannot be explained by economic hardship: ethnic wars occurred in Georgia and Armenia, relative bright spots in the Soviet economy, while most harder-hit areas avoided them. Economic hardship may contribute to ethnic war, but it is not always a necessary precondition.

A third problem with the "economic rivalry" story is that it does not explain why most people mobilize for political action in the first place. If ethnic violence is to be explained as the result of people acting rationally in pursuit of self-interest, as these "instrumentalist" arguments tend to assume, what explains individuals' participation? For most people, getting involved politically is not rational, because the benefit they stand to gain is typically not worth the effort they would have to expend to get it. They should therefore be more likely just to sit back and let someone else do the work. Of course, if everyone sits back, no one acts and no one gains the benefit: this is the collective action problem. Obviously, the Serbian paramilitary groups—all composed of volunteers—found a way to overcome that problem, but self-interest cannot fully explain it: while it might be rationally self-interested to join a group engaged in looting and (for the depraved) rape, pursuit of individual self-interest does not explain torture, murder, or risking one's own life in battle. Ultimately, behavior of this kind must be explained by reference to the factors mentioned in the "ancient hatreds" stories—economic or instrumental rivalry is not enough.

SPIRAL OF INSECURITY

Political scientists who consider the above explanations too simplistic tend to gravitate toward more abstract theories aimed at combining several ideas. The most commonly promoted abstraction focuses on "the structure of the situation," especially the strength of the federal government, as the main explanation for ethnic war. A weak federal government, these analysts point out, is unable to provide a peaceful process for competing groups to resolve their differences, and it is also unable to prevent the groups from fighting with each other should they choose to do so. According to the structural argument, little more is needed to make an ethnic war occur.

The story begins with the insight that some sort of breakdown is the likely outcome of a government that cannot effectively resolve ethnic disputes. What happens then is outlined by MIT scholar Barry Posen:

> "In areas such as the former... Yugoslavia, 'sovereigns' have disappeared. They leave in their wake a host of groups... [that] must pay attention to... the problem of security.... [Thus], there will be competition for the key to security—power. The competition will often continue to a point at which the competing entities have amassed more power than needed for security and, thus, consequently begin to threaten others. Those threatened will respond in turn.... This is the security dilemma: what one does to enhance one's own security causes reactions that, in the end, can make one less secure.... [T]hese strategic problems show that very little nationalist rabble-rousing or nationalistic combativeness is required to generate very dangerous situations."[11]

Posen's logic is that ethnic groups in Yugoslavia found themselves in the situation of "anarchy" faced by hostile independent states. In the absence of a common central government, no group could trust the others not to arm—in fact, someone would inevitably inherit the arms of the Yugoslav army—so all had to arm in self-defense. Their memories of World War II spurred them on in their efforts and promoted a spiral of insecurity as the self-defense efforts of each group increased the insecurity of the others. Once they began thinking in terms of self-defense and the World War II precedent, the groups could not help noticing that whoever attacked first would gain a big advantage, especially over unprepared groups of "enemies" isolated in one's own territory. Eventually, someone was bound to give in to the logic of preventive self-defense and attack first, especially after armed groups of extremists began to appear.

While this story does tell us something about how dangerous the situation was in which the Yugoslav republics found themselves, it says less than meets the eye about the reasons for the danger. First, the Yugoslav republics did not arm themselves because the federal government collapsed. Rather, the federal government collapsed because the republics were mutually hostile enough to arm themselves: anarchy resulted when the federal government lost control of the republics' behavior. Posen's logic is therefore backwards; anarchy was not the cause of the run-up to war, but the result of the run-up to war. This fact is further demonstrated by what did not happen—conflict among the other former Yugoslav republics. Serbia and Croatia fought each other, and tore Bosnia-Herzegovina between them, but security dilemmas did not arise between Croatia and Slovenia despite some border disputes; neither did Macedonia feel compelled to arm itself against Serbia in spite of historical rivalry.

Posen is therefore wrong to say that the security dilemma causes conflicts with "very little nationalist rabble-rousing and nationalistic combativeness." His argument is useful, however, in explaining the results of a security dilemma once it emerges, and in illuminating the factors that may worsen the security dilemma. Once Croats began moving toward independence and reviving their World War II–era symbols, the Serbs in Croatia could not help remembering the genocidal violence carried out under those banners during World War II; this helped motivate them to arm themselves. The Croats realized the advantages of a preventive attack and actually tried to disarm the Serbs within Croatia before the latter could fully organize, but they were prevented from doing so by Yugoslav army threats. That intervention, in turn, increased the motivation of the Croats for independence. A year later, the emergence of armed Serb extremists helped motivate the Bosnian Muslims to go ahead with their dangerous push for independence. In sum, Posen's argument is generally wrong about why security dilemmas emerge, but the idea of the security dilemma is useful for explaining how conflict escalates to war when it does so.

Combining the Stories

It seems clear that a satisfactory explanation of the wars in Yugoslavia and of ethnic war in general must combine these stories into a single theory. The more sophisticated explanations of Yugoslavia's wars do indeed combine them, but none offers a systematic general theory.[12] Building such a theory is the purpose of this book.

The best place to begin is with the concept of symbolic politics.[13] Consider the American "welfare queen" of the 1980s. First, though the term is not explicitly ethnic, it does have a distinctly ethnic connotation, building on stereotypes of African-Americans as lazy and disproportionately likely to be on welfare. Beyond the appeal to stereotypes, however, the term also taps any feelings of hostility that might be present: not only is the recipient black, the term suggests, but in this view "those [insert pejorative term here] blacks" do not deserve help anyway, so hostility to their demands is appropriate. The term appeals, in short, to racist myths. This is how ethnic symbolism works and why it seems linked to "ancient hatreds": it refers to preexisting historical myths in the same way that, for example, the Confederate battle flag refers to American racial myths.

It is important to realize, however, that although the hatred is all too often real, it is not "ancient" but modern. Ethnic hatreds are renewed in each generation by mythologies that are typically modern revisions of older stories with quite different messages. For example, in an article entitled "Modern Hate" (from which I adapted this book's title), University of Chicago scholars Susanne and Lloyd Rudolph find that the mythology behind Hindu extremism in India traces in large part to 1980s television and audio performances recasting the ancient legend of the god Ram into a version more standardized, and in that way less tolerant, than in the past. This new, high-profile recasting of Hindu identity provided the symbols politicians used to spark communal violence.[14] In the Balkans and the Caucasus, the myths used now are similarly modern recastings of narratives that are themselves only a century or two old, though they often recount much older events. American racial politics, so different from these other cases in many ways, also follows this pattern: contemporary controversies over the Confederate battle flag, for example, trace less to the mythology of the Civil War than to the recasting of that mythology to fight racial integration in the 1960s.

Another way ethnic myths and symbols are modernized is to attribute contemporary economic woes to the despised out-group. The symbol of the "welfare queen," for example, appeals to the economic interest of (white) taxpayers by implying that taxes could be cut if money were not wasted on "welfare queens." While there was some substance to that claim, focus on "welfare queens" exaggerated the amount of money spent on antipoverty programs, not to mention the proportion of that sum that went to people with "queenly" standards of living. In India, similarly, Hindu hostility was turned against Muslims by blaming Muslims for the trouble that high-caste young Hindus were having finding jobs. Thus, more than a means of appealing to interests, ethnic symbols are a tool for elites to use in mobilizing ethnic groups, especially their own, in pursuit of policies the elites prefer, but for reasons only partially explained by the tangible interests ostensibly at stake.

The idea of ethnic symbolism is useful, therefore, because it combines the logic of the ancient hatreds, manipulative elites, and economic rivalry stories. Ethnic symbols are tools used by manipulative elites, but they only work when there is some real or perceived conflict of interest at work *and* mythically based feelings of hostility that can be tapped using ethnic symbols. All three elements are needed to make mobilization happen: Without perceived conflicts of interest, people have no reason to mobilize. Without emotional commitment based on hostile feelings, they lack sufficient impetus to do so. And without leadership, they typically lack the organization to act.

The second part of the story is how ethnic politics can escalate from peaceful rivalry to war. Vibrant, emotionally laden ethnic politics are ubiquitous in multiethnic areas, but they very rarely turn to war, even when government breaks down. For example, nine of the fifteen former Soviet republics avoided ethnic war, though all are multiethnic and all were affected by the collapse of the Soviet Union. One of the fifteen, the Russian Federation, itself includes twenty-one ethnic regions, again all multiethnic, but only one of these, Chechnya, experienced overt warfare. When war did happen, the common element was that the politics of ethnic symbolism, shaped by myths justifying hostility against other groups, turned into a contest over who would dominate whom. These hostile myths and extreme goals, not the mere fact of anarchy, created the fears that set off a security dilemma and motivated the drive to war.

Obviously, prejudiced symbolic politics and insecurity feed each other. Thus, ethnic prejudice and hostility make people more likely to see the other group as threatening; while feelings of threat and insecurity contribute to the success of efforts by elites to stir up ethnic extremism. Ethnic wars differ in the extent to which each of these factors is primarily to blame. In some cases, prejudice and hostility are so strong that they result in violence almost as soon as the opportunity arises. In these cases of *mass-led violence,* theories about ancient hatreds seem particularly appropriate. In other cases it is incumbent leaders who play on ethnic prejudice to provoke hostility and violence. Such cases of *elite-led violence* seem more explicable in terms of manipulative leaders.

These are the main elements of my argument: the necessary preconditions for ethnic war are ethnic myths and fears and the opportunity to act on them politically. Ethnic war occurs when the politics of ethnic symbolism goes to extremes, provoking hostile actions and leading to a security dilemma. In some cases, the turn toward extremism is mass-led; in other cases, it is elite-led. Either way, war results from a process in which extremist politics and insecurity mutually reinforce each other in an escalatory spiral.

The rest of the book is aimed at filling in the details: When do such extreme fears arise? How do extremist elites use ethnic symbolism to provoke war? What can outside parties do to prevent or stop such wars? And how, exactly, do these ideas explain the outbreak of ethnic wars, especially in the former Yugoslavia and former USSR?

I begin in chapter 2 by laying out the details of the symbolic politics theory of ethnic war, explaining how the passionate politics of ethnic symbolism can lead to war, why it so frequently does not, and how different paths to war can be blocked. The heart of the book that follows is a series of case studies that explain how these ideas illuminate the causes of ethnic wars in the former USSR and former Yugoslavia. I begin with the mass-led conflicts of the South Caucasus—the Armenian-Azerbaijani dispute (chapter 3) and the civil wars in Georgia (chapter 4). Chapter 5 considers the curious hybrid case of Moldova, which began as a mass-led conflict but required elite manipulation to result in war. The elite-led breakup of Yugoslavia is treated in chapter 6, with a focus on the war in Croatia. Chapter 7 sums up the lessons learned, especially about the options and prospects for war avoidance and termination. The most optimistic conclusion is that while ethnic wars are difficult to stop, they are also difficult to start—which means that it is usually not too difficult, especially for the government of the threatened state, to prevent them from starting in the first place.

[2]

The Symbolic Politics of Ethnic War

Explaining ethnic war requires answering two different but related questions. The first is the question of ethnicity. What exactly is an ethnic group? Why do ethnic groups stick together in politics when individual interests often cut across ethnic lines? Why did ethnic groups become especially important politically only in recent times? The second question concerns the causes of war. How do ethnic wars get started, and why do they happen? Why are people willing to fight and die for their ethnic group?

To be convincing, a theory needs to answer both questions in compatible ways—showing the ways in which the nature of ethnic groups explains how and why they fight. For example, if the theory assumes that ethnic groups act like economic interest groups, it should explain why economic interests motivate people to stick with their ethnic groups and fight. Additionally, the best theory will be supported by evidence at every stage. Thus, for an ancient hatreds account to be convincing, it should show that ethnic groups are ancient, that the hatred is ancient, that their hatred is the motivation for them to fight ethnic wars, and that variations in the amount of ancient hatred explain why ethnic wars break out in some places but not others. The task of this chapter is to assemble these combined theories, pinpoint their weaknesses, and explain how a symbolic politics approach offers a stronger alternative.

Clarifying Definitions

The terminology used in discussions about ethnic conflict is so confused, and confusing, that it is important to sort out the meanings of key terms before beginning the analysis. First, *ethnic group* and *nation* are separate but overlapping concepts. An ethnic group, in Anthony Smith's definition, is a group sharing five key traits: a group name, a believed common descent, common historical memories, elements of shared culture such as language or religion, and attachment (even if only historical or sentimental) to a specific territory. These elements are all tied together by a "myth-symbol complex" (defined below).[1] A nation, by contrast, is a socially mobilized group that wants political self-determination.[2] Thus, not all nations are ethnic groups (some, like the American nation, are ethnically heterogeneous); and not all ethnic groups are nations (many do not aspire to political autonomy). Cases of ethnic war, however, are always cases of competition for political dominance, so they all involve ethnic nations on at least one side. Strictly speaking, therefore, this book is about "ethno-nationalist" wars, but I will stick to the shorter formulation for the sake of simplicity.

Another set of terms relevant to the discussion is *nationalism, chauvinism,* and *hostility*. Nationalism is the belief that one's own group should be politically autonomous—the belief, that is, that one's own nation should take its rightful place among the nations of the world. Chauvinism is the belief that one's own group is *better* than others, and therefore has the right to dominate or displace them.[3] Hostility means relating to another group as to an enemy. The phenomena are separate: nationalists may seek equality for their group, and avoid being chauvinists; chauvinists may be content with their nation's status and see others paternally as "younger brothers" rather than enemies. Frequently, however, extreme nationalists tend to be chauvinists, and chauvinists tend to be hostile to nationalists of other groups.

Central to understanding ethnicity are the terms *myth* and *symbol*. According to Murray Edelman, on whose theory of symbolic politics I build, a myth is "a belief held in common by a large group of people that gives events and actions a particular meaning."[4] The truth or falsity of the myth is irrelevant; its purpose is to help a person understand what a set of events means to him or her. For this reason, it is appropriate to talk about the "myth" of Kosovo or the Armenian Genocide: while these are real events, what affects politics now is less the events themselves than the mythologies that have grown up around them.

A symbol is an emotionally charged shorthand reference to a myth. In Serbian mythology, for example, the meaning of the Battle of Kosovo Field is the martyrdom of the Serbian nation in defense of Serbian honor and of Christendom against the Turks. "Kosovo" therefore is a symbol referring to this myth of Serbian martyrdom; the point of invoking the symbol is usually to express, to communicate, or to evoke among Serbian listeners the emotions, such as pride or a sense of national grievance, associated with the myth. The web of myths and related symbols like these that collectively define what it means to be a Serb forms the Serbs' *"myth-symbol complex."*[5]

Ethnic war, finally, is a war in which the key issues at stake—that is, the express reason political power is being contested—involve either ethnic markers such as language or religion or the status of ethnic groups themselves. A war is organized armed combat between at least two belligerent sides in which at least one thousand people are killed.

Theories of Ethnic Group Origins and Violence

Attempts to explain the origins of ethnic groups and the reasons they fight fall into two basic but diverse categories: rational choice explanations and psychological arguments.

Rational Choice Approaches

Ethnic groups as instrumental

According to the "instrumentalist" approach, ethnic groups are merely coalitions formed in a rational attempt to compete for scarce goods in the context of social changes brought about by modernization.[6] As evidence, instrumentalists point to ethnic conflicts in Africa, which are often essentially conflicts between ethnically defined patron-client networks over economic goods distributed by the state. This is even true, they argue, when the rhetoric of leaders emphasizes such noneconomic issues as cultural autonomy.[7]

In this view, ethnic nations formed in the last two centuries when a "national" language was chosen from among a variety of different dialects, written down, and made the basis for mass literacy in specific states.[8] This was done because industrial society requires a standard means of communication, thus a single standard is set for an entire territory.[9] In empires with many unrelated languages, certain economic classes of subordinate groups promoted literacy and ethnic nationalism in their linguistic groups, thereby creating new ethnic groups.

In sum, the key to this explanation is the self-interested basis of ethnic group formation: elites form people into ethnic nations because of a combination of linguistic and class interests. Furthermore, while all group members share these interests, the elites have an additional interest in organizing the group to pursue them—the elites gain power by leading that pursuit.

Rationalist theories of ethnic war

Rational choice theorists starting from this instrumental understanding of group origins have produced several different theories of ethnic war. I will focus here on three: the "economic rivalry" approach, the "hard rationalist" school, and the "soft rationalist" account.

The economic approach. Arguments that ethnic wars result primarily from economic concerns come in several different versions. One version has it that the issue is distribution: poorer areas might want to secede because they consider the central government to be discriminating against them; and richer areas might want to secede because they do not want to be burdened by union with the poorer ones.

Such arguments have a poor track record empirically. They cannot explain ethnic mobilization in general: analyses find that ethnic groups mobilize under virtually all economic circumstances.[10] Statistical studies come to a similar conclusion: economic discrimination has no significant effect on ethnic group mobilization or on demands for group autonomy.[11] These economic arguments also fail to account for the pattern of violence in the dying Soviet Union, as Table 2.1 shows. Rather, all four of the non-Russian republics that suffered ethnic war—Armenia, Azerbaijan, Georgia, and Moldova—were middle-income republics. There is no pattern among secessionist subregions either: some, such as the Transnistria region of Moldova, were more industrialized and prosperous than the unit they were seceding from; while others, such as South Ossetia, were less so.

Another prominent approach focuses on relative deprivation,[12] and specifically on declines in standard of living. This logic would seem to apply to Yugoslavia and the Soviet Union, both of which experienced serious declines in standard of living in the years before their collapse. It does not, however, explain the pattern of violence, which should show that those areas which suffered more were more prone to ethnic violence.

As Table 2.1 shows, Tajikistan fits the relative deprivation logic—it was second-worst off in both economic performance and national income, and it did experience a civil war—but its conflict was not an ethnic war. On the other hand, Armenia and Georgia, which did experience ethnic wars, actually saw their economies grow relative to Russia's in the years before their wars, while the declines in Azerbaijan and Moldova were minimal. Since the Soviet economy overall grew at a reasonable pace in the 1960s and 1970s, and was stagnant from 1980–88 (the rapid decline began only in 1989),[13] even the mild declines relative to Russia suffered by Moldova and Azerbaijan may not imply absolute decline. The data seem clear: ethnic violence does not correlate closely with economic hardship or economic decline.

In addition to this trouble with the evidence, economic explanations of ethnic war face the additional problem of logical inconsistency: for most people, fighting an ethnic civil war is not economically rational. The reason is simple common sense: fighting a civil war over the benefits of a fragile national economy is obviously likely to destroy that economy. Peaceful ethnic mobilization may make economic sense, but running a serious risk of ethnic war does not because the economic risks vastly outweigh the potential gains, except for would-be profiteers. The Yugoslav conflict of the

Table 2.1. National Income of Soviet Republics
(As a percentage of Russia's national income)

Republic	1962 Income	1988 Income	Change	1988 Rank
Belarusian SSR	63.6	100.5	+37.2	3
Lithuanian SSR	84.8	95.0	+10.2	5
Georgian SSR	69.2	77.4	+8.2	7
Armenian SSR	68.8	75.6	+6.8	8
Russian SSR	100.0	100.0	0.0	4
Kazakh SSR	61.2	61.0	–0.2	11
Azerbaijani SSR	67.1	65.6	–1.5	10
Moldovan SSR	73.1	71.0	–2.1	9
Turkmen SSR	61.2	56.9	–4.3	12.0
Latvian SSR	112.8	107.3	–5.5	1
Kyrgyz SSR	55.6	48.7	–6.9	13
Ukranian SSR	88.9	80.0	–8.9	6
Estonian SSR	114.8	105.3	–9.5	2
Tajik SSR	50.8	39.3	–11.5	15
Uzbek SSR	55.8	43.0	–12.8	14

Source: O. G. Dmitrieva, *Regional'naia ekonomicheskaia diagnosticka* (St. Petersburg: Limbus Press, 1992), p. 79.

early 1990s illustrates the point. That conflict was to a considerable degree triggered by disputes over the distribution of economic goods. However, it very quickly became apparent that almost everyone would lose economically once war began disrupting trade, destroying factories and infrastructure, and turning workers into fighters, refugees, or casualties. In fact, virtually everyone in the former Yugoslavia and the South Caucasus (except for a few profiteers and looters) lost economically from war by every measure. Given the economic costs of postwar hostility, even most of the winners ended up worse off absolutely, worse off than they would have been had the status quo continued, and even worse off than they would have been had they acceded to the rival group's demands.

Hard rationalist approaches. Another rationalist explanation for ethnic war, promoted by Russell Hardin and others, takes a step away from the instrumentalist understanding of ethnicity, arguing that ethnic war is explicable as a function of individuals' rational pursuit not of material benefits but of personal security.[14] The argument suggests that in cases of "emergent anarchy," when the state will not or cannot guarantee people's safety from violence, it is rational for groups to start mobilizing in preemptive self-defense. The result is a security dilemma, in which each group's acts of self-defense threaten other groups, leading to escalating preparations for violence and ultimately to the outbreak of fighting. "Risk-aversion is enough," in this account, "to motivate murderous violence."[15]

The process of mobilization, in this view, is a "tipping process" driven by peer pressure: the more people join in ethnic mobilization, the more they can pressure others into joining, and the more credibly they can argue that it pays to join because their growing movement is likely to succeed. Thus the mobilization process snowballs. And if a group norm in favor of violence somehow emerges, it becomes rational for individual members of the group to engage in murder.[16]

A third argument Hardin makes relies on selective incentives. In this account, people may engage in violent conflict because they are promised rewards for killing or threatened with punishment if they do not kill. To the extent that the participants in Yugoslavia's conflict, for example, were conscripted, this argument explains the conflict as the result of the coercive power of the state, especially Serbia. Criminals may also be useful for aggressive governments, as they can be promised loot or locations for mafia-style operations in exchange for leading their gangs (armed by the state) into battle.[17]

David Lake and Donald Rothchild suggest two additional reasons to think that "emergent anarchy" by itself might be enough to motivate violence.[18] One is information failures: each side has reason to conceal its true desires and strength, but doing so makes it harder to reach a negotiated agreement. The second issue is the problem of credible commitment: even if the sides make promises in good faith, there may be no way to guarantee the promises will be fulfilled later. Added to the security dilemma, these problems make negotiated agreements hard to reach and war more likely.

However, Lake's and Rothchild's understanding of the security dilemma assumes that both sides want to avoid war, and that they are willing to compromise to avoid it. War results, in this logic, only because the sides do not trust each other.[19] The problem with this argument is that I know of no case in which ethnic war resulted from such a process. In every case I am familiar with, security dilemmas were the result of the sides' openly stated pursuit of dominance, not the result of overzealous self-defense under "emergent anarchy." Each side's goals, and expectations about the other, came from hostile interpretations of history encoded in each group's "myth-symbol complex." In such cases, information failures and problems of credible commitment are irrelevant: the sides would rather fight than compromise for reasons that better information and stronger commitments cannot change.

In fact, by focusing on "emergent anarchy," these theorists ignore evidence that they have the causal chain backwards: in ethnic conflict, the security dilemma causes anarchy to emerge, not vice versa. In the Soviet case, for example, there was little evidence of "emergent anarchy" before the

Karabagh crisis exploded into violence in February 1988. It was, rather, the accumulation of ethnic and nationalist disputes across the Soviet Union that eroded the effectiveness of the Soviet state, and finally caused it to break up more than three years later. In most cases—in ten of fifteen Soviet republics and twenty of twenty-one ethnic regions in Russia, all of them ethnically mixed—no ethnic war occurred in spite of the "emergent anarchy" of the Soviet breakup. When violence did erupt, the issue was usually not fear about what rival groups might do, but an open struggle for dominance. This insight explains why nationalism is, in Jack Snyder's words, the "default option" for identification when empires break up:[20] empires break up because the forces of nationalism are already in control.

Another weakness of these "hard rationalist" arguments is that although they begin as arguments about individual self-interest, they end up depending on the emergence of group norms. If groups formed instrumentally merely to seek security, it would be rational for people on the weaker side to switch groups, and for their opponents to let them. It might sometimes be rational, however, for one's own (selfish) co-ethnics to betray one, rendering the whole idea of group self-defense problematic.[21] These problems can only be avoided by assuming that effective group norms prevent such conversions. The switch to group norms weakens the theory, but is supported by the evidence: studies suggest that the values that motivate people to engage in political violence are collective interests, not individual self-interest.[22] The trouble is that these theories do not explain why this happens.

Additionally, this argument requires that group norms justify extreme violence, which then spreads due to a "tipping process." But it would seem more rational for people threatened by violence to reinforce norms against it. Norms can define self-defense in a narrow and immediate sense that does not encourage preemptive mobilization or violence. Rationalists such as Hardin do not explain why violent norms emerge instead. Appealing to a history of conflict does not help: most neighboring groups have some history of past violence that can be used and exaggerated. Alternatively, neighbors can be conflated with mythical enemies, as when Serbs associate Bosnian Muslims with the depredations of the Ottoman Turks.

Soft rationalist approaches. The soft rationalist approach, pioneered by Alvin Rabushka and Kenneth Shepsle, concedes that extremist group values are the core causes of ethnic violence and builds on that assumption.[23] "Rationality" in these models means the rationally calculated pursuit of any consistently defined goals, including those defined by a nationalist ideology. In this version, it is easier to explain why people are willing to join in ethnic movements, since one can appeal to nationalist values to explain people's behavior. Rabushka and Shepsle's argument is that if people have extreme preferences—for example, they want to try to dominate the other group even if trying is very risky—then extremist politicians are likely to outpoll moderates. These extremists, once in power, can then use the machinery of government to organize their willing followers for war.

When preferences are extreme, a "softer" version of Hardin's tipping argument can also be used to explain ethnic wars that start from the bottom up, without government help. Alexander Motyl points out that some people are more strongly nationalistic than others, and they can be divided into "martyrs," "fanatics," "true believers," and "believers of convenience."[24] Nationalist martyrs and fanatics can be counted on to be politically active even in the face of certain repression, so there is always likely to be someone promoting nationalist policies. If political repression decreases, true believers will join in and the nationalist movement will grow. If the incumbent government then shows signs of responding, more moderate nationalists will join as well. The more who join, the greater the incentives for others to join, as a larger movement is both safer to join and more likely to succeed. Martyrs or fanatics may also play an important role by starting the cycle of violence, provoking retaliation which shocks moderates into the belief that extremist policies are necessary.

The inadequacy of rationalist approaches

Available rationalist explanations of ethnic war are inadequate. The economic rivalry argument is logically inconsistent and fails to explain the pattern of ethnic violence. Hardin-style "hard rationalist" arguments fail to explain why ethnic groups hold together. They are also wrong empirically: "emergent anarchy" does not cause ethnic security dilemmas; rather, mutual hostility causes insecurity, ethnic mobilization, state breakdown, and therefore anarchy. Deprived of this argument, these hard rationalist explanations for violence collapse. While the soft rationalist approach works, it does so only by assuming group norms and hostile attitudes, which is most of what the theory is meant to explain.

Rationalist approaches do offer important insights, however. First, they point out that elites, who powerfully shape the course of ethnic conflict, may use ethnicity instrumentally in pursuit of their own personal interests. Second, the mass-led "tipping" process and selective incentives provided by elites are convincing explanations for how mutually hostile groups might mobilize. Finally, information failures and problems of credible commitment can exacerbate interethnic security dilemmas, though rationalists misunderstand the origins of those security dilemmas.

To explain why ethnic groups hold together and hostile attitudes emerge to create security dilemmas, we must turn to psychological theories.

PSYCHOLOGICAL THEORIES

Psychological roots of ethnicity

Primordialism. A powerful statement of the primordialist position is Harold Isaacs's *Idols of the Tribe*, which states, "basic group identity consists of the ready-made set of endowments and identifications that every individual shares with others from the moment of birth by the chance of the family into which he is born."[25] The markers of group identity, Isaacs points out, are basic personal characteristics that fundamentally shape how individuals view the world and how the world views them. Group identity is indeed for most people ascriptive—that is, assigned at birth—and is often marked on the body, either naturally as racial characteristics or carved on by circumcision, tattoo, or other artificial process. Native language provides the words, and therefore the conceptual lens, through which one understands the world. And religion shapes values, identity, and therefore how people define their wants and needs. Walker Connor, who takes a position similar to primordialism, argues that the sum of these markers defines a group which acts like, and indeed claims to be, a kin group.[26] According to this logic, ethnic loyalty taps some fundamental biological drives, such as defense of kin and territoriality. It is these mutually reinforcing bonds which give ethnicity its power in the primordialist view.

The trouble with this argument is that the history and kinship ties are usually fictitious, while most national identities are new. Thus in France, the epitome of a European nation-state, many peasants felt only local rather than national loyalties down to the end of the nineteenth century.[27] National identity can hardly be "primordial" if it is new; and it cannot be genetic if its members are not related.

Constructivism. The constructivist position begins from the insight that the meaning of an ethnic identity—who is included in the group, what its values are, and so on—is a set of ideas. Those ideas, constructivists point out, are generally either newly invented or newly interpreted by ethnic or nationalist intellectuals. It is therefore these intellectuals who "construct" ethnic identity, sometimes by inventing group history from whole cloth.[28] In some parts of Africa and the Soviet Union, even ethnic labels and literary languages were first created by outsiders such as missionaries or anthropologists, and the resulting identity came to be accepted by the groups only after governments began applying the label to them.

This fundamental point is actually conceded by both primordialists and instrumentalists. Thus, the above-mentioned instrumentalist account of the creation of nineteenth-century European nationalisms is also a constructivist account, dependent on the role of ethnic elites and intellectuals in "constructing" nations. And Clifford Geertz, considered the founder of the primordial school, agrees that ethnic markers are culturally rather than biologically determined.[29] The primordialist point is that there is a limit to the plasticity of ethnic identity. Although intellectuals can feel free to invent, reinvent, or obscure their group's past to a large extent, they must build on certain preexisting foundations, such as language, religion, culture, and territory. The trick for the intellectual "cultural entrepreneur" is to link a name and cluster of cultural elements to a history and mythology that both creates ethnic symbols and answers contemporary group needs. In short, while ethnic groups are not permanent and fixed, they are not infinitely malleable either.[30] Weakly supported national identities such as the Yugoslav and Soviet do not survive.

In some cases, ethnic identities may be used to justify conflicts not intended by their creators. For example, myths of "ancient" Sinhalese-Tamil conflict in Sri Lanka were recreated by Sinhalese activist Anagarika Dharmapala in the late nineteenth century to help promote a cultural and Buddhist religious revival among the Sinhalese people, and secondarily to build political opposition to the British colonialists. Decades later, S.W.R.D. Bandaranaike used those myths to mobilize Sinhalese around an anti-Tamil program in the 1956 election campaign.[31] Thus the politicians who exploit ethnic myths may not be the thinkers who created them.

The symbolist synthesis. The different schools of thought about ethnicity are more compatible than normally understood. The barrier to theoretical reconciliation has been the misperception that primordialists see ethnic ties as immutable, genetic links. Understanding that most primordialists see ethnicity as *culturally* rather than genetically determined opens the way to combining all three schools of thought. The outlines of a synthesis were sketched out by Crawford Young in the mid-1970s.[32]

The synthesis begins with the argument that group loyalty is likely to be evolutionarily favored: those who can in a crisis count on fellow group-members' loyalty—including such non-kin as in-laws—were presumably advantaged over strict egoists, who would have died when their groups fractured under stress. "Nationalism gets its force," in this view, "by drawing on [this] primordial sociality." This argument is sometimes caricatured as a simplistic "killer ape" theory of human nature, but in fact its more sophisticated version is consistent with constructivist logic. The argument is not that ethnic violence is somehow encoded in human genes, but that *cultural* tendencies toward collective group self-defense are evolutionarily favored.[33]

Ethnic or national leaders then create nationalist identities, using ethnic symbols to mimic the cues that originally invoked a genuine kinship/

group-defense response—hence the "motherland" and "fatherland" symbols commonly used by nationalists to combine the notions of home territory and family.[34] The core of the ethnic identity is the "myth-symbol complex"—the combination of myths, memories, values, and symbols that defines not only who is a member of the group but what it means to be a member.[35] The existence, status, and security of the group thus come to be seen to depend on the status of group symbols, which is why people are willing to fight and die for them—and why they are willing to follow leaders who manipulate those symbols for dubious or selfish purposes.

Nationalism is further strengthened by the religious nature of ethnic or nationalist ideologies. In this view, what nationalist ideologues create is in some sense a religion. For the nationalist, the nation is a god—a jealous god—to whom one pays homage, venerating its temples (monuments), relics (battle flags), and theology (including a mythical history); and receiving in return a sort of immortality as a participant in what is conceived as an eternal nation.[36]

This synthesis explains why ethnicity is so powerful and ubiquitous: it draws its power from many sources. If cleverly cast, an ethnic or nationalist appeal can claim that the ethnic warrior is fighting simultaneously for self-respect (identity), self-interest (material goods), clan survival, clan territory, the propagation of the faith, and country; and if the fight is successful, the warrior will have achieved immortality (through martyrdom and the defense of progeny) even in death. Ethnic group or nation is, therefore, a god so powerful that it is irresistible to invent him wherever he does not exist. Attempts to create ethnic loyalties are only successful, however, when the symbolic claims seem credible and relevant.

This account also explains why ethnicity is increasingly important today, though ethnic groups have existed for millennia.[37] The key changes are mass literacy and mass media, which made it possible to align the appeal of state and (redefined) tribe, and to mobilize the entire group around the combined ethno-nationalist theme.[38] At the same time, the processes of modernization throw together people from different places, making the markers of ethnicity more salient in daily life, while the increasing role of the modern state makes it more important to mobilize politically—hence the incentive to mobilize on ethnic lines. Finally, international acceptance of nationalism as the main principle legitimizing independent statehood encourages emulation, as groups are induced to say, "we too want our own nation-state." All of these factors contribute to the rising importance of ethnicity.

Psychological explanations of ethnic war

The case for emotional motivations in ethnic war is most effectively argued by Crawford Young and Donald Horowitz.[39] Horowitz starts with Henri Tajfel's finding that, when offered the choice between maximizing benefits for their own group or maximizing the difference between their group and another, people tend to choose to maximize the difference. In other words, people gave up some (potential) benefits for their own group to ensure that the other group gained even less—even when the group is a randomly created one. Horowitz adds that when ethnic conflict turns into such competition for group advantage, the result is frequently a contest for dominance of the state as a way for groups to try to show their superior group worth. The language of the contest is legitimacy, as each group tries to prove its moral and historical claims give it the legitimate right to political dominance in their own homeland.[40] The issue in ethnic conflict, then, is not so much specific economic, linguistic, or other specific benefits, but relative status—superiority over other groups.

Prejudice plays a role as well. In many cases, a group's myth-symbol complex includes prejudice against the other group—that is, stereotypes about the rival group, enhanced by negative feelings about that group. Again, the emotional dimension of prejudice is important: research suggests that negative feelings about the other group are more important than stereotypes in explaining attitudes toward outgroups.[41]

The thinking involved in such conflicts is illustrated by the anecdote of the Russian peasant who finds a genie in a bottle. Offered a single wish, the peasant muses: "Well, my neighbor has a cow and I have none. So—Kill my neighbor's cow." This story illustrates the logic of ethnic war—hostility trumps acquisitiveness. The peasant could have improved both his absolute and his relative position by asking for two cows, but he considered the opportunity to gloat over his neighbor's loss to be worth more than two cows (or a bag of gold) for himself.

Horowitz adds that in cases where conflict leads to ethnic war, there is an additional motivation beyond the contest for dominance: anxiety-laden (that is, exaggerated) fears of group extinction. Such fears tend also to be based on demographic fears and a history of domination by the rival group.[42] Horowitz also agrees with the primordialist view that ethnicity has a "kinship with kinship": ethnic extinction matters, even if one's personal safety is not imperiled, because the future of the kinship group is imperiled. The fear of group extinction, Horowitz argues in sum, leads to feelings of hostility, and then to group violence. Young adds that the atmosphere of hostility and threat is likely to increase group solidarity, encourage the groups to perceive events in ethnic terms, and promote misperceptions across group boundaries.[43]

The insight that the motivation for ethnic war is in part emotional—interethnic hostility resulting from fear of ethnic extinction—helps fill in some of the logical gaps left by rationalist theory. If the issues at stake are defined not merely by economic or linguistic interests, but by a contest for status defined as domination and by anxiety-laden fears of extinction, then it is easy to see why attitudes would be hostile—that is, why groups prefer to weaken or harm other groups even at some cost to their own material welfare.

These insights do not, however, form a coherent theory. Building them into one requires the addition of a theory of choice that incorporates the emotional nature of ethnic bonds. Murray Edelman's theory of symbolic politics offers a way to do so.

A Symbolic Politics Theory of Ethnic War

Symbolic Choice vs. Rational Choice

Rational choice theory is based on several fundamental assumptions. Two of them are that people have stable, ordered preferences; and that in choosing they try rationally to maximize their utility as defined by those preferences. Those assumptions are useful for some purposes, such as explaining most kinds of economic behavior, ordinary diplomacy, or interest-group politics. However, as symbolic politics theory points out, those rationalist assumptions are often false.

Concerning the first assumption, psychologists Irving Janis and Leon Mann argue that people are "reluctant decision maker[s]" because deciding is stressful: people find it hard to handle complexity—especially the complexity of trading off incommensurable values—and they fear that their decision might be wrong.[44] Therefore, people frequently do not make the tradeoff decisions. Because different criteria lead to different preferences, the result is that people's opinions on complex issues are often unstable. For example, polls in 1966 found majorities of Americans in favor both of President Johnson's policy in Vietnam, which involved escalating the war, and of the idea of de-escalating the war.[45] In this case, what determined people's views was how the issue was framed.[46] If the question was one of support for the president, people were inclined to go along. If the question was about what to do in Vietnam, people were inclined to favor de-escalation. The reason for the uncertainty was partly the difficulty of making a tradeoff in incommensurable values: am I sure enough that I dislike this policy to disagree with the president on it?

Regarding the second assumption, psychologists argue that when people choose—and especially when they choose to act—they often do so emotionally rather than rationally. As Susan Fiske and Shelley Taylor put it, "emotion commits one to action more than does the cost-benefit calculation of intellective cognition."[47] Thus people are more likely to participate in a protest rally or write to a politician on an issue that angers them or otherwise stirs them emotionally—an issue that stirs a "hot cognition"—than on an issue that only involves their material interests.[48] This finding is important because of a second effect of emotional decision-making: "emotions . . . divert people from pursuing one goal and point them toward pursuing another goal that has meanwhile increased in importance."[49] Donald Kinder has found, for example, that Americans' feelings of anger against Saddam Hussein during the Persian Gulf War correlated with fewer qualms about the civilian casualties caused by U.S. action, and with greater support for having U.S. troops march to Baghdad to oust Saddam.[50] Emotions change preferences: in this case, anger promoted support for hawkish policies.

Interestingly, even rational choice theorists are inclined to agree that emotions help determine decisions. Thus Samuel Popkin, whose book is entitled *The Reasoning Voter,* notes that "data presented in an emotionally compelling way may be given greater consideration and more weight than data that is statistically more valid, but emotionally neutral."[51] This insight accords with psychological research: for example, one study subtitled "Preferences Need No Inferences" shows that emotional judgments are quicker and stronger than cognitive judgments, people are more likely to remember emotionally keyed information than purely cognitive information, and people may have affective responses to something—liking or disliking it—without even recognizing what it is.[52] Even more important, studies have shown that attitudes which originally formed emotionally are most responsive to emotional appeals.[53] This is the heart of the matter: for some kinds of decisions, people are most likely to base their decisions on emotion.

The core assumption of symbolic choice theory is therefore: *people choose by responding to the most emotionally potent symbol evoked.* According to Murray Edelman, who originated the approach, symbols get their meaning from emotionally laden myths. Myths, as mentioned above, have the role of giving events and actions a particular meaning—typically by defining enemies and heroes and tying ideas of right and wrong to people's identity. Facts, from this point of view, do not matter—either they are redundant, confirming the myth; or else they contradict it and are rejected. To illustrate the point, Edelman uses the example of American attitudes toward the Vietnam War.[54] To those who believed the myth of "America the righteous," the meaning of American military action was a stand against communist aggression, and facts that did not fit that image—American misdeeds of various kinds—were ignored or rejected. To others, the war was symbolized by the napalming of children. They therefore accepted the myth of "Vietnam the victim," the ultimate expression of which was Jane Fonda's visit to North Vietnam, and rejected or downplayed any evidence of North Vietnamese misdeeds.

From this point of view, then, political choice is mostly emotional expression, politics is mostly about manipulating people's emotions, and symbols provide the tool for such manipulation. As a practice, "symbolic politics" refers to any sort of political activity focused on arousing emotions rather than addressing interests. As anthropologist Zdzislaw Mach aptly sums it up, in politics, "symbols are . . . selected and combined so as to achieve a desired state of people's minds; to appeal to values, to refer to ideas, to stir emotions and to stimulate action."[55] Politicians manipulate symbols—wave flags, refer to heroes, kiss babies—in order to induce people to make choices based on the values they are promoting (which are evoked by the chosen symbols), or to associate themselves with those values.[56] Thus politicians supporting a war evoke symbols of the nation's greatness and demonize the enemy, while those opposing it try to evoke sympathy for the casualties and reverse the hawks' identification of heroes and villains.

Symbols are so potent because they have both cognitive and emotional effects.[57] Thus when abortion opponents use the imperiled fetus as the symbol of the issue, they are both framing the issue cognitively as one of the life of the fetus and trying to elicit sympathy for what they consider an innocent and vulnerable baby. Ethnicity is a rich resource for politicians engaged in symbolic politics because it is so emotionally laden. Ethnic groups by definition have myths of shared history, common heroes, and common kinship, as well as symbols that evoke those myths. Furthermore, a threatened ethnic symbol can be used to tap a number of values and emotions simultaneously—especially fellow-feeling among those in the group, shared feelings of superiority over and threat from the out-group—in addition to perceptions of conflict of interests. In short, Edelman argues, symbolic appeals create around conflicts of interest a myth of struggle against "hostile, alien, or subhuman forces" as a way to mobilize support.[58]

THE SYMBOLIC POLITICS OF ETHNIC WAR

The central assumption of symbolic politics theory—that people make political choices based on emotion and in response to symbols—fits closely with the psychologically driven understanding of ethnic war suggested by the work of Young and Horowitz. Horowitz argues that emotions such as fear of group extinction are what drive ethnic violence; Young emphasizes the importance of stereotypes (myths) and symbols in sustaining identity and driving group mobilization. And if ethnicity is an emotional bond evoking kinship feelings, then emotional appeals to that bond should be the basic mechanism by which ethnic mobilization works. Research also shows that people experiencing any negative emotion are more prone to feelings of anger and aggression if ideas justifying anger and aggression are brought to mind.[59] Therefore, if emotional appeals to ethnic themes are simultaneously appeals to ideas that lead one to blame another group, those appeals are apt simultaneously to arouse the feelings of anger and aggression most likely to motivate people to want to fight.

Put together, these ideas create a convincing picture of the psychology of ethnic war. On the individual level, appeals to emotionally laden ethnic symbols are what motivate people to participate in ethnic movements, and appeals to myths blaming other groups are what make people feel aggressive and motivate them to fight in ethnic wars. Those emotional appeals short-circuit the complicated problem of making tradeoff decisions because they encourage people to put ethnic issues ahead of other concerns. At the same time, the social psychology of group membership reinforces these processes for the group as a whole. These processes lead group members to want to gain status relative to other groups, encouraging them to pursue dominance over other groups. Additionally, feelings that the ethnic group is like a kinship group make people willing to fight to defend their group, especially if they believe that the group is truly threatened with extinction.

According to symbolic politics theory, then, understanding whether people will engage in ethnic violence requires that we examine the myths and prejudices that determine which symbols are likely to move them, and what evokes their greatest collective fears.

NECESSARY CONDITIONS FOR ETHNIC WAR

Precisely when, then, does ethnic war occur? The key necessary conditions are:

Myths justifying ethnic hostility

According to symbolic politics theory, people respond to ethnic symbols and mobilize for war only if a widely known and accepted ethnic myth-symbol complex justifies hostility to the other group. The myths justify hostility if they identify a territory as the group's homeland which must be defended and dominated politically and define a mythical enemy with which the other group can be identified. Chauvinism—the belief that one's own group is superior—is typically part of the motivation for the goal of dominance. And if the group's identity includes a warrior ethos, as the Chechen mythos does, for example, that group is likely to be more prone to ethnic violence.[60] In this book, I look for such hostile myths in the key themes in each group's mainstream history texts written before the conflicts began, as well as in dissident sources.

Myths can be and sometimes are recast by chauvinist elites, of course, but this process takes a very long time unless it builds on a myth-symbol complex already made familiar by previous cultural entrepreneurs. Jack Snyder points out that these myths are often molded and propagated by national governments as a way of gaining nationalist legitimacy.[61] In Yugoslavia, for example, the long-standing myth of Serbian martyrdom at the hands of Muslims in the Battle of Kosovo was propagated by the Serbian state in the nineteenth and twentieth centuries, then supplemented and transformed by the fear-invoking slogan "Only unity saves the Serbs," which formed the basis for justifying hostility against Bosnian Muslims and Kosovo Albanians in the 1980s and 1990s.

There does not have to be such a well-developed myth-symbol complex on both sides. Young begins his book with an example of ethnic violence (a conflict between Mbala and Pende in Zaire in 1962) in which one group was relatively well-defined, but the opposing side was essentially a loose coalition of groups that did not long exist as a separate identity. This defines one of the minimum necessary conditions for ethnic war: the existence of at least one group with a myth-symbol complex justifying the pursuit of ethnic dominance (and thus hostility to any who oppose it), and the existence of another group or coalition bound together in opposition to the first group.

Ethnic fears

A fundamental factor causing ethnic conflicts to escalate to war is that first one side, then eventually both sides, come to fear that the existence of their group is at stake. Such extreme fears justify hostile attitudes toward the other group and extreme measures in self-defense, including demands for political dominance. These fears may be anxiety-laden—that is, exaggerated by emotion and by ingroup-outgroup psychology. For example, Horowitz quotes Nigerian Hausa, members of the country's largest ethnic group, as expressing fears at the time of their ethnic war of being "swamped" by minorities from the south.[62] These psychological tendencies explain the power of ethnic fear to motivate ethnic mobilization and murderous violence.

The source of such fear is typically the group's myth-symbol complex, portraying the in-group as peculiarly under threat or peculiarly victimized. In these cases, the more the group's historians emphasize the group's past victimization, the more credible are the emotional charges of genocide that arouse gut-level fears and the more appealing are hate-filled cries for vengeance.[63] Indeed, in most cases of ethnic war, at least one group has been historically dominated by the other,[64] causing fears of ethnic extinction to appear more plausible to the previously dominated, while giving the previously dominant reason to fear revenge. Sometimes both groups have had both experiences: Azerbaijanis fear a return to the Armenian minority's nineteenth-century dominance, while Armenians in Azerbaijan resent twentieth-century Azerbaijani rule.

Demographic threats may also motivate ethnic fears, most insidiously in cases involving an "ethnic affinity problem" in which the minority in a country (e.g., Israel's Palestinians) is the majority in the broader region.[65] The effect of such a situation is that both groups, by viewing borders differently, can think of themselves as potential minorities in danger of ethnic extinction. Mixed settlement patterns also may contribute to ethnic fear,[66] but they only cause a security dilemma if both communities are threatened. If the minority (e.g., Bombay's Muslim community) is seriously threatened, but the majority (Bombay's Hindus) are not, the result is pogroms instead of a security dilemma.[67]

Myths play a key role in the interpretation of these factors, however. Histories of domination can be invented, as the Serbs do when they identify the Albanians of Kosovo, who never dominated Serbia, with the Ottoman Turks, who did. More generally, ethnic histories always contain episodes of peace and of war; which is "traditional" depends on tradition—that is, myth or interpretation—rather than on actual past events. Some groups that are genuinely threatened by demographic trends (e.g., the Latvians) may not resort to violence at all, while other groups (e.g., the Hausa) may distort demographic trends to invent a danger that does not exist. Finally, mixed settlement patterns may contribute to ethnic understanding rather than violence; while ethnic war (as in southern Sudan) may occur where groups are geographically separate. What determines a group's response to its situation is its mythology—which determines its expectations—more than the situation itself.

Once ethnic fears become prevalent among the members of any ethnic group, for whatever reason, they justify and motivate a resort to violence in self-defense. Such fears are a necessary condition for ethnic war because people are much more concerned to avoid loss than to pursue gains, so they are usually mobilizable only when confronted by some threat.[68] This is why leaders of nations, even when they launch aggressive wars, always justify their actions by claiming that it is aimed at averting some mortal danger. Even the Holocaust was justified by an ideology that Jews were not only inferior, but evil and dangerous.[69]

Opportunity to mobilize and fight

Another requirement for ethnic war is opportunity: ethnic groups must have enough freedom to mobilize politically without being stopped by state coercion.[70] Effective policing can prevent violent episodes from escalating, and political repression can prevent ethnic leaders from articulating their demands and mobilizing their followers for conflict. Therefore, as long as a state maintains an effective apparatus of repression and uses it to suppress ethnic mobilization, large-scale ethnic violence cannot occur. Since the relaxation or weakening of political repression opens up political space for all sorts of political entrepreneurs, such relaxation can make ethnic violence more likely. The way Mikhail Gorbachev's policy of *glasnost* provided the political space for ethnic entrepreneurs to mobilize in the Soviet Union epitomizes this possibility.

Of course, if it is the leaders of the state who want to start ethnic violence, they have the opportunity as long as they are in power: Rwanda's Hutu government in 1994 illustrates the point. If the result is to be ethnic war, however, both sides must have the opportunity to organize and arm themselves. Such opportunity requires a territorial base: if one side has no base—either inside the disputed area or across a friendly border—where it can organize its army, it cannot fight. If one side, usually the state, has an overwhelming military advantage, the result is ethnic cleansing, genocide, or more limited riots rather than war.

When foreign patrons are the key cause of violence, they act by changing the opportunity structure, usually by offering material assistance to one side.[71] Foreign countries or groups cannot directly create mass hostility or extremist elites, but they can provide money, advice, and propaganda support to help extremist elites mobilize politically and promote ethnic hostility. They can also provide money and arms to enable chauvinist elites to initiate violence using the few fanatics the elites can mobilize at first. Moldova's Transnistria conflict, as I show in chapter 5, is an example of this potential, with Russia playing the role of the third party. Third parties can also, of course, act to discourage violence; those possibilities are discussed below.

Transnistria and southern Sudan are examples of another point concerning opportunity: ethnic war does not require the existence of government institutions uniting each conflicting group. While groups in conflict often take over existing regional governments where they can, they can create such institutions if necessary (as the Transnistrians did), or they can operate simply as a loose coalition of insurgents (as do the rebels of southern Sudan).

A final related point concerns level of economic development. Jack Snyder has argued that ethnonationalist mobilization is most likely at levels of per capita GDP between $1,000 and $6,000 in 1985 dollars. Below $1,000 in income, he argues, people tend to mobilize as part of patronage networks rather than as ethnic groups; while above $6,000 the growth of an educated middle class damps down tendencies toward ethnonationalist extremism.[72] This correlation does seem to exist, but both the trend and the exceptions to it are best explained in symbolic terms. Purveying a strong nationalist mythology generally requires an effective educational system associated with at least moderate levels of economic development. Sometimes, however, as in Rwanda and Burundi, strong ethnonationalist mythologies exist at lower levels of economic development, and these are the exception to Snyder's rule. At higher income levels, prosperous middle-class groups in democratic states are not usually inclined to pursue ethnic violence—but in cases where ethnic myths and fears are strong, as in Northern Ireland and Spain's Basque region, they do resort to violence.

PROCESSES LEADING TO ETHNIC WAR

If the necessary conditions for ethnic war are myths, fears, and opportunity, the timing of war is explained by an increase in fear, opportunity, or hostility justified by the myths. Hostility and fear rise as a result of symbolic events that activate the myths, such as a violent episode that appeals to ethnic stereotypes (e.g., a murder or beating blamed by one group on another); a leader explicitly manipulating symbols (e.g., waving a flag); a threatening shift in political power (e.g., the election of a minority or extremist candidate); or even the emergence of new information (e.g., publication of a census showing a group's population decline). The alternative possibility is that fear and hostility are already high, but a new political opportunity emerges (e.g., emergence of a reforming leader).

The symbolic politics theory holds that if the three preconditions—hostile myths, ethnic fears, and opportunity—are present, ethnic war results if they lead to rising mass hostility, chauvinist mobilization by leaders making extreme symbolic appeals, and a security dilemma between groups. Different kinds of triggering events work by activating either the hostility or chauvinist mobilization. When myths, fears, and hostility are already strong, a new opportunity and a galvanizing event allow a powerful *mass-led* ethnic movement to emerge. Such movements spur politicians to seek support by making chauvinist symbolic appeals, goading mobilization even if the government opposes it; if the result is a security dilemma, war follows. Other conflicts are *elite-led,* in which a few powerful elites, typically government officials, harness ethnic myths and symbols to provoke fear, hostility, and a security dilemma and mobilize their group for violence. In either case, war results from a vicious feedback loop in which hostility, extremist symbolic appeals, and a security dilemma all reinforce each other to spur violence (see Figure 2.1). If any of the three processes is absent, however—if hostility rises but politicians avoid extremist appeals, or if the population resists such appeals, or if the sides' demands do not cause a security dilemma—war can be avoided.

The way an ethnic security dilemma works is most similar to Jack Snyder's concept of the "imperialist's dilemma" or to what Robert Jervis has called a "deep security dilemma."[73] In contrast to Jervis's more commonly cited formulation, in which the sides prefer not to fight but feel driven to do so by insecurity, the sides in an ethnic security dilemma are openly hostile and are perfectly willing to fight. Violence is not their first choice—they would rather get what they want peacefully. Yet, what each group does to pursue its own security-defined-as-dominance is so threatening to a rival

Figure 2.1 Processes of Ethnic Conflict Escalation

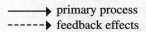

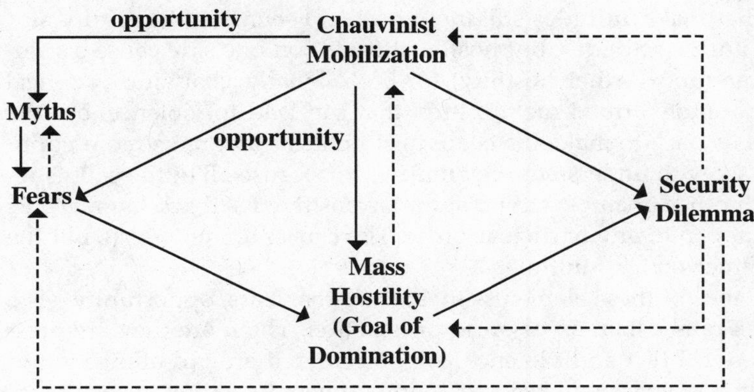

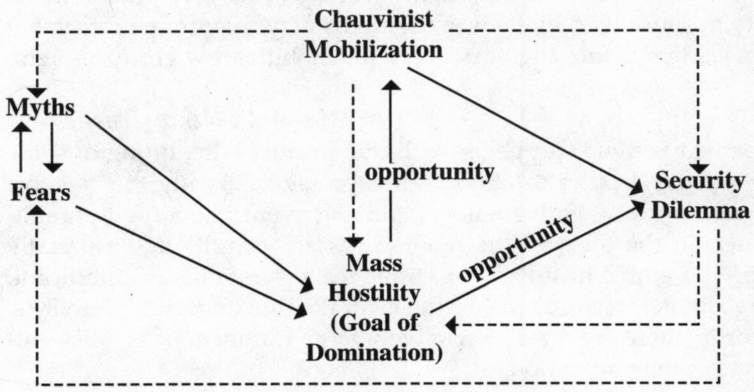

group that the rival increases its security demands in ways threatening to the first. The tragic element is that the groups are spurred by their mythologies to define their security in mutually incompatible ways when more modest definitions on both sides would permit mutual security instead of a spiral of insecurity and violence.

A peculiar feature of the process leading to ethnic war is that it is a process of positive feedback: all of the causes reinforce each other in an escalating spiral of violence.[74] Hostile myths and attitudes are what make chauvinist politics possible, but symbolic appeals to those myths evoke emotions that make attitudes still more hostile. Feelings of insecurity also encourage hostile attitudes, but hostile attitudes on one side cause a security dilemma (and further hostility) for both. Finally, chauvinist political programs promote armed mobilization that can lead to violence; but the violence feeds back to make the chauvinist political programs more popular. This is a key to understanding ethnic war: because all of the causes reinforce each other in an escalating spiral or positive feedback loop, events need not happen in any particular order. The causes are universal, but the paths to ethnic war are multiple.

The existence of these elements—hostile myths, fears, opportunity—is a more-or-less rather than a yes-or-no proposition. The more they are present, the more conflict and violence will be centered around ethnicity and the worse that violence will become. If government breakdown leads to violence but ethnic mythologies and identities are weak, then the violence is likely to be organized around nonethnic coalitions. Also, because the process operates by feedback, different initial mixes of these ingredients can produce war: very strong hostile myths may need very little political opportunity to cause war; while weaker myths may require reinforcement by political leaders before they can serve for mobilizing a group to fight.

Mass-led violence scenarios

Mass-led paths to ethnic war begin with opportunity—the lifting of some previously existing barrier to ethnic self-expression, usually the coercive force of a state—or else with some galvanizing event like a highly publicized murder. In these cases, the other necessary conditions—especially myths justifying ethnic hostility and ethnic fears—are already significant, and nationalism is therefore already the central value of dissident politics. In other words, there are already relatively large numbers of fanatics and true believers in the population.

In these circumstances, long-standing myths justifying group solidarity and identifying threats to group survival suddenly start being articulated publicly. With hostility already high, mass ethnic nationalist movements can spring into being almost overnight, either *de novo* or by pressing previously apolitical organizations into action as vehicles for ethno-nationalist mobilization. A tipping process works to promote that mobilization as the improving safety and prospects for success motivate more and more moderate nationalists to join in. Intraethnic politics then becomes a competition in nationalist symbolism, in which elites in each ethnic group find themselves competing to establish their ethnic *bona fides* and gain adherents by promoting "genuine" nationalist goals—including, if their group fears extinction, the subordination of other ethnic groups to their own.[75] A security dilemma naturally follows from the pursuit of such goals, creating a feedback loop that increases fear, hostility, and extremist symbolic politics on both sides.

There is, however, no single path which all mass-led conflicts follow to ethnic war. In some cases, hostile masses reward elites proposing chauvinist platforms, thereby creating a security dilemma (because the platforms threaten other groups) and leading to violence. This is the likely pattern in cases of *popular chauvinism,* when the group mobilizing first is the majority, as occurred in Georgia (see chapter 4). In other cases, masses engage in widespread but unorganized violence that first creates a security dilemma and only then leads to the replacement of existing leaders with extremists intent on implementing chauvinist policies. This pattern is more typical for repressed minorities—cases of *mass insurgency* such as the Karabagh conflict (see chapter 3). Either way, the first episodes of violence play an important role because they provide vivid evidence supporting previously inchoate fears, and later serve as a symbol of the threat to the group. The emotional impact moves opinion by reinforcing existing myths, often turning latent chauvinism into open hostility.

Elite-led violence scenarios

Elite-led violence involves yet another set of paths. In these cases, leaders motivated either by ideological zeal or by opportunism mobilize their group for ethnic war in pursuit of their own goals. They use the propaganda resources of modern political organizations and mass media to manipulate ethnic symbols and fan ethnic hostility, identifying outgroups with enemies from group mythology and highlighting the "threats" they pose. Thus minor demographic changes can be redefined as mortal threats to group survival, ancient disasters can be recast as current threats, and violent methods can be promoted as the only alternative to group catastrophe.

Additionally, the power of leaders to define the political agenda and control negotiations makes it possible for them to block any potential compromise simply by being intransigent. Blaming the stalemate on the other group then allows them to discredit opponents who promote moderate programs. Eventually, the extremists can organize militias or armies to launch violent provocations which begin a cycle of violence—radicalizing opinion and creating symbols for future use. If the other side responds in kind, a security dilemma spiral fed by violent propaganda takes off. This is most likely to occur in cases of *government jingoism*—epitomized by Slobodan Milosevic in Serbia (see chapter 6)—in which top government officials are the culprits.

Also possible is a process of *elite conspiracy,* in which low-level elites or guerrilla leaders, typically aided from the outside, initiate a similar process. The case of Moldova's Transnistria conflict (see chapter 5) exemplifies this pattern.

EXPLAINING ATROCITIES

The above logic can explain why people are willing to fight in ethnic wars: because they are frightened, and because they become convinced that their group's political dominance is essential to group survival. Such thinking can logically justify killing, and even massacre in extreme cases. Atrocities, however, require something more. While I cannot present a complete theory of atrocities here, it is possible to suggest an explanation based on the logic of symbolic politics.

Some argue that atrocities occur because they are in the interests of the people who commit or order them. That explanation, however, is not adequate. First, atrocities are not very useful, even if one's goal is ethnic cleansing. The Serbs in Bosnia, for example, were in many cases able to use simple threats of murder, accompanied by a few exemplary killings, to accomplish this aim. Dismembering victims or torturing them adds little to the terror created by threats of murder. Second, atrocities do attract moral opprobrium from third parties: all groups in conflict want outside allies and sympathizers, and engaging in atrocities is undeniably costly in driving away potential supporters. Atrocities, in short, are not a useful policy tool.

The symbolic politics theory would suggest an explanation based less on logical than on psychological factors. If the point of ethnic symbolism is to engage supporters' emotions, and the point of such symbolism during violent conflict is specifically to encourage aggressive emotions, it stands to reason that some proportion of people will react extremely strongly to the aggressive symbolism and express it in extreme ways. At the same time, even atrocities have to have a normative basis, which should consist of two components: a mythical belief that the opponent tends to engage in atrocities and a normative view that retaliatory atrocities are morally acceptable. The key is the last part: ethnic violence is always defined defensively, by the claim that the other group is trying to take away what is "rightfully ours"; atrocities have to be justified by the claim that committing them is a legitimate way to defend what is "rightfully ours."

To be sure, not everyone who engages in atrocities has to accept such beliefs. But some must. Even if atrocities are ordered by political leaders and enforced both by peer pressure and by government sanction, at least some of the people carrying out the orders must believe in their legitimacy if they are to exert peer pressure. This is the key point Daniel Goldhagen makes about the Holocaust in *Hitler's Willing Executioners*: while obedience to authority, peer pressure, and other factors do play a role in making such behavior systemic, these motivations are not enough to explain cases in which people take the initiative in committing atrocities, or in which they have the opportunity to evade such "duties" but carry them out anyway.[76] Every plea of "they made me do it" must come attached to a case in which someone willingly applied the coercion.

An alternative explanation for atrocities, and for ethnic wars in general, is that they are carried out primarily by common criminals, thugs who like hurting people and find in such conflicts an excuse to do so. There is plenty of evidence to support this proposition.[77] It is not, however, a complete explanation: behind most warlords employing such thugs (such as Serbia's Arkan) is an ethnic nation and leadership (the Serbs and Milosevic) justifying their behavior in terms of national defense. Furthermore, many atrocities are carried out by otherwise ordinary people. Thuggishness explains some of the atrocities, but the motivating force of ethnic symbolism is necessary to fill in the rest of the puzzle.

Policy Alternatives for Conflict Resolution

The Modest Requirements for Ethnic Peace

One argument of this book is that it is not easy in contemporary times to get people to fight ethnic wars, and it is even harder to get them to commit atrocities. Ethnic war is possible only in the presence of hostile myths, opportunity to mobilize, and fear of group extinction, and it breaks out only if these factors create mass hostility, a within-group politics dominated by extreme nationalist symbolism, and a security dilemma between groups. If any major ingredient is missing, ethnic war cannot occur. If a group's myth-symbol complex encourages cooperation with other groups rather than domination or defensiveness—if, that is, people are reasonable and moderate—mobilization for ethnic war cannot begin because extremist politics is not rewarded. If people are fearful but not extremely so, they are unlikely to resort to violence. And even if people are hostile and fearful, if elites can moderate political demands and restrain violent popular impulses—avoiding extremist political symbolism and preventing the emergence of a security dilemma—violence can still be averted. Ethnic wars only happen when the attitudes of elites and masses are aligned in hostility.

CONFLICT RESOLUTION TOOLS

Given these three key causes of ethnic war—mass hostility, extremist politics, and a security dilemma—a comprehensive approach to conflict resolution would require attempts to ameliorate or prevent all three, either before or after violence breaks out. One way to restrain extremist politics is through *peacemaking*—pursuit of intergroup negotiations and cooperation, whether through mediated talks, building consociational institutions, or some other device.[78] If the problem can be reduced to a classic security dilemma—that is, a situation in which the parties can agree on a preferred outcome but do not trust each other to implement a compromise—then what is needed is *reassurance,* perhaps including *peacekeeping*. If, however, the core of the problem is mutually incompatible security requirements based on hostile myths and fears of extinction, then neither peacemaking nor peacekeeping can lead to a resolution. What is required first in these circumstances is *peacebuilding*—efforts to bring the groups (not just their leaders) together to change their hostile attitudes so they can revise their understanding of their security needs, thereby making peacemaking possible and peacekeeping less necessary.[79] Peacebuilding efforts, I will argue, are unwisely underestimated in conflict resolution practice: while vitally important to make conflict resolution work, they get little attention and few resources. Lack of attention to peacebuilding undermines conflict resolution efforts.

Peacemaking

For leaders faced with managing highly emotional ethnic conflicts, skill and sensitivity in building coalitions, negotiating agreements, and calming volatile passions may make the difference between success and failure.[80] Some political systems may be more likely than others to produce such leaders: the communist systems studied in this book did so only occasionally. The fact that Gorbachev was the first Soviet leader since Lenin to lack leadership experience outside Russia—and lacked therefore the opportunity to develop skill in ethnic conflict management—may be an important reason for the Soviet Union's breakup.

For conflicts that have already exploded into violence, a growing literature explores different modes of peacemaking and different strategies third parties can follow to mediate or broker settlements for ethnic conflicts. One key insight of this literature is that a conflict is "ripe for resolution" only in certain circumstances: if leaders on both sides want an agreement, can find a mutually acceptable formula, are strong enough to "deliver" their constituencies, and have a mutually acceptable process for negotiation. Typically, a mutually hurting stalemate is required for such conditions to emerge.[81]

In this context, there is a long list of things third-party mediators can do, most of which are relevant before violence breaks out as well as after.[82]

Mediators can create a suitable process by convening negotiations, offering a venue, establishing an agenda, and so on. They can suggest possible compromises, propose a formula for resolving the conflict, or set up a conciliation commission to design one. They can make agreement more attractive by offering inducements—resources for reconstruction, rewards for concessions—and by emphasizing the costs of failure to agree. Mediators can also offer to verify and guarantee the settlement. They can even help "deliver" the leaders' constituents by conferring international legitimacy on the process and the outcome—and on the leaders who reach it. More generally, by gaining the parties' trust and helping them communicate, mediators can help the parties reach understandings they might have missed unaided, in part by providing relatively unbiased information. If the parties prove recalcitrant, mediators can try to coerce them by threatening to impose economic sanctions, to aid the other side, or to intervene militarily. Finally, by drawing on international experience, mediators can help structure an agreement to help reduce the dangers that it will collapse in implementation.[83]

There is one problem with this approach, however: it usually does not work for resolving ethnic wars. One study shows that of post-World War II "identity civil wars" that have been settled in some way, over 70 percent were settled by one side's military victory, not by negotiations: and in two-thirds of those cases in which a negotiated settlement was reached, the settlements collapsed and war resumed.[84] Ethnic wars are hard to resolve through ordinary negotiations.

Reassurance

When two sides' goals are compatible but mutual mistrust is an obstacle to resolution, the sides can try to reduce the mistrust with reassuring moves: confidence-building measures such as military reductions or withdrawals; agreement on norms regulating competition; or implementation of strategies such as graduated reciprocation in tension-reduction.[85] The most powerful tool available is for a leader to make a highly visible symbolic gesture of reconciliation, such as Egyptian President Sadat's famous trip to Jerusalem, which started the process that led to the Camp David accords. The trouble, of course, is that by becoming himself the symbol of peace, the leader becomes vulnerable to retaliation by extremists: the assassinations of Sadat and Israeli Prime Minister Rabin are the measure of the incompleteness of Arab-Israeli reconciliation.

For third parties, the most effective tool of reassurance is peacekeeping, the nonviolent use of third-party armed forces to maintain peace among belligerents.[86] In general, peacekeeping only works with the consent and cooperation of the key parties to the conflict: that is, if there is a peace to be kept, and the parties to the conflict want it to be kept, peacekeepers can help by preventing minor incidents between mistrustful belligerents from escalating to renewed war.[87] Interestingly, this rather broad definition—a simplified version of the usual one—applies just as well to domestic policing, and indeed good policing can have this effect. If initial violent incidents play a critical role in provoking fear and motivating further violence, then prompt and fair punishment of violent actors by legitimate authorities can go far in calming fears and undercutting the motives for group violence. The conditions of ethnic warfare presuppose that authorities are unable or unwilling to accomplish this role.

Classical peacekeepers operate differently, by reminding the parties of their agreed obligations, reporting violations, and sometimes by inserting themselves between parties in conflict to prevent violence. In some cases—Macedonia in the mid- and late-1990s is an example discussed below—peacekeepers can be inserted preventively into a peaceful situation to help prevent the outbreak of violence. Peacekeeping has, however, two fundamental limits. First, when peacekeepers are inserted to maintain a ceasefire pending final resolution, the resulting stable ceasefire may remove incentives for the sides to resolve the conflict. The Cyprus conflict, where UN peacekeepers remained for decades in such a situation, is the clearest case. The second limitation is that peacekeeping only works where the parties want it to work: if the parties to a conflict are determined to fight, they can ignore or overrun peacekeepers. Making the parties want peace is the realm of peacebuilding.

Peacebuilding

Many theoreticians and diplomats tend to dismiss peacebuilding as either naive or ineffective, but doing so is a mistake. According to symbolic politics theory, the core causes of ethnic war are ethnic hostility and the myths and fears that promote it. What peacebuilders do is to bring people from opposing sides of a conflict together to replace the myths about the other side with better information, to replace the hostility and fear with understanding, and most of all to build cooperative interethnic relationships to replace stereotyped hostile ones.[88] From the point of view of the diplomatic practitioner, such efforts among grassroots leaders can build a political constituency for the diplomatic peace process so leaders can "sell" a compromise settlement. For mid-level officials, it includes reconciliation commissions or "track II" diplomacy that helps officials who have access to top leaders to work creatively with the other group to create mutually acceptable formulas for conflict resolution. And by building cooperative intergroup relationships, it creates resources that can be drawn on in implementing a peace agreement once reached.

Peacebuilding is an extremely difficult undertaking that has rarely been attempted except on a small scale. It has, however, already shown some results: peacebuilding can change attitudes. The typical formula is to bring people from the groups in conflict together at a neutral site, often to live together for a period of time and to discuss in detail the issues that divide them. What they find time and again is that after heated arguments and initial resistance, most participants—for example, Israeli and Palestinian teenagers (including stone-throwing *intifadah* participants)[89] or religious leaders from northern and southern Sudan—come to an increased mutual understanding, and in some cases move on to creative efforts to help resolve real conflicts. One of the proudest accomplishment of peacebuilding is the 1993 Israeli-Palestinian Oslo Accords, which began as a "problem-solving workshop" involving mid-level officials on both sides. In Mozambique, a much larger grassroots effort including church-sponsored dialogues and a UNICEF-funded "Circus of Peace" helped create the environment in which the peacemaking efforts of top leaders could succeed.[90] The biggest problem peacebuilding faces is the "reentry problem": when participants return to their polarized societies, they find few people receptive to hearing their new insights. The best way to overcome this problem is through a coordinated set of peacebuilding efforts large enough in scale to help a networked constituency for peace emerge.

Another set of possibilities involves efforts to recast ethno-nationalist myths into cooperative and tolerant ones, especially by promoting the writing and teaching of fair-minded history instead of the ethnocentric and scapegoating kind.[91] For third parties, this means attention by governments and international organizations to school curricula in multiethnic countries and open criticism of and pressure on countries that teach hostile myths to their schoolchildren. Such myths, however, may not come exclusively or even primarily from history or social studies classes. On the contrary: since ethnic myths are primarily affective, they may be more effectively transmitted by literature than by history texts. Attention must therefore also be paid to the stories children read and the poems they recite. If they learn to hate in school, it may be more likely to happen in literature class than in history class.

In the shorter term, attention can also be paid to efforts at countering scapegoating propaganda—the twisting of ethnic symbols into symbols of ethnic conflict by chauvinist ethnic elites. Here too the means is primarily open criticism, in this case of chauvinist politicians. Chauvinists always try to equate their views with "true" nationalism; the challenge for outside critics is to make clear their disapproval of such chauvinists without appearing to oppose more legitimate sorts of nationalism. Doing so, indeed, cuts against the grain of symbolic politics, as it is easy for the chauvinist to ask: what right do *they* have to dictate the meaning of *our* national identity? Perhaps the best that can be done is to find ways to support the chauvinists' opponents in order to illustrate and demonstrate the benefits of choosing a more moderate leadership. This approach only works, however, while the chauvinists are out of power; once they come to power, the country is on its way toward elite-led violence, and efforts to head it off become much more difficult.

Crisis management options

Once conflict begins building toward violence, all parties' options for conflict resolution narrow dramatically. If the mobilization is elite-led by government leaders, one option is to offer inducements for peace—a package of political and economic concessions that might help the leaders maintain their power without having to resort to hostile ethnic symbolism. This might be reinforced by deterrent threats to support the other side in case of violence, or by counter-mobilization of peace advocates. If the mobilization is a case of elite conspiracy by leaders of a subordinate group, the most relevant inducement would be co-optation—offering the opposition leaders limited power in exchange for loyalty. Other options include isolating them from outside aid or offering reassurance in the form of new evidence or incentives for government moderation. The trouble with all of these options is that once mobilization takes off, whether under the control of government leaders or of well-entrenched insurgents, the leaders are usually too committed to conflict to be swayed.

Mass-led conflicts may be more amenable to crisis management—if government leaders want to avoid violence. Minorities and majorities are likely to respond to different appeals, however. Mass insurgencies by subordinate minorities, whose fear of group extinction is likely to be relatively well-founded, primarily need reassurance, including from trusted police or peacekeepers, that they will be protected. In Macedonia in the 1990s, for example, United Nations peacekeepers were instrumental in providing such reassurance to the Albanian minority. Dominant majorities, who typically inflate fears of losing control into fears of extinction, are harder to reassure because dominance is the only sort of security their mythology allows. However, peacemaking efforts that grant the majority symbolic dominance while conceding the substantive requirements of security to the minority may be possible; if not, deterrence by the direct presence of superior external force may be the only alternative.

Applying the Symbolic Politics Theory

The symbolic politics theory I have proposed here is a general theory of ethnic war, applicable in any region of the world. Indeed, it is based largely on the ideas of Crawford Young and Donald Horowitz, who write primarily about Africa and Asia. Looking at Africa, for example, the argument that hostile myths and fears of extinction are critical causes of ethnic war holds up well. Sudan's long-running ethnic war is clearly rooted in the mutually antagonistic identity myths of North and South, and where the symbol of "slavery" as the threat to the black southerners is based on a reality of slave trading by Arab northerners that continued into the twentieth century.[92] Similarly, Nigeria's ethnic war of the 1960s was driven by the Hausa-Fulani fear of group extinction, which was based on the stereotype of "pushy" southerners. In Congo/Zaire in the 1960s, in contrast, most violence was ideologically or regionally rather than ethnically based because myth-symbol complexes, and therefore identities, were relatively weak and undeveloped. And South Africa simmered but did not explode in the 1990s in large part because Nelson Mandela and the African National Congress successfully prevented white fears of group extinction from arising, hence avoiding the emergence of a black-white security dilemma (even as elite-led Zulu-Xhosa violence sparked a security dilemma among blacks in Natal).

The rest of this book is aimed at applying the theory to four cases in post-communist Europe. I selected these cases in part to allow a "most-similar systems" comparison: I can control for the type of political institutions and for political opportunity, which were similar in all cases, and focus on how other variables, such as ethnic myths and fears and leaders' behavior, caused ethnic wars. Brief discussions of peaceful counterexamples illustrate how peace was maintained in similar circumstances when myths and fears were weaker or leaders more restrained. Additionally, because many popular theories of ethnic war were formulated to explain the wars in the former Yugoslavia, I want to challenge those theories on their "home ground," showing how the symbolic politics approach offers a more convincing explanation of that case, while also explaining the mass-led wars of the South Caucasus that rival theories cannot explain.

The purpose of these studies is to illustrate the value of the symbolic theory—to show how the theory generates fairly simple, yet different and convincing, explanations for the causes of violence each case. Strictly speaking, they do not represent a test of the symbolic theory because they mostly "search on the dependent variable"—the discussions of cases in which war was avoided are only brief and suggestive. This procedure is warranted, however, because the aim of this book is not primarily theory testing but theory development. The main case studies demonstrate the usefulness of the theory for explaining those important cases, while the brief studies of non-wars provide some suggestive evidence associating ethnic peace with the absence of key variables in the theory. That, plus the theoretical synthesis, is enough for one book; a full test will have to await future study.

One claim I do test is that some conflicts are mass-led while others are elite-led. How can they be distinguished? The critical variable is the attitude of incumbent government officials at the time that ethnic mobilization begins to gather strength. If mass mobilization occurs without government assistance, or even in the face of government efforts to repress it, then the conflict has to be mass-led. If incumbent government leaders are replaced by more nationalist figures as mobilization continues, that would be further evidence of a mass-led process. If, however, there is evidence that government leaders support mass ethnic mobilization from the beginning, then the mobilization is probably elite-led. Since the countries in the study were all communist countries with formal party/government control of the media, the attitude of the media is another indicator: media opposition to ethnic mobilization is evidence of a mass-led process; media support for it is evidence of an elite-led process.

The cases also represent a partial test of the theory in that they look for evidence that the key causes of violence identified in the theory are important in each case. The chapters pay little attention to opportunity, as the opportunities opened up by the death of Tito in Yugoslavia and Mikhail Gorbachev's policy of *glasnost* in the Soviet Union are already well-documented. They do, however, examine in detail the nationalist ideologies and myths in each case and the evidence of ethnic hostility and fear. The explorations of ideology and myth provide the context for examining each group's assertions of its interests and expressions of fear.

The cases also represent a "process-tracing" test, examining in detail how ethnic mobilization happened in order to determine whether the mechanism suggested by the symbolic politics theory actually took place. One key issue is the theory's contention that ethnic mobilization works by a process in which government leaders or dissident intellectuals manipulate ethnic symbols to attract support. By tracing the mobilization process in detail, I can determine whether people responded primarily to appeals to their tangible, individual interests, as rational choice theories assume; or whether they responded to invocations of emotive symbols while ignoring concessions to their material interests, as symbolic politics theory assumes. I also add brief discussions of atrocities to illustrate the plausibility of the symbolic politics explanation of such behavior.

The process-tracing also looks for evidence that ethnic hostility, extremist symbolic politics, and security dilemmas were all present in the cases, and that they all reinforced each other in a positive feedback process to cause the outbreak of violence. If the symbolic politics theory were incorrect, there would be evidence that security dilemmas were the result of groups' uncertainty about each other's motives rather than open hostility, and preparations for war would have been justified with the argument: "we must be prepared because we do not know what they will do." Finally, if the symbolic theory were incorrect, there would be evidence that leaders and followers preferred to avoid war and were willing to compromise to do so, but that structural factors and mistrust caused war to break out anyway.

The case studies support the symbolic politics theory. One of the striking findings of this book is the degree to which emotive symbolic issues—assertions of group or language status, the design of flags, the treatment of "sacred" territory—dominated more tangible issues in motivating participants. Leaders also refer again and again to the importance of emotion in mobilizing followers. People's tangible, individual interests—jobs, housing, education—are frequently irrelevant, and often distorted by ethnic myths even when they are relevant. Security dilemmas arise not from uncertainty about the other side's intentions but from strong evidence of the other side's hostility, usually matched by open hostility on one's own side. This hostility always takes the form of political programs aimed at dominating the other group in the disputed region. Thus war results not from mistrust or miscommunication but from a clash of interests, openly stated and defined as irreconcilable.

Measuring the motivations of the followers of chauvinist movements is, of course, difficult. When opinion polls on relevant issues are not available, the best that can be done is to look at what politicians, activists, and the media were saying at the time. Since we know people mobilized, presumably the themes and issues used at the time were the ones that motivated them. Future studies aimed at probing public attitudes and experimenting with their reactions to ethnic symbols will be necessary to prove or disprove definitively the value of the symbolic politics approach.

THE CAUCASUS IN 1988

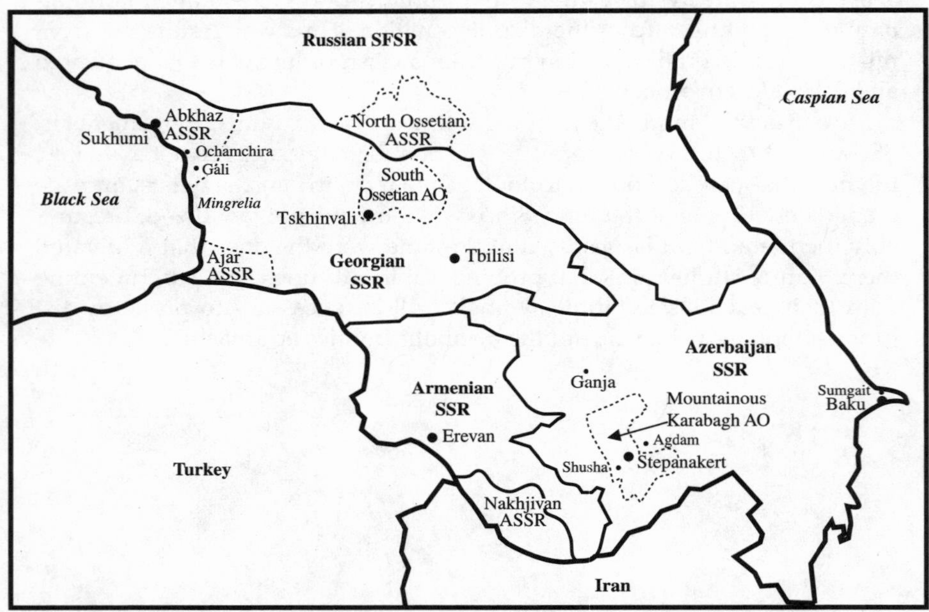

Source: Adapted from Paul Henze, "The Transcaucasus in Transition," RAND Note N-3212-USDP, 1991, p. 2. Reprinted with permission.

[3]

Karabagh and the Fears of Minorities

Since 1988, Armenians and Azerbaijanis have been at war over Mountainous Karabagh, a formerly autonomous region of Azerbaijan populated mostly by Armenians. The conflict over Karabagh is of long standing: the Armenians had been seeking to incorporate the region into Armenia since the end of World War I. Their demands gained international attention in February 1988, when mass rallies in Karabagh spread to the Armenian capital of Erevan, at their peak attracting up to a million demonstrators.

By the end of the month, the conflict exploded into violence—and into the headlines—with pogroms against Armenians in the Azerbaijani city of Sumgait, during which hundreds of Armenians were killed or injured at the hands of mobs of Azerbaijanis (and many more were saved by their Azerbaijani neighbors). The conflict eventually developed into one of the bloodiest and most destructive of the ethnic wars in the former Soviet Union, resulting in some 20,000 dead, over a million refugees, and the almost total "ethnic cleansing" by each side of areas under its control.[1]

The Karabagh conflict is a clear example of the symbolic politics of mass-led violence. Ethnic violence began in spite of the determined opposition of the then-incumbent leaders of Armenia, Azerbaijan, and the Soviet Union and before the emergence of large ethnic nationalist organizations in Armenia or Azerbaijan proper. Indeed, the failure of incumbent leaders to manage the conflict cost them their jobs. The conflict occurred because of a fundamental clash between an Armenian myth-symbol complex focused on fears of genocide and an Azerbaijani one emphasizing the sovereignty and territorial integrity of the Azerbaijani republic. Each therefore defined dominance in Karabagh as vital to its national existence, and saw the other side's aspirations as constituting a threat of group extinction. Karabagh itself thus became, for both sides, a symbol of national aspirations and of the hostility of the other side. The result was first a security dilemma and violence, then a politics of nationalist extremism that led to war.

The Groups and Their History

The Armenian people does not have any close relatives. The Armenian language forms its own branch of the Indo-European language family, has its own alphabet, and was the oldest written language used in the Soviet Union. Most Armenians are Christian, members of the unique Gregorian or Armenian Orthodox church. The Azerbaijanis, in contrast, are a Turkic people whose language was until the 1930s considered identical to Turkish. Azerbaijanis differ from the Turks of Turkey primarily in that, due to a history of Iranian influence, they are traditionally followers of Shi'ite Islam rather than the Sunni form dominant in Turkey.

Historical Background

Like other ethnic conflicts, the Armenian-Azerbaijani conflict over what the Soviets called Nagorno-Karabakh has "historical roots" which include both genuine precedents going back about a century and more dubious interpretations of much earlier history. The complexity of the conflict is implied even in the name of the region: "Kara" is the Turkish word for "black" and "bagh" is Persian for "garden";[2] the "Nagorno"—Russian for "mountainous"—signifies that "Karabagh" previously referred to a larger area. Thus Mountainous Karabagh is the mountainous portion of Karabagh, a region with a mixed Persian, Turkic, Russian—and Armenian—heritage. I refer more loosely to the "Karabagh" conflict because the conflict came to include the grievances of Armenians living in historic Karabagh but outside the Soviet-era boundaries of the Mountainous Karabagh Autonomous Region.

The modern history of the conflict perhaps begins with the 1813 Treaty of Gulistan, which resulted in Persia's cession of most of the contemporary Republic of Azerbaijan, including Karabagh, to Russia.[3] From that time on, "Azerbaijan," the area west and southwest of the Caspian Sea mostly inhabited by Turkic-speaking Shi'ite Muslims, was divided in two: the northern portion under Russian rule and a southern section which remained under Persian rule. The 1828 Russian annexation of the Nakhjivan and Erevan areas impelled further changes, sparking a century-long process of Armenian migration from Persia and the Ottoman Empire to Russian-held territory. The result, over the course of the century, was to change the ethnic composition of regions comprising most of modern Armenia and Mountainous Karabagh from predominantly Muslim to majority-Armenian areas.[4]

The next major turning point was the turn-of-the-century "era of massacres." The first upsurge of Armenian nationalism starting in the 1880s had caused both the Ottoman and the Russian Empires to be increasingly suspicious of the loyalty of their Armenian subjects. Thus, in retaliation for an 1894 uprising in the old Armenian heartland of eastern Anatolia, the Ottoman government organized a series of massacres over the course of two years with, according to Armenian sources, hundreds of thousands of Armenian deaths the result.[5] There followed, during and after the 1905 revolution in Russia, what came to be called the "Armeno-Tatar War," in which Armenians and "Tatars"—i.e., Muslims of the Transcaucasus, mostly Azerbaijanis—fought in clashes all across what are now Armenia and Azerbaijan, with hundreds of villages pillaged or razed and thousands of people killed on both sides.[6] The worst, of course, was yet to come: the genocide of 1915–17 when the Ottoman government, using as an excuse Armenian aid for Russia in World War I, "exiled" over a million Armenian civilians in conditions designed to ensure the death of most of them.

Those Armenians lucky enough to have escaped from Ottoman- to Russian-held territory found themselves on the scene of further horrors as Russian authority in the South Caucasus evaporated in early 1918. A brief Transcaucasian Federation collapsed in May after five weeks of independence, leaving the three separate successor states of Armenia, Azerbaijan, and Georgia. As early as March, however, Armenians and Azerbaijanis had begun committing a series of massacres against each other all across Armenia and Azerbaijan, which soon found themselves at war. Karabagh fell under Azerbaijani authority, but the Armenians of the region repeatedly rebelled. Finally, the Karabagh capital of Shusha fell to Azerbaijani forces in March 1920, and its entire Armenian population was killed or expelled.[7] The next month, with most of the Azerbaijani army concentrated against Armenia, Soviet Russian troops marched into Baku and Azerbaijan was annexed. Armenia followed in November. After the annexations, however, Karabagh remained a bone of contention along with two other disputed territories, Nakhjivan and Zangezur. Soviet officials—meaning, ultimately, Stalin—eventually decided to award the first two areas to Azerbaijan and the third to Armenia.

Karabagh's status remained an issue. Even under Stalin there were sporadic Armenian efforts to raise it. In 1926–27, Armenian émigrés circulated leaflets in Karabagh demanding that the Armenian leadership address the issue. In 1936, Armenian Communist Party First Secretary Khanjyan reportedly raised it again and was shot soon thereafter.[8] In 1945 and 1949, Armenia's new First Secretary, Harutunyan, also approached Moscow with the request that the territory be united with Armenia. There were several petition drives on the issue in the mid-1960s, one of which sparked violent demonstrations in Karabagh in 1963. Armenians attending a 1965 demonstration in Erevan commemorating the 1915 genocide also began crying "Our land!" referring in part to Karabagh.[9] Other appeals were issued in 1967 and 1977.[10] In the early 1980s, Ronald Suny could still report that Karabagh remained "the single most volatile issue" for Armenians.[11]

Conditions for Ethnic War in Armenia and Azerbaijan

OPPORTUNITY

The Armenian view, as illustrated above, is that the Karabagh issue was not newly asserted in 1988; rather, the issue had always been on their agenda. What changed was the opportunity structure: the mere announcement of Mikhail Gorbachev's policy of *glasnost* at the 27th Congress of the Communist Party of the Soviet Union in February 1986 was enough to encourage Karabagh Armenians to launch a new petition drive in quest of official support to change their region's status. Small rallies on environmental and other issues in Erevan in 1987 showed both sides that street demonstrations were permitted in some circumstances as well.

The opportunity to mobilize armed groups followed naturally. Pogrom violence requires relatively little mobilization, and the weapons of riot are ordinary household or industrial items: knives, axes, iron bars. There is evidence that both the 1988 Sumgait and the 1990 Baku pogroms were organized by groups including government officials, but the officials seem merely to have facilitated the pogroms and then ensured that the police stood aside. Later on, a war of raid and counter-raid was easy to organize among mountain villagers, most of whom were armed with hunting rifles and had a tradition of guerrilla warfare. Bribes to or thefts from Soviet soldiers, and the later inheritance of Soviet Army weapons by newly independent Armenia and Azerbaijan in 1992, supplied the means for escalation to full-scale conventional warfare.

MYTHS JUSTIFYING ETHNIC HOSTILITY AND FEAR

Armenian myths and symbols

For understanding ethnic war, the key parts of a myth-symbol complex are its claims to legitimacy (based on claimed indigenous status, past glories, and special merit) and justifications for group hostility. The overtly mythical Armenian story is that Armenians are descended from Haik, a great grandson of the Biblical Noah.[12] A quasi-scholarly counterpart to this story, suggested by Dr. Rafael Ishkhanian (also an activist on the Karabagh issue) claims that Armenians "were the aborigines of the Armenian plateau who have been living there continuously since the fourth millennium B.C.E. at the latest."[13] Similar claims were promoted in nationalist novels such as those of Sero Khanzatian published in the 1970s.[14]

More standard Armenian histories claim the ancient kingdom of Urartu as forerunner to Armenia and emphasize the immigration of the Armenians to the region after that state's sixth-century B.C.E. collapse. Regardless of the specific date they set for the beginning of Armenian history, however, Armenians agree that their long-time habitation of certain territories, including Karabagh—called Artsakh by Armenians—and Nakhjivan, entitles them to possession of those territories regardless of the ethnicity of their current populations.

Though they note *en passant* the role of Armenian Prince Paruir in the conquest of the mighty Assyrian empire in 612 B.C.E., promoters of past Armenian glories make the first-century B.C.E. rise of a great-power Armenian state under King Tigran the Great the real start of their story.[15] The next chapter in that story comes in the early fourth century, when Armenia became the first nation to convert to Christianity—a defining moment about which Armenians proudly boast to visitors. Over the centuries, the Armenian Orthodox Church came to diverge theologically from the views of its neighbors, and that unique and autonomous institution became a central part of the Armenian identity. Largely as a result of the church's influence, the Armenians by the fifth century C.E. clearly formed a single ethnic group with a written language and history as well as a distinctive religion. Another defining glory is the story of David of Sassoun, whose statue sits in downtown Erevan. David's briefly successful uprising against the Arabs in 850 inspired the legend that he would someday return to "liberate his people with his sword of lighting."[16]

Very soon after it emerged, however, the Armenian people developed an ethos as a martyr nation: martyrs, specifically, for their pioneering Christian faith. The foundation of this myth came with the defeat of the Armenian leader St. Vardan by a Persian army at the Battle of Avarayr in 451 C.E.[17] After the Turkish Genocide of 1915, that self-image of martyrdom was vastly strengthened, with "Turks" cast as the timeless victimizer. Earlier history was reinterpreted accordingly. Thus, according to the *Great Soviet Encyclopedia* entry on Armenia, the conquest of Armenia by medieval Turkic groups—the Seljluks in the eleventh century and the Kara-koyunlu state in the fifteenth—led, respectively, to the "annihilat[ion]" and "massive extermination" of the Armenian population.[18] Publicist and historian Ishkhanian has characterized the resulting popular Armenian thinking this way: "[T]o curse at Muslims and especially at Turks, to talk much about the Armenian Genocide, and to remind others constantly of the brutality of the Turks are all regarded as expressions of patriotism. Among the leaders of the past we consider those who curse Turks and killed Turks to be the most patriotic. Our most recent heroes are those who assassinated Turkish diplomats in European cities.... [This] is the dominant mentality."[19]

These strongly anti-Azerbaijani attitudes were not unanimous, but they did show up repeatedly in Armenian political expression.[20] The 1964 petition to Khrushchev on the Karabagh issue, for example, complained of Azerbaijan's "chauvinistic, pan-Turk policy," and concluded that "the policy of discrimination and oppression is engendering justifiable hatred against... the Azerbaijani republic.... [U]ndesirable relationships between nationalities are developing in consequence." Similarly, the 1967 appeal by Karabagh activists to Armenian authorities alleged numerous ethnically motivated murders and even mutilation and concluded by calling Azerbaijan's leaders "chauvinist" and "traitors, spies and their like."[21] Clashes between Armenians and Azerbaijanis, including in 1968 in Stepanakert and again in 1977 and the early 1980s, show that these attitudes repeatedly spilled over into violent action.[22]

Armenians anchor their claim to Karabagh by arguing that the indigenous Christian Albanians were Armenized after the medieval merger of the two churches and that Karabagh is dotted with hundreds of Armenian architectural monuments dating to the twelfth and thirteenth centuries. Karabagh also has great symbolic significance for Armenians because they see it as the only Armenian area to have retained autonomy throughout the dark years of Armenia's decline. Armenian rulers of Mountainous Karabagh were recognized in the fifteenth century by Timur's successors as autonomous "kings," and as late as the 1720s an autonomous Armenian army under Davit Bek fought off Turkish incursions on behalf of Bek's Persian overlords. Karabagh Armenians built on this history a "defiantly martial tradition" which led them to contribute a disproportionate number of war heroes—and war dead—during World War II.[23] According to a British observer, writing in 1919, "Karabagh means more to the Armenians than their religion even, being the cradle of their race, and their traditional last sanctuary when their country has been invaded."[24] The observer knew what he was saying: Karabagh first became part of modern Azerbaijan because temporarily occupying British troops turned Armenian forces under the partisan leader Andranik away from Karabagh in 1918. Promising fair treatment at the Paris peace conference, the British instead assigned the region to Azerbaijan, a decision the Bolsheviks would later uphold. "For the Armenians the historical lessons are clear: Andranik... [was] duped."[25]

Armenian fears

Typically, the strongest ethnic fears are underlain by ethnic affinity problems and histories of ethnic domination. The Armenians of Karabagh faced both: they were a majority in Mountainous Karabagh but a small minority in Azerbaijan. They had been dominated by Baku for seventy years and intermittently by other Muslim Turkic overlords for centuries before that. Armenian fears were particularly acute because both ethnic domination and minority status were associated in their minds with genocide: the "era of massacres" had shown that even brief domination by Turkish extremists could lead to mass slaughter. The fate of Nakhjivan in Soviet times illustrated another threat, subtler but still insidious: Nakhjivan had had a large Armenian minority in Tsarist times, but after seventy years of discriminatory rule from Baku, it was almost entirely Azerbaijani.

Armenians feared that the same thing would happen in Karabagh and used the symbol of "genocide" to refer to the process. Thus they referred to the removal of historic Armenian monuments in Karabagh as "cultural genocide" aimed at eradicating their claim to the territory, and the relative decline of the Armenian population in Karabagh was called "white genocide." Even the pollution problem in Erevan was labeled "ecological genocide" by activists. Alarmists like Zori Balayan tied these fears of genocide to an alleged larger Azerbaijani plan to revive the pan-Turkic movement which would, in the end, annihilate Armenia entirely.[26]

Amidst this danger, however, Armenians also saw opportunity: "Armenians saw in Artsakh [the Armenian name for Karabagh] the symbol for the political, cultural, spiritual and economic revival of our nation; and the people of Artsakh saw in the movement a vehicle for the generation of the popular will to determine their own future."[27] This sentiment was not new: in 1977, the writer Sero Khanzatian attributed to Karabagh Armenians the view, "Let me be poor but be part of Armenia."[28] The power of such sentiments was the reason why the Armenian nationalist movement was, at first, focused primarily on Karabagh.

The nature of Armenian fears is illustrated by the tenor of a petition addressed to Gorbachev by the Armenian Academy of Sciences in 1987—before the outbreak of violence. The Armenian scholars claimed that Azerbaijan was implementing a "Turkish Pan-Islamist" plan to take land from Armenia that had been captured from Turkey by Catherine the Great. "They're not only kicking out Armenian and Russian inhabitants from Nakhjivan and Karabagh, but also, by realizing the plans of NATO member Turkey, they have created a string of Muslim villages which consider themselves Turkish along the Soviet frontier," the appeal insisted.[29] In another appeal, Armenians from Azerbaijan claimed that the government in Baku had "perpetrated genocide against the Armenian population between 1920 and 1987."[30] This connection of the potent symbol of "genocide" with the government in Baku and the Mountainous Karabagh dispute was a major reason why Armenians would prove so easy to mobilize on the issue.

Azerbaijani myths and symbols

In contrast with the Armenians, the Azerbaijani national identity is very recent. In fact, the very name "Azerbaijani" was not widely used until the 1930s; before that, Azerbaijani intellectuals were unsure about whether they should call themselves Caucasian Turks, Muslims, Tatars, or something else.[31] Today, Azerbaijani scholars are inclined to trace their past primarily according to the history of the political structures which have ruled the territory now known as Azerbaijan, though some Azerbaijani mythmakers also try to rival the Armenian claims to ancient cultural roots in the region.

Indeed, some Azerbaijani mythmakers claim to find a distinctly Azerbaijani culture even among the Stone Age inhabitants of the country.[32] The mainstream narrative, however, starts with the "first state formations on the territory of Azerbaijan," those of the ninth-century B.C.E. Mannai (prior, notably, to the Armenian migration into the region). The story continues with the emergence of the Kingdom of Atropatene in what is now Iranian Azerbaijan after the destruction of the Persian Empire by Alexander the Great in the late fourth century B.C.E. Obscuring the fact that Atropatene was culturally Iranian rather than Turkic, the mythmakers claim that "the language of the territory was, apparently, the same as what later became known as Azeri."[33] More important is the kingdom of the linguistically Caucasian people known as Albanians (unrelated to modern Albanians), whose first organized state emerged in the second century C.E.: Azerbaijani mythology uses "Azerbaijan" and "Albania" interchangeably in discussing this kingdom.[34] World War II-era Soviet Azerbaijani propaganda further notes that ancient authors such as Herodotus and Tacitus praised the Albanians' martial prowess.[35]

The key successor state to Albania was Shirvan, which arose in the ninth century C.E. and continued to exist for nearly a millennium. Azerbaijani scholars play down the fact that Shirvan and other local "states" were usually subordinate to larger empires, and that the area did not become ethnically Turkic until after an eleventh-century invasion by the Seljuk Turks. They claim—in spite of the absence of a group name—that "the formation of the Azerbaijani nationality" dates from the century or two after that invasion.[36] Azerbaijani myth also argues that the Albanians were assimilated by the Turkic groups,[37] so modern Azerbaijanis are the descendants of the Albanians. More recent ancestors to Azerbaijan include the fifteenth-century Turkic Kara-koyunlu state and the Safavid dynasty of Persia, which originated in southern Azerbaijan.

The Azerbaijanis root their historical claim to Karabagh primarily on the observation that past administrative boundaries usually placed Karabagh under rulers based in modern Azerbaijan. Indeed, even before 1987, they engaged in an Aesopian debate with Armenian scholars, implying contemporary claims to Karabagh through historical arguments. Thus the ancient

Albanian state, Azerbaijani historians pointedly noted, included "Artsakh."[38] They also argued that Albania had an autonomous church, disputing Armenian claims that the Albanian church was part of the Armenian one.[39] Similarly, in Safavid Iran, the region called Azerbaijan included Karabagh as a subunit.[40] Some Azerbaijani writers also added the point that the city of Shusha in the nineteenth century was a center of Azerbaijani culture (though it was also a center of Armenian culture).[41]

Modern Azerbaijani nationalism, and hence these arguments, first began in reaction to the "Tatar-Armenian War" of 1905–6.[42] In the late nineteenth century, Muslim intellectuals in the region were variously interested in Pan-Islamist, Pan-Turkic, or liberal reformist ideas rather than Azerbaijani nationalist ones. In the Tatar-Armenian War, however, Azerbaijanis were faced with a well-organized opponent in the Armenian nationalist party Dashnaktsutiun, or "Dashnaks," giving them the impetus to form their own organization, aptly named "*Difai*" ("Defense"). The first genuine Azerbaijani nationalist organization, the original *Musavat* ("Equality") party, followed in 1913. The collapse of the Russian and Ottoman Empires in 1918 gave the nationalists their chance to form an independent state, but the nationalist point was really driven home in that year's "March days," when chauvinist Armenian Dashnaks allied with the Bolsheviks carried out pogroms against Muslims in Baku. The turn to nationalism failed, too, of course, when the Bolsheviks marched back into Azerbaijan in 1920.

This historical experience created in many Azerbaijanis a deeply negative attitude toward Armenians. A traveler remarked in 1906 that "Tatar hatred is directed against Armenians more than against Russians" because Armenians were viewed as agents of the tsar, threatening competitors for Azerbaijani traders, and aggressors in the "Tatar-Armenian War."[43] The stereotype was that the "backward" Azerbaijanis were threatened by the "advanced" Armenians, who dominated the urban professions, civil service, and skilled labor positions, became barons of industry and commerce who out-competed Azerbaijanis, and had influence in the developed West.[44] These attitudes remained in the 1980s: one Azerbaijani writer remarked that Armenians "have better connections," and that "The Armenians have always been the first to start conflicts."[45] A Russian resident of Sumgait reported hearing repeated statements by Azerbaijanis such as: "The Turks had it right, they killed them all."[46]

After 1920, Azerbaijani national identity was fundamentally reshaped by Soviet nationality policy. Seventy years of official atheism largely destroyed traditional Muslim beliefs and institutions and fatally weakened prospects for any pan-Islamist resurgence. Instead, Soviet dabbling with creation of an autonomous Azerbaijani region on Iranian territory in 1946 injected a dose of pan-Azerbaijani sentiment into the politics of Soviet Azerbaijan. This irredentist sentiment was strengthened in the 1980s when

Azerbaijani party boss Heidar Aliev, searching for a legitimizing idea to replace a moribund communism, began promoting a "poetry of longing"—longing, that is, for union with the Azerbaijani portions of Iran.[47] At the same time, the central symbol of Azerbaijani nationalism became its "statehood" as embodied in the Azerbaijani Soviet Socialist Republic. It was then that Azerbaijani historians began constructing a history in terms of a specifically Azerbaijani "state."

Azerbaijani fears

As much as for the Armenians, Azerbaijani fears were marked by an ethnic affinity problem and a history of ethnic domination. Thus Azerbaijanis were a threatened and oppressed minority in Armenia and Mountainous Karabagh—the "era of massacres" included massacres of Azerbaijanis by Armenians as well—even if the former were a majority in Azerbaijan. Azerbaijanis also associated tsarist and Soviet rule with the Armenians, who were often the Kremlin's agents in Baku, though the stereotype was much less true in Soviet than in tsarist times.

Azerbaijani fear of Armenians was further inflated, ironically, by the relative weakness of Azerbaijani identity as compared to the Armenian one. Azerbaijanis recognized their "weak sense of solidarity," so Karabagh's bid for succession rankled all the more because the Armenians, the national enemy, were so much better organized and because they were attacking Azerbaijani "statehood"—the main prop for whatever national awareness there was. This Armenian threat became the national obsession, what Mark Saroyan has called the "Karabagh Syndrome," and it was portrayed as a mortal threat to the nation's existence.[48] Audrey Alstadt explains the logic this way: Azerbaijanis "have previously been forced to cede the Zangezur district to Armenia... as well as part of the Kazak district in the north, to Georgia.... [T]he result of continuing such "nibbling away" would be the eventual destruction of Azerbaijan." That the fear was exaggerated—ethnic Azerbaijanis represented 83 percent of the republic's population, so there was little basis for further ethnic fragmentation—was irrelevant. Where the enemy was Armenians, overreaction was to be expected.

DETERIORATING LIVING CONDITIONS

Ethnic problems in Karabagh were, as is typical, exacerbated by material and cultural grievances. In Mountainous Karabagh, Armenian-language education was not easily available, Armenian history was not taught at all, and those who went to Armenia for training were discriminated against in competing for jobs in the province, since even routine hiring had to be cleared with Baku.[49] Underinvestment in the region—also blamed on Baku—meant less economic development and poor infrastructure even by

Soviet standards,[50] and therefore fewer jobs overall, especially for Armenians. Cultural ties with Armenia were strangled in red tape in Baku, and a decision to make Armenian-language television available in the region was left unimplemented.[51] One result of these policies was a continuing exodus of Armenians from Karabagh in search of greener pastures.

Gorbachev's anti-alcohol campaign, which began in 1985, made this situation worse. Fully half of Mountainous Karabagh's meager industrial output before 1985 was in grape processing, and that activity was hit hard by the drastic cutback in wine production demanded by the anti-alcohol campaign. When carried to extremes by overzealous officials, the campaign also resulted in the uprooting of thousands of acres of the "black garden's" vineyards, making the damage much worse.[52]

Azerbaijanis had their own causes for complaint. Azerbaijan ranked nearly last among Soviet republics in virtually every measure of standard of living, earning only 62 percent of the average per capita income and consuming only 59 percent of the consumer goods per capita as compared with the Soviet Union's average. The average monthly income in Azerbaijan was below the wage level of 87 percent of the Soviet population, and it was supplemented by social welfare funds at only 65 percent of the all-union per capita average.[53] Many urban Azerbaijanis lived in dismal shantytowns and amid appalling pollution, the detritus of a century of oil production. While Azerbaijan was not quite uniquely disadvantaged—much of Central Asia was as badly off or worse, and the pollution problem was countrywide—its populace did have much to complain about.

Processes of Ethnic Conflict Escalation

Mass Insurgency in Mountainous Karabagh

Mindful of the past demands for transfer of Mountainous Karabagh Autonomous Region to Armenian control, Azerbaijani officials ensured that the party boss of the region in early 1988, Boris Kevorkov, was a man slavishly loyal to his superiors in Baku. Kevorkov was therefore despised by most of his constituents as a stooge of the Azerbaijanis. He vigorously opposed all efforts to raise anew the question of a territorial transfer, and indeed in 1975 he fired a young official who mentioned in a poem the issue of the other "lost Armenian lands"—the ones in Turkey.[54] Any ethnic mobilization in Mountainous Karabagh would have to be mass-led.

Most key conditions for such mobilization had long been in place: long-standing grievances deeply based in national mythology and made urgent by fear of ethnic extinction. Once the first glimmerings of *glasnost* suggested an opportunity was at hand, mobilization began quickly: one petition for transfer of Mountainous Karabagh to Armenia was reportedly handed to Politburo member Alexander Yakovlev in late 1986. A second followed in January of 1988 with 80,000 signatures—including 31,000 from Mountainous Karabagh, representing some one-fourth of all Armenians in the region.[55] The organizers initially comprised only a loose network of activists, but in February 1988 fifty-five of them created the Krunk (crane) Society, named after the Armenian symbol of longing for one's homeland.[56] Krunk was apparently an organization consisting primarily of intellectuals and others not in power, but its efforts were also assisted by some local Communist Party leaders.[57]

When a senior Communist Party official in Moscow announced in early February 1988 that the petition for transfer had been rejected, Mountainous Karabagh mobilized for a political fight. First, protest placards were posted, then students began boycotting classes.[58] Protest rallies in the central square of Stepanakert, the provincial capital, began and grew daily. Responding to the massive grass-roots pressure, four out of five local soviets (councils) in Mountainous Karabagh passed, between February 12 and February 16, a resolution calling for transfer of the region to Armenia.[59] On February 20, the Supreme Soviet (legislature) of Mountainous Karabagh Autonomous Region endorsed the request, ignoring the concerns of its Azerbaijani members, who were boycotting, and of Azerbaijan's Communist Party boss Kamran Baghirov, who had come to Stepanakert to lobby.[60]

Popular attitudes were ripe for a contest for ethnic dominance. Krunk activists, insistent that Karabagh be joined to Armenia, would consider no compromise. Appalled journalists for *Izvestia,* apparently looking for signs of moderation, heard instead threats to abandon the ruling Communist Party, reject *perestroika,* and begin a guerrilla war. When the journalists suggested consideration of the material costs of such a campaign, they were reminded of the issue's symbolic importance: this was a "sacred cause," they were told.[61] These activists' ability to garner the signatures of so many of the Armenian adults in the province on their petition for transfer suggests that such extreme views were widespread. Meanwhile, Kevorkov was ousted in late February; his replacement, Henrik Poghosyan, soon came out in support of his constituents' demands.

MASS-LED MOBILIZATION IN ARMENIA

While Mountainous Karabagh was mobilizing around the nationalist issue, activists in Armenia were taking a more cautious approach. At first, popular mobilization was limited to issues that were more or less "approved" for discussion in the early years of *glasnost*. Thus the first major issue to be raised was the safety of the nuclear power plant outside the Armenian capital of Erevan: in March 1986, 350 Armenian intellectuals signed a letter urging Gorbachev to order the shutdown of plant, which is situated in an earthquake zone.[62] Protest rallies on that and other environmental issues began in October 1987, drawing at first a few thousand people.[63] When news reached one such rally of the first ethnic clashes in Azerbaijan (at Chardakhlu, described below), however, it quickly turned into a rally on the Karabagh issue—and was soon broken up by police.[64] The streets of Erevan were calmer for some months thereafter.

The Karabagh issue was heating up, however. October 1987 was when the Armenian Academy of Sciences sent the above-mentioned petition on Karabagh to Gorbachev. Throughout the fall, a series of prominent Armenians—scholar Sergo Mikoyan, Gorbachev advisor Abel Aganbegyan, and writer Zori Balayan—raised expectations among Armenians by publicly speculating that the Karabagh issue would soon be resolved.[65] Then, while Armenians in Karabagh began their protests, the environmental issue resurfaced in Armenia, as the republic government reneged on a commitment to close some of the most dangerous sources of pollution. The result was a series of demonstrations in Erevan beginning February 18, 1988 on the environment, with Karabagh also being mentioned.[66] February 20 was the day the Mountainous Karabagh Supreme Soviet requested transfer to Armenia; the following day the Politburo in Moscow rejected the demand.

Now Erevan mobilized. The day after the Politburo decision, 50,000 or more demonstrated in Erevan in protest. The next day, the crowds were twice as large, and they grew daily.[67] Trying to warn of the dangers of nationalist action, Politburo candidate member Vladimir Dolgikh announced on Armenian television on February 24 that there had been "casualties" from clashes in Mountainous Karabagh, presumably referring to two deaths a few days before in Askeran district. The tactic backfired and instead promoted feelings of insecurity that motivated more Armenians to act. February 25 saw rural Armenians beginning to converge on Erevan in large numbers, and on the following day demonstrations were held in Erevan estimated to include as many as a million people. Demonstrations were also held in other Armenian cities.[68] Bowing to the pressure, Gorbachev met that day with Armenian nationalist writers Zori Balayan and Silva Kaputikyan and promised a "just solution" if the demonstrations would stop. The demonstrations stopped at their leaders' urging.[69]

As in Stepanakert, the Erevan demonstrations were organized from below, despite opposition from Armenia's old guard Communist Party First Secretary Karen Demirchyan.[70] *Pravda* later tried to delegitimize the rallies by implying they were merely the result of plotting by provocateurs, reporting that organizers appeared at enterprises, institutes, and schools with timetables for when and where to march and that there was a system for providing food and drink to the enormous crowds with funds to pay the costs.[71] Indeed, protest leaders did manage to recruit numerous organizers—not only from the ranks of the intelligentsia, the group that led the charge, but also in the factories—and to raise money, find transportation for people in the countryside, etc., all on very short notice. But the fact is that the Karabagh Committee, the leading Armenian nationalist organization, with its coherent network of factory and institute committees, did not emerge until March, *after* the February rallies.[72] What made the rallies possible in the face of a hostile government was the mass-led nature of the enterprise: people were eager to help and to participate, so little organization was needed.

The rallies grew so quickly because all the requirements for mobilization were in place. On the one hand, new opportunities allowed expression of long-simmering grievances, hence the slogan "Karabagh Is a Test of *Perestroika*." On the other hand, the emotional mix was right, as old myths and symbols were both adroitly manipulated and found newly appropriate. As one account puts it, "Much of what was heard from the speaker's platform pressed well-known emotional buttons. There were allusions to the glorious past of Karabagh, persecution under the Turkish yoke, and longing for the snow-capped peaks of Mount Ararat."[73] For Armenians, "Persecution under the Turkish yoke" means, more than anything else, the 1915 genocide. The effects of such rhetoric were analyzed by Ashot Manucharyan, one of the Karabagh movement's more insightful leaders: "The boldest, the most emotional speakers became the recognized leaders. It was whoever made the strongest impression on the crowd. Sarukhanyan and others played the role of actors.... The danger, of course, is that actors use appeals to emotion, shifts in the direction of their ideas, simply to boost the emotional level of the crowd without appreciating the consequences."[74]

An ordinary protestor described the crowd's feelings, and inferentially its motivation, more simply: "We are so proud of ourselves. No matter what happens, we are standing on our feet now, instead of being on our knees. For the first time in my life, I feel like a human being."[75] What kept the rallies going and made them grow, therefore, was the interplay between the leaders' rhetoric, based on emotive symbols, and the emotions of the crowd that believed in those symbols—emotions the leaders could only imperfectly control.

OUTBREAK OF VIOLENT CONFLICT

The first violence of the current Karabagh conflict occurred in October 1987 in the Armenian-populated village of Chardakhlu, in Azerbaijan near Mountainous Karabagh, when the local (Azerbaijani) party boss punished a show of dissent from villagers with a "punitive raid" in which women, children and elderly people were beaten up.[76] Possibly in reaction to such incidents, Armenians began driving ethnic Azerbaijanis from their homes in villages in Armenia and Mountainous Karabagh around the same time. Hundreds of Azerbaijani refugees from Armenia soon began accumulating in Azerbaijan and quickly became the catalyst for deadly violence.

The first incident of deadly violence began in Azerbaijan's Aghdam district, also just outside Mountainous Karabagh, which was housing some Azerbaijani refugees from the disputed region.[77] The incident shows that by late February 1988, an interethnic security dilemma was already operating in the region. On February 22, two days after the Karabagh Supreme Soviet requested transfer of the region to Armenia, a crowd of Azerbaijanis surrounded the Aghdam Communist Party headquarters, demanding information about rumors of an Azerbaijani having been killed in Stepanakert. Apparently dissatisfied with what they were told, thousands began marching toward Mountainous Karabagh, "wreaking destruction en route." Several women threw down their headdresses at the front of the column in the traditional signal to avoid violence, but while the move had worked in previous incidents in recent days, this time only part of the mob turned back. The authorities then mobilized roughly a thousand police to stop the riot. The result was a clash in the Askeran district of Mountainous Karabagh that left two Azerbaijanis dead and 50 Armenian villagers, plus an unknown number of Azerbaijanis and police, injured.[78]

The Askeran clash was the prelude to the Sumgait pogroms, where emotions, already heightened by news about the Karabagh crisis, turned even uglier in a series of rallies beginning February 27. Speaking at the rallies, Azerbaijani refugees from the Armenian town of Ghapan accused Armenians of murder and atrocities including raping women and cutting their breasts off. Some speakers called in response: "Death to the Armenians!"[79] Those who tried to calm the crowd, including a leading poet and local Communist Party bosses, were ignored or shouted down, and the mob turned to violence.[80] A television announcement of the two deaths at Askeran then provided the spark that escalated the riot into more than two days of pogroms with Azerbaijanis, armed with iron bars and other makeshift weapons, attacking Armenian residents. The violence was led in part by the refugees from Armenia, who already had a grudge against the Armenians, and many of whom were made even more desperate by being forced to take shelter in the appalling conditions of Sumgait's shantytown.[81] Their equally deprived shantytown neighbors joined in, constituting the bulk of those later arrested.[82] Some aspects of the riots seem planned. The iron bars used as weapons were sharpened in advance, and there were reports of rioters being "recruited" on February 27 for the full-scale violence that began the following day. Armenian activists believe that the Ghapan "refugees" were provocateurs bussed to Sumgait to spread rumors of atrocities and that rioters were given lists of Armenians' addresses.[83] What is known is that Armenians were besieged in their homes for hours, some finding their phones dead, others' pleas for police help ignored for hours.[84] The police malfeasance, in particular, shows some degree of official connivance.

Overall, however, the evidence points more to official incompetence than to careful planning: the "recruiting," for example, began after the rioting started. The key factor was the way the symbol of Armenian atrocities (established in past episodes of violence) played on anti-Armenian attitudes, fanning latent hostile feelings to the point that the mob literally screamed for murder and nonparticipants approved the violence. For example, one young woman whose father was sheltering an Armenian remarked to the Armenian—her neighbor—as they watched the beatings and rapes, "that's what the Armenians deserve." After the rioting, a woman doctor told an Armenian girl who had been gang-raped not to feel sorry for herself: "Your people did even worse things."[85] Against this background, and faced with an enraged mob, city party boss Muslim-zade and his deputy reportedly pleaded with the crowd not to indulge in violence but took no effective action to stop it. Soldiers were introduced into the city by the twenty-ninth but were reportedly not given orders to shoot until later—and as a result some reportedly fell victim to the rioters themselves. Muslim-zade later reportedly confessed that he had not known what to do.[86]

The picture suggests an inept city leadership unable to control the situation, faced with police who sympathized with the rioters, fearful of confronting the crowd's chauvinist mood, and unwilling to admit its own failure to superiors by asking for help. Manipulative leaders with plans for their own future would have remained hidden and not allowed themselves to appear so ineffective. The scale of the resulting carnage is uncertain: the officially announced death toll was 32 people, six of them Azerbaijani, but Armenians claim that evidence from death certificates shows the true number to be over three hundred.[87] What is clear is that Sumgait showed the security dilemma to be already operating in full force in the conflict, provoking further escalation on the Armenian side.

THE POLITICS OF NATIONALIST EXTREMISM

Erevan's reaction to the Sumgait pogrom was relatively calm. The Karabagh Committee's announced moratorium on rallies held, except for a single funeral demonstration which attracted hundreds of thousands of people.[88] But the conflict escalated, producing a continuing stream of refugees fleeing from areas where they were the ethnic minority.[89] In March 1988, the USSR Politburo decided to offer Mountainous Karabagh a package of economic and cultural concessions instead of transfer to Armenia;

new demonstrations in Erevan were averted only by the deployment of thousands of troops in the center of the city before the announcement.[90] The troops did not try to interfere with the traditional but unofficial march on April 24 to the genocide memorial outside town.[91]

New demonstrations in Erevan—and, for the first time, in Baku—came in May, after the sentencing of a few Sumgait rioters: Azerbaijanis believed the 15-year sentence of an Azerbaijani convicted of murder was too harsh, while Armenians protested that the riot's real organizers were not even on trial.[92] In Mountainous Karabagh, May also saw members of local minorities—Azerbaijanis in Stepanakert and Armenians in predominantly Azerbaijani Shusha—being fired from their jobs. Hundreds of Armenians left Shusha for the more hospitable Stepanakert.[93] "Self-defense sentries" appeared on the streets of Stepanakert,[94] and sporadic violence continued.

The May protests ended Gorbachev's patience with the old-style Communist Party First Secretaries in Armenia (Demirchyan) and Azerbaijan (Baghirov). But the new leaders, Suren Harutiunyan in Armenia and Abdul-Rakhman Vezirov in Azerbaijan, found themselves unable to focus on Gorbachev's reform agenda; instead, they were forced to respond to the pressure of the nationalists. This situation gave the Karabagh Committee the opening it had been looking for: it mobilized a crowd estimated at 700,000 people to demonstrate on June 13, two days before a planned meeting of Armenia's Supreme Soviet. The Armenian legislators bowed to the pressure, voting to endorse Mountainous Karabagh's February request that it be joined to Armenia. The Azerbaijani legislature quickly renewed its denial of the request.[95]

Events in July completed the Armenian nationalists' disillusionment with the Gorbachev-Harutiunian leadership. Early in the month, the Karabagh Committee called for rallies and a general strike over Karabagh and the Sumgait trials, and a radical group of protesters occupied and shut down Erevan's airport. Interior Ministry troops were brought in to break up the airport demonstration, but in doing so they killed a protestor. The killing was a watershed: anti-Soviet slogans now began appearing in crowds that had been carrying Gorbachev's portrait just five months earlier.[96]

Armenia's leaders now took the next step in the politics of nationalist extremism, openly articulating their constituents' demands for ethnic dominance, and thereby moving the political center in the nationalists' direction. Thus Armenian Supreme Soviet chairman G. M. Voskanyan went to the mid-July meeting of the Presidium of the USSR Supreme Soviet to argue for the transfer of Mountainous Karabagh to Armenia.[97] Gorbachev and the Presidium rejected the demand. The Karabagh Committee and the Armenian crowds reacted by turning toward more radical nationalism, now demanding democracy and independence from the USSR.[98]

MASS-LED MOBILIZATION IN AZERBAIJAN

As among the Armenians, nationalist mobilization among the Azerbaijanis was mass-led. While actions by Azerbaijani officials helped provoke the Armenian mobilization, those actions were not at first nationalist in intent: the Chardakhlu incident, for example, seems to have been intended as routine Soviet-style repression. For the Azerbaijani population, in contrast, the Karabagh issue was galvanizing from the start: Karabagh symbolized Armenian repression and the Armenian threat to Azerbaijanis. In the Askeran clash, for example, rumors from Karabagh were enough to set in motion a large and violent mob, led by refugees with personal grudges. The Sumgait pogrom illustrates both elite and mass tendencies: while the crowd was pursuing a quarrel with the Armenians, local leaders played along for reasons of their own.

The first hint of a nationalist political agenda did not emerge until May, when protests against the Sumgait trials mushroomed from about 1,000 people to roughly 100,000 in a few days.[99] Azerbaijani intellectuals also began organizing themselves, opposing Armenian scholars' arguments about Karabagh in a document signed by 250 Azerbaijani scholars. However, the tone of the Azerbaijani media—still controlled by local leaders—did not yet differ drastically from the central media in Moscow. As reported in the Azerbaijani press, Sumgait officials were to be held responsible for the violence there;[100] most Azerbaijanis were not chauvinists—rather, many in Sumgait took risks to save Armenian friends or neighbors;[101] and Armenian activist organizations such as "Krunk" were troublemakers who were causing the rise in ethnic tensions.[102] The attitude of the republic's political leaders was covertly discriminatory rather than openly chauvinistic.

The May 1988 protests changed the scale of Azerbaijani popular participation, but not its mostly unorganized character. Thus a virtual siege of Mountainous Karabagh began with the practice of Azerbaijanis in towns between Karabagh and Armenia attacking vehicles and convoys carrying supplies to Stepanakert. These attacks occasionally escalated into larger clashes, such as one in September 1988 in the town of Khojaly, which resulted in the death of an elderly Armenian.[103]

An organized Azerbaijani popular movement did not emerge until the dramatic events of November 1988. The events began with rallies in Baku on November 17, protesting against a reported construction project in the Topkhana area of Mountainous Karabagh. The mobilizing symbols were environmental as well as nationalist: the project was being carried out by Armenians without the approval of Baku, thus violating Azerbaijani sovereignty; the building was allegedly a highly polluting aluminum workshop to be situated in a nature preserve (actually, it was to be a vacation spot for aluminum workers); and its location was proclaimed sacred as the site of a historic eighteenth-century battle by "Azerbaijani" forces against Iran.[104]

Hundreds of thousands of people now began rallying in Baku daily, and for the first time a leader emerged, a charismatic young machinist named Nemat Panakhov. Panakhov's rhetoric was nationalist and reformist rather than chauvinist, focused on the return of Azerbaijani authority and refugees to Mountainous Karabagh, but denouncing the Sumgait riots and the appearance of Islamist symbols. He was also supportive of *perestroika*, calling for "social justice and human rights," cultural reforms, and so on.[105] Of these, the Karabagh issue was the central motivating symbol for participants. Bewildered reporters from Moscow noticed that even in the evening (when the 24-hour rallies were continuing but speeches were not), "the surroundings [would suddenly] shake as tens of thousands of people chant the word, 'Karabagh!'"[106] And in spite of Panakhov's moderation, there were many attacks on Armenians in Baku, and slogans such as "freedom for the heroes of Sumgait" were shouted at rallies.[107]

While Baku was demonstrating, other parts of Azerbaijan exploded into violence in response to the announcement on November 21 of a death sentence for one of the Sumgait rioters.[108] The day after the announcement, Azerbaijani mobs began attacking Armenians in the widely separated cities of Kirovabad and Nakhjivan, and protest rallies spread across the republic. Troops quickly moved to stem the violence, but the security dilemma had already begun to spiral out of control. Violent clashes now spread across Armenia as well, resulting in deaths on both sides, mostly among the locally outnumbered Azerbaijanis.[109] Over the course of a month, 180,000 Armenians fled Azerbaijan, primarily from cities such as Kirovabad and Baku, while 160,000 mostly rural Azerbaijanis left their homes in Armenia, creating a combined refugee population of over a third of a million people.[110] In the midst of the violence came reports of a first, abortive attempt to organize an Azerbaijani Popular Front: an agenda including cultural, political, and human rights and other issues was published in a literary weekly,[111] but government repression prevented the organization from starting its work until months later.[112]

The nationalists had by now taken control of the Azerbaijani press. One report lyrically asserted "Topkhana was the final drop that made the cup of patience overflow," while another accused the Armenian press of fueling the "rampant flame of extremism."[113] The newspaper "Pioneer of Azerbaijan," in theory written for the equivalent of girl scouts and cub scouts, wrote in a similar vein: "when the homeland is in distress and its soil is encroached upon, the descendants of... [Azerbaijani heroes] are ready to fight and perform heroic deeds in the name of their people."[114] An Azerbaijani poet was quoted on Baku radio as claiming, "What has made us all feel uneasy is the foreign hands which are stretched out to [Karabagh]," and "it has been the Azerbaijanis who have been superior throughout history."[115] From this point on, shrill nationalist rhetoric became increasingly common in the regional media on both sides. Indeed Arkadii Volskii, Moscow's representative in the region, quoted one Armenian press report as stating that the riots in Azerbaijan showed "the true nature, the psychology of the Azerbaijanis. There is nothing in their souls besides murder and bestiality."[116]

THE SPIRAL OF CONFLICT

For Armenians, the roller-coaster ride of 1988 was to end with one more catastrophe, a December earthquake that rocked northern Armenia, killing 25,000 and leaving more than 500,000 homeless, especially in the cities of Spitak (nearest the epicenter) and Leninakan. To a large extent, the disaster was manmade: shoddy construction work, attributable in part to massive corruption in Soviet Armenia, was largely to blame for the collapse of many buildings and the death or displacement of their inhabitants. Such hardship inevitably fed resentment against the corrupt communist system that helped cause it. It also contributed to the extremist mood that fed ethnic violence.

To the natural disaster was then added another political one: the Armenian government arrested hundreds of Karabagh Committee activists, including most of the key leaders, on a slender pretext.[117] Nora Dudwick describes the political effects as follows:

> "[A]s the Karabagh Committee was organizing [earthquake] relief efforts, eleven [of its] members were arrested and transferred to prisons in Moscow by the Armenian authorities...in a last-ditch effort to retrieve their crumbling legitimacy. For the next six months, the most salient aspect of political life in Armenia was their detention, which itself triggered further protests and political organization. They were released six months later, in May, 1989, virtually sanctified in the eyes of most Armenians. Under their leadership, the dozens of groups, parties, and political activists who had entered the political scene since February, 1988, came together in autumn, 1989, to form the Armenian National Movement (ANM)."[118]

The year 1989 actually did see some improvement in the situation, especially early in the year. By mid-February, over 48,000 Armenian refugees—over a quarter of the total—were reported to have returned to their homes in Azerbaijan, though only a tenth as many Azerbaijanis returned to Armenia.[119] A special commission, run by Arkadii Volskii and subordinate directly to Moscow, was established in January to rule Mountainous Karabagh, and it began tackling the region's economic problems aided by funds provided in Moscow's special economic package for Karabagh. The Azerbaijani government and media tried to defuse opposition to the special commission, arguing that the republic's sovereignty had not been infringed.[120]

Although the rest of the year still saw relatively little violence, the vicious spiral of increasing mass hostility, the security dilemma, and extreme nationalist politics continued. Armenian politics was roiled by popular dissatisfaction at the arrest of the Karabagh Committee activists until their May release. Trying to appease nationalist opinion, the communist government acted on a number of symbolic issues, proclaiming April 24 a legal holiday for commemorating the 1915 genocide and recognizing the old independence-era tricolor as a symbol of Armenian sovereignty. Then, in early May, ethnic clashes in Mountainous Karabagh broke out again, resulting in three deaths in one instance alone. Armenian officials in Mountainous Karabagh were by now accusing the Volskii Commission of pro-Azerbaijani bias and renewed their calls for transfer of the territory to Armenia.[121] A new general strike again idled most of the Karabagh economy, while an Azerbaijani blockade cut off road traffic to the region from Armenia. In June, Armenian activists began a rail blockade of Nakhjivan, the Azerbaijani region cut off from the rest of Azerbaijan by Armenian territory.[122]

The Azerbaijanis were no happier with the Volskii Commission than the Armenians were—they objected to the loss of sovereignty it imposed. Angered especially by the ethnic cleansing of Azerbaijanis from Armenian areas and by official inattention to that problem, the Azerbaijanis finally succeeded in launching an Azerbaijani Popular Front (APF). The APF had its founding conference in July 1989, where it announced a program demanding democratization and sovereignty over Mountainous Karabagh.[123] August and September saw huge APF-led rallies in Baku, and in a reflection of its increasing radicalization, the APF also helped organize a retaliatory rail blockade of Armenia, severely hampering Armenia's ability to recover from the earthquake, not to mention engage in normal economic activity. The impetus for the rallies again came in large part from those with something personal at stake: media reports suggested that tens of thousands of refugees from Armenia were among the protesters.[124]

Azerbaijan's Communist Party First Secretary Vezirov tried at first to ignore the APF, but events quickly spun out of his control. In response to the pressure, Vezirov's leadership began accommodating the APF's nationalist ambitions with a package of laws to increase the Azerbaijani Republic's sovereignty, including an assertion of the right to disband Mountainous Karabagh's autonomous status. In return, the APF was to have lifted the rail blockade of Armenia, but it found itself unable to deliver on that promise, in part because Armenians resumed attacks on Azerbaijani train crews entering Armenia, who then began refusing to do so.[125]

The growth of the Azerbaijani Popular Front spurred further escalation by the Armenians. By August 1989, in response to an inflammatory appeal by the APF, the Armenian media was back to denouncing the "barbarity and savagery being instigating against" Armenians and to worrying out loud about "the threat to the Armenian population of Azerbaijan's physical existence."[126] Local Communist Party leaders in Armenia jumped on the nationalist bandwagon, denouncing the APF appeal as "an irresponsible… initiative expounding extremely dangerous appeals with harmful effects on interethnic relations."[127] At the same time, also spurred by Azerbaijan's increasing radicalization, Karabagh Armenians formed a shadow government that declared "independence" from Azerbaijan.[128] The newly formed Armenian National Movement tried to slow the escalation by ending the attacks on Azerbaijani trains, hoping the rail blockade of Armenia would also be lifted, but its supporters did not comply: the logic of conflict was now stronger than the logic of self-interest.

Faced with such obstinacy on both sides, the Volskii Commission stopped functioning, and was abolished on November 28, 1989, returning administration of Mountainous Karabagh to Baku. Armenia responded with a decision to annex Karabagh, and on January 8, 1990, it announced a budget for the region. The latter step touched off a revolution in Azerbaijan: activists claiming to represent the APF took over government buildings in the city of Lenkoran on January 11, announcing the dissolution of all government and Communist Party organizations.[129] The next day, a massive wave of attacks on Armenians in Baku got underway, with strong evidence of government involvement[130]—but also with evidence of material motivations, as many rioters appear to have been homeless refugees who occupied Armenians' apartments immediately after ejecting them.[131] The APF eventually managed to get the riots stopped in spite of police complicity and the inaction of interior ministry troops, and to escort the remaining Armenians out of the city. The riots thus completed the "ethnic cleansing" of Baku and left the APF as virtually the only authority remaining in much of Azerbaijan.

At that point, on January 20, 1990, a second bloodbath occurred: Soviet troops moved into Baku under orders from Gorbachev to reestablish Communist Party authority.[132] Imposing a brutal martial law, the troops killed over a hundred civilians and arrested APF activists. Azerbaijan's Communist Party chief Vezirov was replaced by his second-in-command, then-premier Ayaz Mutalibov. With the APF weakened by the crackdown and by accusations that APF actions had provoked it, Mutalibov quickly consolidated power and orchestrated his own election to Azerbaijan's presidency in an unopposed September ballot.[133]

ESCALATION TO WAR

The notable fact about the escalation to full-scale war over Mountainous Karabagh is that it was not a result of government action: neither the Armenian nor the Azerbaijani government had much control over the paramilitary forces that turned the conflict into conventional armed combat. Instead, the escalation from sporadic violence to sustained guerrilla war was a reaction to the disastrous decision in November 1989 to end the authority of Volskii's special commission. The special commission, regardless of its other failings, had at least managed to limit the degree of violence: by one count, only forty people were killed in Azerbaijani–Armenian clashes in 1989—a far better record than that of 1988 and incomparably better than what was to follow.

The abolition of the special commission sparked escalation, with both sides using ever-stronger tactics in pursuit of dominance in Karabagh. Armenia, as noted, moved to annex Mountainous Karabagh in response; Azerbaijan worked to establish de facto as well as de jure rule in the region. The result was to exacerbate the security dilemma: the ethnic cleansing of most of Azerbaijan in 1988 and the Baku pogrom of January 1990 had led Armenians to fear that Azerbaijani control over Mountainous Karabagh would lead to ethnic cleansing there as well—a fear that was reinforced in July 1990 when a high-level Azerbaijani official allegedly proposed such a measure.[134] But the Armenian response, the move to unite Karabagh with Armenia, directly challenged critical Azerbaijani national values—sovereignty and territorial integrity—raising the specter for Azerbaijanis of the dismemberment of their state and the annihilation of their identity. At the same time, of course, Armenian fears of ethnic cleansing and pan-Turkism sharpened memories of the 1915 genocide—and fears of a new one. Fear of group extinction thus began prompting both sides to turn to increasing violence in "self-defense."

The escalation of violence came quickly. Armenian activists accused Azerbaijanis of attacking Armenian villages in November 1989, and in response they began acquiring arms by attacking Soviet military depots and patrols.[135] A wave of attacks across the Armenia-Nakhjivan border in January 1990 marked what might be called the first guerrilla campaign, killing over 200, by one count, in that month alone.[136] It became largely a war of informal sieges, attacks on convoys, hostage-taking, sniping, massacres large and small,[137] and the occasional terrorist bombing, reminiscent of the early stages of Israel's war for independence. Blockade was a key weapon, as the rail blockade of Armenia was never really lifted and the road from Armenia to Mountainous Karabagh had been largely closed since February 1988. Supplies for the Armenians of Karabakh had to be flown in by helicopter. This was especially true for the isolated ethnic-Armenian villages of Shaumyanov district, just north of the Mountainous Karabagh border, and for the town of Getashen, also outside of Mountainous Karabagh. Azerbaijani villages inside Mountainous Karabagh were similarly blockaded by the Armenians.[138]

By spring 1990, Armenians were fighting a real guerrilla war against Azerbaijanis and Soviet troops. The Armenians felt that crackdowns by Soviet Interior Ministry troops were not only aimed against them but also at ethnically cleansing them from some areas, so they increasingly fought back. They also continued their arms-stealing attacks on Soviet troops: by May, Armenian fighters were reportedly equipped with armored vehicles, mortars, and multiple rocket launchers.[139] At the same time, repeated Armenian attacks on Azerbaijani villages were reported,[140] as were Azerbaijani attacks on Armenian ones. By August, heavy weapons were being used, with both sides employing artillery and rocket launchers to attack "enemy" towns.[141]

Meanwhile, the politics of Armenia were being fundamentally reshaped. Parliamentary elections in the summer of 1990 gave a majority to the Armenian National Movement, resulting in the election in early August of ANM leaders Levon Ter-Petrosyan as chairman of Parliament and Vazgen Manukyan as premier—thus marking the final victory of the nationalist elites. The growth of unofficial armed groups, many collected under the umbrella of an unofficial "Armenian National Army," was meanwhile causing increasing anarchy in Erevan, sparking a crackdown by USSR Interior Ministry troops. The government of Ter-Petrosyan was finally driven to use ANM troops to suppress the "Armenian National Army," which announced its "voluntary" disbandment.[142]

The next escalation was spurred by Armenia's decision in March 1991 to boycott the referendum on preserving the Soviet Union, which was to be held that month. The effect of that decision was to turn the Soviet government into an ally of pro-Moscow Azerbaijan.[143] Cross-border raids continued, but now Azerbaijani authorities, backed by Soviet troops, were able to begin deporting Armenians from villages in Mountainous Karabagh and other areas of Azerbaijan, intensifying the security dilemma still more.[144] This campaign was named "Operation Ring" after the tactics employed: villages were surrounded, ostensibly to check the population's documents and to search for weapons; if a village did not submit, it was subjugated by force.[145] Twenty-four Karabagh villages alone were emptied during the offensive, and some villages in Armenia were subject to similar treatment.[146] Predictably, the conflict then escalated, as vengeance-minded paramilitaries—again, outside the control of the Armenian government—sprang up to attack regions from which Armenians had been deported.[147]

The abortive Soviet coup in August 1991, heralding the ultimate collapse of the Soviet Union, then sparked the final escalation to full-scale conventional war. With independence on the horizon, the Azerbaijani government moved to create an army beginning in September, while the Popular Front imposed some sort of organization on the irregular forces doing most of the fighting. In November, the crash near Shusha of a helicopter carrying several high-level Azerbaijani officials was blamed on the Armenians and served as a pretext for further escalation. Azerbaijan now reinstated a full railroad blockade of Armenia, blocked all transportation and communication lines to Stepanakert, and destroyed Stepanakert's water and power plants. The Azerbaijani parliament also officially revoked the autonomy of the Mountainous Karabagh Autonomous Region.[148] Around the same time, Armenian forces in Karabakh joined together to form an "Armenian Popular Liberation Army of Artsakh."[149] In December, Azerbaijan announced a full military mobilization.

Meanwhile, the impending Soviet collapse gave militia commanders means, motive, and opportunity to step up the fighting. The means came from the disintegrating Soviet army, many of whose members joined one side or the other, or else sold their weapons. For example, the Soviet Fourth Army, stationed in Azerbaijan, was reported to be two-thirds Azerbaijani in composition and to be selling arms to Azerbaijan.[150] Similarly, of the men in the 366th Motorized Rifle Regiment stationed in Stepanakert, all three battalion commanders and at least 60 men eventually defected to the Armenian side, bringing 80 tanks and other equipment.

Additionally, when other Soviet troops began to withdraw, their bases were occupied and used to launch further attacks. After the withdrawal of Soviet Interior Ministry troops from around Stepanakert, for example, Azerbaijanis quickly occupied their bases and used them for increasingly intense rocket and artillery attacks on the town.[151] The fluid political and military situation thus created incentives for military commanders to gain as much territory as possible while the opportunity lasted.[152] The result was a spiral of escalation, with an unsuccessful Azerbaijani attack on Stepanakert in late January sparking Armenian counterattacks and ambushes.

It was against this backdrop that the first major conventional battles of the Karabagh war took place: the capture of Khojaly and the massacre of its Azerbaijani population—apparently hundreds of men, women, and children—by Armenian troops in late February 1992;[153] and the Armenian capture and "ethnic cleansing" of Shusha in early April. The key spark for the Khojaly battle may have been the shelling of Stepanakert by Grad multiple-rocket launchers on February 23:[154] the 366th regiment was also hit in that shelling, and elements of the 366th participated in the battle for Khojaly—the alleged source of the shelling—two days later. The disorganized Azerbaijanis lost Shusha five weeks after that.

From this point on, the war was one of conventional ground combat, nominally between Azerbaijan and the Karabagh Armenians, but with Armenia playing a key role in support of Karabagh. Only after that escalation did the politics of nationalism in Azerbaijan take its final turn: in June of 1992, Mutalibov was finally ousted, then replaced in an election by APF leader Abulfez Elchibey. Azerbaijan never did create a disciplined army, which is why it rarely achieved much success. Russia also repeatedly intervened, trying to manipulate the course of fighting to its own advantage and backing a 1993 coup that replaced Elchibey with the less anti-Russian Heidar Aliev, former Communist Party boss of Azerbaijan.[155] By the time a durable cease-fire was reached in May 1994, some 20,000 people on both sides were dead, and the Armenians were occupying about 20 percent of the territory of Azerbaijan, including Mountainous Karabagh and large areas surrounding it.

Moscow as Conflict Mismanager

The Soviet Union government in Moscow spent the first two years of the Karabagh conflict trying, but failing miserably, to manage it. Gorbachev's February 1988 meeting with Balayan and Kaputikyan, in which he persuaded them to put an end to the Erevan rallies, was a good start, but Moscow's proposed solution, announced in March, inevitably dashed the hopes he had raised. The Kremlin decided that the entire problem was due to economic discontent stirred up by outside agitators; it therefore denounced the agitators and proposed a 400-million-ruble, seven-year plan of economic development. The plan addressed most of the biggest economic complaints raised by Karabagh Armenians: it provided for a range of new industrial enterprises to provide jobs, improved roads, a better water supply, new housing, a hospital, cultural center, improved food supplies, and numerous other benefits.[156] But this missed the point of the Armenians' concerns: while the economic gripes were real, their nationalist demands, aimed at communal security, were more important. Besides, even the economic benefits were dubious because of the political situation. The aid money, Armenians noted, would all be funneled through Baku, which was both biased against Armenians and notoriously corrupt, and therefore likely to steal or divert most of the money.[157]

A series of smaller Moscow missteps followed. Moving the trial of the Sumgait rioters to Russia not only violated the sensitive Azerbaijanis' sovereignty, it deprived them of the opportunity to confront their nationalist demons themselves, ensuring that any punishment would be seen as illegitimate. The Armenians, for their part, resented the lack of efforts to find and punish the local officials who abetted the pogrom. This was a mistake even from Gorbachev's narrow perspective, since the culpable officials were surely opponents of *perestroika*. There were also no efforts to punish Armenians responsible for crimes against Azerbaijanis, an issue Azerbaijanis repeatedly raised as further evidence of bias against them. Gorbachev's hectoring tone at the July 1988 USSR Supreme Soviet Presidium meeting did nothing to endear him to the Armenians. Then, when Gorbachev came to visit the stricken sites after Armenia's December earthquake, he allowed himself to be drawn into shouting matches over Karabagh instead of communicating sympathy.

An exchange between Armenian writer Vardges Petrosyan and Gorbachev at the July Presidium meeting illustrates the ineptitude of Moscow in handling the emotions of the time. Petrosyan voiced the common demand of the Armenians that the Sumgait pogrom be officially labeled an act of "genocide." Gorbachev attacked him, exclaiming: "How can you talk about genocide? You know what kind of word it is and the weight it carries. You are flinging around accusations that you will regret for the rest of your life."[158] What renders this exchange so poignant is that while Gorbachev understood the emotional charge carried by the "genocide" accusation, he was utterly oblivious to the fact that Armenians already felt that "genocide" was going on. It was far too late to call demands like Petrosyan's inflammatory; Soviet policy would have to take such perceptions into account if it was to head off further violence. It never did.

Even the establishment of the special commission led by Volskii was mishandled. The idea of putting administration of the province in relatively neutral hands made sense, but in practice it alienated both sides. For the Armenians, direct rule from Moscow meant loss even of the limited degree of autonomous self-government they had previously enjoyed in Mountainous Karabagh. For the Azerbaijanis, it symbolized Baku's loss of sovereignty and Moscow's insensitivity to their concerns: one of Volskii's first acts was to ask Stepanakert's Azerbaijanis to leave for reasons of their own security. If Volskii had kept local self-government in place, limiting his role to what the local Armenians could not do—bulldozing through bureaucratic obstacles in Baku and directing neutral security forces to protect civilians on both sides from violence—he might have been able to avoid exacerbating the situation. In any event, such a commission was in essence a stopgap solution.

What really mattered was what came next—a series of colossal blunders by Moscow. The November 1989 abolition of the Volskii Commission and the return of Mountainous Karabagh to Azerbaijani jurisdiction exacerbated insecurities on both sides, turning the conflict into war. It also set the stage for the tragedy of Baku in January 1990, which of course alienated both sides further: the Soviet troops made no attempt to help the Armenians and were too brutal to maintain much credibility with the Azerbaijanis. Gorbachev then chose to ally himself with the rickety regime in Baku, allowing Soviet troops to assist in raids on Armenian villages—especially the appalling "Operation Ring" in 1991. Gorbachev's aim was apparently to bully the Armenians into signing the Union Treaty, which represented his last hope for preserving the Soviet Union. He succeeded only in ensuring that the Karabagh conflict would escalate further. Finally, the withdrawal of Soviet troops as the Soviet Union collapsed proved the signal for the escalation to full-scale war. There is no evidence that Gorbachev stoked the Karabagh conflict intentionally, but it is easy to see why such policies led to suspicions among local activists that he did.

After the Soviet collapse, the situation for conflict management was, for three years, hopeless. Russian President Boris Yeltsin and Kazakhstan's President Nursultan Nazarbaev visited the region in September of 1991 and induced Armenia and Azerbaijan to sign an agreement, but the fighting started again the next day. A spring 1992 Iranian mediation attempt was only slightly more successful: that cease-fire lasted a week before collapsing.[159] The problem was that formulas for disengagement of forces could do nothing to address the security dilemma: Azerbaijan considered the presence of autonomous Armenian forces on its territory unacceptable, and demanded their withdrawal; and the Armenians refused to give up their means of self-defense. The 1994 cease-fire became possible only when Azerbaijan in effect admitted its battlefield defeat, acquiescing in Mountainous Karabagh's de facto independence.

Could War Have Been Avoided?

The conflict over Mountainous Karabagh was a mass insurgency, a mass-led conflict initiated by a repressed minority group. The conflict was driven by the insecurity of the minority, which demanded change to assuage its fears of group extinction. Averting conflict therefore required reassurance: credible government guarantees that would assuage the minority's fears without stoking the fears of the majority. Unfortunately, the Azerbaijanis and Armenians were disinclined even to acknowledge the other side's fears—let alone assuage them—and the Soviet government led by Gorbachev never understood them.

Perhaps the best hope for a workable compromise came in June 1988: once the Kremlin understood that the March economic package alone was insufficient, it began casting around for better options to resolve the Karabagh problem. The relevant party leaders—Harutiunyan from Armenia, Poghosyan from Karabagh, and Vezirov from Azerbaijan—were therefore summoned to Moscow and presented with a proposal from Gorbachev's deputy Yegor Ligachev. Ligachev's idea was to promote Mountainous Karabagh from an "autonomous region" to an "autonomous republic," with redrawn borders and increased autonomy, but still within Azerbaijan.[160]

If the new borders had been favorable to the Armenians—adding only areas heavily populated by Armenians, plus perhaps a link to Armenia—and if the autonomy on offer had been substantial, they might possibly have been able to accept the deal. The key would have been to allow enough autonomy to Karabagh to ensure that the Armenians' cultural and physical security concerns, including their demand for closer ties to Armenia, were accommodated. Since Azerbaijan's territorial integrity and "sovereignty" would still have been preserved under this arrangement, Vezirov might have been able to accept it as well. But the offer involved adding heavily Azerbaijani areas to the new "autonomous republic" to increase Azerbaijani influence there. Harutiunyan and Poghosyan recognized that the new border would be unacceptable to their constituencies, so they had to reject the deal. The result was the July USSR Supreme Soviet Presidium meeting at which Gorbachev alienated the Armenian representatives, further radicalizing the Armenians. To be fair, the chance for compromise was slim: the Armenians of Karabagh were explicitly determined to gain full de jure union with Armenia, so they may well have rejected even the most generous autonomy package as insufficient. Likewise, the Azerbaijani side might well have mobilized against the plan as it did against the Volskii Commission in 1989. But it is hard to think of any other possible peaceful solution.

As the conflict escalated and increasing numbers of Soviet troops were introduced to provide "security," the key need of the Armenians and Azerbaijanis for symbolic reassurance was overlooked again and again. The Soviet troops apparently tried to defend Armenians during the Kirovabad pogrom of November 1988, but the task was in one sense hopeless: while the troops saved lives, the Armenians had to leave their homes and possessions anyway—the atmosphere made it impossible for them to live in Azerbaijan any longer. By then, the mixture of hostility and fear driving Azerbaijani behavior could have been addressed only if existential fears about Azerbaijani sovereignty and Karabagh's future were addressed. The failure to find a workable compromise convinced both sides they were at risk: the Azerbaijanis constantly suspected that the "well-connected" Armenians would eventually get what they wanted, while the Armenians feared they would not. The result of rising hostility was the virtual ethnic cleansing of Armenia and Azerbaijan proper in November of 1988.

The errors of the Volskii Commission in 1989 have already been discussed, but it is questionable whether a more skillful performance would have made much difference. Feelings were running so strongly on both sides that it may not have been possible to provide enough reassurance to calm them. The abolition of the commission without instituting some sort of guarantees for the Armenians, in the context of the ethnic cleansing in Azerbaijan and Armenia the year before, was monumental in its stupidity; but an alternative scheme may not have been much better: it was probably too late for the kind of resolution that might have worked eighteen months earlier.

A last, slim chance at peace came in the summer of 1991. Faced with their inability to stop "Operation Ring," Karabagh Armenian leaders proposed in

May that "all sides in the conflict reconsider all anti-constitutional decisions regarding Mountainous Karabagh," language both sides interpreted as an offer to submit to Baku. The Armenian parliament approved the initiative two months later, whereupon the Karabagh leaders wrote directly to Mutalibov, proposing talks based on the Soviet and Azerbaijani constitutions. The offer came with a number of tough preconditions, however, and Mutalibov may have doubted that it was made in good faith. In the event, neither side pursued the opening after their first meeting, and one of the Armenian participants in the meeting was assassinated soon after. Armenian moderates took the assassination to mean that hard-line Armenian militia leaders were unalterably opposed to any such deal, so it could never have been consummated.[161] The August coup and subsequent collapse of the Soviet Union then rendered the whole idea obsolete, and the escalation to war followed.

In practice, the conflict was probably unmanageable after 1988. For emotional symbolic reasons, the Armenians were convinced that their security required unification of Mountainous Karabagh with Armenia, while the Azerbaijanis were convinced that their security needs precluded that change. Those perceptions together created a security dilemma that was simply unsolvable.

Kazakhstan: Ethnic War Brewing?

On the surface, relations between ethnic Russians and Kazakhs in Kazakhstan in the 1980s and after seem to parallel the Azerbaijani-Armenian relationship in Azerbaijan. The demographic threat was real: Kazakhs, at 36 percent of their republic's population in 1979, were outnumbered by the 40-percent share of the Russians, and Russian-speaking European groups constituted an absolute majority. Kazakhs had suffered through a century of vicious Russian repression, losing their lands to Russian settlers and the majority of their population during Stalin's collectivization campaign. Then, in 1986, their longtime leader was replaced by an ethnic Russian, Gennadii Kolbin, sparking days of rioting in Alma-Ata, the capital. How was further violence avoided? Conversely, since independence, the Russians have seemed threatened, with their share of the population declining and the government applying pressure to learn the Kazakh language. Why have the Russians not rebelled?

Kazakh Myths and Fears

Theoretically, ethnic war would be motivated largely by hostile myths and fears of extinction. Pre-1991 Kazakh mythology, however, did not justify hostility to Russians. The origins of the Kazakh nation were traced to the separation of a Kazakh Khanate from the Uzbek state in the early sixteenth century. Two centuries later, two of the three Kazakh "hordes" are said to have turned to Russia for help against threatening neighbors from the east, while other Kazakhs joined Russia after rising against domination by the (Uzbek) lord of Kokand in the mid-nineteenth century.[162] Although the late-nineteenth-century Slavic migrations to Kazakhstan were conceded to have had some negative effects, the overall story suggested that if the Kazakhs had national enemies, they were Kazakhstan's Muslim neighbors to the east and south, such as the Uzbeks. This story was in keeping with the divide-and-rule logic of other Soviet-approved national mythologies, like the Armenians' and Azerbaijanis: while hostile myths aimed against local neighbors were tolerable, hostility to the ruling Russians was not. The facts about Kazakh suffering at Russian hands during collectivization and about the anti-Russian Kazakh uprising of 1916 were therefore suppressed. Perhaps as a result of these myths, Kazakhs who expressed chauvinist attitudes tended to be biased more against Jews, Armenians, Tatars, and other Asian groups than against Russians.[163]

Kazakhs also expressed relatively little fear of group extinction in the 1980s. Due to a high birthrate, the Kazakh share of the population had probably surpassed the Russian share by early 1987—a fact that was widely known—and it kept climbing. While the symbolism of a Russian leader rendered the situation volatile in 1987, Kolbin wisely appeased Kazakh concerns where he could, especially by working to improve Kazakh language education, the key nationalist issue of the time.[164] The replacement of Kolbin by the Kazakh Nursultan Nazarbaev in 1988, additional measures to promote Kazakh culture, and finally the achievement of independence in 1991 all offered further reassurance. Ironically, it was after this, in 1992–93, when talk about potential Kazakh "extinction" became commonplace.[165] But since trends were by then moving strongly in the Kazakhs' favor—in particular, because policy was addressing, and ameliorating, the concern—violence did not result.

RUSSIAN MYTHS AND FEARS

Since 1991, it is the Russians who have more cause for concern, and local Russian and Cossack mythology does contain elements justifying hostility toward Kazakhs. One statement of the Russian view is that when the Kazakh SSR was formed in 1936, it "included territories taken from [Russia]."[166] Some believe that this Russian homeland can best be protected by joining Russia and doubt the legitimacy of the current border; though more seem inclined, if pressed, to flee rather than to fight.[167] Although there is no previous history of ethnic domination of Russians by Kazakhs, the Russian perception is that Russians currently face significant discrimination.

Grounds for Kazakh hostility to Russians are also hardening. New histories of Kazakhstan are forthright about the devastating effects for Kazakhs of Stalin's policy of forced collectivization and of the waves of Russian settlement in Kazakhstan.[168] Some anti-Russian feeling also shows up in polls. For example, over 35 percent of Kazakhs would consider Russian in-laws "undesirable," according to one survey.[169] While Russians do not, for now, reciprocate such feelings—they tend to feel superior rather than hostile to Kazakhs—attitudes may change. As one Russian local official put it, "If a person regularly beats you over the head with a stick, would you call that situation stable?... [T]he question is for how long will the Russians living here tolerate the beating, and what will they do once they have had enough?"[170]

Theoretically, the response will be violent only if there is an urgent fear of extinction—a fear for which Russians also have grounds. The "ethnic affinity problem" has turned against them: although they were a majority in the Soviet Union, they are a minority in Kazakhstan. Furthermore, their numbers are declining in both absolute and relative terms, as hundreds of thousands of Russians and Russian speakers have left the country, while the Kazakh population grows. For now, however, Russians perceive a rough balance of power between their group and the Kazakhs, largely because most of Kazakhstan's economic and technical elites are Russian.[171] President Nazarbaev has also gone out of his way to soothe their concerns by co-opting their economic leaders into the political system and enunciating a doctrine that Kazakhstan is a civic state of all Kazakhstanis as well as the national state of the ethnic Kazakhs.[172] There is, therefore, little Russian fear of extinction.

Either of two developments could change this, however. One Cossack official explains that the current rough balance of power is "one of the basic preconditions explaining the virtual absence of ethnically motivated bloodshed" in Kazakhstan.[173] Any shock that changes that perception of balance—a change in Kazakhstani policy, an ethnic riot mishandled, a major surge of Russian emigration—could turn Russian concerns into a visceral fear of extinction and quickly spark escalating violence. Alternatively, a Russian government policy of arming and supporting Russian extremists could easily provoke Kazakhstani repression and a security dilemma spiral of increasing violence. Such a policy would have serious costs for Russia as well, but it is not inconceivable.

President Nazarbaev is aware of the danger. "God grant that nobody will stir up Kazakhstan on ethnic grounds," he has said. "That would be far worse even than Yugoslavia."[174] In November 1999, Kazakhstani police nipped in the bud an abortive effort to do so, confiscating a few weapons and arresting twelve ethnic Russians who were apparently planning to declare an independent Russian republic in East Kazakhstan Province. Other attempts will likely follow.

Conclusion

The evidence for the mass-led character of the Karabagh conflict and for its escalation to war is strong. Armenians in Mountainous Karabagh and in Armenia organized mass appeals for the transfer of Karabagh in spite of the determined opposition of the Communist Party bosses in both. Clashes such as the one at Askeran in February 1988 also resulted from dissatisfaction with official actions. And despite the obvious evidence of official collusion in the pogroms at Sumgait and Baku, that violence, too, was driven primarily by popular passions; the officials did little more than stand back. In neither case could Party leaders have gained from the violence; instead, Muslim-zade in Sumgait and Vezirov in Baku proved their incompetence and were quickly removed.

More to the point, those riots were the reflection of a security dilemma that was already well advanced. Long-standing fears of "genocide" had spurred Armenians to begin expelling their Azerbaijani neighbors as early as 1987. Those Azerbaijani refugees then provided the spark of violence at Askeran, Sumgait, Baku, and elsewhere. The pogroms against vulnerable Armenian populations, in turn, reinforced the determination of Armenians in Karabagh to defend themselves. In the context of deep mutual hostility, the conflict inevitably became a contest for dominance, hardening the security dilemma in place. Importantly, all of this took place while the Soviet government still possessed both the means and (usually) the willingness to intervene with overwhelming force. The later escalations to guerrilla war and then to conventional war required the disengagement of Soviet authority—by then the only remaining restraint on the escalating spiral of insecurity.

The evidence also supports the symbolic model's emphasis on ethnic prejudice and nationalist myths and symbols as key to explaining ethnic violence. While Mountainous Karabagh did suffer from economic and cultural deprivation, its situation was no more severe than that of a hundred other out-of-the-way regions in the Soviet Union, which is why Soviet officials, good materialists all, were convinced that a generous package of economic and cultural concessions would "resolve" the problem. But in Mountainous Karabagh, Armenians were easily mobilizable because of ethnic prejudice—long-standing stereotypes of Azerbaijanis as oppressors aiming ultimately at genocide against Armenians, combined with emotional hostility toward Azerbaijanis. Karabagh became a symbol of how much Armenians had already lost to genocidal attackers, and of the lands and national existence they still had to lose. Later, Karabagh Armenians' self-image as fierce and proud fighters also played a role in encouraging them to fight. These attitudes were called to support a long-standing nationalist ideology which promoted a simple, symbolic solution to all of their perceived problems: "reunification" with Armenia. The attitudes had existed throughout the Soviet period; all that was required for them to be expressed was the opportunity afforded by Gorbachev's policy of *glasnost*.

The reaction of the Azerbaijani government to Armenian demands was ordinary: all Soviet republics opposed secessionist movements within their borders. The extraordinary intensity and immediacy of the Azerbaijani people's response resulted not from material deprivation—other parts of the Soviet Union had comparably bad standards of living—but from a long-standing prejudice harnessed by myths emphasizing the importance of defending the nation's integrity. Azerbaijanis had long viewed Armenians as "troublemakers" and resented them for their power and wealth. At the same time, Azerbaijanis' fragile sense of nationhood was bound up tightly with defense of their territorial integrity, which Armenian demands threatened. These attitudes helped turn Karabagh into the most important symbol of the Azerbaijani nationalist movement, with great emotional power.

Again, the ill-housed refugees who led the pogroms in Sumgait, Baku, and elsewhere were motivated partly by material conditions—i.e., to occupy their victims' apartments. But these motives are not sufficient to explain such violence: there were ill-housed refugees all over the Soviet Union by 1990, but in few other places did they indulge in pogroms. Only in Azerbaijan was the sense of deprivation fueled by prejudice, harnessed by a nationalist ideology that justified violence against the hated group, directed by symbolic appeals, and impelled by an interethnic security dilemma.

What is striking about the Karabagh case is the relative unimportance of the national leadership in mobilizing people on either side. Since the nationalist ideology, especially on the Armenian side, was widely understood and of long standing, neither a long period of time nor wide exposure in the media was required to persuade people of the rightness of the Karabagh cause—a few leaflets or speeches were enough. More strikingly, governments were not important in mobilizing people for war: guerrilla war was well underway in the spring of 1990, before nationalists came to power in either Armenia or Azerbaijan. Only in Mountainous Karabagh did nationalists consolidate their power early, with the February 1988 appointment of Henrik Poghosian. Elsewhere, the strength of nationalist ideology, especially on the Armenian side, was enough to enable unofficial organizations to create militia groups and motivate them to fight in spite of government opposition.

This is the most important finding of this chapter. Prejudice, fear, and a hostile myth-symbol complex can create a contest for dominance and an interethnic security dilemma even in an apparently stable country, which the Soviet Union was in 1988. There was no previous hint of emergent anarchy, so theories about "structural security dilemmas" based on anarchy do not work in this case. The Armenians flatly rejected Moscow's generous economic package, proving that economic benefit was not their central goal. And nationalist mobilization occurred against the efforts of incumbent leaders to squash it, showing that elite-led explanations cannot account for the conflict. Ethnic politics and war are sometimes driven by hate and fear. No theory focused primarily on elite calculations, material interests, or "structural" security dilemmas can capture that dynamic.

At the same time, the symbolic theory explains why Kazakhstan in the 1980s remained stable: neither Russians nor Kazakhs suffered from fears of extinction, nor did they have nationalist mythologies identifying the other as an enemy. Unfortunately, that situation has begun to change. Kazakh nationalist mythology now has anti-Russian elements, while Russian (especially Cossack) mythology encourages the Russians to defend their perceived rights. If the Russian population begins to see a tilt toward the Kazakhs in the current balance of ethnic power, or if local extremists receive arms from Russia, a security dilemma spiral will become not only possible, but virtually unavoidable.

[4]

Georgia and the Fears of Majorities

None of the other post-Soviet republics has been riven by as many different violent political conflicts as has Georgia. These have included one civil war between factions of Georgians; two civil wars between Georgians and minority ethnic groups in Georgia with foreign military intervention; and numerous smaller clashes between various ethnic groups and among rival warlords and criminal groups. All of this violence has been connected, resulting from the rise of nationalism among Georgians and minority groups in the context of a slow collapse of legitimate authority in Georgia during and after the breakup of the Soviet Union.

The central cause of these conflicts was the emergence by 1989 of a strong Georgian nationalist movement with a program calling for the political dominance of ethnic Georgians and for restricting the political autonomy and cultural opportunities of Georgia's ethnic minorities. When the minorities, especially the Abkhaz and Ossetians, mobilized in response, the demands of Georgian nationalists became even more extreme. In 1990, a nationalist government in Georgia led by longtime dissident Zviad Gamsakhurdia took power. The assumption of power by Gamsakhurdia quickly sparked a guerrilla war in the autonomous region of South Ossetia. Gamsakhurdia's incompetence, however, led to his ouster in a bloody 1991 coup by a coalition of the informal Georgian militias that had been fighting the Ossetians; the result was a civil war among Georgians centered in Gamsakhurdia's ancestral region of Mingrelia beginning in 1992. The new leadership headed by Eduard Shevardnadze quickly arranged a ceasefire in South Ossetia, but soon after started the war in Abkhazia while still fighting the pro-Gamsakhurdia forces known as "Zviadists." The resulting three-sided civil war among the Abkhaz, the Zviadists, and the warlords supporting the new Georgian government led the country to plumb the depths of chaos in 1993.

In spite of the complicated context, however, the two ethnic conflicts (in Abkhazia and South Ossetia) are well explained as the result of symbolic politics. At the center of ethnic mobilization and ethnic violence was a struggle over nationalist symbols summed up in the competing groups' pretensions to "statehood," pretensions dating to the period of the Russian civil war of 1918–20 but with roots in the much more distant past. *Glasnost* created the opportunity for these long-standing desires to be raised, so nationalist counter-elites on all three sides seized the opportunity. The nationalist mobilization was, therefore, mass-led for all three groups: incumbent leaders in each initially tried, without success, to restrain mobilization and prevent interethnic violence. Violence quickly resulted anyway because hostile feelings and attitudes led the groups to rule out compromise. Instead, they chose new leaders who defined their core demands about "statehood" to mean their own dominance in disputed territories, creating a security dilemma which fed fears of ethnic extinction among all three groups. Meanwhile, intervention by Moscow worked intermittently to promote all of these causes of ethnic violence, ultimately making it possible for the Ossetians and Abkhaz to fight and (de facto) win their secessionist wars against Georgia.

Georgia's Peoples and Their History

georgia's ethnic groups

More than Armenia and Azerbaijan, Georgia reflects the Caucasus region's remarkable ethnic diversity. Though ethnic Georgians comprise about 70 percent of its population, Georgia has substantial minority populations of Armenians, Russians, Azerbaijanis, Ossetians, Greeks, and Abkhaz; and smaller populations of Kurds, Laks, Avars, and others. Additionally, the Georgian category includes an array of politically important subgroups, especially Mingrelians, Svans, and Ajarians.

The Georgians are an ethnic group indigenous to the Caucasus region. They count among their forerunners the kingdom of Colchis from which, according to Greek myth, Jason and the Argonauts stole the Golden Fleece more than three thousand years ago. The Georgians' languages are also unique to the Caucasus region, together forming a separate Kartvelian branch of the Caucasic language family. Most Georgians speak *kartuli,* or "Georgian," and are Orthodox Christian in religion. The Mingrelians of western Georgia speak Mingrelian, a related language but one incomprehensible to *kartuli* speakers. Mingrelians, however, consider themselves

Table 4.1 Ethnic Composition of Georgia and Autonomous Regions in 1989

Group	Georgian SSR Population	%	Abkhazian ASSR Population	%	South Ossetian AO Population	%
Georgians	3,787,000	70.1	242,000	46.2	29,000	29.0
Armenians	437,000	8.1	77,000	14.6		
Russians	341,000	6.3	74,000	14.2	2,000	2.2
Azerbaijanis	307,000	5.7				
Ossetians	164,000	3.0			65,000	66.2
Abkhaz	95,000	1.8	91,000	17.3		
Greeks	100,000	1.9				
Others	212,000	3.1	40,000	7.7	3,000	2.7
Total	5,433,000		524,000		99,000	

Source: Georgia data is from Stephen F. Jones, "Georgia: A Failed Democratic Transition," in *Nations and Politics in the Soviet Successor States,* Ian Bremmer and Ray Taras (New York: Cambridge University Press, 1993), p. 289. Abkhazian and Ossetian data is from Paul B. Henze, *The Transcaucasus in Transition* (Santa Monica Calif.: Rand, 1991), pp. 37–38.

Georgians and, since Mingrelian is not a literary language, they read and write in Georgian. The Laz and Svans are smaller groups speaking Kartvelian languages less closely related to Georgian. Ajarians are not technically (by Soviet definition) an ethnic group, but are distinctive among Georgians in that many of them are Sunni Muslim.

The Abkhaz are another group indigenous to the Caucasus region and speaking a Caucasic language. The linguistic connection to Georgian is, however, distant: Abkhazian is closely related only to the languages of certain North Caucasian peoples, and only faintly (the Abkhaz say not at all) related to the Kartvelian languages.[1] Some Abkhaz are Christians and the rest are Sunni Muslims, though the religious divide is relatively recent and not deep.

The Ossetians, speakers of an Iranian language entirely unrelated to Georgian (it is most closely related to the language of Afghanistan's Pathans), are divided by the Caucasus Mountain range: almost three-quarters live in the Republic of North Ossetia, a component part of the Russian Federation; most of the rest live in Georgia. Most Ossetians are Christian, though some, mostly in North Ossetia, are Muslim.[2] They trace their ancestry to the Alans, an Indo-European people which appeared in the North Caucasus—north, that is, of Georgia—in the sixth century C.E. Groups of Ossetians began crossing the Caucasus Mountains into Georgia after the Mongol invasions of the thirteenth century and descended from the mountains to the Georgian plains in the seventeenth and eighteenth centuries. In 1989, most of Georgia's Ossetians (about 100,000 out of 160,000), lived not in Georgia's South Ossetia Autonomous Region but in other parts of Georgia.[3]

HISTORICAL BACKGROUND

The first durably united Georgian kingdom emerged in the eleventh century C.E., when a prince of Abkhazia, who already ruled most of western Georgia, inherited most eastern Georgian lands as well. There followed a two-century "golden age" of Georgian cultural achievement and political unity, which ended in the early thirteenth century with the Mongol conquest. Georgia regained its independence a century later, but internal conflict divided it again into eastern and western pieces in the mid-fifteenth century, and the western portion was in turn divided into several autonomous principalities. One of these was Abkhazia, which remained under the rule of the Shervashidze family for the next four centuries. A century later, the rising Safavid Persian and Ottoman Turkish Empires divided Georgia between them, the Safavids gaining suzerainty over eastern Georgia and the Ottomans over the west (including Abkhazia).[4] A rising Russia then won control of all of Georgia between 1783 and 1810. After Russia revoked Abkhazian autonomy in 1864, the Abkhaz launched a series of rebellions, provoking suppression so harsh that tens of thousands were forced into exile in a great migration the Abkhaz call the *Mohajirstvo*.

Georgia regained its independence in the spring of 1918 in the chaos of the Russian Revolution. Abkhazia was torn between supporters of a short-lived union of North Caucasian peoples, a pro-Russian Bolshevik faction, supporters of a short-lived Turkish invasion (led by a scion of the Shervashidze family), and a pro-Georgian Menshevik group.[5] The short-term winners of power were the Mensheviks, who had organized a pro-Georgian Abkhaz People's Council in November 1917; that council negotiated a June 1918 union with Georgia which gave autonomy to Abkhazia. The Abkhaz People's Council soon proved disloyal to Georgia, however, and was suppressed by the Georgian troops whom it had invited to eject the Bolsheviks, Turks, and Russian Whites. Abkhazia's autonomy was abrogated, and the population subjected to brutal Georgian repression. Fighting continued intermittently until 1921, when Georgia was invaded and annexed by Soviet Russia.

The South Ossetians, supported by Bolshevik Russia, were also a major source of dissent for Georgia's Menshevik government, launching Bolshevik-backed uprisings each year from 1918 to 1920 and suffering brutal repression after each. The 1920 rising was especially bloody, resulting in 5,000 Ossetian dead in fighting and reprisals and another 20,000 taking refuge in North Ossetia.

The new Soviet government gave special autonomous status to the Ossetians and Abkhaz. For the Ossetians it created within Georgia a South Ossetia Autonomous Region, with its capital at Tskhinvali. In March 1921, Soviet authorities made Abkhazia a Soviet republic separate from Georgia, with its capital at Sukhumi. In December 1921, however, Abkhazia signed a special treaty delegating some of its "sovereign" powers to Georgia. Georgia and Abkhazia were at the same time subordinated not only to Moscow but also to an intermediate "Transcaucasian Republic," while Georgia had a third autonomy, the Ajarian Autonomous Republic, created in its southwestern corner. In 1931, Abkhazia was demoted to the status of an Autonomous Republic and incorporated unambiguously into Georgia.

The Stalinization policies that followed devastated the interests of Georgia's minorities, who were forced to assimilate into Georgian society. Thus while "other non-Russians had their alphabets 'Cyrillicized,' the Abkhazians had theirs 'Georgianized' and all the native language schools in Abkhazia and South Ossetia were closed."[6] Stalin's five-year plans also resulted in the inflow of many Russians, Georgians, Armenians, and Greeks into Abkhazia to work in the growing agricultural sector, dramatically reducing the Abkhaz share of the local population.[7]

Although some minority rights were restored following the death of Stalin in 1953, Georgians continued to dominate, holding the controlling positions in Tbilisi and getting the lion's share of support for cultural projects.[8] In protest against these policies, Abkhaz organized public demonstrations or strikes in 1931, 1957, 1965, 1967, and 1978—a record of public discontent surpassed by few other Soviet groups. The 1978 protests included massive indoor and outdoor rallies in several locations demanding transfer of Abkhazia from the Georgian to the Russian republic. Moscow and Tbilisi responded with economic concessions, appropriating an extra 500 million rubles over seven years for economic investments such as a road-building program for infrastructure-poor Abkhazia, and cultural benefits such as the creation of an Abkhaz State University, a State Folk Dance Ensemble in Sukhumi, and Abkhazian-language television broadcasting. The package also set aside many government posts to be staffed by ethnic Abkhaz.[9] Despite these concessions, Abkhaz fears were not assuaged, so Abkhazia remained at the start of the 1980s one of the most volatile areas in the Soviet Union.

Conditions for Ethnic War in Georgia

Opportunity

Different people assess the same opportunity structure differently. For the Karabagh Armenians, as discussed in chapter 3, the first announcement of *glasnost* in 1986 was enough to encourage mobilization around a petition drive and pioneering protests on environmental and other issues a year and a half later. The Georgians and the Abkhaz required even less encouragement: the Abkhaz had launched major protests in every decade since the

1950s in the face of Khrushchev's and Brezhnev's repression; and the Georgians also had engaged in mass nationalist demonstrations in 1956 and 1978. As Georgian nationalist leader Nodar Natadze put it regarding Georgia's small community of nationalist activists: "there was no year when no political group was arrested."[10] The effect of *glasnost* was to encourage participation in such activities: in Natadze's words, "The fact was that it was becoming less and less dangerous" to join in public protests. By 1988, it was possible to establish public protest organizations and arrange campaigns of mass political rallies. Those same protest organizations were also capable of organizing ethnic riots, as was to occur in Abkhazia in July 1989.

The opportunity to mobilize for ethnic war came later. People armed with hunting weapons and organized by nationalist groups carried out the first skirmishes and guerrilla campaigns. Ownership of such hunting weapons was common on all sides, as Abkhaz, Georgians, and Ossetians all shared the general Caucasus Mountain culture in which hunting and gun ownership are accepted, indeed encouraged. One Abkhaz intellectual explained: "the Caucasian way of thinking, it's different. My grandpa used to carry a gun all of the time.... It was against the law, but people used to do it."[11] Georgian paramilitary leader Vazha Adamia confirmed that his followers began their campaigns in Abkhazia and South Ossetia with hunting weapons. Cloud-seeding rockets and explosives used to control mountain avalanches soon followed.[12]

The later escalation to guerrilla war, and then full-scale conventional war in Abkhazia, required first a further deterioration in the authority of the Soviet state. As discipline in the Soviet military slackened, it became increasingly easy to buy automatic weapons—and later, virtually any sort of military equipment—from poorly motivated Soviet soldiers, many sympathetic to one or another side in the conflict. Meanwhile, the curious inaction of Soviet troops against the Georgian paramilitaries' first attacks in South Ossetia in late 1989 surely encouraged escalation of such activities later. Other sources of arms were, according to some accounts, the KGB (secret police) and GRU (Soviet military intelligence), though the truth and significance of such activities remains uncertain.[13] Ultimately, the conventional war in Abkhazia was supplied on both sides by the Soviet Army: the Georgians used their share of the divided Soviet Army arsenal in their invasion of Abkhazia; while the Abkhaz received their weapons directly from military units and through Chechen sources.

MYTHS JUSTIFYING ETHNIC HOSTILITY AND FEAR

Georgian myths and symbols

Georgian national mythology begins with the claim that from the second millennium B.C.E., western Transcaucasia was dominated by a single "Colchian" culture, which was linguistically and therefore ethnically Kartvelian (Georgian). The kingdom of Colchis, which existed from the sixth to the first centuries B.C.E., is therefore presented as the first Georgian state. The first united Georgian state was created by a king of Kartli, known in the Georgian chronicles by the name of Parnavazi, who briefly united eastern Georgia and brought Colchis (Western Georgia) under its influence in the third century B.C.E. The successor state to Colchis, in Georgian tradition, is the Kingdom of Egrisi (in Greek, "Lazica," kingdom of the Kartvelian Laz), which ruled western Georgia including Abkhazia from the second to the sixth centuries C.E.[14] Georgian mythology emphasizes the "statehood" of these ancient kingdoms, playing down their frequent subjection to the larger powers of the region such as Persia and Rome.[15]

Another crucial event in Georgian national mythology is the fourth-century conversion of Kartli and Egrisi to the Christian faith by St. Nino, establishing Georgia as a bastion of Christianity in a region bordered—and threatened—first by pagan and then by Muslim powers.[16] After the seventh-century conquest of the country by the Arabs, Georgian mythology emphasizes the "struggle of the Georgian people for liberation,"[17] a goal finally achieved three centuries later.

Georgian mythology emphasizes next the golden age of Georgian unity beginning in 1008. David the Builder (1089–1125) unified all of modern Georgia and beyond, receiving the Ossetians (in modern North Ossetia) into vassalage and ejecting the ruling Seljuk Turks, which permitted the Georgian population to return to the lowlands from their mountain hideouts. Georgian historians emphasize David's religious tolerance, noting that Muslims lived no worse under his rule than under Muslim rule. But Georgian historical pretensions are more grandiose. Noting that "the brother peoples of the Caucasus were ready... to join the Georgians against their common [Seljuk] enemy," one Georgian text claims that Georgia was at that time given "the great historical mission for the liberation of the Transcaucasian peoples."[18]

Under David's greatest successor, Queen Tamar (1184–1212), Georgia achieved "military superiority in the Near East" and also reached its greatest cultural glories, including the creation of Georgia's great epic poem, Rustaveli's "The Knight in the Panther Skin." Indeed, the name of Queen Tamar herself became an important symbol in Georgian popular culture, and the one artifact known to be associated with her, a small jeweled cross, is the most treasured piece in Tbilisi's art museum.[19] A poll shows the importance of this golden age more generally in Georgian popular culture: almost 20 percent of contemporary respondents chose that period as the model which the new independent Georgia should follow.[20]

Georgia's relations with Russia provide a more recent set of historical symbols. First is Russia's decision in 1801 to violate its treaty with Kartli-Kakhetia (eastern Georgia) and abolish its monarchy rather than making it a protectorate as agreed. Even Soviet-era textbooks convey, in muted form, the Georgian outrage: "Tsarist Russia finally deprived Georgia of political independence, foisting on her someone else's regime."[21] Redemption came in 1918, when Georgia finally regained its independence as a single, united state led by the Menshevik Noe Jordania, creating another, albeit short-lived, exemplar of Georgian statehood. Georgia's independence was recognized by Soviet Russia in a 1920 treaty, but the Russians perfidiously abrogated the treaty a few months later, invading Georgia in February 1921 and annexing it de facto. This, then, is the iconography of Georgian nationalism. The ancient Colchian and Kartlian kingdoms give Georgians a claim to over two thousand years of "statehood," and the conversion to Christianity gave Georgia a mission as "defender of the faith" in a mostly non-Christian region. The golden age under David the Builder and Queen Tamar symbolizes the strength of Georgian statehood and the greatness of Georgian culture; and provides an example of the tolerance of the Georgian people while also justifying Georgian pretensions to leadership over other peoples in the region. The two Russian annexations (1801 and 1921) prove Russian perfidy and imperialism, while the Menshevik republic of 1918–21 represents the legitimacy of modern Georgian independence, which is clinched by the Russian consent embodied in the 1920 treaty.

Georgian mythology about Abkhazia claims that Abkhazia was historically merely a part of Georgia. It emphasizes that in the first millennium B.C.E., Abkhazia was part of ancient Colchis.[22] The second century C.E. subordination of Abkhazia to the Kingdom of Egrisi is said to strengthen the Georgian claim. Georgians also see the Abkhazian kingdom that united Georgia in the eleventh century as a Georgian kingdom: Abkhazia ruled western Georgia—so most of its inhabitants, even before unification, were western Georgians, and the language of administration was Georgian (there was as yet no written Abkhazian language). Therefore, "the 'Abkhazian kings'... were Georgians, culturally and politically speaking."[23] The more extreme version of this mythology claims, based on a bogus theory first proposed in Stalin's time, that the ancient "Abkhazians" were actually a Georgian tribe, and that the ancestors of the contemporary Abkhaz are recent interlopers, arriving in Abkhazia from the North Caucasus only in the seventeenth century.[24]

Most importantly to Georgian apologists, the fact that the Menshevik Abkhaz People's Council chose to unite Abkhazia with Georgia in 1918 legitimized Georgian rule over the area in 1918–21, and by extension Georgian rule today.[25] Georgians defend their more recent record of rule in Abkhazia by noting that ethnic Abkhaz occupied most leadership positions in Abkhazia in the 1980s, though they were only 17.3 percent of the population of the region; and that Georgia ensured the economic and cultural development of Abkhazia. Rather than being repressed, the Georgians charge, the Abkhaz were in fact repressing Georgians in the region.[26]

Regarding the Ossetians, David the Builder's relationship with them summarizes much of the Georgian attitude: the Ossetians were a people of the North Caucasus; Georgians had good relations with them; and the Ossetians were subordinate to Georgia. The Ossetians who successfully invaded Georgia in the thirteenth century were expelled in the fourteenth, so the current settlement of Ossetians in Georgia, in the region Georgians call Inner Kartli, dates only to the early seventeenth or eighteenth century, making the Ossetians newcomers in Georgia. The name "South Ossetia" is not appropriate—a coinage only of the late nineteenth century—for referring to an area that was the heartland of eastern Georgia for centuries. Ossetian revolts against independent Georgia in 1918, 1919, and 1920 were all connected to foreign intervention, especially by Soviet Russia. And the creation of the South Ossetian Autonomous Region by Stalin was part of the Bolshevik "divide and rule" strategy aimed at controlling Georgia, thus the autonomous region was not a legitimate structure in Georgian eyes.[27] Expressions of Ossetian national pride were not considered appropriate: Shevardnadze complained in 1983 about South Ossetian writers "glorifying 'moribund attributes of antiquity'".[28]

Georgian fears

Georgian fears stem from a history of domination and ethnic affinity problems in relation to two traditional Georgian enemies: Muslims and Russians. The former Muslim powers of Turkey and Iran are currently relatively weak and restrained, but Georgia is still surrounded and outnumbered by Muslim peoples: Turks and Iranians to the south, Azerbaijanis to the east, and the Muslims of the North Caucasus to the north. Furthermore, the fastest-growing ethnic groups in Georgia are Muslim minorities. The Georgians fear that with their lower birthrate, they might eventually be lost in a Muslim sea.[29] Historical trends do not justify the Georgians' concerns: from 1939 to 1989, Georgians *increased* their share of Georgia's population, from 61 percent to 70 percent, so there seems little rational reason to worry about any threat of being relegated to minority status.[30] Nevertheless, worry Georgians do: even Shevardnadze worried aloud in 1983 that the demographic situation had "worsened catastrophically."[31]

Regarding Russia, Georgians believe that the Russian aim has always been not only to dominate Georgia but to annihilate the Georgian people through assimilation. They see nineteenth-century Russification policies as attempts to implant "a Russian soul in [each] Georgian body."[32] Intellectuals believed that this policy of Russification threatened the very existence of the Georgian nation while it was part of the USSR. They refer to the autonomies in Georgia—Abkhazia, South Ossetia, and Ajaria—as "mines" planted in Georgia, set to explode in order to weaken Georgia and frustrate any attempt to escape from Russian domination. The Georgians' self-image that they are a tolerant people blinds them to the possibility that these minority groups might have legitimate grievances, so they believe almost unanimously that minority restiveness can only be explained by the actions of a malevolent "third force"—Moscow.

The importance to Georgians of symbolic issues and existential fears, especially in the late 1980s and early 1990s, is illustrated by the results of a 1990 poll of Tbilisi residents.[33] Of seven issues mentioned by Tbilisians as of major concern at that time, five were symbolic nationalist issues such as "Preserving Georgia's territorial unity" [from ethnic separatists], mentioned by 88.5 percent; interethnic conflicts, mentioned by 86.5 percent; and the "demographic problem," mentioned by 77.5 percent. Only two issues related to individual interests ranked with these symbolic concerns: ecological problems, mentioned by 86.9 percent of respondents, and "filling the stores with quality merchandise," mentioned by 86.6 percent.

Georgian chauvinism and mass hostility

Because of the deserved Georgian reputation for tolerance, Georgians feel hostile toward those who make what they consider unjustified or dangerous claims. Thus one intellectual claimed for Georgians "an instinct for genuine chivalry," simultaneously admitting that this self-image was "inflated" but claiming that "in developed western countries people are struggling toward" these Georgian qualities. Similarly, Georgians are proud of their emotional honesty but are therefore unashamed at framing the issue of ethnic politics unambiguously: "The question we all wait to see answered is: Who will dominate?"[34] Thus the Georgian understanding of tolerance is essentially: you submit to our power, and we will magnanimously treat you as well as you ought to expect. In this view Ossetians, present in Georgia in significant numbers for three or four centuries, are essentially "guests" without the right to expect political autonomy. More precisely, the existence of the South Ossetia Autonomous Region "countered the very interests in survival for Georgia."[35]

The Abkhaz were in fact autochthonous inhabitants of the region, but since Georgians consider Abkhazia to be "Georgian land," they find it easier to believe that the Abkhaz are in fact newcomers as well. So sure of their essential good faith are Georgians that even after the war in Abkhazia, they dismiss as a "fairy tale" or "speculation" the notion that Abkhaz might fear the reimposition of Georgian rule—in spite of the widespread looting and occasional atrocities in which Georgian troops in Abkhazia indulged during the war.[36] That these attitudes are motivated in part by hostility toward both the Abkhaz and the Ossetians is indicated by survey research: one 1990 survey found 32 percent of Georgians willing to state a "negative" attitude toward Ossetians (versus 26 percent positive), and 38 percent stated a "negative" attitude toward Abkhaz (versus 22 percent positive)—this two years before the 1992 outbreak of war in Abkhazia.[37] Abkhaz have tended to cite those Georgians who have been much more direct in their hostility: claiming, for example, that "Abkhazians...suck the juices from Georgia" or propounding racist theories contending that Georgian "blood" is superior to that of other peoples.[38]

Abkhaz myths and symbols

Abkhazian national mythology starts from the view that the Abkhaz are the aboriginal inhabitants of the area[39] and it traces the Abkhaz linguistic heritage to the Hurrians and Hattians of the Middle East's second and third millennium B.C.E. It identifies Abkhazia's political roots in a series of small principalities that emerged in the first century C.E. and developed into a united Abkhazia (subordinate to Byzantium, not Lazica) in the eighth century.[40] "By the eighth century," the *Great Soviet Encyclopedia* claims, "the Abkhazian nationality had basically been consolidated."[41] After a brief "genuine Abkhazian national period," Abkhazia took control of western Georgia and eventually united all of Georgia. Abkhazian mythology emphasizes that these unifiers of Georgia were an Abkhazian dynasty: even Queen Tamar gave her son Georgii the second name "Lasha"—Abkhazian for "bright" or "enlightened."[42]

Abkhazian nationalists next emphasize that Abkhazia regained its independence under the Shervashidze dynasty in the seventeenth century, maintaining autonomy (though under Ottoman suzerainty) until its 1810 union with Russia. The next great symbolic event was the *Mohajirstvo*, for which the standard Soviet estimate is that 32,000 of 78,000 Abkhaz were expelled in 1877 alone following the Abkhaz uprising of that year.[43] One Abkhaz source puts the total number of expulsions over several decades at over 100,000, characterizing the event as the Abkhazians' "deepest popular tragedy" which confronted them with the "threat of physical extinction." Colonists of other ethnic groups then resettled the best Abkhazian land.[44]

The next great tragedy for the Abkhaz followed the Russian Revolution. In the Soviet-era Abkhaz telling, the Menshevik government represented "occupiers from the south" against whom "all Abkhazia arose." After the Abkhaz were suppressed in 1918, the Mensheviks instituted a "regime of white terror" which did not allow "any kind of rights" to the Abkhaz while pursuing a "resettlement policy" of importing more ethnic Georgians into Abkhazia.[45] Menshevik rule and the Menshevik flag thus became symbols of Georgian "imperialism" and brutality.

Obviously, the Abkhaz assessment of the Soviet period could not be published before the conflict with Georgia began, but since most of it occurred in living memory, some views of the period were known and later written down. In the Abkhaz telling, Abkhazia was subordinated to Georgia in 1931 due to the machinations of Stalin, a Georgian, and his Mingrelian henchman Lavrentii Beria—who was the party boss of the Transcaucasian Communist Party machine until 1938 and then secret police chief until 1953. Teaching in the Abkhazian language was banned, and forced immigration of Georgians and other ethnic groups was accelerated. During the terror of the late 1930s, the Abkhaz claim, 80 percent of those victimized in Abkhazia were ethnic Abkhaz, far out of proportion to their share of the population.[46]

The icons of Abkhazian mythology are therefore symbols of an ancient and distinctive people whose existence is under threat. Abkhaz are the original inhabitants of their land; they established independent principalities of early medieval and early modern times; and their distinct culture is reflected in Queen Tamar's son's Abkhazian name; they faced the tragedy of the *Mohajirstvo;* gained legal autonomy from Georgia in the 1920s; and were repressed by Menshevik and Soviet Georgia.

Abkhaz fears

Although the Abkhaz population grew both absolutely and as a proportion of Georgia's population between 1939 and 1989, it was still only 17.3 percent of the population of Abkhazia by 1989 due to continuing immigration of other groups, especially Georgians. From the Abkhazian point of view, cultural policies in the region disproportionately favorable to them were necessary to maintain their cultural heritage. Policies of Georgianization, in contrast, could create a mortal threat to their communal existence. Thus in their 1977 appeal to Moscow (which led to the 1978 mass protests), a group of Abkhaz intellectuals expressed concern that Georgian "policy is leading to the complete Georgianization of Abkhazia"—that is, the complete assimilation of the Abkhaz people.[47] For the Abkhaz, an example of what might happen to them is provided by the fate of the Ubykhs, a closely related ethnic group whose former territory bordered on Abkhazia to the west: the Ubykhs were all deported to the Ottoman Empire in the *Mohajirstvo*, their territory (including what is now the Black Sea resort town of Sochi) resettled by Russians, and they themselves assimilated by other peoples in Turkey. The Ubykhs, in short, were annihilated as a people; and the Abkhaz fear that the same will happen to them.[48]

Abkhazian mass hostility

There is clear evidence of Abkhaz hostility toward Georgians throughout the Soviet period, due in large part to these demographic fears. Even Orjonikidze noted the Abkhaz "mistrust" of Georgians (a 1967 Abkhazian dissident letter complains about the "chauvinist poison of a definite portion of the Georgian intelligentsia,") and chauvinist Georgian policies in Abkhazia.[49]

The intensity of this attitude is difficult to measure, but one indication is from the lighthearted collection of stories, *Sandro of Chegem*, by the popular Abkhaz writer Fazil Iskander. In the following passage, "Chegemians" are Abkhaz from the village of Chegem and "Endurskies" are Georgians.

> [T]he Chegemians were sure that all of Abkhazia dreamed of becoming related to them. Not to mention the Endurskies, who dreamed not so much of becoming related to the Chegemians as of subjugating them, or not even subjugating but simply destroying the flourishing village, turning it into a wasteland, and then taking off for home, so that they could go around saying that there had never been any Chegem, frankly speaking, it was a fabrication....
>
> Any response from the Endurskies was perceived as a crafty, but also a stupid, attempt to conceal their true, allegedly most often malicious, attitude toward everything that alarmed the Chegemians.
>
> None of this prevented them from maintaining quite friendly relations with their Endursky aliens in normal times, but in a difficult moment the Chegemians would begin to suspect the Endurskies of secret intrigues.[50]

The last sentence sums up the real Abkhaz attitude toward Georgians, as confirmed in interviews: while ordinary people got along well in quiet times, including in the early and mid-1980s, Abkhaz fears of Georgians' political intent was never far below the surface. Such an attitude makes comprehensible the 1967 protests in Abkhazia, which seem to have been sparked by the revival in a prominent Georgian periodical of the theory that Abkhazia was originally populated by Georgians, with the Abkhaz having arrived only in the seventeenth century.[51] Similarly, during Abkhazia's 1978 protests, Georgian-language signs in Abkhazia were defaced, and graffiti on a Georgian school denounced Georgian as a "dog language." Some Georgians were reportedly attacked, and a few killed, in the same period.[52] Such attitudes continued into the 1980s: a moderate Georgian politician reports, for example, that once when he spoke Georgian to Abkhaz in a shop, he was "told to speak Russian, because they did not understand 'my dog's language.'"[53]

Ossetian myths and symbols

Ossetian mythology traces the Ossetians' ancestry to the first Iranian people to reach the Caucasus region, the ancient Scythians, who were present in the North Caucasus by the eighth century B.C.E.[54] This genealogy is dubious, but their claim to descent from the Sarmatians, who arrived in the region some five centuries later, seems better-founded. The existence of an Alan kingdom in the North Caucasus in the seventh century C.E. is well documented, and indeed it became a major power in the North Caucasus after the fall of the Khazar kingdom in the eighth century.[55] The Ossetians emphasize this tie.

The rest of Ossetian historiography reinterprets accepted history more than inventing it. Claiming that there was some Sarmatian presence in modern South Ossetia for over two millennia, they admit that the major migration of proto-Ossetians south across the Caucasus Mountains began after the Mongol invasion of the thirteenth century. A pamphlet by Yuri Gogluyti, "Foreign Minister" of South Ossetia in the late 1990s, traces the first militarily significant Ossetian presence only to the early seventeenth century, not far from the western interpretation. The Ossetians' main point is to emphasize their eighteenth-century conflicts with Georgian kings, and their at least intermittent autonomy from those kings.[56] Ossetian mythology emphasizes that the name "South Ossetia" dates from this period rather than being a nineteenth-century or Bolshevik invention, as claimed by the Georgians.[57] Other strands of Ossetian mythology note that Ossetians and Georgians were sometimes allies against their Muslim neighbors in this period, but the implication is of Ossetian friendship spurned by the chauvinist Georgians.

Ossetian mythology about the eighteenth and nineteenth centuries emphasizes disappointment with Russian policy: Ossetians had looked to Russia as a counterweight to the Kabardians in the north and to the Georgians in the south, but Russian rule provided little relief. The Russian punitive campaign of 1830 against one of many Ossetian uprisings (in North and South Ossetia) is especially remembered. In the south, the Ossetians were further disappointed to note that Russian policy seemed to support Georgian pretensions.[58] Ossetians, like the Abkhaz, have negative memories about Menshevik Georgian rule: they especially emphasize the bloody suppression of their 1920 rebellion (insisting that it was an Ossetian, not a Bolshevik, uprising); and the Menshevik flag came to be for Ossetians, as for Abkhazians, a symbol of chauvinist Georgian rule.

Ossetian attitudes toward Georgians

Unlike the Abkhaz and the Georgians, the Ossetians seem to have shown little evidence of hostility toward their ethnic rivals. The Ossetians' nineteenth-century national poet Khetagurov did worry that his people were on the edge of extinction,[59] but that concern does not seem to have persisted into Soviet times. The bloody events of 1920 were, just barely, within living memory of Ossetians in the 1980s, but even nationalist Ossetians report that before that time Ossetian dissatisfaction with Georgians was inchoate and not strongly felt or articulated.[60] Ossetians outside of South Ossetia—who comprised the majority of Georgia's Ossetians—were increasingly Georgianized linguistically, apparently with little resistance.[61] Ossetian hostility of the 1980s was primarily a reaction against the chauvinistic tendencies present in the reviving Georgian nationalism of the time.

ECONOMIC AND LIVING-STANDARD GRIEVANCES

For two of the nationalist movements in Georgia, those of the Georgians and Abkhaz, economic concerns per se played a very small motivating role. Georgia was relatively prosperous by Soviet standards, and foodstuffs in particular were abundant, with a wide variety of foods easily available.[62] The Georgian standard of living was undoubtedly affected by the Soviet economic doldrums of the 1980s (thus minimally fulfilling the requirement of economic decline), and the wine-loving Georgians were surely discomfited by Gorbachev's anti-alcohol campaign, but these purely economic issues did not figure in the rhetoric of nationalists. As noted above, polls showed Georgians with more symbolic nationalist concerns than economic ones.

From the Georgian viewpoint, Abkhazia, too, was a prosperous corner of the Soviet Union, a tourist mecca often favored by Soviet bigwigs—and therefore well connected in Moscow. There were problems, however. Especially before 1978, economic growth and public investment per capita were lower in the Akbhazian Autonomous Republic than in Georgia proper. As a result, Akbhazia's factories were proportionately fewer and more often obsolete than in Georgia proper, and the roads were poorer. Furthermore, ethnic Abkhaz benefited less from economic growth than did other groups: as late as 1970, over 50 percent of ethnic Abkhaz were peasants, and only 30 percent were industrial workers; Georgians, by contrast, were more likely to be better-paid industrial workers (41 percent) than peasants (33 percent).[63]

After 1978, however, the Abkhaz were more concerned about the national implications of economic issues. Abkhaz nationalists often complained about economic development projects, including even the siting of a subtropical studies institute in Sukhumi, because they spurred immigration of non-Abkhaz ethnic groups and further diluted the Abkhaz share of the local population. Abkhaz also complained about Tbilisi's tendency to dictate every detail of economic policy, which distorted Abkhazia's economy.[64] Finally, Abkhaz also believed that Georgians were favored in gaining many sorts of jobs, especially the more desirable ones, and in getting housing in Sukhumi. The Georgians, in contrast, complained that it was they who were discriminated against in hiring: for example, two-thirds of government ministers and 71.4 percent of Communist Party department heads were ethnic Abkhaz.[65] The Georgians also claimed that the Abkhaz were trying to discourage Georgian immigration—to preserve the demographic balance—by denying housing permits to Georgians.[66]

South Ossetia, unlike Abkhazia, was truly economically disadvantaged. The South Ossetians argued in the 1980s that the budget for South Ossetia had declined as a share of the overall Georgian budget, resulting in lower living standards for South Ossetians than for people in other parts of Georgia.[67]

That difference was graphically brought home to South Ossetians in May 1988 when an inadequate water treatment system caused an outbreak of typhoid in their capital of Tskhinvali.[68]

In none of these cases did economic concerns play an important role in political mobilization, however. Both Georgians and Abkhaz mobilized around almost entirely noneconomic issues in 1988; those economic issues that did come up were primarily proxies for issues of ethnic balance or political power. And while the Ossetians were disadvantaged, their mobilization was a reaction against rising Georgian chauvinism, not against longstanding economic discrimination.

The Escalation of Ethnic Conflict

Mass-Led Mobilization among Georgians

Georgia's nationalist mobilization in the 1980s was primarily a mass-led phenomenon. Georgian nationalist sentiment had long been strong: there were mass demonstrations on nationalist themes in Georgia in 1956 and 1978, for example, and a small dissident Georgian nationalist movement remained active throughout the 1970s and 1980s. According to one dissident source, even high-level Communist Party officials in Georgia—up to and including then-First Secretary Eduard Shevardnadze—had to at least pay lip service to Georgian nationalism in private in order to maintain their credibility with Georgia's educated elite.[69] All that was required to make large-scale nationalist mobilization possible was the political space afforded by *glasnost*.

The early phase of Georgia's nationalist mobilization, following the pattern of other Soviet republics, centered on apparently nonnationalist issues: the first major issue, for example, raised publicly in 1986, was the construction of a railroad line across the Caucasus mountains, which critics claimed was damaging the environment.[70] In 1987 the nationalists took on a more formidable opponent, the Soviet army, demanding the closing of a firing range which was causing damage to a nearby monastery of historical significance. At first the dissidents had access to the press only through a few outlets, such as the Georgian Writers' Union newspaper *Literaturuli Sakartvelo*, but the debate over such issues quickly spread to other media sources—and then to other issues. By 1988, substantial and growing nationalist rallies were being held: commemorating the anniversary of Georgia's 1918 declaration of independence (May 26), calling for closing the firing range (September), and so on.[71] The September demonstrations lasted for two days and attracted as many as 10,000 people.[72]

The mass-led nature of this movement is shown by the reaction of Georgia's communist leadership to it. Communist leaders repeatedly used police to break up nationalist rallies, and they tried to mobilize the press to discredit nationalist leaders, especially Zviad Gamsakhurdia, a veteran dissident and son of a popular Georgian novelist. When the government took steps that were in line with the nationalists' agenda—ending construction of the disputed railway, rejecting a proposed amendment to the USSR constitution that would have limited the right of republics to secede—they did so only under intense pressure. The USSR constitution issue came up in November 1988, sparking a protest rally by tens of thousands of people on November 12 and a week-long series of demonstrations and hunger strikes November 23–29.[73] The Georgian leadership finally acceded to the protesters' demands in a feeble attempt to separate moderate from more extreme nationalists.[74]

By this time, however, the nationalists were invoking fears of group extinction and demanding ethnic dominance. Speakers at the November 1988 rallies warned about the "expansionism" of other ethnic groups and the "problem of physical survival" of the Georgian people, and demanded secession from the Soviet Union and the independence of Georgia. By the following spring, slogans at rallies included "The Soviet Union is the Prison of Nations," "Long Live a Free, Democratic Georgia," and, most famously, "Georgia for the Georgians."[75] These themes were apparently popular with ordinary Georgians and worked to attract growing crowds to nationalist demonstrations.

The April 1989 rallies marked a major turning point. Initially reacting against Abkhaz demands for independence from Georgia, Georgian nationalists organized a series of rallies of growing size which again demanded Georgian independence from the USSR as well as suppression of Abkhazia's autonomy. While there was no single umbrella organization of Georgian nationalists, leaders of the various competing groups—such as Gamsakhurdia, Merab Kostava (another prominent longtime dissident and lifelong friend of Gamsakhurdia), Gia Chanturia (author of the "Georgia for the Georgians" slogan), and Nodar Natadze (leader of the Georgian "Popular Front")—met periodically to coordinate their activities, especially regarding mass demonstrations.[76]

While evidence on the motives of ordinary protesters is thin, it seems to indicate simple nationalist sentiment was the major factor. One protester explained his motives to a western journalist as follows: "The Soviet system has tried to take away not only our nationality, they've tried to take away "us" from us. Our own individuality. It's not surprising now that we have a little freedom that we want back the first thing they tried to take away, our country."[77] The protest leaders understood that this was the participants' motivation: in retrospective interviews, they report that the shift of slogans from anti-Abkhazian to pro-independence was critical in attracting the massive crowds to those protests.[78] The motivating force was the powerful symbolism of statehood. Indeed, even reporters for *Pravda* and other Soviet newspapers, anxious to discredit the demonstrators, had to admit that the demonstrations were successful in appealing to people's emotions, "inflaming the atmosphere, [and] getting people all worked up and excited."[79]

Apparently feeling threatened, the Georgian leadership under Party First Secretary Jumber Patiashvili sent an envoy to negotiate with the organizers of the demonstrations, but the organizers refused to end them. Patiashvili therefore requested and received authorization from Moscow to use force to break up the rallies. The Soviet troops waited until the middle of the night, when the crowd was the smallest, to launch their attack, but the result was a massacre.[80] On April 9, 1989, Soviet troops wielding sharpened shovels and a toxic gas waded into the crowd of unarmed demonstrators and killed nineteen Georgian civilians—sixteen of them women.[81] Rather than crushing the Georgian independence movement, this massacre confirmed Georgian suspicions of the Soviet government and demonstrated the need for independence. Patiashvili was forced to resign, and the Georgian Communist Party's authority never recovered.

MASS-LED MOBILIZATION AMONG ABKHAZ

The Abkhaz, long active in promoting their nationalist aspirations, also took the opportunity provided by *glasnost* to begin mobilizing. They began with innocuous steps such as forming a youth group concerned with the environment, but they quickly became active on nationalist issues: one early effort of the youth group was to organize a march commemorating the nineteenth-century *Mohajirstvo*.[82] At the same time, Abkhaz were increasingly concerned about the direction of the Georgian nationalist movement, especially slogans such as "Georgia for the Georgians," which implied suppression of minority political and cultural rights.

The Abkhaz nationalists' next move was a June 1988 letter to the special Communist Party Conference in Moscow. In the letter, 58 members of the Abkhazian Communist Party requested that Abkhazia be made a union republic independent of Georgia.[83] They justified their demands by claiming that due to Georgian hostility the economic and cultural programs initiated ten years earlier had failed to meet their goals of Abkhazian cultural revitalization. As a result, they argued, the Abkhaz nation remained on the brink of extinction. Both the Soviet and the Georgian Communist Parties rejected the Abkhaz demands, and the Georgian population in Tbilisi responded with large demonstrations advocating Georgian independence and protesting discrimination against Georgians by ethnic minorities.

Around the same time, growing Georgian fears about the demographic situation led to increasingly bizarre policy proposals. One infamous article published in the Tbilisi press advocated a coercive policy of restricting non-Georgians to no more than two children per family as a way of addressing Georgians' demographic concerns. Unused to *glasnost*, many Abkhaz, Ossetians, and other minorities believed that the article's publication in an official newspaper meant the idea had official endorsement, raising fears that such policies would actually be implemented.[84]

Meanwhile, over the course of 1988, the Abkhaz formed a popular front organization called *Aidgylara*, patterned after similar organizations in the Baltic states. In December of that year they organized a mass assembly, appointing the prominent but politically naive writer Alexei Gogua as its first president.[85] The organization quickly adopted an extreme line: ignoring voices suggesting that "sovereignty" (to which Abkhazia was legally entitled) might be a less provocative interim goal than an Abkhazian republic fully independent of Georgia, most of the leaders opted to demand full independence from Georgia from the beginning.[86] The role of Gogua and other cultural leaders was to put these demands for dominance over the local Georgians into beautiful, poetic language.

In March 1989, *Aidgylara* organized a mass rally that attracted some 30,000 people in the town of Lykhny, historic site of the start of an 1866 uprising in Abkhazia, to repeat the demand that Abkhazia be granted union republic status independent of Georgia.[87] Under duress, virtually the entire communist leadership of Abkhazia signed the resulting Lykhny appeal, even though the appeal criticized them.[88] Even Konstantin Ozgan, a known nationalist and Communist Party chief of Guadauta District where the rally was held, was not involved in organizing the rally: he was informed about it only a day or two in advance and claims to have bent the rules to approve the rally but otherwise not to have helped arrange it.[89] Rather, *Aidgylara* had already established a network of cells throughout Abkhazia, and the small, close-knit Abkhazian people found it easy to spread the word about the rally—and gather some one-quarter of their entire population plus thousands of non-Abkhazians—without any official help.[90] The official leaders of Abkhazia apparently signed the appeal only due to the pressure from this public outpouring.

The Abkhaz demand provoked large counter-rallies of ethnic Georgians in Sukhumi, the Abkhazian capital, and in Gali, a district center in Abkhazia populated mostly by Georgians.[91] According to an Abkhaz source, one of these rallies featured Georgian nationalist leader Merab Kostava, who allegedly said, "let [the Abkhaz] say thank you, that they live on our land," and "we will teach the Abkhaz reason." A local Georgian leader was quoted as saying, "if the Georgian government will not [defend us], we are doomed to destruction, and then blood will have to be shed." The Abkhaz, meanwhile, denounced the protesters' flying of the Menshevik flag, which represented for them the Mensheviks' "policy of terror and physical annihilation of the Abkhazian people."[92]

The Lykhny rally also occasioned the Tbilisi rallies that culminated in the April 9 massacre: Georgian nationalists in Tbilisi were now demanding abolition of Abkhazia's autonomy.[93] One of the Georgians' fears was that Moscow would side with the Abkhaz as a way of weakening the Georgians' growing pro-independence movement.[94] Responding to popular demand and its own perception of "nationalism" in the Abkhazian Communist Party organization, the Patiashvili leadership in one of its last acts removed Abkhazian party chief Boris Adleyba—who was not in fact much of a nationalist—on April 6; his replacement, the "inert" Vladimir Khishba, did nothing to improve the situation in Abkhazia.[95]

OUTBREAK OF ETHNIC VIOLENCE IN ABKHAZIA

The Georgian leadership team headed by Givi Gumbaridze, which took over after the removal of Patiashvili, was almost completely lacking in popular legitimacy. In one poll, 71 percent of the respondents viewed Georgia's party leadership negatively, while another poll found that 42 percent of Georgians claimed the Communist Party never made decisions in the public interest—the most negative view of any ethnic group in the USSR.[96] This lack of legitimacy forced communist leaders to make ever-greater concessions to the popular Georgian nationalists in order to remain in power.

For example, egged on by nationalist leaders in Tbilisi, Georgian students at Abkhaz State University in Sukhumi launched a hunger strike soon after the April 9 tragedy, demanding that the Georgian-language sector of their institution be spun off and made into a branch of Tbilisi State University (i.e., that it be controlled by Georgia instead of Abkhazia). The students' demand was part of a larger campaign of Georgian cultural separatism, which quickly led to the division of other cultural institutions in Abkhazia along ethnic lines, including the soccer team (which had Georgian and Abkhaz players) and the theater (which had Georgian and Russian-language troupes).[97] The university issue, however, required Tbilisi's approval, and after ethnic Georgian schoolteachers and researchers at the Subtropics Institute in Sukhumi joined in a strike on the issue, the new Georgian government agreed on May 14 to establish the new Sukhumi branch of Tbilisi university.[98]

The status of the university was so symbolically important to the Abkhaz, however, that a backlash was inevitable.[99] It began with a series of Abkhaz demonstrations immediately after the May decision. When Georgian students and faculty moved into new premises and began organizing admissions examinations for their new university, Abkhaz of all ages began a sit-in. Foreseeing the possibility of violence, local officials began a campaign to collect hunting weapons from the population—especially, the Abkhaz believed, from Abkhaz. A special commission of the USSR

Supreme Soviet came to investigate the university dispute in early July and concluded that the Georgian government had no legal right to authorize the new university—it was the prerogative of the Soviet government. Despite that conclusion, and threats by the Abkhaz, the Georgians decided to go ahead with a new entrance exam for the school that was scheduled to be administered on July 15.[100]

The result was a riot, possibly planned on both sides. In Sukhumi, initially peaceful demonstrations came to blows when an Abkhaz photographer tried to take a picture of the Georgian demonstrators and was beaten by Georgians. The two crowds immediately clashed, and the Abkhaz demonstrators attacked the school building where the entrance examinations were being held, beating up members of the examining commission. That evening, Abkhaz and Georgians began mobilizing all over Abkhazia and western Georgia. Svans from northeastern Abkhazia and Abkhaz from the city of Tkvarcheli (near Svanian territory) clashed in Sukhumi in a shooting spree that lasted all night and intermittently for several days afterward.

Meanwhile 30,000 Mingrelians from Mingrelia (in western Georgia) and the Gali district (the easternmost part of Abkhazia, bordering on Mingrelia and populated mostly by Mingrelians) began marching toward Sukhumi, led by Merab Kostava, a Georgian leader based in Tbilisi. An armed group of Abkhaz (whose hunting weapons had just been returned) blocked the marchers (some of whom were armed as well) at a bridge outside the ethnically mixed town of Ochamchira. Kostava stopped the march, averting even more violence, and Soviet interior troops were called in to reestablish order. Yet fighting did not stop until two weeks of intermittent violence had left at least 15 dead and 500 wounded on both sides.[101]

These escalatory steps all resulted primarily from mass-led political pressures. The change in the university's status came not because the Georgian government was nationalist, but because it was under pressure from nationalist demonstrators and hunger strikers in Sukhumi and Tbilisi. It had to respond to attempts by dissident elites to discredit it as "antinational." The Mingrelians' march was openly organized by Georgian informal organizations under the slogan of "defending Georgians' rights," and the Georgian government did not dare to stop it. The nationalist Abkhaz leaders, under pressure from Tbilisi, dared not take overt action either, but under pressure from below they also could not block the protests of their own nationalists. Thus when Abkhaz crowds "attacked" militia (police) posts to get access to weapons, the militia reported no casualties—suggesting that, with official sympathy, they sometimes failed to resist the "attacks."[102] The example of a local procurator in Ochamchira who ordered the return of Abkhazians' hunting weapons is only an extreme case of this official connivance.

The July 1989 violence reinforced the Abkhaz in their determination to find allies. In August, therefore, they organized an "Assembly of Mountain Peoples of the Caucasus" in Sukhumi, looking for help from their ethnic kin in the North Caucasus. The first head of this organization was Musa Shanibov, a Kabardian, member of a group ethnically related to the Abkhaz.[103]

Meanwhile, as reflected in the press, Georgians in Tbilisi reacted with their usual wide-eyed chauvinistic innocence. One curious article asked how and why the Abkhaz could organize, acquire arms, and attack Georgians without noting that Georgians also organized themselves, acquired arms, and attacked Abkhaz.[104] A poem entitled, "Till When?" and published in the official Communist Party newspaper captured—and reinforced—the mood of self-exculpatory denial:

We don't want to be slaves of others....
Surely, that is not why we are guilty,
Or guilty in what?
We gave shelter and warmth to other peoples,
We shared their grief and joy....
And in response?
In response, shooting and killing....[105]

This apparent inability of Georgian public opinion to accept that Georgian actions might be contributing to ethnic hostility seems to be one of the main reasons for later Georgian immoderation. So was the attitude of the official Georgian press, which by August could print an article claiming that many Abkhaz were really Georgians who changed their nationality in order to get jobs reserved for ethnic Abkhaz. The symbolism was explicit: Georgians are discriminated against in hiring, while those who get jobs are those who "turn their backs on their mothers."[106]

MOBILIZATION AND VIOLENCE IN SOUTH OSSETIA

Ossetians responded to Georgian mobilization soon after the Abkhaz did by forming a popular front called *Ademon Nykhas* ("Popular Shrine") in January 1989 under the leadership of a college instructor named Alan Chochiev.[107] Tensions between Ossetians and Georgians rose dramatically when Chochiev wrote a letter in an Abkhaz newspaper in April 1989 saying that Ossetians sympathized with the Abkhazian efforts at autonomy and hoped that their success would set a precedent for other regions that wished to join the Russian Republic.[108] This letter defined the conflict as a contest for dominance: *Ademon Nykhas* wanted secession from Georgia and dominance over local Georgians, while Georgian nationalists wanted to abolish South Ossetia's name and autonomy. Violence soon followed: on

May 26 a group of Georgians traveled to Tskhinvali, the South Ossetian capital, to celebrate Georgia's 1918 independence from Tsarist Russia—which the South Ossetians, of course, had opposed. Provoked by the display of Georgian flags—the flag of the old Menshevik government, and a symbol of oppression to the Ossetians—some Ossetians attacked the Georgians, grabbing the flags and wiping their shoes with them.[109]

At first, this seemed an isolated incident. Georgian nationalist leader Nodar Natadze, a shrewd if biased witness, observed an Ossetian nationalist rally in early June and reported a small crowd of only two or three hundred participants and "no emotional ground" for the rally, which advocated secession from Georgia and union with North Ossetia.[110] Simple nationalism, if this account is accurate, was not motivating many Ossetians at this time. However, in July, during the clashes over Abkhaz State University in Sukhumi, Georgians began circulating rumors that Ossetians were aiding the Abkhaz in Sukhumi, while Ossetians passed rumors that armed Georgians were headed for South Ossetia.[111] These beginnings of a security dilemma caused mass tensions to start escalating.

Incumbent leaders on both sides worked hard to reduce those tensions. South Ossetia's Communist Party leader Anatolii Chekhoev denounced the demands of *Ademon Nykhas* for union with North Ossetia, while the Georgian press denounced the rumors about plans for ethnic violence. Even nationalist organizations on both sides, including *Ademon Nykhas* and Georgia's Ilia Chavchavadze Society, issued appeals for nonviolence and "the fraternal brotherhood of nations."[112]

In August 1989, however, the Georgian government—responding to its people's fear of ethnic extinction and to nationalist leaders' charges that its policy was "antinationalist"[113]—approved a *State Program on the Georgian Language*.[114] The plan, calling for the use of Georgian in all aspects of public life, was denounced by *Ademon Nykhas* as "anti-democratic and discriminatory" since most Ossetians lacked working knowledge of Georgian. The South Ossetian legislature, pressured by demonstrations and strikes, countered in late September with an act making Ossetian the official language of the region, while *Ademon Nykhas* appealed to the Soviet government for unification of South and North Ossetia. More moderate South Ossetian nationalists campaigned for upgrading their status to that of an autonomous republic within Georgia, while Georgian nationalists demanded the complete abolition of Ossetian autonomy.[115] Georgian-language street signs in South Ossetia were defaced, and slogans for Ossetian unification became increasingly common. Georgian leaders went to Tskhinvali to try to calm the situation, but to no avail.[116]

Indeed, under pressure from below, leaders on both sides soon returned to pursuing their nationalist programs, rendering their calls for conciliation hollow. In November, a coalition of South Ossetian officials sent a petition to the Georgian Supreme Soviet demanding that the region be upgraded to an autonomous republic. Ossetian extremists saw autonomous republic status as the first step toward reunification with North Ossetia. The Georgian leadership responded by illegally removing South Ossetian party chief Chekhoev from office. Two days later, in response to additional nationalist protests, came the Georgian claim of the right to veto USSR laws and of the right to secede—both considered threatening by Ossetians, who did not want to be separated from their kin in North Ossetia. The Georgian government also agreed, under nationalist pressure, to hold a referendum on independence.[117]

A new round of violence followed. On November 23, 1989, thousands of Georgians led by Gamsakhurdia and others piled into busses to hold a rally in Tskhinvali. The followers of Merab Kostava, who had been killed in a suspicious auto accident the month before, were led by Vazha Adamia, a charismatic but fanatical physician and former sidekick to Kostava. In spite of the slogan of some Georgians that the Ossetians should "head through the tunnel" (through the Caucasus Mountains to North Ossetia), Adamia claimed later with loopy logic that the aim of the rally was to show that "we are brothers."[118] But a counter-rally of Ossetians and the presence of some Interior Ministry troops stopped the busses, so the Georgians returned home. What followed is murky, but both sides were soon accusing the other of "atrocities": Georgians claimed that a Georgian infant was shot in its cradle by an Ossetian.[119] Adamia mobilized an armed group that tried to blockade Tskhinvali but was persuaded to pull back in January 1990. The clashes remained low-level, with only a few killed before Adamia's retreat stabilized the situation.[120] Unable as usual to understand the reason for opposition to their efforts, Georgian nationalists blamed the Ossetian reaction on KGB manipulation.

VICTORY OF GEORGIA'S NATIONAL CHAUVINISTS

By March 1990, the Georgian nationalist movement was split. Gamsakhurdia was the leader of the Round Table/Free Georgia coalition that had agreed to compete in the upcoming Georgian Supreme Soviet elections, but he was opposed by Gia Chanturia, leader of the more radical Georgian National Independence Party and National Forum. Chanturia's slogan was the inflammatory "Georgia for the Georgians," which neatly summed up the chauvinistic mood of many Georgians. Its implication was that non-Georgians had no particular rights in Georgia, except what might be magnanimously granted by Georgians. Chanturia and his ally Irakli Tseretelli, a pair of young extreme nationalist dissidents, argued that Georgians should boycott the upcoming official elections because communist-organized institutions should not be lent the legitimacy; they proposed instead elections for an alternative National Congress that would lead Georgia to independence.[121]

Seeking to capitalize on the nationalist split by developing a cautious pro-independence stand of their own, the communist government postponed the elections for the Supreme Soviet until fall.[122] Meanwhile, the communists began making other nationalist moves, voting in June to denounce the Soviet annexation of Georgia in 1921, to assert economic autonomy, and to set up a commission to pave the way for Georgian sovereignty.[123] Then, following an extensive railroad blockade and strike orchestrated by Gamsakhurdia in July, the Georgian Supreme Soviet passed a controversial electoral law for the elections scheduled for October 28. Included in the law were provisions barring the participation of the Abkhazian Popular Front *Aidgylara* and the South Ossetian movement *Ademon Nykhas.* Despairing anyway about what could be achieved in a parliament dominated by extreme Georgian nationalists,[124] both Abkhaz and Ossetians decided to boycott the election.

In the October elections, Georgian voters gave Gamsakhurdia's Round Table/Free Georgia coalition 54 percent of the vote; the Communist Party came in second with 30 percent.[125] Something more than simple charisma was operating here: Gamsakhurdia had by now achieved such status as an icon of Georgian nationalism that one Georgian intellectual later reported having been afraid to admit that he had voted for someone else.[126] Indeed, in the personalistic context of Georgian politics, Gamsakhurdia himself now symbolized Georgian nationalism, and opposition to one was seen as opposition to the other. Supporters of Gamsakhurdia soon began hailing him as a national savior in the religious sense. His minister of culture, for example, called Gamsakhurdia "the messiah and leader of the nation, for whom this role was predestined from above" and said he was "happy to be Gamsakhurdia's slave."[127] In this atmosphere, most other parties fell short of the 4 percent minimum vote needed for representation in parliament. Besides the two big blocs, only Natadze's Georgian Popular Front and a party called "Democratic Georgia" made the cut.[128]

After Gamsakhurdia's election victory, further escalation of ethnic conflicts came more easily, as the Georgian government began promoting if not precisely organizing ethnic violence. Gamsakhurdia did make one important gesture to the moderate opposition, naming as premier Tengiz Sigua, a respected academic (and boyhood acquaintance of Gamsakhurdia). But Gamsakhurdia also began ruthlessly consolidating his power, taking over television and radio stations and former communist newspapers; and creating a Georgian National Guard commanded by another old friend, Tengiz Kitovani, whose previous career as a sculptor provided dubious preparation for this new military responsibility. The next month, the extremist opposition National Congress, backed by their own paramilitary organization known as *Mkhedrioni,* began demonstrations against restrictions placed on them by the new government. The *Mkhedrioni* were led by Jaba Ioseliani, a warlord, ex-convict, and holder of a Ph.D. with a habit of attacking police stations and Soviet military installations to procure weapons.[129] The trio of Sigua, Kitovani, and Ioseliani was to prove of decisive importance in Gamsakhurdia's, and Georgia's, future.

Meanwhile, Gamsakhurdia was stoking Georgian fears about the demographic growth of Georgia's Muslim and other minorities. At one late 1990 rally he said:

> A Lakization process has begun in Kakhetia, in the very heart of Kakhetia. Kakhetia has always been a very demographically pure region, where the Georgian element has always predominated and always wielded power. Now things have taken shape there in such a way that we are wondering how to save Kakhetia. Tatardom is rearing its head there and measuring its strength against Kakhetia, there are Laks in one place, Armenians in another, Ossetians in a third place, and they're on the point of swallowing up Kakhetia. That's what these Communists, these traitors, have done to us.

More frightening still was his proposed remedy:

> They should be chopped up, they should be burned out with a red-hot iron from the Georgian nation, these traitors and venal people...Strength is on our side, the Georgian nation is with us; we will deal with all the traitors, hold all of them to proper account, and drive all the evil enemies and non-Georgians who have taken refuge here out of Georgia![130]

Gamsakhurdia's concern was not, of course, strictly with Laks in Kakhetia, but with Georgia's ethnic affinity problem: while Muslim groups such as Laks were small minorities in Georgia, Muslims in general—"Tatardom"—surrounded and outnumbered Georgians in the broader region, and some Muslim ethnic groups in Georgia were growing in population faster than were Georgians. By the same logic, Gamsakhurdia said on another occasion that mixed marriages constituted a threat to the survival of the Georgian nation.[131] It was the general demographic "threat" from "Tatardom" that worried nationalistic Georgians—and the emotional power of the Muslim threat, symbolically labeled "Tatardom," which interested Gamsakhurdia. Unfortunately, he was not above incitements to violence as a way of harnessing that emotion.

WAR IN SOUTH OSSETIA

In spite of Gamsakhurdia's rhetoric and a June 1990 mass rally in Tskhinvali calling for union with North Ossetia, South Ossetia avoided violence for most of the year. But when Georgia passed its August 1990 election law, barring *Ademon Nykhas* from participating in the upcoming Georgian parliamentary elections, tensions again started to rise. Feeling increasingly threatened, the South Ossetian legislature proclaimed in September the establishment of the "South Ossetian Soviet Democratic Republic." A month later it appealed for the Soviet parliament to recognize its separation from Georgia, which both the Soviet and Georgian parliaments quickly branded unconstitutional.[132] Soon-to-be Georgian parliamentary chairman Gamsakhurdia continued his threatening rhetoric, promising to guarantee the safety of non-Georgians in the republic only as long as they did not "violate the interests of the Georgian people," a condition the South Ossetians could not meet.[133] Indeed, anti-Ossetian paramilitary leader Vazha Adamia was a member of Gamsakhurdia's Round Table coalition, and would be made chief of the committee overseeing the Interior Ministry in the new parliament—as the fighting in South Ossetia began to heat up again.[134]

Effectively shut out of the October 1990 election in the Republic of Georgia, the Ossetians held their own on December 9. On the eve of the election, Gamsakhurdia remarked, ominously: "if [Ossetians] do not wish to live peacefully with us, then let them leave Georgia."[135] They tried: the South Ossetian legislature voted again on December 11 to subordinate the region directly to Moscow—independent of Georgia. Partly in response, the Georgian Supreme Soviet voted the same day to abolish South Ossetia's autonomous status, in spite of Gamsakhurdia's recent promise not to do so; the next day Georgia imposed a state of emergency on Tskhinvali as armed clashes again erupted.[136]

Again, the struggle for political dominance—this time, South Ossetia's bid for secession from Georgia—was what prompted the fighting. Georgian paramilitaries such as Adamia's Merab Kostava Society and the pro-Gamsakhurdia "Society of the White George" quickly mobilized, and by early February 1991, they had achieved a total blockade of Tskhinvali. They blew up a cliff to block the road to North Ossetia and sniped at construction crews to prevent its reopening, while blockading all other roads and cutting off all electricity and most natural gas supplies to the city.[137] They also began a campaign of forcing Ossetians out of villages surrounding Tskhinvali, creating thousands of refugees. Georgian police seem to have participated in the continuation of the siege.[138]

Gamsakhurdia, meanwhile, justified the abolition of Ossetian autonomy by claiming, "They [Ossetians] have no right to a state here in Georgia. They are a national minority. Their homeland is North Ossetia. . . . Here they are newcomers."[139] The Ossetians' prediction of isolation was proved as even the "moderate" opposition in the Georgian parliament led by Nodar Natadze voted in favor of the dissolution of Ossetian autonomy. Natadze's retrospective judgment: "we had no right not to" abolish Ossetian autonomy, because it was illegitimately imposed by the Bolsheviks.[140]

By now, as mass hostility rose, neither side was showing much interest in compromise. Georgian nationalism was so radical that even relatively moderate figures such as Natadze had little resonance with voters, and even the moderates strongly favored abolition of South Ossetian autonomy. The firebrands Chanturia and Tseretelli, had they participated in the elections, might well have proven more popular than these "moderates." Thus Gamsakhurdia was in the center of the nationalist spectrum, trying to project a statesmanlike image—by promising, for example, not to abolish Georgia's autonomies. Gamsakhurdia's major contribution to the fighting was an omission: he was the one person in Georgian politics who had the moral authority to convince the Georgian people to restrain themselves and accept compromise, but he failed to try. Instead, he promoted the abolition of Ossetian autonomy (violating his promise not to do so), failed to restrain the paramilitaries, and allowed the Georgian Interior Ministry to assist them. Those decisions were a central reason why the violence occurred.

But what motivated the rank-and-file fighters in the Georgian paramilitaries? On the Ossetian side, personal self-preservation was obviously a motive: Ossetians were terrorized by the Georgian paramilitaries and took up arms in self-defense. But what motivated the Georgian fighters patiently to maintain a blockade for months? Banditry was one motivation: local Ossetian villages were sacked and looted, as were convoys of supplies on their way to Tskhinvali. But people motivated only by profit would not have shown the discipline and determination to persevere in dull blockade duties for months at a time, especially in winter, and local Georgians who were defending their homes were too few to be militarily important. Those from other parts of Georgia must have been motivated by the nationalist charisma of paramilitary leaders like Adamia, who spoke of defending fellow Georgians and defeating the "separatists." In short, the same sort of extremist nationalism that led Georgians to vote for Gamsakhurdia or his fanatical opponents also led some of them to fight.

MOSCOW'S EFFORTS AT CONFLICT MANAGEMENT IN SOUTH OSSETIA

Soviet government policy in South Ossetia was highly inconsistent. On the one hand, Gorbachev called in January 1991 for Georgian forces to leave South Ossetia but did not simultaneously move to disarm the Ossetian paramilitary forces.[141] Similarly, the Soviet military forces stationed in the region were said to have brokered a ceasefire following Gorbachev's January order but were later apparently fighting on the side of the Ossetians.[142] Soviet institutions such as the State Bank gave funding to South Ossetia,[143] which could be seen as aiding in its separatist efforts. On the other hand, the bank funds may have constituted efforts simply to keep South Ossetia's economy, suffering badly from the blockade, working at some minimal level. And in March and April 1991, Soviet interior troops in the region were reportedly active in disarming militias on both sides, imposing a brief calm on the region in the spring.[144] Since the conflict was caused primarily by popular chauvinism, which is best stopped by forceful deterrence—inserting troops to oppose the aggressive side with the threat of force—it may be most appropriate to criticize Gorbachev for not having intervened sooner and in greater force to oppose the poorly disciplined paramilitaries.

Gamsakhurdia's oft-repeated view was that the Soviet government was inciting the South Ossetians as a way of forcing Georgia to sign the Union Treaty and remain in the USSR.[145] The charge may have been true: Gamsakhurdia claimed Gorbachev had made the connection explicitly, and there is evidence (discussed in chapter 5) that Gorbachev was using such tactics against Moldova as well.[146] Still, Moscow's role was not wholly negative: worse violence was probably prevented by Soviet interior troops, who helped keep the two sides apart and worked to break the blockade of Tskhinvali.[147] But ironically, if Gorbachev's priority was to pressure the Georgians, he still would have been wiser to intervene in greater force, stop the violence, and then bargain about the removal of Soviet forces in exchange for Georgian cooperation. It is hard to know why Gorbachev did not do so, though he may either have been hesitant to insert Soviet forces into another quagmire like Mountainous Karabagh, or hesitant to act more strongly without Georgian approval.

GAMSAKHURDIA'S FALL AND CIVIL WAR IN GEORGIA

Despite the unrest in South Ossetia, Gamsakhurdia pushed Georgia closer to independence from the Soviet Union in 1991. He barred Georgians from taking part in the all-Union referendum, instead holding a March referendum on whether to restore Georgia's 1918 independence declaration. Election officials claimed a vote of 98.93 percent in favor of independence, a tally which might be accurate given some minorities' boycott of the poll and given that Gamsakhurdia had threatened to revoke the citizenship and residence permits of ethnic minorities in regions that voted "no."[148] Ten days later—on the second anniversary of the Tbilisi massacre—the Georgian parliament unanimously passed a declaration of independence. On May 26, 1991, Gamsakhurdia was elected president of the new republic with 86.5 percent of the vote.[149]

Although Gamsakhurdia seemed to enjoy a high level of popular support, his constraints on the opposition began alienating key constituencies. He demonstrated an increasing intolerance of criticism, alienating Georgia's intelligentsia by branding virtually all critics as agents of Moscow. This became a joke, as intellectuals began greeting each other, "Hi, Kremlin spy!" Gamsakhurdia also appointed people (like Kitovani) without relevant experience or qualifications to high posts based solely on perceived personal loyalty. Further, he failed to carry out his proposed economic program, failed to manage the Ossetian problem, and needlessly criticized Gorbachev and foreign leaders. One particular foreign policy blunder was to assert that Karabagh belonged to Armenia, thus alienating Azerbaijan, which had been supplying Georgia with oil. On August 18, Prime Minister Tengiz Sigua resigned in disgust at these and other blunders.[150] Days later came the attempted coup against Gorbachev, to which Gamsakhurdia seemed halfheartedly to acquiesce: this was the final straw for Kitovani and a large portion of the National Guard he commanded, who renounced Gamsakhurdia and left Tbilisi. Kitovani was also reacting in part against Gamsakhurdia's attempt to curb his power by subordinating the National Guard to the Georgian Interior Ministry, but the result was the same: Gamsakhurdia was increasingly bereft of allies.[151]

The situation quickly deteriorated in September as pro- and anti-Gamsakhurdia demonstrations crippled Tbilisi and became increasingly violent, while the opposition, backed by the National Guard, seized the television station. By December, Gamsakhurdia was under siege in the parliament building. When the fighting was over at the beginning of January 1992, over 200 people were dead, the center of Tbilisi was in ruins, and Gamsakhurdia himself had fled into exile.[152] A Georgian military council controlled by Kitovani, Ioseliani, and Sigua declared a state of emergency and said it would assume control until elections could be held.

Their actions did not, however, end the dispute with Gamsakhurdia's supporters, the "Zviadists." Support for Gamsakhurdia after his ouster was sustained by two critical factors. First was the intense personalism of Georgian politics, as illustrated by the following vignette:

> One of the enduring images of the first winter of Georgia's terrible freedom begins like this: a man, one leg amputated at the knee, is being interviewed on television after he has walked, on crutches, 300 kilometers from his village to the capital...in January 1992....His language was as poor as his worn dark clothes and he could not explain the force that had propelled him onwards to Tbilisi. He gave up looking for the right words and instead began to chant as if in prayer, "Zviadi, Zviadi." He hopped up and down on his crutches until, transported, he let go and hovered in mid-air for a dangerous instant. But he found his balance, backflipped onto his palms and resumed his chanting, "Zviadi."[153]

Half a dozen years after these events, I met one Zviadist—still loyal to the dead Gamsakhurdia—who continued to feel such passions: when discussing Georgian nationalism, she began weeping uncontrollably, exclaiming, "I want to die" because of the fractured condition of Georgian statehood.[154]

Gamsakhurdia's status as a semi-religious messiah figure probably helps explain such passion. Regardless of their source, however, the fact that such powerful personal loyalties were commanded by Gamsakhurdia, and to some extent by his opponents, meant that a quick coup was out of the question; civil war was inevitable. The nature of the civil war was shaped by a second factor, the strong regionalism of Georgian politics. Gamsakhurdia was a Mingrelian, thus his main base of support was among Mingrelians, who had their own version of local chauvinism: one Mingrelian described his group as "Georgians of a higher type."

The location of the Zviadist base among Mingrelians meant that the focus of opposition activity shifted from Tbilisi—where protests continued but were not influential—to areas where Mingrelians lived, especially Mingrelia itself and Abkhazia. A massive campaign of civil disobedience quickly erupted in those regions, and in western Georgia more generally, after Gamsakhurdia's flight. Factories, airports, and rail lines were shut by strikes, which quickly erupted into a full-scale Zviadist uprising. After the military council government sent National Guard and *Mkhedrioni* troops to reestablish its authority, the Zviadists were quickly repressed where they did not simply fade away, but the new government did not unambiguously gain authority as a result: the National Guard and *Mkhedrioni* were wholly undisciplined and contained a substantial proportion of simple criminals, who engaged in widespread looting wherever they were sent.[155]

These events were pregnant with importance for Georgia's ethnic conflicts, as were subsequent events in Tbilisi: in March 1992, the military council leaders, to bolster their dubious authority, invited Eduard Shevardnadze to return to Georgia to assume control of a newly created Georgian State Council.[156] Despite a brief upsurge in fighting between Georgians and Ossetians and some friction with the Russians, Shevardnadze managed to reach a ceasefire agreement with the Ossetians on May 14.[157] By mid-July, a tripartite peacekeeping force consisting of Russian, Georgian, and Ossetian troops was in place, ending the fighting if not resolving the conflict.[158] Over the following months, Shevardnadze managed to consolidate his power and, bolstered by an election victory in October 1992, he succeeded in reestablishing some kind of order in most of Georgia. In Abkhazia, however, he failed utterly.

THE WAR IN ABKHAZIA

In 1990, the Abkhaz-Georgian conflict had moved from the streets to the legislatures, mostly following the pattern of the "war of laws" going on at that time throughout the Soviet Union. Thus after Georgia adopted an August 1990 decree that Georgian would be the only language spoken in the Georgian Supreme Soviet, Abkhaz delegates to Abkhazia's Supreme Soviet voted, in the absence of their Georgian colleagues, to declare Abkhazian "sovereignty" (as most Soviet republics and autonomous republics in Russia were also doing). The next day, the Georgian parliament annulled that declaration, and a week later, the ethnic Georgian deputies to the Abkhazian Supreme Soviet met and rescinded their colleagues' sovereignty declaration.[159] The Abkhaz nationalists, meanwhile, continued their quest for allies and convened a second Congress of Peoples of the Caucasus in October 1990.[160] In December, the Abkhazian Supreme Soviet elected as its chairman Vladislav Ardzinba, a charismatic but excitable figure popular among Abkhaz but believed by some Georgians to have helped instigate the violence of the previous July. In the same session, the Abkhazian parliament also passed a new Declaration of Sovereignty and other acts furthering the legal separation between Abkhazia and Georgia.[161]

The legal struggle continued the next year: in February, Gamsakhurdia tried to institute a system of prefects—representatives of Tbilisi's authority—in each district of Georgia, but the Abkhaz resisted on the grounds that the prefect would threaten Abkhazia's autonomy.[162] Abkhazia also participated in the all-Union referendum in March of 1991, in spite of Georgia's boycott: 52.4 percent of those eligible—presumably Abkhazia's non-Georgian population—voted, and 98.4 percent of them cast their ballots in favor of the Union.[163] The issue of the referendum—whether Abkhazia would stay in the Soviet Union—became increasingly heated during the summer, as Georgia was bent on independence and on taking Abkhazia with it. The view of Abkhazian nationalists, as represented by *Aidgylara* leader Sergei Shamba, was that existing forms of autonomy were no longer adequate. One version of the Georgian response was articulated by Georgian Minister of Education Temur Koridze at an early August rally in Sukhumi: he threatened that if Abkhazia signed the impending Union Treaty, "rivers of blood would flow."[164] The failed Moscow coup rendered that particular issue irrelevant, ensuring that no union treaty would be signed.

In spite of ethnic antagonism, legal experts from both sides managed to reach an agreement that summer on a consociational scheme for structuring a new Abkhazian parliament. The concept was first proposed by a Georgian, Professor Levan Alexidze, and, "in a usually forgotten moment of flexibility," approved by Gamsakhurdia.[165] According to the new scheme, seats in the Abkhazian parliament were to be divided according to ethnic group, with the Abkhaz receiving 28, Georgians 26, and "others" 11. A two-thirds majority was to be required to pass "important legislation," thus ensuring (in principle) that both Abkhaz and Georgians would have veto power over key decisions.[166] Gamsakhurdia ironically rejected a less convoluted Abkhaz proposal for a bicameral parliament on the grounds that it would set an undesirable example for Georgia. The Abkhaz settled for what they could get, and elections for the new parliament followed in two rounds, in October and December, 1991.[167]

Some such system might have had a chance to work, but this one had three strikes against it from the beginning. First, it began its work just after the dissolution of the Soviet Union in December 1991, so some critical and sensitive issues—most importantly, the disposition of Soviet troops in Abkhazia—had to be decided quickly, before delegates could establish a working relationship. Second, it started meeting immediately after the January 1992 ouster of Gamsakhurdia, who had a stake in making it work because he had approved it. Relatedly, it first convened during the worst of Georgia's post-Gamsakhurdia chaos, which was to play a critical role in sparking war. Third was the gross disproportionality of representation in the new parliament: Abkhaz represented 18 percent of Abkhazia's population but held 43 percent of the seats in parliament, while the smaller minorities together accounted for 36 percent of the population but only 17 percent of the seats; Georgians were also slightly underrepresented. Most Georgians opposed the new parliament from the beginning, branding it an "apartheid" parliament. Indeed, a coalition of anti-Gamsakhurdia Georgians issued an appeal in December 1991, before the new parliament even met, calling for "peaceful political opposition to the Supreme Soviet and civil disobedience to the government of Abkhazia."[168]

The new Abkhazian Supreme Soviet started meeting in January of 1992 in an atmosphere of ill will exemplified by the Georgian civil disobedience campaign. Georgian members soon began complaining that the two-thirds voting rule was being ignored and that an ethnic Georgian had not, as promised, been appointed premier. By the end of the month, the body was debating secession from Georgia. Its members also began bickering over the highly symbolic issue of the design of the Abkhazian flag: would it include the Georgian tricolor scheme (with its negative associations for the Abkhaz) or the symbols associated with the 1917 Mountain Republic (to which the Georgians objected)? Even more ominous to the Georgians were the new leadership's military moves: as early as December 1991, Ardzinba signed orders asserting Abkhazian control over Soviet military units stationed in Abkhazia. Georgians present these orders as open efforts to start a war,[169] but in fact Ardzinba had to act quickly: someone had to take responsibility for the troops after the Soviet government evaporated, and the Abkhaz could not trust the Georgians to act with restraint if they did so. In practice, it was the Russians who retained control of the troops, so the Abkhazian Supreme Soviet later voted to create a National Guard staffed purely with ethnic Abkhaz.

Other moves by the new Abkhazian government were less justifiable and nearly as offensive to the Georgians. Ardzinba's government tried to bring criminal charges against members of Georgian groups denouncing his rule.

It also began replacing ethnic Georgian administrators with Abkhaz, especially in top positions—moves local Georgians labeled "provocations."[170] Abkhazian deputies, meanwhile, objected to the Georgians' habit of consulting with Tbilisi on most of their decisions: again, the Georgians wanted to minimize Abkhazian autonomy from Georgia by coordinating with Tbilisi, while the Abkhaz grew to resent the Georgian deputies as agents of Tbilisi instead of representatives of local Georgians.[171] By May 1992, the isolated Georgian deputies began boycotting parliamentary sessions, and Georgians in Sukhumi announced another campaign of civil disobedience.[172] The Abkhazian Interior Ministry chief and ethnic Georgian, Givi Lominadze, triggered further demonstrations when, complaining about discrimination against Georgians, he refused to obey an order from the Supreme Soviet to resign his post. Lominadze was eventually ousted by force: on June 24, Abkhazian National Guard troops entered his office, hit him in the throat with a rifle butt, and removed him from the building.[173]

In spite of these increasing tensions, all sides made efforts, at first, to avoid confrontation. When Zviadists began blocking railroads in western Georgia and Abkhazia, the Georgian military council asked permission for Georgian National Guard troops to enter Abkhazia to suppress them, and Ardzinba granted it. The troops entered in early February, and the Zviadists were duly suppressed, but the ill-disciplined Georgian troops also indulged in a spree of looting, increasing Georgian-Abkhaz tensions.[174] According to Tengiz Sigua, then-Georgian premier, Ardzinba made a point of seeking the approval of Tbilisi for many of his actions until around March, when Eduard Shevardnadze returned to Georgia.[175] The Abkhaz view is that Shevardnadze interfered more in Abkhazian affairs than did Gamsakhurdia, which increased tensions in the relationship.[176]

In fact, the key move on the Georgian side was probably the decision in February 1992 to return to Georgia's 1921 constitution, which did not specifically mention Abkhazia at all, and therefore had no provision for Abkhazian autonomy. This was of course unacceptable to the Abkhaz. In June, therefore, Ardzinba sent to the Georgian State Council a draft Abkhazian-Georgian treaty which would have established a loose federation or confederation between the two but, at least in principle, would have maintained Georgia's territorial integrity. Georgia, still in disarray, sent no formal answer.[177] After waiting a decent interval, the Abkhazian parliament voted on July 23 to reinstate the Abkhazian constitution of 1925, according to which Abkhazia was "united with...Georgia on the basis of a special union treaty."[178] The decision could have been cast as a moderate one, leaving the door open to compromise, but Ardzinba typically insisted on declaring symbolically, "Abkhazia is a sovereign state. And it will build its relations with Georgia solely on a treaty basis"[179]—implying little intention to maintain any sort of union at all. The Georgian state council immediately annulled the Abkhazian decision, charging that it was "aimed at kindling a new, serious hotbed of tension in the country";[180] and a week later, a meeting of the Georgian members of the Abkhazian parliament also declared the decision void.[181]

By now, public opinion among Georgians seems to have been ready for war. One Georgian observer summarizes later Georgian public opinion as follows: "Despite... the long-standing Georgian tradition of tolerance... the Abkhaz ungratefully chose secession and have fostered intolerance and hatred toward Georgians.... If the separatists refuse to accept Georgian jurisdiction in Abkhazia, then it is within Georgia's legal rights to restore sovereignty by force." At the same time, Georgians were "not prepared for federalist and multi cultural solutions,"[182] due to what another observer labels the Georgian body politic's "disdain for compromise."[183] The Georgian delegates to Abkhazia's parliament were, at the same time, increasingly demanding forceful intervention by Tbilisi.[184] The Georgian self-image of tolerance did not, however, permit a forthright initiation of war. Leaders like Shevardnadze and Ioseliani therefore insisted that while Abkhazian behavior was unacceptable, it would be dealt with by peaceful means.[185] The Georgian public was unwilling to compromise and ready to fight, but war would first have to be "forced" on it.

Mounting Zviadist opposition to the Shevardnadze government helped provide the pretext. A March 1992 uprising was quickly squashed, but in the summer came a series of guerrilla actions—kidnappings of Georgian government officials and banditry on the railroad lines—that were harder to prevent. Shevardnadze tried conciliation first, announcing in early August an amnesty for supporters of the former government, but the response of hard-core Zviadists was a further round of hostage-taking.[186] Shevardnadze then pronounced the amnesty a mistake and on August 12 dispatched 3,000 Georgian troops under National Guard chief Tengiz Kitovani to Mingrelia to find the hostages and reestablish order on the railroads. Information quickly surfaced indicating that the hostages were being held in the Mingrelian-inhabited region of eastern Abkhazia, so Shevardnadze called Ardzinba to request Abkhazian cooperation in another Georgian operation against the Zviadists in Abhkazia. What was said in that phone call remains contentious, but one result was the removal of the Abkhazian border post at the Inguri river, the border between Abkhazia and Georgia proper:[187] the Abkhaz would not oppose the Georgian troops' search. That night, August 13–14, the railroad bridge over the Inguri was blown up, apparently by Zviadist guerrillas, cutting the only direct rail line from Georgia to Russia.

The next day, August 14, 1992, Georgian National Guard troops invaded Abkhazia. The Georgians claimed that the troops entered only to search for the hostages and to secure the rail line, but that claim is nonsense. With the bridge over the Inguri destroyed, the railroad line was out of commission, so there was no urgency to policing it. And instead of searching for hostages, the bulk of the Georgian troops—accompanied by armored vehicles—stayed on the main road, arrested the head of administration of the city of Ochamchira, skirmished with Abkhaz outside the city, and drove straight for Sukhumi.[188] This behavior shows that the Georgian explanations were a smokescreen: one does not use tanks and armored cars to police a dead rail line, and there was never any claim that the hostages were being held west of Sukhumi, so the armored assault on Sukhumi could only have been meant as an attempt to secure control of Abkhazia by military means. Further, if the Georgians had been expecting Abkhazian cooperation, as they claimed, they would have stopped and negotiated with the envoys dispatched by Ardzinba to meet them instead of capturing the envoys and continuing their drive to Sukhumi.[189]

Ardzinba was shocked by the Georgian incursion.[190] Once he was sure of the aim of the Georgian troops, the volatile Abkhazian leader secured a parliamentary vote branding the Georgian incursion "aggression against Abkhazian statehood on the part of a hostile state" and ordering Abkhazian interior troops to "offer armed resistance to the 'aggressor.'" He also recorded a television and radio address calling on the people of Abkhazia to wage a "patriotic war" against the "enemy." Shamba, the newly appointed defense chief, followed with a call for mobilization of all men age 18 to 45.[191] Ardzinba's earlier rhetoric had been aimed at using the "statehood" symbol to gain support for his government's course of political confrontation; he now added the symbolism of national self-defense against an "enemy aggressor" to mobilize his people for war.

Shevardnadze, for his part, declared that "We have done the right thing."[192] He interpreted the Abkhazian attacks on Georgian troops and Ardzinba's fiery declaration of war to mean that it was the Abkhaz who had started it. Having thus claimed the role of victim, Georgia could go ahead with prosecuting the war: it was now a war of "national defense" for Georgia, too. Kitovani made clear that he was determined to stop Abkhazian "separatism" and also declared ambiguously that his troops would need a few days to "satisfy themselves."[193] What remains unclear is whether Shevardnadze actively ordered the attack or merely decided to support actions by Kitovani that he could not control. The war, in any case, was now on: the two sides agreed to a ceasefire on August 17, but the troops never stopped firing. Instead, the Georgian troops reentered Sukhumi the next day and began "satisfying themselves" by engaging in rape, looting, and arson of Abkhazian cultural artifacts.

Foreign intervention in the Abkhazian conflict

Given the suddenness of the outbreak of war in Abkhazia, it is difficult to see what might have been done to prevent it. What is clear is that the war escalated and lasted over a year largely because it quickly became internationalized. The Georgians had inherited a substantial arsenal from the Soviet army, so they were well-armed and at first had the sympathy of Russian troops. Soon after the fighting began, however, a Russian airborne division arrived in Abkhazia to help evacuate Russian vacationers and drew fire from Georgian armed formations; unsurprisingly, Russian sympathies began to change.[194] An increasing number of troops from the Confederation of Mountain Peoples, especially the well-armed Chechens, as well as Cossack fighters, supported the Abkhaz from the first days of the war. And as ceasefire after ceasefire was violated and fighting continued, evidence accumulated that elements of the Russian military were also actively supporting the Abkhaz. The Georgians captured some Russian officers in the fighting, unidentified (probably Russian) ships shelled Georgian positions, and planes bombing Georgian positions proved, when shot down, to have been piloted by Russians.[195]

Russian forces stepped up their support of the Abkhazian separatists in December 1992 when Georgian forces shot down a Russian helicopter evacuating Russian refugees from the area, killing all aboard—most of them women and children.[196] The fighting continued into 1993 as the Abkhaz started an assault on Georgian-held Sukhumi. Following an initially cautious approach to the conflict and numerous attacks from the Russian right wing in the press, Yeltsin also became more assertive, saying in February that it was time "to grant Russia special powers as the guarantor of peace and stability in the region."[197] In May, Shevardnadze was finally able to remove Kitovani and Ioseliani from the Defense Council and start negotiations for a ceasefire agreement, with mediation by the Russians. Another ceasefire was signed in late July 1993, calling for both sides to withdraw their heavy weapons, a provision the Georgians followed but the Abkhaz did not.

In mid-September—as Boris Yeltsin's showdown with the Russian parliament was approaching its climax—the Abkhaz, aided by Confederation of Mountains Peoples and Russian troops, broke the ceasefire and launched their final offensive to retake Sukhumi.[198] Eleven days after the assault began, the Georgian forces were forced to retreat, only to be intercepted by resurgent Zviadist forces who seized their weapons. Most ethnic Georgians in Abkhazia followed their retreating troops, most fleeing from fear, others forced out by Abkhazian troops or their allies. (Most of the remaining Georgians, concentrated in the Gali district, would suffer the same fate after a new series of clashes in May 1998).

Facing an economic crisis, a refugee crisis, and internal dissension from the Zviadists and other militias, Shevardnadze finally submitted to Russia in the fall of 1993, accepting membership in the Commonwealth of Independent States (CIS) and the stationing of Russian troops in Georgia in exchange for Russian support against the Zviadists. With Russian support, the Zviadist forces were defeated by November,[199] and Gamsakhurdia committed suicide the following January. A UN sponsored *Memorandum of Understanding* was signed by Abkhazia and Georgia in Geneva on December 1, 1993.

The puzzle of atrocities

People are as inventive in devising torture and other atrocities as they are in any other field of activity; the sorts of things they do are depressingly well known. Still, even the beginnings of an explanation demand some attention to what people actually do. The following are some examples of atrocities purportedly committed in the war in Abkhazia.

> Pieces of a human body were hanging on long wires from the trees.... [T]hose were the remains of two skinned men.... In the same woods,... there was found the corpse of a pregnant woman. She had been raped and disemboweled.
>
> The poor souls were stabbed all over before being dispatched. They had "Columbian Ties." It is an ordinary thing to be done—an incision of the throat is made, five centimeters below the chin, and the victims' tongues are pulled out through the hole.[200]
>
> They raped everybody beginning with little girls and up to elderly women.[201]

The motives for such acts were, of course, mixed. In some cases, atrocities were profit-motivated. Most Abkhaz charges against Georgian troops, for example, focus on thievery and on the murder or torture of those who tried to resist. Indeed, the Abkhaz view was that the Georgian forces consisted primarily of common criminals: one witness quoted a Georgian soldier as saying, "We came here not to serve, but to 'work.' We are not subordinate to anyone, not Shevardnadze, not Kitovani." Still, other motives were at work: Georgian troops made a point of destroying Abkhaz cultural artifacts, and there were examples of Abkhaz being "ethnically cleansed" from their villages. One witness reports a Georgian soldier indulging his particular prejudice by threatening to "kill all the Armenians."[202]

Since these acts were not part of a policy of terror or ethnic cleansing on either side, explanations for them must focus on the motivations of the individual perpetrators. Evidence is thin, but it supports the idea that the same processes of symbolic mobilization that generate ethnic warfare also, when taken to extremes, motivate ethnic atrocities. In one example, "a truck stopped; armed Abkhazians were in it; a young fair man jumped down from it and headed to my seventeen years [*sic*] old son Nukri. He first struck him and then shot. He kept firing at him, already dead, shouting and cursing, 'In this way we shall kill all the Georgians, [including]...your mother.'"[203] We know that "killing all the Georgians" was neither Abkhazian policy, nor even the intention of this killer—after all, he released the mother, who later told the story. However, if the purpose of nationalist rhetoric is to engage the listeners emotionally, then the killer's behavior can be understood in this context. The killer is agitated, shouting and shooting fruitlessly at a dead body, motivated by the idea of "killing all the Georgians," who are the national enemy—and whose army had engaged in an orgy of looting and destruction while it occupied Abkhazian territory. National defense requires much less, however, so when he calms down, he lets the rest of the family go.

Another class of atrocities is rape. We know that in civilian life, rape is usually motivated not by sexual desire but by a desire to degrade the victim and assert power over her.[204] This fits the case of ethnically motivated rapes as well: the soldier motivated by sexual desire is unlikely to choose an elderly woman or young girl as his victim. However, for the fighter in a war for ethnic domination, it is psychologically consistent with the purpose of the war to assert domination by raping "enemy" women. What makes it seem so is a twisted exaggeration of the myth-symbol complex of ethnic war: defending the nation's "statehood" means asserting the nation's sovereignty and control over all the people on the national territory—including enemy women.

Azerbaijanis and Ajarians: The Wars Avoided

In 1989, ethnic Azerbaijanis in Georgia numbered about 307,000, more than the Abkhaz and Ossetians in Georgia combined. They were Georgia's third-largest minority group, constituting about 5.7 percent of Georgia's population. In three districts of southern Georgia bordering on Azerbaijan, collectively called Kvemo Kartli by Georgians, they constituted an absolute majority of the population.[205] The combination of this compact geographical base, a ready supply of weapons available from neighboring Azerbaijan, and the political space created by the dissolution of Soviet and Georgian authority in 1991 meant that the Azerbaijanis had the opportunity to engage in ethnic war with the Georgians. There were repeated episodes of Georgian-Azerbaijani violence from 1987 to 1991, giving Azerbaijanis reason to fear Georgians. And partly as a result of all this the Azerbaijanis did formulate political demands: in early 1989, they requested the formation of an Azerbaijani autonomous republic within Georgia, with its capital in the city of Rustavi.[206]

Some conditions for ethnic war were present on the Georgian side as well. Georgians obviously had the means and opportunity to attack the Azerbaijanis, and they had a symbolic grievance in the form of illegal Azerbaijani immigration into Georgia. Indeed, the rate of growth of the ethnic Azerbaijani population in Georgia—which was double the rate of growth of the overall population of Georgia—was a key component in the Georgians' demographic fears, articulated by Gamsakhurdia as the threat of "Tatardom" encroaching on Georgian land. When the Azerbaijanis demanded an autonomous republic, they further fed the ethnic fears of Georgians. And Georgians' attitudes toward Azerbaijanis were not enormously more positive than their attitudes toward Ossetians—26.5 percent expressed negative attitudes toward Azerbaijanis, as compared with 32 percent who felt negatively toward Ossetians—and these attitudes did spill over into Azerbaijani-Georgian ethnic violence several times,[207] prompting Gamsakhurdia to declare a state of emergency in the region in November 1991.

The one ingredient that was missing in the Azerbaijani case, and the key reason why scattered ethnic violence did not escalate to ethnic war, was the absence of an Azerbaijani mythology justifying hostility toward Georgians or claiming an Azerbaijani homeland in Georgia. The Georgians had such a mythology regarding Azerbaijanis stemming from their history of conflict with Muslim powers. Many did feel hostile toward Azerbaijanis—and political leaders including Gamsakhurdia articulated that hostility—but the Azerbaijanis had no reciprocal mythology. Azerbaijani nationalist mythology, as explained in chapter 3, focuses on Armenians as the national enemy and land within Azerbaijan as the territory critical to Azerbaijani statehood. Kvemo Kartli was part of Georgia, not Azerbaijan, so it had no symbolic power to mobilize Azerbaijanis. As a result, Azerbaijani demands for autonomous republic status was never pursued vigorously. Instead, Azerbaijanis in Georgia seem to have focused on the Mountainous Karabagh conflict—disrupting supply routes, railways, and gas pipelines running through their territory to Armenia. Azerbaijani mythology, in sum, identifies Armenians, not Georgians as the national adversary, so Azerbaijanis directed their efforts against Armenians.

The reason for peace in Ajaria is similar: there was no official "Ajarian" nationality in the Soviet Union,[208] so Ajarians did not develop a strong sense of national identity or a nationalist mythology. They were simply Muslim Georgians. Lacking mobilizing myths and symbols, they could not be welded into a fighting force. Ajarian strongman Aslan Abashidze therefore concentrated on maintaining stability in his fiefdom and on consolidating his own power there.

Conclusions

Georgia's ethnic conflicts fit the category of mass-led violence and, specifically, of popular chauvinism. Not only did the Georgians have a national mythology justifying hostility against Abkhaz and Ossetians and fears of ethnic extinction, large numbers of Georgians actually felt ethnic hostility, according to poll results. Rather than following from extremist elite appeals or media manipulation, these attitudes preceded such appeals: even when Georgia's communist leaders and communist-run press were hostile to nationalism, counter-elites like Gamsakhurdia found that appeals to national chauvinism were effective for mobilizing large crowds at nationalist rallies. The only opportunity required was the political opening offered by Gorbachev's reforms. The fact that the Georgian national movement was from the beginning aimed at ethnic dominance posed a real threat to the Ossetians and Abkhaz. The Abkhaz, of course, had their own nationalist myths and were already mobilizing politically; the increasing threat from the Georgians spurred both their mobilization and that of the Ossetians. The result was a security dilemma, as each side's fears of extinction led it to make demands threatening to the other. Ultimately, Georgian nationalist leaders put in place by their nationalist movement chose to go to war to try to resolve the conflicts.

In the case of the South Ossetian conflict, the mass pressure was at first mostly on the Georgian side. The Ossetians also had their nationalist mythology promoting ethnic hostility and providing potent ethnic symbols, real ethnic fears, and serious economic grievances. The Georgians felt that "immigrants" such as the Ossetians threatened their status as the majority people of Georgia and that only policies aimed at Georgianizing and disfranchising Georgia's minorities could protect their status. The Ossetians, conversely, felt that such Georgianizing policies were threatening to them, and they also resented Georgia's move toward independence from the Soviet Union, since it would create political barriers between South Ossetians and their ethnic kin in North Ossetia. But the Ossetians did not mobilize until after the Georgians did, and mostly in response to the Georgians. This was a case of popular chauvinism: chauvinist ideas on the part of the masses of the majority group were the driving force of ethnic conflict.

The conflict escalated due to a security dilemma spiral driven by the push for ethnic dominance. Georgia's nationalist opposition leaders, more popular than the incumbent communist leaders, constantly pushed the Georgian government to implement increasingly chauvinistic policies, which the minority Ossetians found increasingly threatening. Each move the Ossetians took in self-defense was seen as threatening to the Georgians, who escalated the conflict even further in response. Much of the escalation was driven by the actions of unofficial paramilitary organizations outside the control of top leaders: Vazha Adamia, one of the Georgian paramilitary leaders, boasts that even Gamsakhurdia repeatedly tried and failed to convince him to withdraw his forces.[209] The South Ossetians understandably mobilized in response. The conflict never escalated beyond the point of guerrilla violence only because of the interposition of Soviet Interior Ministry troops who kept the two sides largely apart until the advent of a more reasonable Georgian leader made it possible to establish a ceasefire.

The Abkhaz-Georgian conflict, in contrast, was driven as much by Abkhaz as by Georgian behavior and its escalation was due as much to elite behavior as to mass preferences. The conflict was, to be sure, driven by genuine mass passions, which had been expressed on both sides as recently as 1978—only a decade before. Thus Abkhaz nationalists were able very quickly to mobilize some 30,000 people (25,000 of them Abkhaz, comprising over a quarter of the entire Abkhaz people) to the Lykhny rally to support their demands for separation from Georgia. The Georgian nationalists, for their part, were able while still out of power to mobilize thousands in Abkhazia and hundreds of thousands in Tbilisi to oppose the Abkhazian demands; and to do so within weeks of the Lykhny appeal. And, more than was the case with Ossetia, the two sides' security needs really were mutually exclusive: the Abkhaz probably are faced with the threat of group extinction, and their survival probably did depend on a certain degree of discrimination against the ethnic Georgians in Abkhazia's population. Faced with a chauvinistic, nationalist Georgia intent on political dominance in theoretically autonomous Abkhazia, they probably had little choice but to try to expand their autonomy if they wanted to survive as a people. The sheer anarchy of Georgia's situation in 1992, with poorly disciplined National Guard, Zviadist, and Abkhazian troops often terrorizing their adversaries, made confrontation even harder to avoid.

And yet, in many ways the war in Abkhazia was highly artificial. Ardzinba's fiery rhetoric certainly played a role, but if the Abkhazian leadership was repressive and disinclined to concede much power to Tbilisi, it was at least willing to concede the principle of maintaining Georgia's territorial integrity. More importantly, Georgian leaders such as Kitovani clearly wanted war—it was his attack on Sukhumi that started the war—and Shevardnadze failed to restrain him. Russia then caused the war to escalate, especially by enabling the massive Abkhazian counteroffensive that swept the Georgians out of Abkhazia. In sum, if mass passions were driving political conflict and personal confrontation, individual leaders' decisions turned those elements into war and made possible the Russian intervention that determined the war's outcome.

The peculiarly fractious political culture of the Georgians—and its extreme embodiment in the personality of Zviad Gamsakhurdia—also contributed. Gamsakhurdia polarized Georgian politics by branding all dissenters as traitors, eventually creating a coalition of most political forces in Georgia against his arbitrary and dictatorial ways. Yet even after combining to oust Gamsakhurdia and replace him with the more supple and skillful Shevardnadze, Georgian leaders could not curb their penchant for warlordism—and their followers did not cease to follow them into combat against fellow Georgians. Georgian troops were first sent to Abkhazia not to confront the Abkhaz but to combat the forces of the ousted Gamsakhurdia. Those troops attacked Sukhumi not in their capacity as instruments of the Georgian government but as the personal followers of the Defense Minister-cum-warlord Kitovani, who may or may not have been under orders from Shevardnadze. The course and outcome of the war was then shaped by the multisided battle among what became virtually the personal forces of Gamsakhurdia (and his heirs), Kitovani, Ioseliani, and Shevardnadze; divided, they had no chance against the Russian forces supporting the rebel Abkhaz.

Emotive slogans played a critical role in making all of this happen—exactly what symbolic politics theory would lead us to expect. Reminiscing about the conflicts in interviews, leaders on all sides again and again returned to the importance of symbolic slogans in motivating participation in political activity. Themes such as "independence" or "statehood" were what attracted crowds to protests, and "national self-defense" prompted them to fight, not to mention the more extreme semi-religious claims about Gamsakhurdia as national savior. But perhaps the most loaded and effective of all was "Georgia for the Georgians," which so neatly encapsulated for both sides the Georgians' chauvinistic nationalist goals. It was mentioned more than any other slogan as the one that brought Georgians into the street—and even more, that prompted the backlash among Ossetians and Abkhaz that led eventually to war. The goals captured by such slogans also defined the nature of the security dilemma in these conflicts: it was not uncertainty about rivals' goals creating insecurity, but the open determination of the sides to dominate the disputed territory, which all sides claimed as their exclusive homelands. Without understanding the central role played by these emotive slogans and uncompromising goals, it is impossible to make sense of ethnic mobilization and ethnic war in Georgia.

Moldova

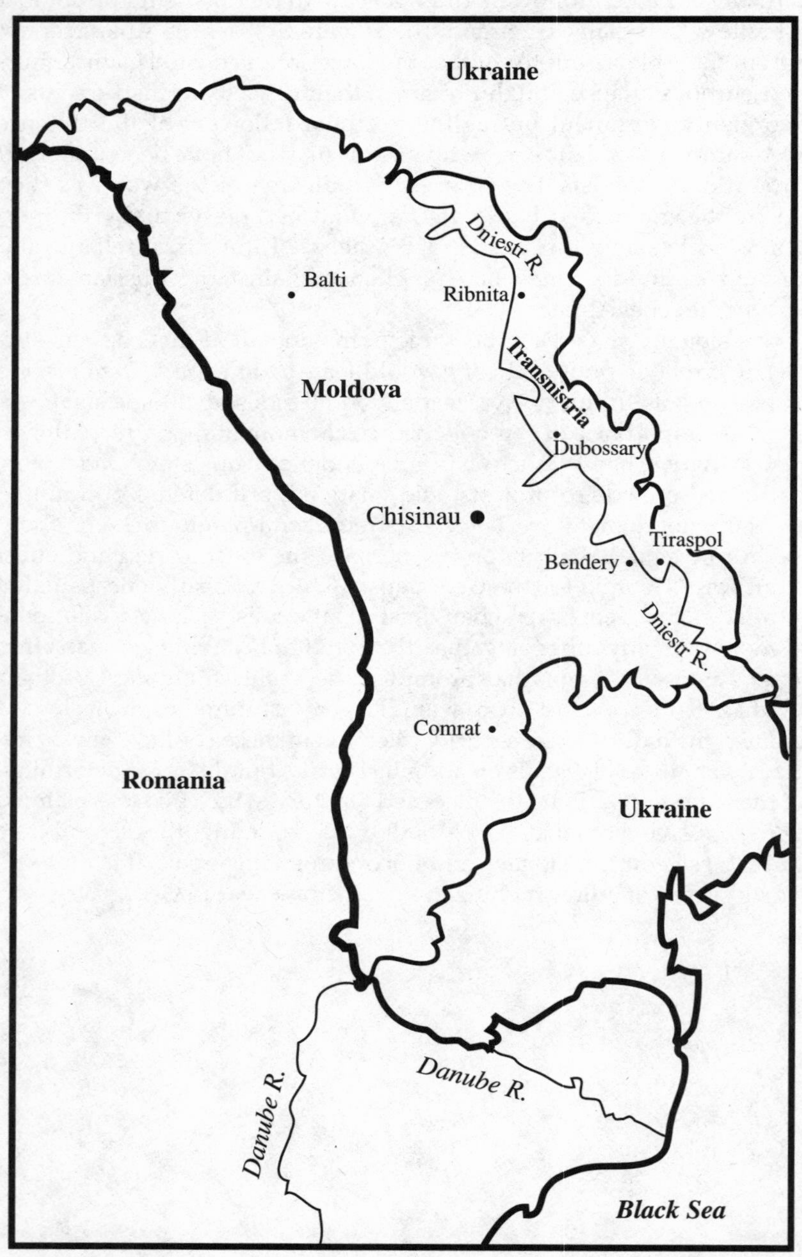
Ukraine
Dniestr R.
Balti
Ribnita
Transnistria
Moldova
Dubossary
Chisinau
Tiraspol
Bendery
Dniestr R.
Comrat
Romania
Ukraine
Danube R.
Danube R.
Black Sea

[5]

Elite Conspiracy in Moldova's Civil War

Moldova's civil war was the shortest and least bloody of the conflicts examined in this book, lasting only about seven months in 1991–92 and costing the lives of about 1,000 people. The conflict began as a mass insurgency by ethnic Moldovans against rule by Russians and from Moscow. Appealing to fears of ethnic extinction roused by Soviet policies of Russification, Moldovan nationalists began a campaign for political dominance of the territory of the Soviet Republic of Moldova by ethnic Moldovans. But demands among some Moldovans for unification with Romania provoked fears of forced Romanianization among non-Moldovans. Feeding those fears and exaggerating the dangers, self-interested local leaders in the Transnistria region—the part of Moldova northeast of the Dniester River where ethnic Russians and Ukrainians together formed a majority of the population—quickly organized a counter-mobilization aimed ostensibly at defending the interests of "Russophones," those who spoke Russian but not Moldovan. These elite conspirators, assisted by Russia—especially by the Fourteenth Russian Army, which was stationed in the area—then contrived a separatist crisis and eventually launched a secessionist war.

The war was not terribly bloody, however, because although ethnic fears were strong, ethnic hostility was not. Moldovans and Russians did not hate each other; they only feared governments dominated by the other. Hence there were no pogroms and no spontaneous efforts at ethnic cleansing. For these reasons, the Transnistria conflict was also the most avoidable of all the post-Soviet ethnic wars: had either the Transnistrian or Moldovan leaders been more moderate, the fighting could easily have been avoided.

Moldova's Peoples and Their History

moldova's ethnic groups

All of Moldova's main ethnic groups are traditionally Orthodox Christian by religion; they are distinguished primarily by language and historical experience. The Moldovans, comprising 64 percent of the population in 1989, speak a Romance language essentially identical to Romanian. The Ukrainians (14 percent of the population), the Russians (13 percent) and the Bulgarians (2 percent) are all, of course, Slavic-language speakers; the Ukrainians and Bulgarians are, in addition, heavily Russified. Finally, the Gagauz (4 percent of the population), speak a unique Turkic language, though they share the Orthodox Christian culture of their neighbors and most speak Russian as well. The Gagauz and Bulgarians migrated together from Bulgaria to what is now southern Moldova in the late eighteenth and early nineteenth centuries.[1]

A complexity of Moldova's ethnic war is that the Transnistrians are not an ethnic group. The population of the Transnistrian region before the war was over 40 percent ethnic Moldovan, 28 percent Ukrainian, and 25 percent Russian; the Transnistrian side in the conflict is usually labeled the "Russophone" side. The Transnistrian Russophones were the group, including Russified Moldovans and Ukrainians as well as Russians, that considered Russian its language and the Soviet Union its country. Its "national" myths and symbols were thus Soviet myths and symbols. However, most of Moldova's Russians lived outside of Transnistria, and both sides in the conflict insist that the conflict is not an ethnic but a political one over issues like language status. Because of this and the relatively low group hostility and absence of pogroms, some scholars characterize the conflict as "regional" rather than ethnic.[2]

The ethnic conflict label also fits, however. The conflict was about the nationalist demands of the ethnic Moldovan side—for priority of their language, for political independence, and so on. These are classic ethnic demands which led to classic ethnic conflict dynamics. The fact that the Transnistrians are not an ethnic group is not critical: identities are frequently made and remade in the crucible of ethnic conflict, and it is not unusual for ethnic mobilization of one group to prompt the creation and mobilization of a diverse opposing "group" whose identity may well fade away as soon as the conflict is over.[3] As long as both sides—or the constituent groups on each side—can appeal to ethnic or nationalist myths and symbols in the course of mobilization, and as long as the issues at stake are relevant to those myths and symbols, the ethnic conflict label is appropriate. The fact that the group identities of both sides were redefined in the course of the conflict makes Moldova not an exceptional but a typical case.

HISTORICAL BACKGROUND

The first Moldova (spelled "Moldavia" in Russia and in the West during the Soviet period) was a medieval and early modern principality which emerged in the fourteenth century. It extended roughly from the Carpathian Mountains to the Dniester River and the Black Sea, embracing much of what is now northern Romania and pieces of modern-day Ukraine, in addition to all of the territory of the current Republic of Moldova except Transnistria. Along with its neighbor to the south, the principality of Wallachia, Moldova was populated primarily by Romanian-speaking peasants. Both had fallen under Ottoman suzerainty by the early sixteenth century, but they maintained their autonomy for the next two centuries. Transnistria, a strip of land on the left or northeastern bank of the Dniester—the area across the river from the Principality of Moldova—was mostly depopulated until the late seventeenth century, when Romanian-speaking peasants from the southwest and Ukrainian peasants from the northeast began settling in the region.[4] In 1792, Russian troops under the famed General Suvorov entered Transnistria, and the Russian government promptly annexed the region and established the Dniester River as the border between Russia and Ottoman-controlled Moldova. Cossacks were then added to Transnistria's ethnic mix, as they established military settlements in Tiraspol and other border posts.

In 1812, Russia annexed the portion of old Moldova between the Dniester and Prut Rivers, inventing the name "Bessarabia" for the province. Russian administration radically changed the face of Bessarabia, as massive immigration changed the ethnic balance: by the 1897 census, the towns were about 37 percent Jewish, 24 percent Russian, 16 percent Ukrainian, and only 14 percent Romanian-speaking Moldovan; even the countryside was only 53 percent Moldovan.[5] Meanwhile, what was left of old Moldova united with Wallachia in 1859 to form the first Romanian state, with the Prut River forming the Russian-Romanian border until 1918. Thus while Wallachians and southern Moldovans were forming a Romanian national identity for the first time, the Bessarabians, living in a very different cultural milieu, developed a distinct if inchoate Moldovan regional identity.[6]

During the Russian Civil War, this sentiment led the provisional Bessarabian parliament, the Sfatul Tarii, initially to declare autonomy within Russia. However, a January 1918 Sfatul request for (White) Russian troops to help establish order in Bessarabia led to the dispatch of allied Romanian troops instead, as Russian troops were in short supply. The presence of the Romanian troops, plus threats of annexation from a temporarily independent Ukraine, influenced the Sfatul to vote in April 1918 for conditional union with Romania. That December, under heavy Romanian pressure, a pro-Romanian rump of the Sfatul decided in a midnight vote to unite unconditionally with Romania and dissolve itself.[7] The Soviet Union, however, refused to accept the loss of formerly Russian imperial territory: in 1924, Stalin created the Moldavian Autonomous Soviet Socialist Republic (MASSR) in the portion of Soviet Ukraine then bordering Romania, including the current Transnistria and some adjoining territory. This "republic" symbolized the continuing Soviet territorial claims on Bessarabia.

The Soviet opportunity came when the 1939 Molotov-Ribbentrop Pact granted Nazi approval for the Soviet Union to annex Bessarabia. In 1940 Stalin did so, grabbing at the same time the neighboring region of Northern Bukovina. The Soviet government then redrew all of the local boundaries, establishing the borders that exist to this day. Northern Bukovina and the northern and southern ends of Bessarabia, populated mostly by Ukrainians, were given to Ukraine. The rest of Bessarabia was united with Transnistria—the part of the MASSR with most of the ethnic Moldovans—to form the Moldavian Soviet Socialist Republic as a unit of the USSR. The Romanians did not give up: in 1941, the quasifascist Romanian government joined in the Nazi invasion of the Soviet Union, reoccupying Moldova, including Transnistria, until expelled by Soviet troops in 1944.

Conditions for Ethnic War in Moldova

opportunity

The issue of Moldova's status emerged again in the 1980s only because Mikhail Gorbachev's policies of *glasnost* and *perestroika* gave the peoples of Moldova the opportunity to mobilize. As one nationalist leader put it, Gorbachev "took away the fear."[8] Thus when Moldovan intellectuals beginning in 1987 banded together to form cultural clubs, Moscow tolerated them. When they formed a "Democratic Movement in Support of *Perestroika*" the next year, Moscow even lent some support—including, allegedly, from KGB agents who were trying to generate pressure on the hard-line boss of the Moldovan Communist Party, Simeon Grossu.[9] When the Transnistrians counter-mobilized, they had the same atmosphere of *glasnost* and the support of hard-liners in Moscow: hence political space was no problem. The timing of Moldova's conflict is unquestionably explained by *glasnost*.

The opportunity to mobilize armed groups came later, and for the same combination of reasons—the liberalization of Soviet policy and assistance from variously disposed groups or bodies in the Soviet government. Most significant in this regard was the capture of the Moldovan Republic's government machinery by the Moldovan side, and assistance from the Soviet military for the Transnistrian side. The need for a territorial base was an important factor shaping how violence broke out. Fighting happened only in Transnistria, because only there were the Russophones sufficiently concentrated to gain control of enough territory. Indeed, the fighting was from the beginning over the control of territory, as the Transnistrians tried to establish their authority over the entire territory of the area, and the Moldovan authorities tried to resist.

MYTHS JUSTIFYING ETHNIC HOSTILITY

Moldovan myths and symbols

Soviet-era Moldovan historiography, unlike that of Georgia or Armenia, was not allowed to express Moldovan nationalism unambiguously: because of the Moldovans' close ties to Romania, Soviet authorities were unable to decide whether to encourage a separate Moldovan identity or to suppress it and Russify the inhabitants. In practice, it did a bit of both, allowing the main elements of a Moldovan nationalist mythology to emerge but tying it especially strongly to alleged close connections to Russia. At the same time, some Moldovan intellectuals kept alive a different, pro-Romanian mythology emphasizing the identity of the Romanian and Moldovan peoples. To this day, the Moldovan nationalist mythology remains divided into these two distinct versions: the mythology of "Moldovans as a distinct people" versus the concept of "Moldovans as part of the Romanian nation."

In both versions, Romanian and Moldovan history begin with the Roman Emperor Trajan, who invaded the country of Dacia in 101 C.E. and annexed it to Rome. The Dacians, who occupied the territory of modern Romania including Bessarabia, learned from the Romans the Latin language, which they never abandoned. Through the Dark Ages after the Roman collapse, these people came to be known as "Valakhs" or "Vlachs"—that is, Wallachians.[10] The self-image of the Moldovans starts from the belief that they are the modern-day descendants of the ancient Dacians,[11] with the legitimacy that is to be attached to over two thousand years of residence in the country—even though modern Moldova was never part of Roman Dacia. The assumption is part of popular culture with, for instance, one of the leading hotels in Chisinau named the "Dacia."

For the pro-Romanian version of Moldovan mythology, the figure of Moldovan prince Stefan the Great (1457–1504) also plays an important symbolic role, as Stefan, whose statue now dominates Chisinau's central square, maintained Moldova's independence against great-power neighbors such as Poland and the Ottoman Empire. Even the Great Soviet Encyclopedia allows that he "waged a fierce struggle against Turkish aggression."[12] Moldovans point to the story of the later Moldovan Prince Dmitrie Cantemir to suggest what Moldovan-Russian relations should be: Dmitrie, in the Moldovan view, impressed Peter the Great's court with his erudition and was rewarded with a treaty of alliance against the Turks which recognized the sovereignty of Moldova.[13] Alas, the story has a tragic ending, as Peter was quickly defeated by the Turks and ejected from the Balkans, while Moldova and Wallachia lost their autonomy and were subjected to a much more repressive direct Ottoman rule.

The myths justifying hostility to the Russians stem primarily from more recent history. Moldovans, of course, had been dominated and ruled by Russians for a century and a half—from 1812 to 1918, 1940 to 1941, and 1944 to 1991—providing ample grounds for resentment and fear. The nineteenth-century Romanian view is most vividly expressed in the work of Mihai Eminescu, considered the national poet of Romania. A Romanian admirer, not incidentally a Romanian Orthodox cleric, characterizes his political views this way:

> Eminescu... wrote a book against Russian czarists as occupiers of the Eastern part of Moldavia, called by them "Bassarabia," since 1812; he explained with many historical documents and geographical maps, why Panslavism wanted to enslave the Romanian territory... So our greatest poet and national visionary gave us, the Romanian people, his testament, put into all his poems and writings, pointing out our rights and where the most dangerous enemies are. He helped us to see clearly that these enemies are entrenched, hostile to the Romanian people, and are ready, at any time, to destroy our country and to assimilate the Romanian nation.[14]

According to the pro-Romanian version of Moldovan mythology, therefore, the 1918 unification of Moldova with Romania expressed the will of the people: the Sfatul Tarii invited the Romanian troops, and its "intention [to unite with Romania] was clear from the start." Indeed, "from a Romanian point of view, the reunion of Bessarabia and Bukovina with the mother country was the final act in the struggle for reunification of the Romanian land and people."[15]

The purely Moldovan version of the nationalist mythology claims, in contrast, that the Moldovans already had a separate identity at the time. For example, in May 1917, a group of local teachers addressed as "Romanian brothers" responded, "We are not Romanian, we are Moldavian."[16] More significantly, Romania's rule over Bessarabia in the interwar period was inept and deeply unpopular, partly because the Romanians looked down on Bessarabians as "poor country cousins." A French observer said of Romanian government in Bessarabia: "By lack of method and political know-how, and total lack of honesty, it has alienated the sympathies of the population."[17] This experience led to lasting negative memories among some Moldovans about union with Romania.[18]

The two versions of Moldovan mythology agree, however, about Soviet rule, though of course these experiences were passed down only orally, since they could not be published before *glasnost*. One of the most potent symbols of the period is the Molotov-Ribbentrop Pact of 1939 which gave Stalin the opportunity to annex Bessarabia. In the aftermath of the annexation came the brutal Stalinization of the region, accompanied by "mass annihilations, exiles, organized famine and other crimes against humanity."[19] A related complaint, frequently repeated, is that the borders of modern Moldova were drawn by Stalin specifically to complicate any future Romanian counter-claims, as Moldova was to include territory (Transnistria) that had never been part of Romania, while territory which had been Romanian was given to Ukraine.

In order to justify the Soviet annexation of Bessarabia, the pro-Romanian version of the mythology continues, Stalin decreed that the Romanian-speaking peasants in Soviet Moldova were Moldovans, linguistically and historically different from the Romanian peasants on the other side of the Prut. The key difference between Romanians and Moldovans, Soviet apologists claimed, was that the "Moldovan" language was Slavicized, using the Cyrillic alphabet (which was duly imposed) and including a large number of Russian loan words (which were also duly imposed).[20]

To maintain control of Moldova, both versions of the mythology then argue, Soviet authorities imported Russian and Ukrainian cadres wholesale to run the government and Communist Party bureaucracies and sent Russian and Ukrainian workers to run the new factories being built in Moldovan cities (which were largely depopulated due to the war, the Stalinist Terror, and the Nazi Holocaust against the Jews, who were the previous urban majority).[21] The result of Soviet policy was that two-thirds of Moldova's Communist Party members were Russian or Ukrainian in the 1960s, as were 54 percent of industrial workers in 1977[22]—not a congenial situation for the indigenous Moldovans. Ethnic Russians even dominated local cultural life, since continuation of indigenous Romanian culture was forbidden.[23]

Many people first heard this mythology in the 1980s, but it so resonated with their experience that it was quickly internalized. Russian immigration and political domination, linguistic and cultural discrimination, the living memory of the Terror, and the denial of the obvious identity of the Romanian and Moldovan languages were facts so obvious that they needed only to be articulated to attain status as basic myths. The language issues were particularly important. The Cyrillic alphabet symbolized the imposition of Russian rule and cultural Russification (even though Romanian had been written in Cyrillic until the nineteenth century). The status of the language mattered, too: it simply was not possible to use the Moldovan language very often; for most public and official purposes, people had to use Russian.

Finally, there was the issue of the flag: Soviet Moldova's flag, dominated by the Soviet hammer and sickle in a field of red, meant little to Moldovans, while the traditional tricolor flown by Romania resonated more deeply, at least for some.

Russophone myths and symbols

Russophone—that is, Soviet—mythology about Moldova emphasized the theme of Russian-Moldovan friendship, but with the Russians in a clearly superior role. Thus the *Great Soviet Encyclopedia* emphasizes the early medieval presence of Slavic tribes in Moldova among the ancestors of the Vlachs and claims that Russia's Ivan III "the Great" helped Moldova's Stefan the Great in the latter's war against Poland in 1497.[24] More significant is the story of Peter the Great and Dmitrie Cantemir: in the Russophone telling, the treaty between them established a Russian protectorate over Moldova.[25] The idea of a protectorate is significant in two senses: on the one hand, Russia was to protect Moldova against common enemies; on the other hand, Russia thereby gained sovereignty over Moldova.

If the Moldovans are considered historical friends, however, Romanians are another matter. According to the Soviet version of history, when Bessarabia was part of Romania in the interwar years, Romania "introduced a military-police dictatorship and pursued a colonial policy in Bessarabia."[26] When Romania again occupied Moldova—including Transnistria—during World War II, its government was heavily influenced by the atmosphere that had given rise to the fascist Iron Guard, and its occupation policy toward Russians was harsh—not to mention its policy of sending Moldova's Jews to Romanian-run concentration camps. Soviet mythology often referred, therefore, to the "iron guardist" regime, and the standard characterization of Romanian wartime rule was that "The German and Romanian fascists restored the rule of the landowners and capitalists, and a terrorist regime was established."[27]

Another key element of the Russophone mythology is the history of the Moldavian ASSR (MASSR), which included Transnistria, from 1924 to 1940. The history of Tiraspol as displayed on billboards outside Tiraspol's City Hall starts from the city's founding by Suvorov, and is marked from this point of view by the formation of the MASSR (1924), the establishment of Tiraspol as its capital (1929), and the promulgation of the MASSR constitution (1938). Thus the precedent of an autonomous political unit centered on Tiraspol became an important element in justifying the creation of a Transnistrian Moldavian Republic in 1990. Significantly, though, while the Russophones defined Transnistria as a Russian and Ukrainian homeland, they did not consider the rest of Moldova to be so—another reason why ethnic war did not expand much across the Dniester River.

Ethnic fears

The most intense ethnic fears stem from histories of ethnic domination and ethnic affinity problems: both were present in Moldova. The history of domination has already been discussed: Russians ruled Moldovans from 1812–1918, 1940–41, and 1944–91, while Romanians ruled Russophones from 1918–40 and 1941–44. The ethnic affinity problem is equally apparent: the Moldovans, from their point of view, were the local majority (in Moldova), but the minority in the Russian-dominated USSR. The Transnistrian Russophones, for their part, considered themselves collectively as the local majority in Transnistria but a threatened minority in Moldova—especially if, as was openly discussed in the late 1980s and early 1990s, Moldova were eventually to unite with Romania.

The Moldovans were explicit in stating a fear, stemming from these and other facts, that their existence as a people was threatened. Soviet policies of Russification were particularly blamed for this; one account cites "the widely held view among the Moldovan intelligentsia . . . that 'either we return to the Latin script and get the state language, or else we shall disappear as a language and as a nationality.'"[28] The immigration of other ethnic groups, generally Russophones, was held to contribute to this trend, and it gave rise to the view that political autonomy for the Moldovans (symbolized, of course, by the Romanian flag) was necessary to give them control over such processes as immigration and language policy. Even in retrospect, Moldovan intellectuals felt that the threat of ethnic extinction through assimilation was a real one before the successes of the Moldovan nationalist movement. These fears were important, though statistical data did not support them: a roughly stable 98 percent of ethnic Moldovans reported Moldovan to be their mother tongue in Soviet censuses—hardly evidence of a disappearing nation.[29]

Addressing this fear was particularly difficult because the measures the Moldovans wanted were threatening to Russophones: imposing the priority of the Romanian language (from which Moldovan is virtually indistinguishable once the alphabet is changed) and the Romanian tricolor flag (also flown by Romania in World War II) seemed the harbinger of the chauvinist policies of fascist Iron Guard Romania; and giving better jobs to Moldovans meant taking them from Russophones. Thus these symbolic issues worked to recast powerful, emotive group stereotypes held by both groups: Moldovans labeled Russians and Ukrainians as "migrant" interlopers or communists, while Russians saw echoes of 1940s-style fascism in every manifestation of pro-Romanian nationalism. Still, ethnic hostility between Moldovans and Russians was limited: intermarriage rates were high, and even after the violence, in 1993, only 9 percent of Moldovans and 3.5 percent of Russians answering a Chisinau survey said they considered mixed marriages between the groups undesirable.[30] Thus while the groups were hostile to each other's political aspirations, they did not feel hostile to individuals of the other group.

DETERIORATING LIVING STANDARDS

Ethnic problems in Moldova in the 1980s were tangled up with and exacerbated by economic grievances. One legacy of Soviet domination was that ethnic Moldovans were underrepresented in many of the more desirable professional, managerial, and industrial production jobs, while they dominated the poorer agricultural sector. For example, in 1977 non-Moldovans accounted for 54 percent of industrial workers, 57 percent of leadership posts, and 68 percent of those employed in the sciences.[31] Thus economic facts gave the Moldovans simultaneously a symbolic grievance ("the Russians get all the good jobs"), a political grievance ("we do not have the power to run our own lives"), and an economic grievance ("my job prospects, and my children's, are not good"). Moldovan elites particularly resented the priority that incoming Russian cadres received for scarce apartments in Chisinau, at the expense of Moldovans who might have been waiting for years.[32]

This situation did begin improving by the 1970s, but the economic hardships of the 1980s made further progress for ethnic Moldovans—and economic security for Russophones—seem problematic. The Soviet economy stagnated in the 1980s, and Moldova's important wine industry was particularly hurt by Gorbachev's anti-alcohol campaign, during which some vineyards were torn up and wine sales drastically curtailed. As the economic pie stopped expanding, competition for larger shares of the existing pie—competition which could easily be cast in ethnic terms—was bound to intensify.

HOW ETHNIC CONFLICT ESCALATED

MASS-LED MOBILIZATION AMONG MOLDOVANS

The initial mass-led nature of the Moldovan nationalist movement is hard to dispute. On the language issue—the first issue to result in ethnic conflict—the hostile perceptions resulted from personal experience, not propaganda: Moldovan students often could get an education only in Russian; would-be managers found their career paths blocked by Russophones; and intellectuals confronted the "degraded" state of the Moldovan language.[33] Nationalist organizations, therefore, did not need massive propaganda efforts to gather support. Nor could they mount any: before they came to power, the nationalists controlled only a few publications, such as the literary weekly *Literatura si arta*; most of the official media remained conservative until after nationalist leaders came to power in late 1989.[34]

In fact, the conservative Moldovan leadership led by Communist Party First Secretary Simeon Grossu did everything it could to stifle the growth of Moldovan nationalism. As late as July 1989, the Moldovan Communist Party Central Committee and the Council of Ministers issued a joint resolution calling on citizens in Soviet-style language to "rebuff nationalists."[35] The conservative tone of the mass media was aimed at reinforcing that view. But the situation was already out of the control of the Communist Party, as Grossu admitted;[36] former party activists were by then polarized into opposing Moldovan and Russophone nationalist groups.[37]

What happened was a classic example of mass-led political mobilization. It began in 1987 and 1988, when Moldovan intellectuals, taking advantage of *glasnost*, formed a few informal discussion groups, such as the Alexei Mateevici Literary-Musical Circle. These groups paved the way for the Democratic Movement in Support of Perestroika, an independent but pro-Gorbachev political organization. Spreading through networks of contacts in cultural organizations and even local Communist Party cells, the Democratic Movement could muster over 300 support groups throughout the country by early 1989.[38] Too big to be suppressed, it then changed its name to the Moldovan Popular Front and became an opposition movement: in August 1989 it mobilized a crowd of at least 100,000 people—some estimate 300,000 or more—at a "Grand National Assembly" to demand that Moldovan be made the state language of Moldova.[39] Already feeling the pressure of smaller rallies, the previously rubber-stamp Moldovan parliament had a month earlier elected Mircea Snegur, a Moldovan Politburo member newly reborn as a moderate Moldovan nationalist, to be its chairman. In September 1989, the parliament passed a pair of laws enshrining Moldovan as the state language and defining the state language's functions.

Throughout this process, emotive national symbols played a critical role. The first big protest demonstration organized by the Democratic Movement, on March 12, 1989, focused on the symbolism of language, promoting the slogan "Language, Script," as well as "Down with Grossu" and "Down with Communism." Fear of group extinction was also an important mobilizing theme: the Democratic Movement called in its platform for putting a stop to "the assimilation of smaller nationalities through uncontrolled immigration and encroachment on their rights."[40] The first rally of the Popular Front, in June 1989, evoked a more controversial symbol: the Molotov-Ribbentrop Pact, said to prove the Soviet government to be an "occupation regime." At that rally, tens of thousands of protesters waved Romanian tricolor flags at half-mast and wore mourning clothes in commemoration. Two days later, on the anniversary of the Soviet annexation, the Popular Front blocked the official Soviet celebration and organized an opposing "march of silence" to the statue of Stefan the Great, hero of Moldovan independence.[41]

The demands of the August 1989 "Great National Assembly" were also largely symbolic and called among other things for real sacrifice by those supporting the demands.[42] The main demand was for Moldovan to have the status of the state language, a demand of little practical significance but of great symbolic importance as an indicator of group status: it was the first step toward demands for political dominance by ethnic Moldovans. Protest leaders, however, also had an important interest at stake: the demand implied that government officials would have to be able to speak Moldovan, which would guarantee the jobs to members of the Moldovan intelligentsia—including protest leaders—at the expense of the frequently monolingual Russophones. Ordinary protesters had much less at stake; for them, the symbolic demands were more important. Indeed, the demand to replace the Soviet-style flag with the Romanian tricolor was entirely symbolic. And the final demand, that the Cyrillic alphabet be replaced by the Latin, called for real sacrifice by ordinary protesters: many Moldovans were not fluent in reading and writing the Latin alphabet, so making the switch would represent quite an inconvenience for them. Evidently, they felt the symbolic value of the alphabet change outweighed the inconvenience.

The driving force behind the language demand was fear of ethnic extinction. Thus the Popular Front concern that the Moldovan nation faced extinction if Moldovan were not designated the state language using the Latin script was actually incorporated into the text of the September 1989 language laws. Some ethnic Moldovans invested extraordinary hope in that law: one former Popular Front leader later reported that "people were expecting this law like the Second Coming of Christ. People fainted, held their chests, ..."[43] What began to drive nationalist extremists to violence was the specter of resistance, first by the conservative government and later by Russophones, to measures like the language law that they considered necessary for their group's survival but that the Russophones saw as a step toward ethnic Moldovan domination. Thus during the debate on the language law, when Russophone deputies left the parliament building in protest, the nationalist crowd outside the building tried to attack them.[44]

Changes in the nationalist agenda, and the initial episodes of violence, followed the same bottom-up pattern. The Moldovan nationalist leaders were originally aiming for moderate reform, and rallies that remained under their control in early 1989 were praised by authorities for their moderation. Later in 1989, however, while the nationalist leaders' rhetoric generally remained moderate, their rallies had banners telling the local Russians, "Suitcase—Train Station—Home." When protests began turning violent, leaders of the Popular Front worked to calm their followers,[45] but they began to lose control, with one protest outside police headquarters in November 1989 leading to a bloody clash with police. That violence was the final blow for the antinationalist Grossu, who was replaced as Communist Party chief by Petru Lucinschi, who was more willing to work with the nationalists. By May 1990, Snegur and Lucinschi had in turn been outflanked and forced to acquiesce in the appointment of the extreme nationalist Popular Front leader Mircea Druc as prime minister. This is the pattern of mass-led mobilization—mass organizations built from the ground up pushing their leaders into political power.

Moldova's mass-led nationalist hysteria reached a peak in April 1990, when the law replacing Moldova's Soviet-style flag with the Romanian tricolor was passed. There was a continuous rally outside the parliament building during the days of debate on the flag law, and while Snegur failed to ensure order, the Popular Front activists seemed to feel that "anything was accepted"—including violence—if done in the nationalist cause.[46] Some members of parliament were reportedly intimidated into supporting nationalist positions,[47] and some Russophone members who resisted were roughed up by the crowd. As a result of this atmosphere, even those ethnic Moldovan deputies who were not Popular Front supporters voted with the Popular Front, rejecting any compromise in favor of adopting the Romanian tricolor as Moldova's state flag (though a commission was appointed to design a Moldovan crest to add to that flag).

After the flag law was passed, ethnic conflict escalated even more. When cities in Transnistria passed laws refusing to fly the new flag, the Popular Front organized a May 20 rally aimed at marching on Bendery, one of the defiant cities, to forcibly raise the tricolor there. Besides pro-Romanian slogans, they also bore the banner, "Let the CPSU [Communist Party of the Soviet Union] Live at Chernobyl!" Their way was blocked by a counter-demonstration, and the opposing crowds scuffled.[48] Two days later, a Russian student was beaten to death in the streets of Chisinau.[49]

THE PERFORMANCE OF MOLDOVA'S NATIONALIST LEADERS

Moldovan leaders did try to prevent violence. In 1989 and the first half of 1990, Popular Front leaders repeatedly pulled demonstrators back from clashes with the police and Russophone crowds.[50] Their efforts were usually successful because, as noted above, Moldovans and Russophones were not mutually hostile, so the mass impulse to violence was limited. Indeed, even at the height of the Transnistrian conflict, Moldovans favored granting a wide array of language, cultural and political rights to Russophones—more than, for example, their Romanian neighbors were inclined to grant to Romania's ethnic Hungarians.[51]

What Moldovan leaders failed to do was to find appropriate compromises. Popular Front leaders in parliament did compromise on some key provisions of the 1989 language law, against the opposition of their own extremists, but they did not go far enough. The final wording of the law still needlessly harmed Russophones' interests. Worse, as the Moldovan government later admitted, the implementing regulations required that virtually all workers be tested for proficiency in the Moldovan language within four years—a possible threat to the jobs of virtually all nonnative speakers of the language.[52] In the flag controversy of 1990, Moldovan leaders contributed to the conflict's escalation when they responded to Transnistrian defiance by ordering criminal sanctions, increasing the penalty for desecration of the flag to up to three years' imprisonment.[53]

The climactic issue of 1990–91—the choice between the Soviet Union, independence, or a union with Romania—allowed less room for compromise. Conservative Russophones demanded that Moldova sign Gorbachev's Union Treaty and remain in the USSR, but they were marginalized outside of Transnistria. Rather, it was the radical pro-Romanian nationalists who were on the offensive. They organized a "bridge of flowers" demonstration in May 1990 in which people on both the Romanian and Moldovan sides of the Prut River surged past border posts and across the bridges linking the two countries, symbolizing their desire for closer ties—and, to the radicals, political union. In July, the Popular Front adopted a platform branding the Communist Party illegal, labeling the Soviet army "occupation troops," and applying the name "Romanian" to the people and language of Moldova.

By December, the Popular Front's pro-independence rhetoric sounded like this: "Will we accept slavery for centuries or choose the path of freedom? Will we legalize the 1940 act of occupation by signing the Union Treaty or embark upon the path of our state and national independence? Will we accept with humiliation and shame the terms dictated by the empire or oppose them?" Later that month, the Popular Front proclaimed at a massive demonstration that signing a new Soviet union treaty would constitute "treason" and that instead the "integration of the Romanian nation"—a euphemism for political unification—"is an imperative of our days."[54] That euphemism was telling: the Moldovan nationalist movement was united in insisting on separation from the Soviet Union, but divided over whether the ultimate goal was Moldovan independence or reunification with Romania.

This three-way tug-of-war among pro-Soviet, pro-Romanian, and pro-independence activists was tearing Moldova apart. Prime Minister Druc, representing the pro-Romanian radicals in the government, became locked in a power struggle with President Snegur, leader of the pro-independence forces. By March 1991, Snegur had won an increase in his power, as the Prime Minister's office was subordinated to the Presidency. In May, Druc was ousted altogether, charged with destroying the Moldovan economy and with "Russophobia" in personnel policy—his leadership team had consisted almost entirely of ethnic Moldovans.[55] Druc was replaced as prime minister by the more moderate Valeriu Muravschi, but leadership on the key issues of ethnic policy was taken by President Snegur personally; Muravschi was primarily given charge of the economy.

During this tense conflict over fundamental political values, Moldova's political leaders repeatedly showed themselves to be either inept in or ignorant of conflict management techniques. They knew enough to call for a "round table" discussion among all political groups in spring 1990, but the benefits—dubious in any case, according to one participant[56]—were immediately squandered in the handling of the debate on changing Moldova's flag. Thus Snegur, the parliamentary chairman during legislative debates on the issue, excluded deputies from Transnistria from the debate by "failing to notice" when they wanted to speak; and he failed to protect them effectively from the mobs outside the parliament building.[57] Although Snegur condemned the violence against members of parliament, he asked for improved security not for them but for himself.[58] To add insult to injury, the decision was made to fly the Romanian flag temporarily while a commission discussed adding the Moldovan crest. To those for whom union with Romania was anathema, this move seemed to be a prelude to their worst fears.

Most damaging of all to prospects for compromise, Snegur repeatedly refused to discuss offering political autonomy to Transnistria. Instead, when a group of officials from Transnistria met in an extraordinary congress to demand autonomy, Snegur sent deputy parliamentary chairman Victor Puscasu to the Transnistrian congress to threaten criminal action against its participants.[59] In September 1990 he had the parliament declare a state of emergency and "presidential rule" so he could try to suppress the region's move toward autonomy.[60] An authoritarian temperament resulting from Snegur's Communist Party background probably explains this choice of tactics. As one former advisor to Snegur put it, the general climate was one in which "compromise [was] a symbol of weakness and humiliation."[61] Another reason for Snegur's course was his judgment that the Transnistrian leaders were similarly inflexible: Snegur's retrospective view was that the Transnistrians were "not talking about compromise" and that had he made concessions, they would simply have made more extreme demands.[62] But by ruling out compromise and relying on coercive threats that could not be carried out, Snegur succeeded only in making violence more likely.

Some government and nationalist leaders later admitted that some of their actions exacerbated the situation. As one nationalist leader put it, the "style of categorical formulation" used by the nationalist camp—the frequent appeals to "historical right" and denial of legitimacy to opposing views—alienated too many people.[63] Valeriu Muravschi, prime minister during the 1991–92 fighting, perhaps gets to the nub of the matter when he admits, "We were not ready, on the moral-psychological plane, to recognize some kind of administrative territory [in Transnistria]. We were not ready to broaden their political rights."[64] Because such figures—who later formed the political center—were taking such extreme positions in 1990–91, there effectively was no political center at that time. The Popular Front's street protests helped to prevent one from forming until after the chastening experience of the war.

Other Moldovan leaders forthrightly organized what violence there was before the 1991 Moscow coup. In October 1990, when the Gagauz of southern Moldova were preparing to vote on an autonomy referendum, Popular Front leaders called for volunteers to stop the vote by coercion. Prime Minister Druc agreed under pressure to legalize the volunteer detachments and subordinate them formally (but not practically) to the Moldovan Ministry of Defense. In response, the Transnistrians also began mobilizing volunteers, sending some of them to "assist" the Gagauz. Others set up roadblocks on a bridge across the Dniester near Dubossary. The interposition of Soviet armed forces blocked the Moldovan volunteers from the Gagauz regions, but some turned north and on November 2 clashed with Transnistrian volunteers in Bendery. On the same day, Moldovan Interior Ministry troops acting on the authority of Druc and Moldovan Interior Minister Costas tried to open the Dubossary bridge by force, attacking the better-armed Transnistrian volunteers. They failed, leaving about six dead.[65] These decisions seem to have resulted from a combination of incompetence and malice: even Costas's colleagues perceived him as too anti-Russian, while aides viewed Druc as "inexperienced" and "emotional."[66] Russians also suspected the pair of having ordered the police not to interfere with the mobs attacking the Russian members of parliament in April 1990.[67]

These events are best understood as symbolic politics *par excellence*. People mobilized for rallies and engaged in violence over the most symbolic and least practical of issues—e.g., the raising of a flag—when they had no individual interests at stake. Their leaders repeatedly characterized their motivation as "euphoria" or "romantic enthusiasm,"[68] which suggests emotional commitment to promoting their group's status. Indeed, one moderate nationalist leader reports nearly being assaulted by his own erstwhile supporters when he tried to suggest that they compromise. His explanation was that his followers had adopted a Soviet mentality, which created "enemy images," and infused it with an anti-Soviet Moldovan nationalist content: thus Russians or Soviets were the enemy, and compromise was betrayal.[69] Such followers perhaps were, in Motyl's terminology, fanatics, but there were tens of thousands of them on both sides.

Leaders were similarly single-minded, aiming at maximizing either their own power or their nationalist values, apparently without admitting the need for tradeoffs. One Moldovan nationalist leader, for example, while insisting that his side's demands for eventual union with Romania represented "historical right," refused to accept that Russians might feel threatened by such union. He asserted that claims about such fear were mere "speculation," and that the conflict in Transnistria was due to outside interference (implicitly, by Russia) rather than to any genuine opposition among the people of the region.[70] Other Moldovan nationalists applied double standards to maintain the logical consistency of their preferences. Thus one, while justifying Moldova's independence by insisting that Russians and "Romanians" were not compatible, and therefore could not live together in one state, also insisted that Transnistrian separatism was due entirely to self-interested leaders and the intervention of Moscow rather than to any concerns the Russophone population—though allegedly incompatible with Romanians—might have.[71]

In sum, the escalation to low-level violence on the Moldovan side was driven by a combination of mass sentiment, elite temperament, and counter-elite manipulation. The mass sentiment on nationalist issues was real enough, but its expression in mass protests on particular issues, especially in 1990–91, was largely the result of decisions by the Popular Front leadership. Given the atmosphere thus created and the inexperience of many Moldovan leaders, no political center could emerge at the time. Then, the authoritarian instincts of leaders such as Snegur, Druc, and Costas inclined the leaders to try coercion as an early response to Transnistrian secessionism. They literally did not perceive compromise as a viable alternative. On the other hand, given the temperament of the leading Transnistrian officials, compromise may well not have been feasible.

ELITE-LED VIOLENCE IN TRANSNISTRIA

The mobilization process worked very differently on the Transnistrian side than it did with the Moldovans. The preconditions for hostility and fear—the ethnic affinity problem, history of domination, contentious symbols, and potentially hostile mythology—were equally there, but on this side the process was elite-led. Instead of insecurity leading to extremist politics, as happened on the Moldovan side, Russophone elites mobilized people against ethnic Moldovan demands, turning politics into a contest for ethnic dominance. Their goal was to create a security dilemma for both sides as a way to preserve and increase their own power. They succeeded due in large measure to support from hard-liners in Moscow, though provocative actions from the Moldovan side also helped.

As on the Moldovan side, the first major issue for the Russophones was the language law. The law made Moldovan the sole state language, raising its symbolic status above that of Russian: place names were to be written in

Moldovan only, and officials were made personally responsible if their subordinates failed to implement language requirements at work.[72] Moldovan was also to be the main language of government and industry, though there was a provision that local governments could, if they gained the approval of the Council of Ministers in Chisinau, make Russian the business language in their localities. Finally, all political leaders, economic managers, service workers, and some others would have to be bilingual within five years (a period the implementing regulations at first reduced to four years). As noted above, these categories were interpreted so broadly that most workers were included in one of them.

The provisions for exemption were significant: if applied to the cities of Transnistria, the exemption would have relieved Russophone workers of the most onerous burdens of the language law. Most Transnistrian Russophones could have continued using Russian when dealing with the local government, and factory workers could have used it on the job as well, though officials and managers would still have had to know Moldovan for dealing with Chisinau. The symbolic subordination of the Russian language was galling, but that fact did not lead to separatist violence anywhere else such laws were passed in the collapsing Soviet Union. It need not have done so in Transnistria either.

Separatist violence occurred largely because Russophone elites stood to gain power by promoting it, while they could lose everything—their jobs, their influence, and their perquisites—if they were to submit to the language law. Transnistrian elites therefore chose to turn the language issue into an ethnonationalist struggle for group dominance. Thus they immediately acted to challenge the authority of the Moldovan government, stating their demands in absolute terms: instead of voting to exempt their constituents from key provisions of the language law, city councils in Transnistria voted to defy the law itself. They justified this move by claiming that the language law expressed a "scornful attitude toward the rights of non-Moldovans," and that they were merely defending "the equality of all peoples before the law."[73] The real political agenda was already declared, however: the city council of Bendery, politically but not geographically part of Transnistria, announced as early as September 1989 "the beginning of work on creating a national-territorial region."[74] These tactics made accommodation difficult to achieve, eventually making secession the Transnistrians' only alternative to submission.

While Transnistrian politicians were voting to defy the language law, strikes protesting the law broke out in factories throughout the region. Curiously, the strikers were mostly industrial workers—i.e., workers to whom exemptions could have been applied. That they struck was due less to their own interests than to elite pressure: the strike committees were dominated by the workers' de facto bosses—the leaders of enterprise

Communist Party and labor union organizations, or even deputy factory directors.[75] In some places, presumably where workers did not take the hint, managers reportedly resorted to a lockout to initiate the "strike."[76] The strike organizers found powerful allies in other places as well: one Moldovan leader claims that prostrike leaflets were distributed in Tiraspol by (government) helicopter.[77]

The local Transnistrian media was another powerful tool for Russophone elites: by playing on the symbolic issues at stake and stirring up anti-Moldovan chauvinism, the media played a key role in building popular support for the Transnistrian cause. For example, in Tiraspol—the hotbed of Russophone separatist feeling, and soon the Transnistrian capital—the leading newspaper was saturated with rhetoric that aroused Russians' fears and reinforced their intransigence in the face of Moldovan demands. The newspaper promoted the myth of Peter the Great's "protectorate" treaty with Dmitrie Cantemir in 1711[78] and encouraged the strikers to continue their walkout.[79] It repeatedly alleged that the language law was only the first step in a grander chauvinist Moldovan scheme to reduce Russians to second-class citizenship and deprive them of human rights,[80] and repeated the most extreme slogans of the Popular Front demonstrators such as "Banish the migrants!"[81] Finally, it hinted at—and promoted—fears of extinction, stating that Popular Front demands for secession "cause well-founded uneasiness among the Russophone part of the population about its future, the future of its children."[82] Since this newspaper was still controlled by the Tiraspol city Communist Party organization, there can be no doubt that its editors were acting on orders from above.

This is not to say that all of the Transnistrian elites' claims were false: one reason their secessionist bid gained popular support was because they had some claim to legitimacy. Unlike any other Russian or Russophone minority in the former Soviet Union, the Transnistrians could appeal to a history of autonomous existence—in the Moldavian Autonomous Soviet Socialist Republic of the 1920s and 1930s. They argued, therefore, that though the rest of Moldova might claim that its inclusion in the USSR was the illegitimate result of the Molotov-Ribbentrop Pact, Transnistria had been part of the USSR since the founding of the Soviet state. Ergo, they claimed, if the rest of Moldova wanted to revert to its pre-1940 status outside the USSR, then Transnistria should have the right to revert to its own pre-1940 status—as an "autonomous republic" in the USSR.

Another tool the Transnistrian leaders used effectively to build a ruling coalition was communist ideology. Some supporters, like Grigore Maracuta, later the Transnistrian parliamentary chairman, were ethnic Moldovans but hard-line communists who felt more comfortable in Tiraspol's political atmosphere and chose to migrate there. Others, such as Tiraspol's industrial managers, were suspicious of Moldova's economic reformism and drift away from integration with the Soviet economy. They therefore supported the Transnistrian government's efforts to keep the region in the Soviet Union, and to resist market reforms. For conservative politicians in Russia, like General Albert Makashov, both the ideological and the ethnic issues were useful for making Transnistrian separatism into a politically useful *cause célèbre*. Thus the ethnonationalist conflict in Moldova (Moldovan vs. Soviet or Russian nationalism) was reinforced by a coinciding ideological divide (communists vs. anticommunists).

The Transnistrian elite's main approach to justifying itself, however, was not ideological but military: it stoked violent conflict by manufacturing a security dilemma, then cast itself as the region's only defender. By defying the language law and moving toward self-proclaimed autonomy, Transnistrian leaders symbolically threw down the gauntlet, turning the issue into one of political dominance in Transnistria. This tactic exacerbated the greatest fears of the Moldovan nationalists—that they would not be able to escape from Moscow-backed policies of Russification. Indeed, the timing of the first Transnistrian moves toward autonomy prove the disingenuousness of their justifications. The Transnistrians argued that they moved toward autonomy in reaction to the June 1990 Moldovan declaration of "sovereignty." But the first official moves toward secession—referenda in the Transnistrian cities of Rybnitsa and Tiraspol in favor of forming an autonomous region—came in December 1989 and January 1990, six months before the Moldovan sovereignty declaration.[83]

When the Transnistrian leaders voted to defy the flag law, they managed to provoke precisely the reaction they wanted: the May 1990 Popular Front march aimed at raising the new Moldovan flag on Transnistrian territory by sheer force of numbers. That march—which its organizers tried to stop when a violent confrontation seemed about to occur—made Transnistrian Russophones feel that they were directly threatened by Moldovan nationalism.[84] That feeling was then used to justify expansion of the volunteer defense groups which had successfully stood off the Popular Front marchers. It was these volunteer groups—by then armed—that participated in the violent confrontation with Moldovan volunteers in November of 1990.

Meanwhile, Transnistria had gone much further in its separatism. In early June 1990, a special congress of Transnistrian leaders proclaimed the establishment of an autonomous Transnistrian region within Moldova. Three months later, a second such congress upped the ante, proclaiming the establishment of a Transnistrian republic independent of Moldova but within the USSR. The congress also established a provisional parliament and elected Igor Smirnov as its president.[85] This growing threat of Transnistrian separatism, combined with the growth of Transnistrian armed groups, worked to increase further the feelings of threat on the Moldovan side.

Throughout this period, the Transnistrian press continued to encourage feelings of threat and inclinations toward a violent response among the Transnistrian population by manipulating nationalist symbols. During the furor over the flag law, Tiraspol's leading newspaper repeatedly invoked memories of Romanian fascist occupation of the region during World War II, recalling how Russians had fought against the Romanian flag (identical to the new Moldovan flag)—"the flag of the fascist occupiers."[86] The equally controversial glories of the Soviet-style red flag—a symbol of freedom, one journalist claimed without intending irony—were rehearsed ad nauseam.[87] To make the point clearer, the newspaper also compared Popular Front slogans to those of Romania's fascist Iron Guard movement of the 1930s and 1940s[88] and alluded to a threat of "genocide."[89] Every Moldovan move to build its security forces was blasted (not always inaccurately) as part of a plot against Transnistria, and accusations that the Moldovans were aiming at assimilation or expulsion of the Russophone population grew ever more explicit.[90] False claims that the Moldovan government had decided to unite with Romania further fueled Transnistrians' fears.

The fears engendered by this media onslaught were mostly baseless. Most Russophones in Moldova live not in Transnistria but in Bessarabia—especially in the capital, Chisinau. While these people were touched by the emotions of the time, their lives were actually little affected by Moldova's nationalist movement. Except for a few tragic incidents, there was no violence against Russians even in the capital, the cockpit of Moldovan nationalism. Had Transnistria chosen to seek a modus vivendi with Chisinau, it could have found one.

CREATION OF A SECURITY DILEMMA

Instead of seeking compromise, both sides acted to exacerbate the security dilemma. Russophone elites provoked the volatile Moldovan nationalist movement into overreacting, then used that overreaction to justify further moves toward secession. After the 1990 Dubossary clash, for example, the Tiraspol press repeatedly invoked the "victims of Dubossary" to promote fear among Transnistrian Russophones and to justify further violent confrontations.[91] Those moves prompted even more extreme Moldovan nationalist attempts to suppress the Transnistrians, making ordinary Transnistrians feel even more threatened. The result was an escalating security dilemma that pushed Transnistria to the edge of large-scale violence—and which the Russophone elites used to justify the expansion of their own power.

A significant fact about Moldova's interethnic security dilemma is that it was not the result but rather the cause of emergent anarchy. Throughout 1990, Interior Ministry troops subordinate to Moscow were capable of preventing interethnic violence: they did so both in September in Transnistria and in October in the Gagauz region. For this reason, fears about physical insecurity were exaggerated on all sides, especially among Russophones and the Gagauz. What drove those exaggerated fears was not the absence of effective security troops but elite manipulation and provocations. False claims about plots to unify with Romania or oppress Russians played an important role in mobilizing the Russophones, as did the provocations of violence. To be sure, on the Moldovan side the conflict was largely mass-led, with extremist rhetoric merely the tool rather than the cause of mobilization. But as long as the Soviet Union existed, the threat to Russophones was small and distant enough that violence remained limited. Real war broke out only after ethnonationalist mobilization, driven by the insecurity of the Moldovans and other Soviet minorities, caused the Soviet Union to break up.

After the failed August 1991 coup, a real international-style security dilemma emerged in Moldova: the Russophones' fears of Moldovan repression were more justified than ever, while the Moldovans saw Russophone resistance, in part correctly, as part of an attempt by Moscow to deprive Moldova of its hard-won sovereignty. So the conflict escalated, beginning with another Moldovan government overreaction. Using the Transnistrian leadership's support for the coup as an excuse, Moldovan police agents abducted Transnistrian leader Igor Smirnov from Kiev, where he was visiting, and placed him under arrest. The arrest enormously boosted Smirnov's dubious prestige, elevating him in Transnistria to a heroic stature he had previously lacked.

The Transnistrians' reaction was to blockade the rail lines to Moldova proper and demand Smirnov's release before they would allow the trains to run. Upon his release, Smirnov organized a fall 1991 referendum on Transnistrian independence from Moldova, still within the Soviet Union. The purpose of the referendum was not to consult local opinion on the future status of Transnistria; rather, it was an attempt by the Transnistrian leadership to bolster its bargaining position. The proposed end state for Transnistria, "independence" within the USSR, was a mirage unless the major Soviet republics signed a union treaty, which was already unlikely. Promising such a chimera did, however, have the virtue for Transnistrian leaders of creating a fait accompli of popular "insistence" on independence from Moldova which would obstruct any future compromise with Chisinau.

Though the referendum went the leaders' way, it is doubtful that most Transnistrian residents wanted war. The ethnic Moldovan population actually constituted a plurality of the local population (over 40 percent), and although the Transnistrian leaders claimed to represent the Russians (25 percent) and Russophone Ukrainians (28 percent), there is evidence that not all Ukrainians supported the leadership's policies.[92] Leaders tried to manipulate the voters by using the local press, warning Russophone voters that the alternative to independence was to submit to a "new inquisition" by Moldovan authorities in the short run and eventually to be swallowed up in an extreme nationalist Romania.[93] Leaders proclaimed that the vote showed a majority in favor of Transnistrian "independence," and that separatist leader Smirnov had won a separate vote for Transnistrian president.[94] However, balloting was not really secret, so considering elite and media pressure and the Soviet habit of voting as one is told, that result cannot be taken as a real measure of public opinion.[95]

Starting around this time, opposition to the Transnistrian leadership was increasingly suppressed. Leaders of the ethnic Moldovan community who tried to oppose the Russophone leadership were subjected to intimidation—in one case mysteriously murdered; in another case abducted in an official car.[96] In one celebrated case in June 1992, the prominent activist Ilie Ilascu was arrested and later subjected to a Stalinist-style show trial.[97] The Transnistrian leaders' ability to organize such repression substantially increased in the months after August 1991, as former Soviet OMON special police officers, many wanted elsewhere for human rights abuses, started arriving in the region. One of these officers became, under the *nom de guerre* "General Shevtsov," the Transnistrian "Minister of National Security."[98]

ESCALATION TO WAR

Smirnov now proceeded with Transnistria's war of independence. Armed with the show of "popular support" from his election and the pro-independence referendum, and with increasing help from the local Soviet military unit, the Fourteenth Army, Smirnov began a military campaign to capture the entire Transnistrian region, including the predominantly Moldovan countryside. The Transnistrians perceived a security dilemma: control of areas in Transnistria by police units loyal to Chisinau represented to them possible bases for an oft-threatened Moldovan attempt to suppress them by force.[99] Smirnov, therefore, set about eliminating those pro-Chisinau policemen. That was the focus of the entire war: Transnistrian forces would attack pro-Chisinau police posts; Chisinau would send reinforcements, which would frequently be ambushed; and the fighting would escalate. Much of the fighting centered on rural areas around the city of Dubossary: the countryside here was populated mostly by ethnic Moldovans loyal to Chisinau, but Smirnov needed to control it because it would otherwise split Transnistria in two.[100] In these cases, the goal of the fighting was often not just police stations but entire villages.[101]

As the conflict escalated, outside groups joined in. As early as October 1991, Cossack revivalists were flocking to Transnistria to defend "Russia." They were sponsored by pro-Cossack enterprises and private firms in traditionally Cossack areas such as Sochi and Rostov, and encouraged in their actions by Russia's Vice President Alexander Rutskoi and by the Soviet (later Russian) Defense Ministry as well.[102] The role they played in Transnistria remains murky, but there were reports that they did not always follow Tiraspol's orders. Sometimes opposing the Cossacks were Moldovan guerrillas acting independently of Chisinau.[103] The Moldovan side also received some assistance from Romania, the main effect of which was to increase Russophone fears about impending unification. Thus, uncontrolled elements and foreign actions on both sides acted to escalate the conflict, stoking the security dilemma and magnifying ethnic hostility.

The most serious fighting occurred at the end of the war—during and after the climactic battle for Bendery, a city on the Chisinau side of the river with Transnistrian sympathies. The reasons for the battle are disputed, but evidence suggests a degree of bad faith on all sides. The Moldovans claim they received word on June 19, 1992, while negotiations to resolve the conflict were taking place, that pro-Chisinau police in Bendery were under attack.[104] Transnistrian representatives denied there was an attack and proposed a joint fact-finding mission.[105] Some on the Moldovan side also doubted the reported attack,[106] but the Moldovan response was to launch a counterattack aimed at capturing the entire city.[107]

The resulting battle seems not to have been planned by either side. Moldova's then-Deputy Defense Minister Creanga reports employing little more than a battalion in the critical battle at the Dniester River bridge, and then-Moldovan National Security Advisor Chirtoaca later recalled that some units, including the artillery, got lost on the way to the battle. Yet Creanga's account does not sound like a well-designed Transnistrian attempt to trap the Moldovan troops, either. Over a full day of artillery bombardment and numerous attacks were necessary to dislodge the small Moldovan force from the bridge, and the process destroyed much of the city. Ultimately the Transnistrians, with their first open assistance from the Fourteenth Army, drove the Moldovans out of the city altogether. If the Transnistrian side is guilty of having intentionally provoked the battle, which is credible, then Moldovans are equally guilty of having been too easily provoked.[108]

The battle in Bendery sparked violent clashes all along the line of contact. Together with the Bendery battle itself, these clashes accounted for the majority of casualties during the entire war. Intervention by the Fourteenth Army ensured that the result overwhelmingly favored the Transnistrians: by the time a cease-fire was imposed, Tiraspol controlled virtually all of Transnistria, plus an enclave across the river around Bendery. What made their victory possible, as I detail below, was Russian help.

CONFLICT MANAGEMENT AND CONFLICT PROMOTION BY RUSSIA

The Soviet government faced a difficult conflict-management problem in Moldova. Although Moscow wanted to avoid ethnic violence of the type already underway in Karabagh, it also wanted to maintain its own authority in the region and to guarantee the status of the Russophones, who were, after all, Moscow loyalists. However, in the context of a strong Moldovan nationalist movement insistent on independence, these goals were incompatible. Moscow could only have maintained its authority by the massive use of force, which it was not prepared to do, and it could only support the Russophones by interventions that the Moldovans would see as efforts at "divide and rule."

By the time of the first Transnistrian declaration of independence from Moldova in September 1990, Moscow had adopted the "divide and rule" strategy: henceforth, every major escalatory action by the Transnistrians was preceded by a show of support from Moscow—support that was often decisive for the Transnistrians' success. Moscow used this aid as a lever not only to try to gain Moldova's "voluntary" agreement to remain in the Soviet Union but also to promote a peaceful resolution of Moldova's conflict with its Russophones. Gorbachev's proclamations, for example, were not one-sidedly pro-Transnistrian, and troop deployments acted not only to help the Transnistrians but also to avert violence. The final military involvement by now-independent Russia in June 1992 had a similar dual character, putting a stop to the violence, but doing so by decisively supporting Transnistria.

In the early stages of the conflict, during the 1989 battle over Moldova's language law, the best conflict management approach would have offered reassurance to the Moldovans that perceived threats to them could be averted, while offering the Transnistrian elites inducements to settle while they were cut off from military help. Interestingly, this seems to have been what Gorbachev tried to do. During the preliminary debate on the language law, Gorbachev phoned Moldovan party chief Grossu to lobby for a compromise in which Moldovan would be the state language—the Moldovans' key demand—but Russian would remain the "language of inter-ethnic communications."[109] Gorbachev's reaction to the Transnistrians' strike over the issue was to send Soviet Deputy Prime Minister Lev Voronin to talk with the strikers and to phone a leader of striking railwaymen in Bendery personally. Gorbachev asked the railroad workers to return to work and promised to consider their situation.[110] Assured of such attention, strike leader Vladimir Rylyakov announced that the strike had achieved its aims, and the workers returned to their jobs.[111]

Unfortunately, overall policy from Moscow had the longer-term effect of stoking rather than ameliorating the conflict. While making Russian the language of "interethnic communications" sounds like a fair compromise, Moldovans objected because it would mean that for many purposes Moldovans would have to learn Russian but Russophones would not have to learn Moldovan. Such a provision would provide the Transnistrian leaders the inducement to desist—their jobs would be protected—but it would not allow the Moldovans to reassure themselves that their nationality was safe from the threat of Russification. Given the strong Moldovan insistence on this point, Gorbachev ultimately had to give way, and the law was passed without the provision for Russian. When all was decided, Gorbachev had lost credibility with both sides: his initial opposition to the Moldovan side cost him their support; while his betrayal of the hopes of the Transnistrian strikers meant they would never again be so easily persuaded by his promises.

Further cause for Moldovan distrust of Moscow came from the attitude of Moscow's conservative press, which openly sympathized with the Transnistrians.[112] *Pravda,* for example, claimed that in passing the language law, the Moldovan side had "succumbed to powerful and prolonged conditioning from the nationalistically-minded ideologists of the Moldavian Popular Front"—an odd claim since *Moskovskie Novosti* (*Moscow News*) reported that even several months later the Moldovan media was still biased *against* the Popular Front.[113] The bias of the Moscow press was significant because it reinforced the biased messages reaching residents of Transnistria from their own local press. As a result, they had little access to sources of information that might have moderated their perceptions.

By the summer of 1990, the conflict had entered a new phase: with nationalist Mircea Snegur as parliamentary chairman and extremist Mircea Druc as prime minister, the mass-led Moldovan nationalist movement was now clearly dominant in Moldova. Moscow was reduced more and more to the role of an outside intervener rather than a sovereign authority. Theoretically, to help avoid violence in such a situation, the intervener needs to deter any aggressive moves by the insurgents. Moscow did just this on two occasions. First, in early September 1990 the Soviet Interior Ministry dispatched troops to Tiraspol to protect the congress of Russophone elites that declared the "Dniester Republic" independent of Moldova within the Soviet Union.[114] This move deterred a threatened Moldovan attempt to disrupt the gathering and imprison the Transnistrian leaders and thereby prevented the violence that would have resulted when armed Transnistrian formations opposed the Moldovan move. Similarly, in late October, when the Gagauz were organizing (illegal) elections for their separatist region, Moscow interposed Interior Ministry troops between Druc's ethnic Moldovan volunteers, who were coming to disrupt the elections, and the Gagauz volunteers defending their territory and election process. Again, violence was averted.

Moscow's frank support for the Transnistrian position, however, cost it the credibility it needed to promote conflict resolution. Thus the Soviet military newspaper *Krasnaia zvezda* (*Red Star*) quickly signaled its recognition of the Transnistrian "republic," in spite of its illegality.[115] The Soviet government's position, as expressed by Gorbachev, was more qualified—he supported Moldova's "integrity as a part of a union of sovereign states"[116]—but he bluntly told Snegur in private that if he did not sign the Union Treaty, there would be a Transnistrian Republic.[117] USSR Supreme Soviet (i.e., parliament) Chairman Anatolii Lukyanov, at that time a Gorbachev ally, delivered a similar message to other Moldovan leaders.[118] In short, Moscow was still attempting to divide and rule.

The aid to the Transnistrians arrived through many channels. Probably as early as 1990, the Soviet civil defense organization and the official paramilitary DOSAAF organization started supplying the Transnistrian volunteers with weapons.[119] Meanwhile, the Transnistrians had also secured the sympathy of the Fourteenth Army by resisting Chisinau's antimilitary legislation. The local troops were encouraged by the Soviet Defense Ministry's open tilt toward Tiraspol, as signaled by the military newspaper *Krasnaia zvezda*.[120] Thus, by the time the first Moldovan-Transnistrian armed confrontation took place outside Dubossary in November 1990, the Transnistrian Russophones had not only their own armed volunteer formations but also the expectation of support from Soviet troops. Soviet officers were also active in aiding Moldova's other separatist movement, the pro-Soviet Gagauz, as Lukyanov had also threatened would occur.[121]

In the meantime, the Soviet government was not willing to undermine its tool even by noting its illegality. Vadim Bakatin, the liberal interior minister of the Soviet Union, did remark on the Transnistrian Republic's "unconstitutionality";[122] and more significantly, he granted the Moldovan interior minister autonomy to command and reform the Moldovan police forces;[123] but Bakatin was an exception. The "compromise" promoted in the fall of 1990 by Soviet Premier Ryzhkov and by Gorbachev's military aide, Marshal Sergei Akhromeyev, was less favorable to Chisinau. Instead of branding the Transnistrian "Republic" as illegal or unconstitutional, Ryzhkov and Akhromeyev called for freezing further steps on either side—thereby freezing the Transnistrians' gains in place.[124] Indeed, the Transnistrians felt free to ignore even the minimal degree of restraint requested by Moscow: Akhromeyev was sent partly to prevent them from holding (technically illegal) elections for a parliament in November of 1990, but the election went forward anyway.[125]

Gorbachev now again misplayed his hand. Snegur was not personally opposed to signing a union treaty—he favored signing a suitable one as late as May or June 1990[126]—but he was caught between pressure from below for independence and Gorbachev's refusal from above to help shut down Transnistrian separatism. Even in November, Snegur agreed to a Gorbachev-sponsored deal to respect the Soviet constitution in return for Smirnov not "dismembering" Moldova; and the Moldovan parliament signaled its openness to such a deal, voting to reconsider the language law and continue Union Treaty negotiations if Moldova's integrity was protected.[127]

Gorbachev, however, reneged, canceling a late November visit to Moldova in the face of Transnistrian recalcitrance. That decision gave further impetus to a December 1990 "National Assembly," at which hundreds of thousands of Moldovans rallying in Chisinau called for independence from the USSR and rejection of any union treaty, essentially forcing the Moldovan government to take that course. Only then, after it was too late, did Gorbachev concede even Snegur's legal point, issuing a decree annulling both Moldovan sovereignty and the establishment of the Transnistrian "Republic."[128] Both sides ignored it.

In the Soviet Union's last year, the Transnistrian "Republic" continued to receive aid from the Soviet government. When the Transnistrians decided to assert their financial independence from Chisinau, they had the helpful support of the Soviet Agro-Industrial Bank, which aided them in setting up their own national bank. This bank enabled the Transnistrians to begin withholding all tax payments to Chisinau in April 1991, crippling Moldova's government budget.[129] Around the same time, parliamentary Chairman Lukyanov instructed the KGB and interior ministry to unite their local operations with the Transnistrian "Republic's" structures; though apparently that order was not fully carried out.[130]

After the failed August 1991 coup in Moscow and Moldova's declaration of independence, the Transnistrians won the military backing that ensured the success of their counter-secession. In September, a group of Fourteenth Army personnel expressed "readiness, at the request of the people, to come to the defense of the population of the [Transnistrian] Republic and of the legitimate [*sic*] local bodies of power."[131] The source of this sympathy was to a large degree community loyalty: the majority of Fourteenth Army officers and enlisted men were Transnistrian residents.[132] At the same time, the commander of the Fourteenth Army, Major General Gennadii Yakovlev, was proving massively corruptible: Yakovlev drove in the streets of Tiraspol in a white Mercedes, presumably paid for with the sale of weapons available to the Fourteenth Army.[133] According to then-Prime Minister of Moldova Valeriu Muravschi, legislators from Russia were at this time encouraging Transnistrian negotiators to be intransigent in negotiations with Chisinau.[134] Since the Fourteenth Army's show of support occurred before Smirnov's election as Transnistrian president in December 1991, it probably helped reassure Transnistrian voters that Smirnov's confrontational course was safe—they were, after all, under the Army's protection.

Stunningly, Smirnov also managed briefly to secure the services of Yakovlev himself as Transnistrian Minister of Defense while Yakovlev retained his Fourteenth Army command.[135] Yakovlev's immediate superior pronounced the general's ministerial moonlighting to be "his own business."[136] Moscow announced Yakovlev's new job was "news to the leadership of the Defense Ministry" and ordered him to Moscow, but he was returned to his command before finally being removed for corruption.[137] With their supplier gone, the Transnistrians had to resort to stratagem in their quest for additional weapons. In one incident, a Soviet civil defense major loyal to Smirnov led a raid on an Interior Ministry depot to provide arms for the Transnistrian Guards.[138] In another case, Transnistrian guardsmen, obviously tipped off by officers of the Fourteenth Army, seized forty-one military transport vehicles at the train station when they arrived in Tiraspol by rail; Fourteenth Army officers looked on benignly.[139] Another tactic was for women activists and their children to lie down in the path of Fourteenth Army tanks to "force" the soldiers to part with the vehicles.[140]

General Yakovlev's successor as Fourteenth Army commander, Major General Yuri Netkachev, proved something of a contrast to Yakovlev. He tried at first to keep his troops from intervening directly in the ongoing fighting and repeatedly declared the Fourteenth Army's neutrality.[141] Snegur believed him,[142] and so was not deterred from continuing the fight. Netkachev, however, had difficulty controlling his own troops, and seems to have been out of his depth throughout his brief tenure of command. After April 1, 1992, when President Boris Yeltsin took over control of the Fourteenth Army for Russia, its units increasingly often supplied the Transnistrians with weapons and, when necessary, intervened directly to support them in combat.[143] From that point on, the Transnistrians prevailed in battle after battle. Indeed, the Fourteenth Army was so generous in "loaning" personnel and equipment to the Transnistrian forces that it became difficult to tell where one force ended and the other began.[144]

By this time also, most of the Moscow media were unabashedly spreading anti-Chisinau propaganda. False claims abounded that Moldova was about to unite with Romania,[145] in spite of denials by Muravschi and Snegur, now Moldova's president. Moscow television falsely accused Romania of military intervention. Charges of "genocide" were also published.[146] Undoubtedly, such "information" coming from a presumably trustworthy and friendly Moscow acted further to inflame the Transnistrians' fears and passions: Moldovan leaders visiting the area heard genuine expressions of fear, especially about the prospects of union with Romania.[147] At the same time, this propaganda built support in Moscow for military aid to the Transnistrians.

Russia also faced another problem in choosing its policy in Transnistria. As illustrated by the continuing defections of Russian troops to the Transnistrian side, Moscow faced the possibility of losing control of the Fourteenth Army.[148] This was a serious problem: while the Army consisted of only one division of troops, about 6,000 men, it had enough weapons, mostly in the Transnistria region, to equip several more divisions, so the implications of Tiraspol gaining control of those weapons would have been highly destabilizing. Yeltsin's April decision to subordinate the Fourteenth Army to Russia instead of to the Commonwealth of Independent States was apparently part of an effort to prevent it from defecting wholesale to the Transnistrians. This combination of facts—rising political support in Russia for the Transnistrians and rising concerns over keeping control of the Fourteenth Army—help to explain the increasing Russian support for Transnistria, including the tolerance of Cossack activity and the drift of the Fourteenth Army toward intervention on Tiraspol's side. As early as March 1992, Russian financial aid for Tiraspol was also renewed, according to the Moldovans.[149]

Not until the battle at Bendery, however, was Transnistrian victory inevitable. Even moderate Russian opinion was outraged by Moldova's Bendery attack, in spite of the provocations that had preceded it. The result locally was to push the Fourteenth Army decisively toward open intervention; it was Fourteenth Army tanks and artillery that played the decisive role in driving the Moldovans from the city.[150] It later became clear that the Army's intervention was not merely a local initiative but was directed from Moscow.[151] The effect of the battle, and of open Russian intervention, was to end Moldovan hopes for military success, and thereby to end the war. The replacement of Major General Netkachev by Major General Aleksandr Lebed was a further blow to Chisinau's prospects. Lebed quickly emerged as an extreme Russian nationalist, denouncing Snegur as a "fascist," plumping for the revival of the Soviet Union and/or Russian annexation of Transnistria, and refusing to allow his army to be withdrawn for at least 10 to 15 years.[152] Meanwhile, Russia began more overtly financing the Transnistrian "Republic."[153]

Once the Transnistrian side had captured essentially all of the territory it wanted, the Russian government intervened to broker a ceasefire agreement favoring Tiraspol, sending pro-Tiraspol Vice President Alexander Rutskoi to act as mediator. The agreement's chief features were that the Fourteenth Army would revert to "neutrality," while the ceasefire would be monitored by multilateral "peacekeeping" forces, primarily from Russia—and therefore partial to the Transnistrians.[154] Contrary to promises that the Fourteenth Army would be gradually withdrawn, Lebed was allowed to increase Fourteenth Army manpower by mobilizing local reservists.[155]

As Russia's support for his dubious republic became more clear, Transnistrian "President" Smirnov's position hardened: by October, he was insisting not on federation with Moldova but on confederation—de facto independence—with Tiraspol given its own army. As Snegur noted, Smirnov had little incentive to compromise given that he had "the complete military, political, and economic support of Moscow."[156] Russia's introduction of "peacekeepers" ensured the status quo would not change in Chisinau's favor.

COULD WAR HAVE BEEN AVERTED?

Although some conflict over ethnic issues in Moldova was inevitable, the history of the Transnistrian conflict is littered with opportunities to avert ethnic violence. The 1990 clashes could have been averted if the Transnistrians were less provocative in defying the language law and mobilizing armed groups, or if the Popular Front had refrained from organizing aggressive marches, or if the Moldovan government had used its Interior Ministry troops to restrain the Popular Front marchers instead of attacking the Transnistrians. The most serious violence of 1990, the Dubossary bridge incident, could have been avoided if the Moldovan government had resorted to patient negotiations or to assistance from the more-respected Soviet Interior Ministry troops. Moscow, too, could have prevented these clashes by taking the initiative to deploy interior troops to separate the sides before the clashes occurred: they had enough warning time to do so. Chisinau and Tiraspol were simply too aggressive, and Moscow too passive.

Those clashes, however, were minor; the important question is whether the serious fighting of 1991–92 could have been avoided. Again, the answer is that all three sides—Moscow, Tiraspol, and Chisinau—had their chance. For a third party—Moscow, in this case—the key tactic for stopping an elite conspiracy of the Transnistrian sort is to isolate the conspirators from outside help. Instead, Moscow aided the elite conspirators—providing troops to protect their illegal congress, financing to their illegal "republic," and propaganda support to boost their local legitimacy. Without such aid, the creation of the Transnistrian "Republic" would have been impossible, so ethnic war could not have occurred. However, the Soviet government under Gorbachev was more interested in creating pressure on Chisinau to sign the Union Treaty, so Moscow did provide the aid. After the August 1991 coup, the situation changed: while the Fourteenth Army had the power to disarm the Transnistrians, or at least to deny them heavy weapons, Yeltsin and Netkachev did not fully control it. The Fourteenth Army became so dominated by local residents that denying weapons to the Transnistrians or acting as neutral peacekeepers was impossible.

Tiraspol did, however, have choices about what to do with the Fourteenth Army's support. A security dilemma did exist, resulting especially from the fear of a new Moldova-Romania union. But the repeated assurances of Snegur, Muravschi, and other Moldovan leaders that union was not under consideration meant that Tiraspol had time; preemptive action to assure de facto independence was not essential for Transnistria. Smirnov and his colleagues, however, wanted independence for their own reasons, so they initiated the war. It is critical to note that most of the fighting came at the initiation of the Transnistrian side: while Chisinau could be said at times to have overreacted, Tiraspol started most of the battles. The Transnistrians could have used the threat of Fourteenth Army intervention to negotiate an autonomy arrangement, which would have become possible once tempers on both sides cooled. They chose instead to start a war.

The Transnistrian side does not deserve all of the blame, however; greater flexibility on the part of Moldova's leaders could also, most likely, have averted war. The Transnistrians' position as late as spring 1992 was to demand autonomy in a federal Moldova within the CIS[157]—a position Moldovan President Snegur was willing to accept by 1994. But in 1992, when the offer was made, Snegur refused even to discuss it.[158] The sides did set up a commission to discuss a ceasefire and separation of forces in June 1992, but it is doubtful that either side was yet ready to be flexible. For example, Pavel Creanga, deputy minister of defense and one of the negotiators on the Moldovan side, took the position that a political solution had to be reached before he would agree to pull his troops back from the area of conflict. If he pulled his troops back first, he feared, the Transnistrians could quickly move to occupy areas Creanga's troops had just vacated, especially Chisinau's remaining toeholds across the Dniester, should the agreement break down.[159]

GAGAUZIA: THE WAR AVOIDED

Absence of Gagauz myths and symbols

While the Gagauz have their own language and a distinctive history (flowing from their migration from Bulgaria), they did not have widely known nationalist myths and symbols before the 1990s. Indeed, there was virtually no literature about them at all before World War II. Instead, they were typically lumped together with their Bulgarian neighbors, whose customs they shared and from whom they were distinguished only by language. Subject to a forced Romanianization campaign under Romanian rule from 1918–40, the Gagauz did not have the opportunity to start developing a myth-symbol complex until a Cyrillic alphabet was created for them under Soviet rule in 1957.[160]

Even then the Gagauz did not formulate a coherent national narrative. One of the few 1950s-vintage books about their history, for example, continued to lump them together with the Bulgarians.[161] Similarly, instead of a myth of national origin, they were offered a dozen different theories that competed to explain their roots. The now-prevailing view is that the Gagauz descended from the Pechenegs and other medieval Turkic tribes from southern Russia; but others have claimed that they were Christianized Anatolian Turks, while still others have maintained that they were Turkicized Bulgarians. Furthermore, the Gagauz hardly had a national literature at all: only thirty-three books were published in the Gagauz language in Soviet times, and education for Gagauz children was solely in Russian.[162]

Political conflict, not war

As it did for others in the USSR, *glasnost* gave the Gagauz the opportunity to mobilize politically. The Gagauz also suffered economic hardship—

theirs was among the poorest regions in Moldova. They also had a realistic fear of extinction: virtually the only Turkic-speaking people who are Orthodox Christian in faith, the Gagauz are small in numbers (about 150,000 in Moldova), and their compatriots in Romania are mostly assimilated. Moldova's Gagauz could reasonably fear the same fate. Given that the experience of Romanian rule was within living memory, the Gagauz did not need a written nationalist mythology to fear union with Romania when that seemed a realistic threat, especially in 1990–92.

Indeed, in reaction to the Popular Front's chauvinistic rhetoric, the Gagauz mirrored many of the separatist moves of the Transnistrians, provoking several violent clashes. First, when repeated Gagauz demands for political autonomy were rejected in 1990, Gagauz elites announced the creation of a Gagauz republic separate from Moldova. As outlined above, that announcement prompted tens of thousands of Moldovan volunteers to converge on Gagauz areas that October to try to stop the Gagauz elections. Opposed by Gagauz and Transnistrian volunteers, the Moldovans were balked, but there were still a few violent clashes until leaders found a compromise, easing the strain. Smaller violent clashes recurred until 1993.

The Gagauz also had extremist elites, most significantly Stepan Topal, the leader of their secessionist movement. Gagauz elites had real reason for concern: while the language law was not particularly threatening to ordinary Gagauz (mostly peasants), it was much more threatening to elites, who spoke Russian but not Moldovan: their careers (like those of the Transnistrian elites) depended on maintaining the status of the Russian language. The combination of ethnic hostility and elite extremism was enough to spark a security dilemma: Moldovans feared the dismemberment, north and south, of their republic; while Gagauz feared assimilation and ethnic extinction.

But in spite of all these factors, there was no war. Instead, an autonomy arrangement—meant by Chisinau as a model for Transnistria—was signed in late 1994. Why no war? Some suggest that the Gagauz were too rural, or too few, to mobilize effectively, but this is not true: rural Moldovans mobilized en masse, and the South Ossetians and Abkhaz of Georgia, even fewer in number than the Gagauz, fought an enemy equally numerous. A more important reason was that less support from Moscow made for a less favorable opportunity structure: the Gagauz had fewer direct political and economic connections in Russia, therefore less economic and propaganda aid; and most of all, they lacked the Fourteenth Army and the weapons it could provide.[163] But South Ossetians too were at first isolated and poorly armed, and still they fought. The Gagauz could have had all the military help they needed from the Transnistrians; they did not want it.

A key reason why was elite attitudes. The fact that the Moldovans were from the start sympathetic to Gagauz concerns and willing to compromise made confrontation easier to avoid. This was in part because the Moldovans found the Gagauz less threatening. And the Gagauz elites, for their part, were also relatively flexible: though they did make moves toward separation from Moldova in 1990 and 1991, they continually signaled a willingness to compromise. Therefore a series of compromises, starting with one that ended the October 1990 standoff, succeeded in restraining the conflict long enough for the sides to reach the 1994 autonomy deal.

The basic factor underlying that elite moderation, however, was the absence of emotive myths needed to sustain mobilization and of the political symbols leaders could use to rally the public. The immediate physical threat to Gagauz was also limited: unlike the Georgian paramilitaries fighting the Ossetians, the Moldovans did not maintain military pressure on the Gagauz. The conflict was at first strictly about language policy, and later about the Gagauz separatist leaders' perquisites of office; it was not really about nationalism. Therefore, the Gagauz did not sustain their mobilization: Gagauz nationalist rallies never exceeded about 10,000, far fewer than for the Transnistrians. Absent large-scale nationalist mobilization, war could not occur.

Conclusions

The war in Transnistria was in no sense inevitable. The situation did include all of the key preconditions for ethnic violence: opportunity to mobilize, mutually hostile mythologies generating emotive symbols of conflict, and ethnic fears stemming from ethnic affinity problems and histories of ethnic domination. These conditions produced a politics of nationalist extremism and some ethnic hostility. But these conditions also existed in many places that did not explode into violence in the aftermath of the Soviet Union's collapse: Transnistria was the only case in which Russian-speaking separatists turned politics into a contest for group dominance and created an autonomous unit which went to war for its independence. What was different about Moldova?

The first factor is opportunity: Moscow made Transnistrian separatism and ethnic war possible by providing crucial help to Tiraspol at every stage of the conflict and on every key dimension. It gave diplomatic support, military protection, economic aid, arms, and propaganda assistance. That help was not, however, entirely the result of a coherent policy: different groups in Moscow favored different policies, and many of the Fourteenth Army's actions were taken either because Moscow did not control it or was trying to regain control of it. Nevertheless, the combination of Russian assistance to Transnistria, ethnonationalist extremism on the Moldovan side, and fears of union with Romania on the Russophone side created a security dilemma, which caused a spiral of fears that led each side to resort to coercion in "self-defense."

But the nature of that security dilemma is crucial: leaders in Chisinau and Tiraspol threatened each other's security because of the requirements for security they set and the way they pursued it. If, in spite of all the other factors, leaders in Chisinau and Tiraspol had been willing and able to search for peaceful methods of conflict management and to compromise instead of fighting for dominance, then there would have been no war. Popular Front leaders deserve some of the blame for pushing their government to spurn compromise and attempt to suppress Transnistrian separatism by force. Moldovan government leaders such as Snegur and Costas deserve even more for refusing to engage in an open dialogue, for being closed to the kinds of compromise that might have headed off violence, and for their frequent threats to use force—not to mention their repeated resort to it, most disastrously at Bendery in June 1992.

But most of the blame lies with Transnistria's self-seeking elites. Meddling from Moscow was successful only because of the efforts of communist leaders in Transnistria, who aroused their followers' fears and reawakened memories of conflict. Transnistrian leaders used their control over the media to pound home images of conflict, and they used their political and economic positions to mobilize supporters. They thus managed to define the stakes as dominance or submission, in spite of large reservoirs of moderate opinion available to be mobilized. And they defined submission to mean exploitation by fascist Romanians, in spite of abundant evidence that there would be no unification with Romania. The point of defining issues in such nonnegotiable terms was to ensure that negotiated solutions would not be found. The conflict, in short, was elite-led.

But even elite-led conflicts need followers. The Moldova case also shows the critical importance of nationalist mythologies and highly emotive symbols in motivating people for ethnic violence. Mobilization began over symbolic demands to raise the status of the Moldovan language and to shift to a symbolically important script. The first violent clashes resulted from the most symbolic of all acts: attempts to raise Moldova's national flag. Appeals to historical symbols mobilized people to fight, with current adversaries identified with historical ones: the Russophones were labeled "imperialist occupiers" as from Tsarist days, while Moldovans were "fascist occupiers" as from World War II. Elite-led violence only happens when elites' use of such emotive symbols make people want to come out and fight. Unfortunately, in Moldova such emotive symbols were available, and they worked. Among the Gagauz, such symbols were not available, and war was avoided.

Yugoslavia in 1988

Austria
Hungary
Slovenia
Ljubljana
Zagreb
Croatia
Romania
Vojvodina
Slavonia
Krajina
Novi Sad
Belgrade
Bosnia and Herzegovina
Serbia
Knin
Dalmatia
Sarajevo
Montenegro
Pristina
Kosovo
Adriatic Sea
Podgorica
Bulgaria
Skopje
Macedonia
Italy
Albania
Greece

[6]

Government Jingoism and the Fall of Yugoslavia

The civil war in the former Yugoslavia was the worst outbreak of violence in Europe since World War II. The human costs of the fighting in Croatia and Bosnia-Herzegovina included about a quarter of a million dead, millions of refugees, mass rapes and other atrocities, and devastation of entire cities and regions. The political costs included the embitterment of Balkan politics, serious splits within the western alliance and the United Nations over how to respond, and a major contribution to a Europe-wide refugee problem. Unlike the other cases examined in this book, the Yugoslav collapse was a major focus of the attention of outside powers, so great-power failure to prevent the violence raised the question: Did Yugoslavia sink into war because the West is helpless in such conflicts, because the West failed in Yugoslavia, or because Yugoslavia's problems were particularly intractable?

The answer centers on the ambiguously elite-led nature of Yugoslavia's ethnic wars. On the one hand, the nationalist myths of Serbs and Croats encouraged mutual hostility, as did the living memory of the last round of intercommunal violence during World War II. On the other hand, ethnic hostility was not high at first. Confrontation occurred because the leaders of republics and regions, especially Serbia's Slobodan Milosevic, intentionally stoked hostility and organized violent conflict so they could build ruling coalitions based on making other Yugoslav peoples scapegoats for the problems of their own populations. These actions encouraged followers to insist on extreme outcomes, which turned politics into a contest for dominance. At the same time, in their negotiations with each other, ethnic leaders adamantly insisted on those extreme demands, thus blocking any compromise. Indeed, their tactics of deception and duplicity acted to discredit the very ideas of negotiation and compromise.

These dynamics also created a security dilemma. The scapegoating rhetoric and discriminatory policies of the leaders led ethnic groups to mobilize against each other, causing residents of ethnically mixed areas to begin seeing their neighbors as threats. As ethnic tensions rose, these mixed communities, aided by extremist leaders, engaged in a kind of arms race that quickly led to the outbreak of violence. What made the security dilemma still worse was the fact that there were so many different ethnic conflicts in Yugoslavia, all interconnected, so that all had to be settled if the settlements of any were to be stable.

In sum, Yugoslavia's ethnic conflicts were particularly intractable, but mostly because its leaders were determined to make them so. The challenge for the West as a would-be third party conflict manager was, therefore, nearly impossible. To make a compromise settlement possible, western governments would have had to force key Yugoslav leaders to change not only their bargaining tactics but their central policy goals and ruling strategies. The absence of appropriate international institutions to coordinate policy and the absence of norms sanctioning such interference in internal Yugoslav politics further interfered with western efforts to exert what leverage they had. For all these reasons, forcing a peaceful Yugoslav settlement was probably beyond the West's power.

Yugoslavia's Peoples and Their History

YUGOSLAVIA'S REPUBLICS AND ETHNIC GROUPS

At the time Yugoslavia started to come apart, it was a loose federation consisting of eight "federal units"—the six republics of Serbia, Croatia, Bosnia-Herzegovina, Slovenia, Macedonia, and Montenegro; plus two autonomous provinces inside Serbia: Kosovo and Vojvodina. Five of the six republics were inhabited primarily by the national group for which it was named. The exception was Bosnia-Herzegovina, which had no ethnic majority, but its largest single group was Yugoslavia's "Muslims," who lived predominantly in that republic. Kosovo and Vojvodina were also established on an ethnonationalist basis: Kosovo was primarily inhabited by ethnic Albanians, and Vojvodina had substantial minorities of Croats and Hungarians.

The largest of Yugoslavia's ethnic groups according to the 1981 census were the Serbs (8.1 million people), followed by the Croats (4.4 million), and the "Muslims" (1.99 million) of Bosnia and neighboring regions.[1] All three groups speak the same language, Serbo-Croatian, although most Serbs and Muslims write it in the Cyrillic alphabet while most Croats use the Latin script. The main ethnic marker distinguishing them is religious tradition: Serbs are traditionally Eastern Orthodox in faith, the Croats are Roman Catholic, and the Muslims identify with Sunni Islam. The Montenegrins

(570,000 people) are also Eastern Orthodox speakers of Serbo-Croatian, and they traditionally maintained an ambiguous attitude toward their identity: they have been described as being unsure about whether they are a separate nation based on their distinct history, or whether they are simply the toughest Serbs. During the rule of the communists in Yugoslavia, the decline in religious faith among all of these groups and the promotion of the ideology of Yugoslavism worked to erode all of these identities. As a result, many people, especially government officials, military officers, and children or partners in mixed marriages, began declaring themselves "Yugoslav" by nationality: there were 1.2 million such people in the 1981 census.[2]

The other major groups all speak different languages. The Slovenes (1.75 million people) are traditionally Catholic and speak a Slavic language related to but distinct from Serbo-Croatian. The Macedonians are traditionally Orthodox, speaking a Slavic language closer to Bulgarian than to Serbo-Croatian. Finally, the Muslim Albanians (1.7 million people) and the Catholic Hungarians both speak languages unrelated to those of any of the others.

In spite of the nominal equation of national group with republic or province, the ethnic borders were not at all neat.[3] Only Slovenia (about 90 percent Slovenes) could be considered effectively homogeneous. Croatia was only 75 percent Croat, and its traditionally restive 12 percent minority of Serbs was mostly concentrated in the region that came to be known as the "Krajina." Bosnia, whose population was roughly 44 percent Muslim, 31 percent Serb, and 17 percent Croat in 1991 (plus 5.5 percent "Yugoslav," many of them Serbs),[4] was a patchwork quilt of ethnic diversity. Within Serbia, Kosovo was 90 percent Albanian in population, but Serbs feel strongly that it is the "cradle of their nation," so its status has long been disputed. Macedonia also has an Albanian minority representing upwards of 20 percent of the population. Serbia, Croatia, Bosnia, and Macedonia all faced serious ethnic tensions as a result.

HISTORICAL BACKGROUND

The history of Yugoslavia's conflicts begins with the medieval kingdoms of Croatia, Serbia, and Bosnia.[5] The Croatian kingdom reached its peak in the early tenth century, but was annexed by Hungary in the early twelfth century after its ruling dynasty died out.[6] The Serbian kingdom emerged somewhat later: founded in the eleventh century, it reached its peak under Tsar Stefan Dusan, who controlled much of the southern Balkans and was preparing for an attack on Constantinople at the time of his death in 1355. An independent Bosnia, meanwhile, already existed at the time of Dusan and reached its peak under King Tvrtko (1353–91), when it controlled most of modern Bosnia-Herzegovina and beyond.

All of these kingdoms were crushed, starting in the late fourteenth century, by the rising power of the Ottoman Turks.[7] As a result of their defeats, Orthodox Christian Slavs (whose descendants would identify themselves as Serbs) began migrating north to land held by Christian Austria. In the late seventeenth century, after the Turkish-Austrian border stabilized roughly on the current border between Croatia and Bosnia-Herzegovina, the Austrians established the *vojna krajina*, or military frontier, where they settled these Orthodox Christian migrants and gave them the job of defending the border from the Turks.

Hostility based on religious difference was historically high. A seventeenth-century English traveler reported, for example, that in Bosnia "the hatred of the Greek Church for the Romish was the [cause of the] loss of Belgrade... and is so implacable as he who in any Christian warre upon the Turke should expect the least good will from the Christians in those parts would finde himselfe utterly deceived."[8] Throughout the century, the Croatian Sabor, an assembly composed of Croatian noblemen, repeatedly protested the introduction of Orthodox settlers into Croatia's *vojna krajina*. In the early eighteenth century, this tension spilled over into religious riots, in which groups of Catholics or Orthodox attacked institutions of the other's religion. Such clashes recurred in the 1890s. Nevertheless, by 1905 Serbs and Croats had formed a coalition which became an important force in local elections in Croatia over the next decade.

The wars of the nineteenth and early twentieth century, in which Serbia regained its independence and expanded its power over Serbian lands, continued a practice which had been commonplace in earlier centuries: ethnic cleansing. During and after each of the major Serbian-Turkish wars, hundreds of thousands of people migrated from areas controlled by the other religious faith to areas controlled by their own. All told, over the course of the nineteenth century roughly one million Serbs migrated to lands controlled by Serbia, and a similar number of Muslims fled newly conquered Serbian lands for territories still held by the Ottomans. Many of those who did not flee were massacred. The Balkan Wars of 1912–14 kept the tradition alive: after Serbia captured most of Macedonia, a series of gruesome massacres led to the flight of roughly 200,000 Muslims from Serbian-held territory.[9] World War I elicited still more communal bloodletting.

As World War I ended, the Austro-Hungarian Empire fell apart. Faced with the choice of being treated as enemies by the Allies or joining with Serbia in a new South Slavic state, the Croats and Slovenes chose union with the Serbs as the lesser evil. The resulting "first Yugoslavia" had a troubled history, however. The Croats and Slovenes wanted autonomy within a federation, but the Serbs successfully insisted on a unitary state which they could control. The Croats' discontent rose further with the assassination of their national leader, Stepan Radic, in the national parliament by a Serbian deputy. In 1934, however, the Croats got their revenge as Yugoslavia's Serbian King Alexander was assassinated by an underground fascist Croat organization known as the Ustasha. Serbs and Croats then began groping toward a compromise, agreeing in 1939 on a new, if imperfect, constitution which gave Croatia autonomy.[10]

When the Nazis invaded in 1941, this fragile Yugoslavia fell apart. The Nazis installed the fascist Ustasha as a quisling regime in Croatia (including much of Bosnia), an act greeted with "a wave of enthusiasm" among Croats.[11] There followed a many-sided war of uncommon savagery. The Ustasha government began a frankly genocidal campaign of murder and terror against the Serbs, with one minister declaring, "there are no methods that we Ustasha will not use to make this land truly Croatian, and cleanse it of the Serbs."[12] Indeed, Ustasha tactics were so horrifying that even Nazi SS reports labeled them "bestial." The Nazi invasion and Ustasha terror resulted ultimately in the deaths of over 300,000 Serbs in Croatia and Bosnia, including many at the infamous concentration camp of Jasenovac.[13]

Meanwhile, a new Serbian guerrilla force, calling itself the Chetniks after Serb guerrillas of previous eras, tried to oppose the Nazi occupation but, dissuaded by the ruthlessness of the Nazi response, ended up focusing its enmity on Josip Broz Tito's communist-led Partisans instead. When Soviet advances in Hungary forced the Germans to withdraw from Yugoslavia, Tito's Partisans were left in control of Yugoslavia, where their first order of business was to massacre tens of thousands of Ustashas and Chetniks who fell into their hands.[14] Responsible estimates suggest that all told a bit over one million people in Yugoslavia died during the war, about half of them Serbs.[15]

After the war, Tito reestablished Yugoslavia as a country, handling the nationality problem by setting up a federalist system granting some cultural and political autonomy to the main national groups. He also, at first, suppressed any mention of nationalist ideas other than the Yugoslav idea and established himself, the national war hero, as the ultimate arbiter of ethnic disputes. When a resurgence of nationalist sentiment in Kosovo and Croatia in the late 1960s and early 1970s threatened to get out of hand, Tito ruthlessly suppressed it.[16] Then, in 1974, he conceded many of the nationalists' demands by vastly increasing the political autonomy of Yugoslavia's republics and provinces.

By the time Tito died in 1980, his legacy to Yugoslavia's nations was a mixed one. Ethnic tensions among individuals was relatively low, and intermarriage, especially in ethnically mixed areas, was high and increasing. But nationalist ideas had reemerged: each nation's writers and historians tended to trumpet the heroic deeds of their nation's history while obscuring its past atrocities and exaggerating the historical crimes of other groups against theirs.[17] Nationalist resentments were further encouraged by republic media campaigns in the 1980s which relentlessly harped on the aspects of federal economic policy that disfavored their own republics. In short, each national group was being encouraged to feel uniquely worthy, but uniquely disadvantaged, by the Yugoslav system. This potpourri of resentments was explosive: after Tito's death, Yugoslavia's weak central institutions lacked any mechanism for handling them.

Conditions for Ethnic War in Yugoslavia

opportunity

The political space that opened up in the Soviet Union as a result of Mikhail Gorbachev's policy of *glasnost* came a bit earlier to Yugoslavia as a result of the death of Tito. In the highly decentralized system established by the 1974 constitution, Tito himself had been the main restraint on ethnic self-expression, as he had shown by purging the Croatian leadership in 1971 and the Serbian leadership in 1972—in both cases on charges of nationalism. Tito was replaced by a collective presidency consisting of representatives of each of the eight federal units; such a body could not and did not have the authority to restrain nationalist excesses in any given federal unit. Tito's death made possible the nationalist politics that were to come.

The fighting, when it came, was organized by existing institutions—the federal army, the republic governments, and the Serbian communist organization (later transformed into the Socialist Party of Serbia). The fact that most of the participants controlled republic governments meant that each protagonist had a ready-made territorial base, and each was able to use the machinery of the government to form an army on the basis of republic police or civil defense organizations, using imported (at first, smuggled) arms. Slovenia and Croatia in particular took this approach. Serbia and the Bosnian Serbs had it easier because they inherited most of the former Yugoslav army as well. The Serbs in the Krajina region of Croatia were the exception: lacking both a government organization and a military force, they needed (and received) substantial help from Serbia to organize themselves politically and militarily.

myths justifying ethnic hostility and fear

Since this study focuses on the outbreak of Yugoslavia's conflict among Serbs, Croats, and Slovenes, it is their myths that are most pertinent here. Discussing the wars in Bosnia and Kosovo would require a separate study.

Serbian myths and symbols

The medieval Serbian kingdom left a legacy that was to shape Serbian identities down through the centuries. First, the establishment by Saint Sava, son of the first Serbian king, of an autocephalous (autonomous) Serbian Orthodox Church in 1219 decisively defined the Serbs as an Eastern Orthodox people distinct from their Catholic neighbors to the west. Sava also compared his later-canonized father to the biblical patriarch Abraham, suggesting that the Serbs were a divinely "elected people" whose land was promised to them by God.[18] Serbian legend also has it that had Stefan Dusan not died suddenly in 1355, he would soon have conquered Constantinople and been crowned Emperor, and his empire would have survived for centuries.

The most powerful myth of all for Serbs is the Battle of Kosovo Field. According to Serbian folk legend, the Serbian leader, Prince Lazar, was offered a choice by the Prophet Elijah:

Lazar, glorious Emperor,
which is the empire of your choice?
Is it the empire of heaven?
Is it the empire of earth?
If it is the empire of the earth,...
attack the Turks,
and all the Turkish army shall die.
But if the empire of heaven,
weave a church on Kosovo,...
take the Sacrament, marshal the men,
they shall all die,
and you shall die among them as they die.[19]

Lazar is said to have thought, "the empire of earth is brief, [but] heaven is lasting and everlasting," and therefore to have chosen the empire of heaven. Over five hundred years later, a Serbian Orthodox bishop praised that choice, saying of Kosovo, "Beside the name of Christ, no other name is more beautiful or more sacred."[20]

This song captures much about the glorious irrationality of Serbian national mythology. It casts the Serbian people as martyrs, eternally victims and eternally sanctified by God (reinforcing Sava's idea about Serbian sanctity). It also defines the Serb ethos as that of defenders of (and martyrs for) the Orthodox Christian faith against the oppressors, the Muslim Turks. By claiming moral superiority, it provides a psychologically useful way of rationalizing a terrible practical defeat. Finally, the moving poetry does exactly what a myth is supposed to do: give meaning to a confusing, and in this case painful, reality. In doing so, of course, it overlooks such embarrassing events as the Battle of Nicopolis where, in 1396—just seven years after Kosovo—Serbian forces, now subordinate to the Sultan, played a key role in helping the Ottomans defeat a combined French and Hungarian Crusader force.

The implied priorities, furthermore, are bizarre in secular terms: the way the poem describes it, Prince Lazar and his nobles chose sanctification for themselves over saving their families and their nation from five centuries of Ottoman domination. That medieval chroniclers should have glorified such a choice is unremarkable, since honorable if futile death in battle was highly regarded by medieval norms. But the fact that Serbs still praise a violent course of action which led to their own destruction—just because it allows them to uphold a belief in their own sanctity—is unfortunately relevant for explaining their behavior today.

A further wrinkle on the Kosovo legend, also important as part of Serbian mythology, is the myth of the traitor Vuk Brankovic. According to this myth—which is not entirely compatible with the myth of Lazar's choice of the kingdom of heaven—the Battle of Kosovo was lost because the traitor Brankovic betrayed Lazar and the Serbs. This myth has no basis in fact,[21] but it represents another important strand in Serbian thinking: that Serbia is repeatedly the martyr because it is repeatedly betrayed. This myth encourages a tendency in Serbian political culture constantly to suspect plots and treachery, and therefore to be suspicious of negotiations or deals of any kind, since they might involve betrayal.

In the nineteenth century, promoted by the newborn Serbian state,[22] the Serbian myths about their moral superiority began to take on a political connotation, implying that Serbs should rule a Serbian empire. The mid-century Serbian statesman Ilia Garasanin proposed several justifications for this thinking. His first argument was based on the historical myth of Stefan Dusan: "Historically speaking, the Serbian rulers, it may be remembered, began to assume the position held by the Greek Empire and almost succeeded in making an end of it, replacing the collapsed Eastern Roman Empire with a Serbian-Slavic one.... But now,... this process must commence once more. "Additionally, Garasanin claimed, "The Serbs were the first of all the Slavs of Turkey to struggle for their freedom with their own resources and strength; therefore, they have the first and foremost right to further direct this endeavor."[23]

Vuk Karadzic, a nineteenth-century Serbian linguistic reformer, added another argument for creation of a Greater Serbia. According to his linguistic theories, all speakers of the main Serbo-Croatian dialect of "stokavian" were Serbs—meaning that most people who identified themselves as Croats or Slavic Muslims were in fact Serbs, while the Croats of western Croatia were actually Slovenes. Karadzic admitted that Croats and Muslims identified themselves as such and not as Serbs; he just asserted that their self-identification was wrong.[24] Serbian politicians used these arguments to assert that all areas so identified as "Serbian" should be part of Serbia. Karadzic himself implied that the Serbian identity should be forced on such people: "Those of the Roman Catholic Church find it difficult to call themselves Serbs but will probably get used to it little by little, for if they do not want to be Serbs they have no other choice."[25]

The alternative to becoming a Serb is made clear in a Serbian literary epic of the time, *The Mountain Wreath,* which celebrates events of a century before, in the early eighteenth century. At that time, resurgent Montenegrin forces had captured some Muslim villages, and the Metropolitan of the Orthodox Church, Danilo, was uncertain how to treat the Muslim villagers. In the end, the prince tries to persuade the Muslims to convert to Christianity. All who refuse are killed, and the Metropolitan rejoices at the "victory." This poem "is still celebrated as one of the pinnacles of Serbian literary achievement" and is taught in schools.[26]

Serbia entered Yugoslavia with this goal of dominance intact. Thus in 1918, Serbian Prime Minister Nikola Pasic, who would soon be Prime Minister of Yugoslavia, said: "Serbia wants to liberate and unite the Yugoslavs and does not want to drown in the sea of some kind of Yugoslavia. Serbia does not want to drown in Yugoslavia, but to have Yugoslavia drown in her."[27]

The experience of World War II, in which Croatian troops refused to fight the Nazis while the Ustashas collaborated with them and massacred Serbs, naturally strengthened the Serbian self-image as a martyr nation always victimized by betrayers (the fact that there was also a Serbian quisling regime in Belgrade is conveniently forgotten in this context). But World War II also added a new set of symbols to the Serbian myth-symbol complex: the murderous Ustasha and the traditional Croatian red-and-white checkerboard flag, the *sahovnica,* which they adopted as their emblem. Given the documented and undeniable horrors of Ustasha rule, the Serbs had little need to exaggerate. Nevertheless, exaggerations and questionable stories came to form the core of Serbian mythology about the Ustashas. Thus, if responsible estimates suggest about half a million Serbs died during World War II, Serbian popular mythology asserts that one million Serbs were killed at Jasenovac alone. The depraved brutality of Ustasha leader Ante Pavelic is illustrated by an oft-told story of dubious authenticity which has it that Pavelic kept on his desk a basket containing "a present from my loyal Ustashis. Forty pounds of human eyes."[28]

To some extent, of course, mythologizing about the Ustashas was hardly necessary: the experience was within the living memory of many in the late 1980s, especially of Serbs still living in Croatia or Bosnia. But the myths and stories kept the experience, along with other elements of the Serbian myth-symbol complex, alive as part of Serbian discourse for decades to come. Thus Serbian novelist Dobrica Cosic, later the godfather of the Serbian nationalist revival, claimed in 1961: "Unification is for [Serbs] a creation of privileges for their language, and the assimilation of smaller nations,... and in unification they seek to obtain their 'historical rights' and 'state-building aims.'"[29]

Croatian myths and symbols

The Croatian founding myth is based on an assertion by the tenth-century Byzantine historian-emperor Constantine Porphyrogenitus that the Croatian people were led by seven siblings, five brothers and two sisters, in their migration to modern Croatian territory in the seventh century C.E. In the ninth century the Croatians were converted to Roman Catholicism, and a duchy of Croatia emerged as a part of Charlemagne's empire.[30] The conversion was considered by later Croats to have been a seminal event: Croatia's Catholic hierarchy was to be a mainstay of the national identity through the coming centuries, and in 1979 the Croatian Catholic Church organized a celebration of the 1100th anniversary of the conversion.[31] The first king of Croatia was Tomislav (910–c.929), who ruled a kingdom including modern Croatia, Bosnia, and the coast of Montenegro, and was described by the Emperor Porphyrogenitus as a major power in the region. This history established the basis for a self-image of military potency as a part of the Croatian national mythology.

The rise of the Ottoman Empire and the fall of the Serbs and Bosnians to the advancing Turks gave Croatia a new enemy. Indeed, one account has it that "If there is a Croatian national myth it is that of the *Antemurale Christianitatis,* that is to say the 'outer wall' or bulwark of Christianity."[32] The myth has some basis in fact, as Croatia was on the Austrian-Turkish border for some four centuries until Austria's 1878 de facto annexation of Bosnia-Herzegovina. Additionally, the continued existence of the Croatian Sabor and of the traditional office of Ban, or viceroy, was used to support the assertion of a millennium of essentially uninterrupted Croatian "statehood."

The first stirrings of Croatian national sentiment came when a few sixteenth- and seventeenth-century clerics and noblemen, dissatisfied with Habsburg failures to regain traditional Croatian lands from the Turks, began promoting the idea of a general Slavic or South Slavic community (they used the term "Illyrian" for the latter) which could join together against the Turks. Remarkably, many of these Catholic clerics were promoting the idea of Croatian unity with the Serbs or even the Russians, in spite of these other Slavic peoples' Orthodox faith. This was, in fact, a major difference between Croatian and Serbian nationalist thinking: while Serb identity was overwhelmingly defined by the Orthodox religion, the only all-Croatian institutions were the Sabor and the office of the Ban, so Croatian identity was more closely bound to the state and had to include all the peoples living in it; this factor made Croatian nationalism more inclined to pan-Slavic or pan-Yugoslav thinking.[33]

A brief occupation of Dalmatia (Croatia's province on the coast of the Adriatic Sea) by Napoleonic France in the early nineteenth century encouraged a rekindled interest in nationalist ideas in Croatia, which had died down in the previous century. One of the first of the modern Croatian nationalists was poet Ljudevit Gaj, who wrote in 1831:

Still Croatia has not fallen
We are in her still alive
Long she slept, but she's not vanquished
We shall wake her and revive.[34]

Far from being a Croatian chauvinist, however, Gaj came to promote a more egalitarian pan-Yugoslav nationalism. Considering the Croatian label too narrow (it did not at the time even embrace Slavonia, which is part of contemporary Croatia), he instead promoted an "Illyrian" identity, harking back to the earlier Croatian "Illyrianists" and relying on a popular myth that all Slavic peoples were descended from the ancient Illyrians. Additionally, when faced with a choice of which dialect to establish as the Croatian literary standard, Gaj and his colleagues chose stokavian, the one spoken by most Croats and Serbs—and the one promoted by the Serbian linguist Karadzic—instead of the dialect of their native region. Their ideal was to create a single, common South Slavic language. Ultimately, however, their primary focus on Croatian interests caused the failure of this part of their program, which attracted few Serbian intellectuals.[35]

The Illyrian tradition ultimately counted on Habsburg imperial assistance for its progress; when the monarchy turned to reactionary policies after the 1848 revolutions, those hopes were dashed, and a narrower Croatian nationalism began to gain adherents. Promoted by publicist Ante Starcevic, this approach mirrored the chauvinism of the Serb Karadzic: instead of labeling all speakers of stokavian as Serbs, Starcevic labeled them all Croats—hence to him, most Serbs were really Croats. Opposing Starcevic was a new generation of "Illyrianists" led by Bishop Josip Strossmayer and using, for the first time, the label "Yugoslavism."[36] The successors to this faction were later to promote a Croatian-Serbian coalition beginning in 1905 and to advocate the merger into a united Yugoslavia in 1918.

Many Croats immediately regretted that merger, however, as grievances against Serbian-dominated Yugoslavia's policies coalesced into a myth of Serbian chauvinism. Croatia was at first placed under martial law, and corporal punishment was reintroduced (the Habsburgs had banned it a half century earlier). Police beat some Croats for political offenses such as espousing a republic (in place of the Serbian monarchy in Yugoslavia) or even objecting to the term "Great Serbia." Croatian officers and the Latin alphabet were disfavored in the army, which became Serbian-dominated.[37] The list of complaints grew so long so quickly that Stjepan Radic, political heir of Starcevic and the lone Croat opponent of the Yugoslav idea in 1918, quickly became the Croatian national champion in Yugoslav politics in the 1920s until his assassination.[38]

Croatia's initial support for the Ustasha regime during World War II was partly the result of Croatian frustration with Serbian oppression. Ustasha savagery, however, was widely unpopular with Croats, leading some to join with Tito's Partisans in opposition to it. Franjo Tudjman, the ex-Partisan who became Croatia's nationalist hero, summed up Croatian ambivalence this way: the Ustasha regime was "not only a quisling organization and a Fascist crime, but was also an expression of the Croatian nation's historic desire for an independent homeland."[39] The symbol of this ambivalence is the figure of Zagreb's Archbishop Alojzije Stepinac, who was at first a Croatian chauvinist and supporter of the Ustasha. Later, Stepinac began openly denouncing the genocidal Ustasha policies, on one occasion famously confronting the dictator Pavelic and declaring, "The Sixth Commandment says, thou shalt not kill." He never, however, denounced the Ustasha regime; only its policies. As Tito's Partisans were coming to power, Stepinac, knowing that he would be blamed for his role—the communist regime was to label him "the priest who baptized with one hand and slaughtered with the other"—chose to stay and meet his fate.[40] For that choice, he became a Cardinal and a Croatian national hero; the anticommunist Pope John Paul II later moved to canonize him.

Slovenian myths

Unlike the Serbs and Croats, the Slovenes had no independent premodern history; their lands were simply provinces in the Habsburg domains for most of a millennium. The idea of a Slovenian identity based on the Slovenes' distinctive language was first formulated in the sixteenth century, but the real flowering of Slovenian identity came in the late nineteenth century with the start of a nationalist movement aimed at gaining the unification of all Slovene lands in a single autonomous unit within the Austro-Hungarian Empire.[41] The first Yugoslavia recognized the Slovenes' identity—it was originally called the "Kingdom of the Serbs, Croats and Slovenes"—but Slovenian politicians were usually marginalized in Yugoslav politics.

The nationalist myths that led Slovenia to independence in 1991 were primarily a product of the 1980s. For instance, Slovenes had presumably long recognized that the Serb-Croat arguments about the Ustasha past or over territorial borders had little to do with them: their boundaries were not in dispute, and they were neither perpetrators nor victims of the Ustasha terror. Similarly, while Slovenes had difficulty interpreting the meaning of the unique Slovenian popular music culture of the mid-1980s, they did agree that it was distinctively Slovene. The republic's government had a more specific issue: Slovenia was the most prosperous of the Yugoslav republics, and so, the leaders felt, it was unfairly taxed to provide funds for economic development in the poorer areas. Dissidents, meanwhile, pointed out that if Slovenia had not been subjected to the Ustasha terror, it was subjected to the communist terror. Thus overtaxed, overlooked, and repressed Slovenia could be seen as "a sacrificial offering on the altar of Yugoslavism."[42]

These ideas were eventually brought together in the simple slogan, "Europe now!" which like any good symbolic slogan, had multiple meanings. The implication was that Slovenia was historically part of the Austrian Empire—part of Central Europe—and was not historically connected to the Serbs' and Croats' Balkan squabbles. Slovene culture (including its popular music) was, furthermore, unique, and Slovenia had joined Yugoslavia to defend that culture; if Yugoslavia oppressed Slovenia instead, the Slovenes could think about independence in a new, integrated Europe. Finally, as Yugoslavia's most prosperous republic, Slovenia was already closer to the European Community than the others, so its economic troubles would be better addressed by joining the rich European Community rather than being dragged down by its poorer fellow Yugoslav republics.

FEARS OF ETHNIC EXTINCTION

One result of Yugoslavia's history is that every group has a history of having been dominated and repressed. The Serbs, of course, built this into a cult of victimhood, expressed to one journalist as follows: "We have been overrun, tortured, killed and stolen from by the Turks, the Austrians, the Bulgarians, the Germans, Tito..."; not to mention the Croats under the Ustasha regime.[43] The Croats and Slovenes, meanwhile, had also experienced Austrian and German (and for the Croats, Hungarian) domination and had in addition nearly a century's worth of resentment against Serbian dominance in Yugoslavia. Tito's Yugoslavia, as these litanies make clear, was considered oppressive by all three groups. Serbs felt discriminated against because Serbia was the only republic deprived of authority over autonomous provinces and because Tito was half Croatian and half Slovene—he did, after all, suppress Serbian nationalism. The Croats and Slovenes, in contrast, argued that the Serbs dominated most Yugoslav institutions.

The Serbs and Croats also faced an ethnic affinity problem. Serbs were the plurality in Yugoslavia as a whole—threateningly to the Croats—while they constituted potentially vulnerable minorities in Croatia and Bosnia-Herzegovina. Since it was those Serb communities which had experienced the Ustasha terror in living memory, fear of potential Croat dominance was no mere theoretical matter for them. The Slovenes faced a different sort of demographic issue: while they themselves posed no threat to other Yugoslav nations, they felt vulnerable to linguistic pressure from Yugoslavia's majority of Serbo-Croatian speakers. If Slovenia seceded from Yugoslavia, however, the Croats would lose a key ally against Serb efforts at domination, so Slovene fears indirectly affected the Serb-Croat security dilemma.

These conditions made it possible for fears of ethnic extinction to arise in all three communities. Economic conditions helped make it more likely that such fears would emerge.

Economic rivalries and declining living standards

The Yugoslav economy deteriorated badly in the 1980s, after having performed much better in the previous decades.[44] Unemployment rose from 14 percent in 1979 to 17 percent by 1988, while national income stagnated for a decade before beginning a serious decline in 1990. Inflation, already high in the 1970s, topped 100 percent annually from 1986 through 1990. This stagflation economy hit living standards hard: 84 percent of middle-class people saw their living standards decline in this period. Such economic hardship obviously contributed to people's willingness to mobilize politically.

Because the Yugoslav economy was primarily state-owned, improving it was primarily a state problem. And since the state made decisions on the basis of agreement among (ethnically defined) federal units, economic policy debates tragically became defined on ethnic lines. Regional trade-offs, for example between primary product exporters (mostly located in the poorer south) or exporters of manufactured goods (concentrated in the affluent north), would have arisen in any system, but this system gave them an ethnic tinge. Furthermore, since the federal government was toothless and all decisions depended on consensus, intransigence was rewarded—everyone who wanted a decision had to "buy off" the intransigent one just so the decision could be made. If a republic did not benefit from a particular policy, it could stop contributing to its implementation. Thus the republics stopped making contributions to the federal budget as early as 1986. And they argued for reforms that would benefit them: Milosevic's Serbs, for example, wanted to centralize power in the federal central bank to get a handle on the country's money supply and thereby control inflation. The Slovenes and Croats, in contrast, argued for more decentralization and marketization, maintaining that high taxes, government misinvestment, and overspending on social welfare (mostly in the south) and defense (mostly demanded by and benefiting the Serbs) were drags on the economy. Both sides were right, but neither side would concede the points of the other. The result was gridlock in economic decision-making throughout the 1980s and a politics of blaming other ethnic groups for economic problems. The rise of Ante Markovic to the premiership in 1989 finally ended the logjam, as Markovic devised some helpful policies, but by the time they began to show results, it was too late to stop Yugoslavia's descent into war.

How Ethnic Conflict Escalated

GOVERNMENT JINGOISM IN SERBIA

The first ethnic violence after Tito's death was the result of arguably the most intractable dispute in Yugoslavia—the Serb-Albanian dispute over Kosovo. Kosovo, as an autonomous province of Serbia, was symbolically subordinate to Serbia but after 1974 was its equal in practical terms. The Albanians resented the symbolic inequality—they were far more numerous than the Macedonians or Montenegrins, who had republics—and they blamed their economic underdevelopment on Serbian discrimination. Tension over these issues reached a new peak in 1981 when Albanians rioted all over Kosovo, with some demanding full republic status and others calling for independence. Given Kosovo's mythological importance to the Serbs, neither change was acceptable to them; government reaction was to increase repression in Kosovo.[45] The situation never really settled down: the Serbian minority in Kosovo was constantly demanding more protection, and by the spring of 1986, they were able to mobilize a crowd of 10,000 people to protest the arrest of one of their activists.[46]

Later in 1986 came the first step in a broader Serbian nationalist mobilization—the publication of a "Memorandum" on Yugoslavia's situation by the Serbian Academy of Art and Science. Most of the "Memorandum" was dedicated to Yugoslavia's economic problems, proposing a more centralized Yugoslav government as a remedy. Its most explosive portions, however, played on Serbian nationalist mythology. It asserted that there was an anti-Serb conspiracy causing "genocide of the Serbian population in Kosovo," and that, "but for the period of the existence of the NDH [Ustasha regime], Serbs in Croatia have never been as threatened as they are now."[47] The fact that the respected Academy made such charges gave them a weight in public opinion that protesters in Kosovo lacked. At the same time, the resonance of the charges with Serbian nationalist mythology and the asserted threat of ethnic extinction inflamed Serbian public opinion. The Serbian media added to the furor by printing unsubstantiated charges of brutal rapes of Serbs by Albanians in Kosovo.

This situation represented a political opportunity. While Serbian President Ivan Stambolic feared playing with nationalist fire, his deputy and erstwhile best friend, Serbian communist organization chief Slobodan Milosevic, was more daring. Sent by Stambolic in 1987 to quiet another rally of Kosovo Serbs, Milosevic saw an opportunity. Arranging for yet another rally, Milosevic dramatically sided with the crowd, shouting, "No one should dare beat you!" referring to the ethnic Albanian policemen who were protecting his group from the mob. The crowd immediately began shouting, "Slobo! Slobo!," joyfully picked up rocks they had trucked to the site, and began stoning the police. The Serbian media, already under

Milosevic's control, replayed the flattering bits of the episode on television, turning Milosevic instantly into a popular nationalist leader in Serbia. Opposed in this nationalist gambit by his old friend Stambolic, Milosevic quickly organized a coup to oust his longtime patron and moved up to take the presidency of Serbia for himself.[48]

Milosevic now adopted the platform implied by the Academy's "Memorandum"—which he had at the time quietly denounced[49]—blaming Serbia's problems on internal and external scapegoats. He argued that Serbs were uniquely disadvantaged by the Yugoslav order because Serbia alone contained autonomous provinces it did not control. Further, he claimed, Serbs were suffering from a political and economic system that did not work because it was too decentralized. Milosevic's proxies, meanwhile, began claiming that various enemies, named and unnamed, were conspiring against Serb interests, and they hyperbolically repeated the accusation of Albanian "genocide" against Kosovo Serbs. Milosevic's proposed solution was to reassert Serbian control in Kosovo and Vojvodina and to recentralize power over the republics in a Serbian-dominated federal government.

An important point about Milosevic's rise is that, while he was playing on real grievances, he was not carrying out a freely developed consensus of opinion. Milosevic had risen to power as a communist bureaucrat, and although his coup against Stambolic did ride on a wave of nationalist paranoia, that wave was in part the result of false media reports and staged demonstrations. After he took power, Milosevic used the state-controlled media, especially television, to build further an atmosphere of resentment, hatred, and fear among Serbs by purveying a distorted picture of ethnic relations.[50] The media identified Muslim Albanians, for example, with the old Turkish threat as the vanguard of a new Islamic menace to Serbs.

Milosevic combined his scapegoating policies with national chauvinism, encouraging extreme nationalist pride while demonizing other ethnic groups and encouraging Serbs to fear them. Even while Croatia was still ruled by antinationalist communists, for example, the Belgrade *Literary Gazette* featured cartoons depicting Croats as sadistic Ustasha thugs who delighted in dismembering Serb children.[51] To press home the point, Milosevic had mass graves of victims of the Ustasha terror opened and their remains exhumed in front of television cameras. After the nationalist Croatian Democratic Union (HDZ) came to power in Croatia, Milosevic's proxies focused their attention on it, labeling its members "executioners,"[52] while Milosevic labeled Slovenian policy "fascistic."[53] These charges of murder and "genocide" and endless invocations of the slogan "only unity can save the Serbs" created and fed the fear of ethnic extinction that is the driving force of ethnic violence.

Milosevic used all of the old emotional Serbian nationalist symbols in this propaganda campaign. He had the bones of Prince Lazar, the doomed hero of Kosovo Field, toured around ethnically Serbian parts of the country. He revived the double-headed white eagle symbol of the Serbian royal house—which had also been used by the World War II *chetniks*. Then, to solidify his claim to the mantle of Serbian royalty, he held a massive rally on the 600th anniversary of the Battle of Kosovo, at the battle site itself. His speech was an open appeal to traditional Serbian chauvinist martyrology, containing the usual distortions of history:

> Serbs in their history have never conquered or exploited others. Through two world wars, they liberated themselves and, when they could, they also helped others to liberate themselves.
>
> The Kosovo heroism does not allow us to forget that at one time we were brave and dignified and one of the few who went into battle undefeated.
>
> Six centuries later, again we are in battles and quarrels. They are not armed battles, though such things should not be excluded yet.[54]

Milosevic's purpose in all of this was the pursuit of power: he could consolidate his power in Serbia and extend it to other federal units by manipulating the symbols of Serbian nationalism. His bid to expand his power began in 1988 and early 1989, when he suppressed the autonomous Kosovo government and staged massive street demonstrations to push his supporters into power in Serbia's other autonomous province, Vojvodina, and also in Montenegro.[55] Since Kosovo and Vojvodina had a status equal to that of the republics in the collective federal presidency, Milosevic by this point controlled four of the eight votes in that body—just one short of a majority which would have enabled him to assert Serbia's dominance in the whole system.

His next step, at the end of 1989, was to increase the pressure on his most energetic opponents, the Slovenes. Serbian activists allied with Milosevic announced they would hold a "truth rally" in the Slovenian capital that December—the same sort of rally that had brought down the Montenegrin government less than a year before. The Slovenes would have none of it, working with the Croats to stop the trains carrying the (mostly Serb) protesters from reaching Slovenia. Frustrated, the Serbs canceled the rally and organized a boycott of Slovenian products.[56]

SLOVENIA'S ABANDONMENT OF BALANCING

Sabrina Ramet describes Yugoslavia after World War II as a kind of balance-of-power system among the eight federal units. When one republic seemed to endanger the system, either by threatening to dominate it or to leave it, the others coalesced against the threat in order to maintain the system. When the threat from Milosevic became clear, the remaining federal units, led by Slovenia, reacted at first by trying to balance against him.[57]

There was, however, a problem: As Ramet puts it, "Slovenes did not really consider themselves part of Yugoslavia."[58] Thus the Slovenes had two choices for escaping Milosevic's power: they could balance against Serbia or try to secede and destroy the entire system. Some incentives pointed in each direction.

Into this delicate situation stepped the Yugoslav People's Army (YPA), which managed to alienate both the Slovenian government and the Slovenian opposition by its bungled handling of a 1988 controversy over a leaked document. The Slovenian opposition claimed, with solid evidence, that the document was an army plan to declare martial law in Slovenia and force out the Slovenian government. (A similar plan was soon actually employed in Kosovo.) Indeed, the information was probably leaked by Slovenian President Milan Kucan himself as a way of fending off the army plot. Adding insult to injury, the YPA insisted on conducting the trial of the accused men—two journalists and a noncommissioned officer—in the Serbo-Croatian language rather than in Slovene as called for by the Yugoslav and Slovenian Constitutions.[59] Partly in response to the apparent YPA ambitions revealed in the disputed document, President Kucan publicly suggested a few months later that Slovenia should perhaps consider secession.[60]

Milosevic's later assaults, such as the planned rally of December 1989, pushed the Slovenes further toward secession. At the January 1990 Congress of the League of Communists of Yugoslavia, (the official title of the country's communist party), Milosevic tried again to assert control, this time by demanding increased centralized discipline over communist organizations in all the republics. The Slovenes were ready: they had come armed with a demand that the League be reorganized into a loose association of independent parties (a prelude to reorganizing Yugoslavia as a loose confederation). The Slovenes were not just defeated, but humiliated—every one of their proposals, even the most innocuous, was automatically voted down by Milosevic's solid Serbian bloc. The Slovenes stalked out of the Congress, and it collapsed.[61] The League of Communists did not survive the year.

VICTORY OF SLOVENIAN AND CROATIAN NATIONALISTS

The spring 1990 elections in Croatia and Slovenia brought to power governments fully as obstinate as Milosevic's. The new governments, led by Kucan in Slovenia and Franjo Tudjman in Croatia, declared as their goal the reorganization of Yugoslavia as a "confederation of sovereign states" roughly comparable to the European Community. Both republics further asserted that they had the right to secede entirely.[62] One purpose of such a confederal system, besides the salving of nationalist pride, was to make it impossible for Milosevic to grab control of the other republics. But the effect in Croatia was to counter Milosevic's plan for ethnic Serb dominance over Yugoslavia with a plan for Croatian dominance over the Serbs in Croatia.

Furthermore, the leadership in both republics was more extreme than public opinion. While only 26 percent of Slovenes reported feeling a strong attachment to Yugoslavia, 58 percent wanted autonomy within Yugoslavia rather than secession.[63] In Croatia, the discrepancy was larger: while the leaders pushed toward independence, 48 percent of ethnic Croats felt attached to Yugoslavia, as, presumably, did virtually all of Croatia's 12 percent minority of ethnic Serbs. At the same time, Croats did not at first believe the propagandistic claims that they were inferior in their own republic: according to one 1990 survey, 51 percent believed that Serbs and Croats were equal, and an additional 14 percent felt that Serbs and Croats were both repressed. Only about a third—34 percent—felt ethnically disadvantaged.[64] Most Croats wanted to stay in Yugoslavia and were not inclined to make the Serbs their scapegoats.

Tudjman's Croatian Democratic Union, however, had a substantial advantage in the election campaign, as it was able to tap the Croatian émigré community—many the descendants of former Ustasha officials—for campaign funds. It was therefore the best-funded party competing in the 1990 elections, with the most extensive organization.[65] One effect, according to a visitor, was that the HDZ had an enormous publicity advantage, with posters and advertisements everywhere far outnumbering the ads of competing groups.[66] Combined with Croatia's single-member district election system, this organizational advantage enabled the HDZ to translate its 42 percent of the popular vote into two-thirds of the seats in Croatia's parliament, giving Croatia a government much more nationalistic than its population.

At the same time, Tudjman's manipulation of Croatian nationalist symbols did strike a chord.[67] The fierce debate over Archbishop Stepinac's relationship with the Ustasha had reignited the year before as Milosevic's Serbian nationalist campaign was heating up.[68] Into this polarized context stepped the HDZ, which boldly revived the *sahovnica,* the red-and-white checkerboard flag, which was a symbol of past Croatian statehood so important in Croatian nationalist mythology—and a symbol to the Serbs of Ustasha genocide. The HDZ also tapped directly into the theme, represented by the Stepinac controversy, of the Croat nation's links to the Catholic Church, promoting the slogan, "God in heaven and Tudjman in the homeland."

The religious symbolism reached a climax at Tudjman's 1990 inauguration, when Tudjman was introduced with the words: "On this day [Palm Sunday] Christ triumphant came to Jerusalem. He was greeted as a messiah. Today our capital is the new Jerusalem. Franjo Tudjman has come to his people."[69] Additionally, Tudjman's party resolved to erect monuments to nationalist heroes. Even his intimations of chauvinism—his refusal to apologize for Ustasha crimes, his statement at a campaign rally, "Thank

God my wife is not a Jew or a Serb"—went down well with a nationalist electorate tired of being forced to reject its nationalism because of the fascist past.[70] A public willing to countenance a comparison of Tudjman to Jesus was willing to countenance much else.

CREATING A DEADLOCK

While leaders were manipulating nationalist symbols and creating a contest for political dominance, publics remained open to compromise. In Serbia, for example, one 1990 poll showed that Serbs considered economic growth more important than pushing Serbia's views on nationality issues, and in another poll, 71 percent of Serbs reported feeling an attachment to Yugoslavia.[71] Among Croats, a poll found that only 15 percent wanted independence, while 64 percent wanted to keep Yugoslavia as a confederation and 13 percent actually wanted a stronger central government.[72] Slovenian public opinion was harder-line, but still, a September 1990 poll showed most Slovenes favoring confederation over independence.[73]

Instead of heeding public opinion, however, Yugoslavia's leaders acted to make compromise impossible. In the view of Milosevic and the Serbian nationalists, for example, a confederation of the sort proposed by the Slovenes and Croats was unacceptable—it meant the end of the Yugoslav state. Furthermore, it would leave the Serbian minorities in Croatia and Bosnia-Herzegovina unprotected from the apparently chauvinist Croat and Muslim leaders in those republics. Should the other republics move to create a confederation, Milosevic therefore threatened, Serbia would declare independence and protect the interests of Serbs outside Serbia—implying the dismemberment of Croatia and Bosnia-Herzegovina to incorporate into Serbia areas inhabited by Serbs.[74] He later made this threat explicit.[75] Again, most Serbs clearly wanted to save Yugoslavia, but Milosevic had different priorities—he preferred a centralized Greater Serbia to a weak Yugoslavia. Meanwhile, he moved to strengthen his control over Serbia's provinces.[76]

Provoked rather than deterred by Milosevic's behavior, Kosovo and Slovenia reacted by declaring "sovereignty" in the summer of 1990, asserting that neither Serb nor Yugoslav laws applied to them. The connection was typical: though Kosovo was a province legally subordinate to Serbia, while Slovenia was a republic legally equal to Serbia, the Slovenes saw a threat in Milosevic's moves and were determined not to allow Serbia to do to them what was done to the Albanians of Kosovo. Serbia's response, a further crackdown in Kosovo and dissolution of the provincial government,[77] reinforced Slovene determination. In mid-November 1990, Slovenia announced that it would hold a plebiscite on independence in December,[78] the point of which was to preempt negotiations by creating a *fait accompli* of popular "insistence" on independence. Milosevic's response was to revive his attacks on "enemies... who are leading us to civil war."[79]

Tudjman, coordinating his action with the Slovenes, soon took a similar stand. In early December 1990, he declared that he, too, no longer believed a confederal Yugoslavia would be sufficient to safeguard Croatian "independence."[80] On December 23, Slovenians took the next step and voted overwhelmingly for independence. Three days later, the Slovenian parliament declared Slovenia "independent."[81]

Intriguingly, as this process unfolded, Milosevic was forced to moderate his rhetoric at home as the Serbian election campaign heated up in the fall of 1990. Confronted for the first time with the need to win votes and challenged on the nationalist right by the fiery Vuk Draskovic, Milosevic portrayed himself as the moderate in the race. Instead of continuing his scare tactics, Milosevic declared that the Croats and Slovenes could not be blamed for Yugoslavia's economic troubles—the opposite of his earlier message.[82] Draskovic followed his lead, calling for negotiations with Croatia and with the Albanians in Kosovo.[83] This episode suggests that the Serbian people did not really support Milosevic's confrontational policies.[84]

THE SECURITY DILEMMA AND ELITE CONSPIRACY IN THE KRAJINA

Rather than erupting from popular discontent, extremism was manufactured by the creation of a security dilemma in ethnically mixed areas of Croatia. The first step was the promotion of extremist propaganda on both the Serb and Croat sides. In the atmosphere of hostility created by an unrelenting drumbeat of hate messages, people who had lived peacefully as neighbors for decades were increasingly encouraged to see their ethnic cousins as a threat. In the context of Milosevic's national chauvinist propaganda and aims, how could Croats feel safe if their local police were mostly Serbs? When those police were replaced by local Croats—mostly national chauvinist true believers—how could their Serb neighbors feel safe in a Croatia unapologetically reviving Ustasha symbols? In a situation where the Serbian and Croatian republics were mutually hostile and popular mistrust that originated from propaganda was reinforced by scattered incidents of violence, a security dilemma emerged as each side began defining its security needs in ways that threatened the other side's security.

The security dilemma spiral began in earnest in the aftermath of the spring 1990 elections. At the time of the elections, the opinion of Croatia's Serbs was relatively moderate: like the ethnic Croats, most of Croatia's Serbs were inclined to see Serbs and Croats as equal.[85] Most therefore voted for the reformed communist party, which was led by an ethnic Croat but ran on a supra-ethnic platform. As a result of the Serbs' vote, the communists sent twenty-four Serbs to the Croatian National Assembly, and the vice president of that body was their leader. A smaller number of Serbs voted for the more radical "Serbian Democratic Party" led by Jovan Raskovic—a protégé of Serbia's nationalist novelist Dobrica Cosic—which sent five representatives to Zagreb.[86] But even Raskovic, the fiery Serb nationalist in the race, was neither chauvinist nor warlike: he wanted what amounted to legal equality and cultural autonomy for Croatia's Serbs.[87]

After taking office, however, the nationalist HDZ government continued its revival of Croatian national symbols associated with World War II-era Croatian fascists: a famous film clip, for example, shows the newly inaugurated President Tudjman kissing the *sahovnica.* The man who considered himself "the Messiah of the Croatian people" could hardly be counted on as a protector of minority rights.[88] And others in the HDZ were worse, some prone to making frankly racist anti-Serb statements.[89] Tudjman himself was famous for his work as a historian minimizing the number of Serbian victims of the Ustasha concentration camp at Jasenovac.[90] Soon after his election, Tudjman lent further credence to Serb fears by forming a 5,000-man "Guards" unit in the Croatian police which the Serb population feared was intended to be used against it.[91] And local Croatian authorities in outlying areas were often even more extreme than the government in Zagreb, occasionally intimidating and threatening or even bombing Serb residents and property. At the same time, ethnic Serbs were purged from government jobs, especially the police.[92]

Problems escalated further in late July 1990, when Croatia amended its constitution to assert "sovereignty." The local Serb majority in the old *vojna krajina* responded the same day by setting up a "Serbian national council," which Raskovic described as "a Serbian uprising without weapons." In August, Raskovic's Serbian Democratic Party (SDS) organized an unofficial referendum (declared illegal) on autonomy for their region, now simply called the Krajina. The referendum was clearly bogus: one Serb mayor claimed that 125 percent of his constituents voted in favor of the autonomy plan.[93] The point, of course, was to counter Tudjman's policy of Croat dominance in Croatia with a policy of Serb dominance in the Krajina.

Croatian bungling played an important role in feeding Serb anxieties: Tudjman repeatedly promised cultural autonomy to the Serb minority[94] and wrote that promise into the Croatian constitution of December 1990 after consultation with a board of Serb and Croat intellectuals.[95] But what the new constitution gave with one hand it took back with the other, dropping specific mention of the Serbs as a constituent nation in Croatia. It also specified that the only official language was the "Croatian language and the Latin script," thus excluding the Serbian literary variant and eviscerating the value of cultural autonomy by curtailing linguistic rights.[96]

This Croatian bungling opened the door for elite conspirators in the Krajina. Raskovic's deputy leader in the SDS was Milan Babic, a dentist from the city of Knin and a violent national chauvinist with ties to Milosevic's Socialist Party of Serbia. Belgrade had begun supporting the organizing efforts of such figures in Croatia as early as 1988,[97] but now they came into their own. Babic, soon Mayor of Knin, with his cronies established a Krajina militia that forcibly took control of neighboring Serb-populated towns. They also promoted rumors and fanned fears among Serbs about the allegedly genocidal intentions of Tudjman's government. An early provocation came when Milan Martic, a Knin police inspector and soon-to-be leader of the Krajina militia, wrote a letter effectively refusing to take orders from the Croatian Interior Ministry. Croatian police tried to reestablish their authority by force, but the Yugoslav People's Army turned back the Croatian police helicopters. The outcome was ideal for the Serbian extremists: not only had they gained de facto autonomy, but they had increased ordinary Serbs' fears by provoking the Croatian government into threatening action.[98]

Later, Milosevic's Serbian Socialist Party openly set up a special fund to "help"—that is, organize and arm—that militia and the Krajina government. A key purpose of those groups was to organize incidents of ethnic violence and provoke counterviolence in order to make more credible their warnings about threats to Serbs. In some cases, such as riots before a Serbian-Croatian soccer game in Zagreb in May 1990, violence was organized on both sides.[99] On the Serb side, important roles were played by a small minority of organized nationalist fanatics led by such men as chauvinist ideologue Vojislav Seselj. Seselj and his band were based in Bosnia, but, aided by Milosevic's secret police, they initiated the violent clashes in Croatia that made moderates on both sides feel obliged to fight in self-defense. Meanwhile, as late as May 1991, there were large Serbian protests in Krajina against the extremist leadership there—many Croatian Serbs were still willing to compromise.[100] Tudjman may have been willing, too, but the extremists in Knin, armed by Milosevic, ensured that compromise would be impossible.

Meanwhile, the YPA repeated its insistence that Slovenia's and Croatia's paramilitary forces were illegal and must be demobilized. In the fall of 1990, this demand had led the YPA to attack Slovenia's Defense Ministry building. In January 1991, the YPA unveiled an apparently doctored videotape of Croatian Defense Minister Martin Spegelj allegedly plotting terrorist operations and used the "evidence" to demand the demobilization of Croatian troops and the arrest of Spegelj.[101] The Spegelj issue was never resolved, and the question of republican military forces caused the collapse of virtually every agreement on the Yugoslav future, as the YPA continued to insist that the Slovenes and Croatians disarm, while the latter two, insistent about their "sovereignty" and mistrustful of the YPA, were reluctant to allow the YPA to maintain order on their territory.

INTERDEPENDENCE OF NEGOTIATIONS

The fact that the key leaders were actually aiming for confrontation was what made Yugoslavia's ethnic war happen. Their task was made easier, however, by the fact that the issues in Yugoslavia were so closely intertwined: none could be settled unless virtually all were settled. The secession of Slovenia alone, for example, was enough to start a wider war, because its absence would have given Serbia a majority voice of four votes against three in the collective presidency. Once that threat arose, Croatia had to rush into independence to avoid Serbian dominance. Once Croatia seceded, in turn, the position of Bosnia-Herzegovina became impossible. On the one hand, the majority of Bosnia's population was Croats and Muslims who feared Serbian domination and thus wanted secession. On the other hand, Serbs and Croats (who together also formed a majority) did not identify with the Bosnian "state."[102] Thus both Croatia and Bosnia-Herzegovina had to secede, and so became battlefields because their armed Serb minorities preferred war to separation from Serbia. Once Milosevic and the Slovenian leadership both concluded that they wanted Slovenia to secede, in short, the fall of most of the other Yugoslav dominoes became inevitable.

The Kosovo problem made matters still worse. The Serbs would never agree to make Kosovo an Albanian-dominated republic, especially not in a confederal Yugoslavia, and the Albanians were unwilling to settle for anything less. But the interim solution—continued repression of the Albanians—was not acceptable to Slovenia and Croatia, because they were determined to integrate with the European Community, which demanded respect for human rights in Yugoslavia, including Kosovo. Making matters worse still, the players least inclined to compromise were also the least likely to suffer the consequences of conflict: the most intransigent sides were the Slovenes and the Serbs, but it was Croatia and Bosnia-Herzegovina which, in the short term, paid the most in blood. The ultimate result in Kosovo was the brutal 1999 war, leading to the temporary expulsion of most Albanians, followed by the counterexpulsion of most Serbs after the NATO victory.

THE FAILURE OF NEGOTIATIONS

Given these complexities, the various negotiating fora set up by Yugoslav leaders looked increasingly hopeless. In fact, the Yugoslav leaders themselves had no faith in them at all. As early as October 1988, for example, then-president of Slovenia Janez Stanovnik remarked, "Earlier I advocated the view that we should talk to Milosevic. I'm sorry to say I don't see any more the point of talking."[103] The Slovene leadership had already concluded that any agreement by Milosevic to some confederal formula would merely set up a future attempt at establishing Serbian dominance.

This suspicion needs to be understood in the context of Yugoslav political culture. As one Slovene politician put it, "let us not forget we are in the Balkans, where lies and deceit are the highest moral values."[104] While obviously meant hyperbolically, there is more than a grain of truth in the claim, as shown by the blatant bad faith of all sides in the 1990–91 negotiations (discussed below). Milosevic was understood to be the master of the Balkan politics of deception,[105] which meant that all compromises with him were "rotten," to use Stalin's term—that is, they were subject to revision as soon as Milosevic found it convenient. Eventually, these suspicions led his interlocutors to decide to risk war rather than agree to any inherently unstable compromise.

The negotiating process was, therefore, rendered utterly fruitless by mendacity and bad faith on the part of all the key players in the months before the civil war. The Slovenes' record on the issue is exemplary. They agreed to a series of "roundtable" negotiations on the future of Yugoslavia in December 1990, but their parliament declared Slovenia "independent" on the day the roundtable talks began,[106] thus preemptively deciding the issue the negotiations were supposedly about. They found flimsy excuses to boycott the next two rounds of talks, then in February their parliament annulled all their legal obligations to Yugoslavia.[107] The next day, Slovenian President Kucan accepted a compromise proposal to save Yugoslavia that was incompatible with the parliamentary actions.[108] Another roundtable agreement, reached on June 6, was held up by a Slovenian boycott of the next round of talks, then destroyed by the definitive Slovenian declaration of independence on June 25. The Slovenes were encouraged in this behavior by Milosevic, who was intentionally pushing them to secede. As President Kucan later remarked, by January 1991 "It was obvious . . . that the Serbs would not insist on keeping Slovenia within Yugoslavia."[109]

Milosevic, meanwhile, was compiling an unexcelled record of duplicity in the negotiations. Soon after having gained election as a "moderate," Milosevic tried in January 1991 to force through Yugoslavia's collective presidency authorization for the YPA to disarm Croatia by force. Yugoslav Defense Minister Kadijevic was ready to do so, but the anti-Croatian coalition could not get a majority in favor of the proposal: Milosevic's four henchmen voted in favor, but none of the autonomous members did, so the proposal was shelved.[110]

Temporarily balked, Milosevic agreed on February 22 to a compromise plan suggested by Yugoslav Prime Minister Ante Markovic.[111] Just a week later, however, Milosevic's allies used a March 1 Serb-Croat battle in the Croatian town of Pakrac as a pretext to demand again that the YPA be authorized to disarm Croatia by force. Again there was no agreement, but the

YPA did act to stop the fighting after separatist Serbs had gained control of their neighborhood, securing the Serb gains from any possible Croatian counterattack. A frustrated Milosevic then declared that he no longer recognized the presidency's authority—contradicting his own insistence on maintenance of an effective Yugoslav government.

A few days later, massive anti-Milosevic protests organized by the regime's most prominent rival, Vuk Draskovic, almost shook Milosevic's hold on power—evidence of the unpopularity of Milosevic's policies. However, Borisav Jovic, Milosevic's chief lieutenant and Serbia's representative on the collective Yugoslav presidency, managed to trick and browbeat the Bosnian and Macedonian representatives into authorizing the YPA to put down the protests by force. The tanks rolled, the opposition was crushed, and Milosevic's hold on power was secured.[112]

Later in March, Milosevic met with Tudjman and agreed to stop supporting Krajina separatists,[113] but he showed that promise to be worthless a week later when he allowed Krajina to declare itself part of Serbia.[114] In May, Milosevic crippled the collective presidency by blocking what should have been the routine succession of the Croatian representative, Stipe Mesic, to the position of president of the collective presidency. By the time Mesic was elected, the war had already begun.

Croatia's Tudjman was, meanwhile, negotiating in equally bad faith. Tudjman matched many of the Slovenes' insincere moves, steadily moving toward independence and frequently boycotting negotiating sessions in between occasional incompatible agreements on Yugoslavia's future. A key move came in May 1991, when Croatian leaders borrowed a page from the Slovene tactical handbook and organized a referendum on their demand for a confederal Yugoslavia. The point, of course, was to narrow the field of potential compromise with the Serbs once the voters—encouraged by a pro-independence blitz in the media—predictably approved the demand. Just as important, a local Croat police commander decided on May 2, just weeks before the referendum, to attack the Serb-held village of Borovo Selo. The attack was bungled badly, and a dozen men were killed. Croatian official rhetoric now escalated from chauvinistic to hysterical, the media routinely referring to Croatia's Serbs as "chetniks" or "terrorists." In that atmosphere of nationalist fervor, the vote for Croatian independence was predictably overwhelming.[115]

On the strength of the referendum results, Croatia proclaimed its sovereignty on May 30, thus making its demands irreversible. Tudjman's willingness to risk war in this way was in part the result of miscalculation: according to journalist Misha Glenny, Tudjman seemed convinced that in the end, the YPA would not really fight.[116] If it did fight, Tudjman suggested, he would expect western military help.[117] In short, the Croatian government concluded that compromise was not worth pursuing, while a confrontation would not be too risky. Thus Tudjman reached an agreement with Milosevic on Yugoslavia's future on June 6, but abrogated that agreement only nine days later instead of giving it a chance to work.

In these conditions, where several parties had no intention of honoring their commitments or of acting in good faith, negotiations were worthless.

War

Even in these tense circumstances, war erupted only because key leaders intentionally provoked it. The first combat deaths came on March 31, when Milan Martic, by now the military chief of the self-declared Krajina region, sent a force of armed militiamen to take control of a national park in ethnically Serb territory. When Zagreb predictably sent a force of special police to eject the militiamen, the Serbs ambushed the Croats: one combatant on each side was killed in the ensuing firefight. The May battle at Borovo Selo, in the Eastern Slavonia region of Croatia near the border with Serbia, was the first serious battle of the war. It too resulted from violent provocations on both sides. On the Croat side, for example, Gojko Susak, an HDZ official close to Tudjman, personally went on a midnight foray toward the Serb-held village in mid-April, firing three shoulder-launched missiles at it with no apparent military purpose. Then, on May 1 and 2, incursions by Croatian police into the Serb-held village led to the death of a dozen Croatian men in an ambush. In the Croatian nationalist frenzy that ensued, Josip Reichl-Kir, the moderate Croatian police chief of the region who had tried to prevent violence, was gunned down by some of his own men; Susak, in contrast, was later made Croatia's Minister of Defense.[118]

There were last-minute attempts in May and June to head off the war that now loomed, but the Slovenes were determined to secede—they euphemistically called it "dissociation"—and when they declared independence on June 25, the YPA acted. The well-prepared Slovenes were unexpectedly successful, and Milosevic pulled the rug out from the YPA: Milosevic did not want to save Yugoslavia by confronting the Slovenes; he wanted to build a Greater Serbia by confronting the Croats. The YPA was forced to back down, and the war in Slovenia was ended by an agreement brokered on the island of Brioni by European intermediaries.

The withdrawal from Slovenia set the stage for the much more serious war in Croatia. Now that it was too late, Tudjman tried to avoid war, but the Serbian side was determined to fight. After months of intense warfare punctuated by the traditional savagery of the Balkans—ethnic cleansing, murder of civilians, torture, mutilation, senseless bombardment and destruction of entire cities, mostly by the Serbs—a ceasefire agreement was reached in January 1992 which left the Serbs in control of most of the Croatian territory they wanted. The Croatian ceasefire, in turn, set the stage for the immeasurably worse horrors of Bosnia. The Serbs prosecuted that war with their traditionally inflexible, self-defeating belief in their own unassailable righteousness, alienating in the process every ally they had. This gave the Croats the opportunity for revenge: when the end came in 1995, the Serbs were the victims of their own tactics, driven out of their centuries-old communities in the Krajina and western Bosnia-Herzegovina. The result was not a Greater Serbia, but a Greater Croatia.

Atrocities

In Yugoslavia's wars, the "shock troops" of ethnic cleansing and atrocity were the paramilitary groups under two infamous leaders, Vojislav Seselj and Zeljko Raznatovic, alias "Arkan." Between them they represent three of the key explanations for atrocities in ethnic war. Seselj is an example of the fanaticism that drives many fighters and that motivates atrocities. Seselj was a brilliant scholar who was jailed in 1984 for advocating a reorganization of Yugoslavia that would allow for Serbian domination. He named his group the "chetniks," harking back to an older tradition, and boasted on television of gouging out the eyes of his victims. Arkan, in contrast, was a career criminal specializing in bank robbery who was motivated largely by wartime "business" opportunities. The motivations did overlap: ironically, it was the mafia chieftain Arkan who led a well-disciplined group of fighters who were also the shock troops of ethnic cleansing, while the true believer Seselj led a slovenly, ill-disciplined lot good only for looting and terrorizing unarmed civilians. Both groups were well armed and well supplied by Serbia because they were useful to Milosevic: Arkan operated under supervision of the Serbian Interior Ministry, and Seselj worked under the YPA umbrella.[119] While atrocities were not specifically required by Milosevic's policy, these men were the available tools for starting a war to establish greater Serbia, which *was* Milosevic's policy. If atrocities came with the package, Milosevic did not object: when they became embarrassing, he denounced them and their perpetrators.

A vivid illustration of the mythological motives for atrocities is provided by Dragoslav Bokan, a soft-spoken psychopath and nationalist ideologue who committed atrocities on a smaller scale in Croatia. In one Croatian town, a unit led by Bokan killed and mutilated forty-eight Croats, either chopping them up with axes, burning them alive, or gouging out their eyes, afterwards leaving them on display to show off their handiwork. The specific choice of mutilation tactics comes from Serbian mythology, as these particular tactics are enshrined in memories about Ustasha atrocities during World War II. Bokan's explanation of his behavior makes clear the role of nationalist mythology in his motivation: "You must know where you stand. Are you a hero or a coward?...Will the nation honor you or shame you as a deserter?"[120] For men like Bokan, the hero and the righteous warrior is one who murders and mutilates.

Macedonia: The War Avoided

In the 1990s, Macedonia, with roughly a quarter of its population composed of ethnic Albanian Muslims, faced a situation very nearly as explosive as Bosnia's. The country was riven by deeply felt ethnic hostility between the two groups, ethnic Macedonian fears of extinction, and Albanian secessionism and resentment at government discrimination. So how did it avoid war?

The key fact about Macedonian nationalism is that it is new: in the early twentieth century, Macedonian villagers defined their identity religiously—they were either "Bulgarian," "Serbian," or "Greek" depending on the affiliation of the village priest.[121] While Bulgarian was the most common affiliation then, mistreatment by occupying Bulgarian troops during World War II cured most Macedonians of their pro-Bulgarian sympathies, leaving them open to embracing the distinct Macedonian identity promoted by the Tito regime after the war.[122] According to the new Macedonian mythology, modern Macedonians are the direct descendants of Alexander the Great's subjects. They trace their cultural identity to the ninth-century Saints Cyril and Methodius, who converted the Slavs to Christianity and invented the first Slavic alphabet, and whose disciples maintained a center of Christian learning in western Macedonia.[123] A more modern national hero is Gotse Delchev, leader of the turn-of-the-century Internal Macedonian Revolutionary Organization (IMRO), which was actually a largely pro-Bulgarian organization but is claimed as the founding Macedonian national movement.

One effect of this mythology is that it does not focus Macedonian enmity on the Albanians. The Macedonians had a long history of domination by Muslims: Macedonia was ruled by the Turks until 1912, and repressive Albanian lords had often acted as Ottoman agents in Macedonia. Macedonians' fear of group extinction, however, is focused as much on the fact that their neighbors are continuing the identity arguments of a century ago. The Serbs insist that Macedonians are misguided Serbs and want to renew Belgrade's rule over the region; while the Bulgarians, whose irredentist pretensions are better-concealed, claim Macedonians are really Bulgarians. Greeks, finally, argue that the term "Macedonia" can only apply to Greeks, so they annihilated their ethnic Macedonian minority through expulsions and forced assimilation and refused to recognize the Macedonian state by that name, imposing an economic blockade in the early 1990s that almost brought Macedonia to its knees.[124] Macedonians' greatest fear, in this context, is that Albanian demands for autonomy threaten the eventual dismemberment and destruction of the state by its neighbors, the "four wolves," perhaps by renewing the World War II pattern when Albania was given western Macedonia and Bulgaria ruled the rest.

The Albanians, for their part, probably are the descendants of an ancient people of the region, the Illyrians, so they claim western Macedonia as historically theirs. According to their national mythology, they have never accepted foreign rule: their national hero, Skanderbeg, led their fight against the Ottomans in the fifteenth century, and their nineteenth-century nationalist "awakening" was directed as much against the Turks as against the Serbs.[125] These ideas inclined them to reject Macedonian authority as well. There is, in addition, a deep cultural divide due to the two sides' mutually unintelligible languages and radically different styles of life, leading to ethnic hostility on both sides. Indeed, the savagery of the Balkan Wars of 1912–13 took place largely in Macedonia, so a twentieth-century precedent of extreme mutual violence was also present. But in the 1990s, violence took the limited form of occasional riots and police brutality against Albanians.

This was because several necessary conditions for war were absent in Macedonia. First, the Macedonians' political power assuaged their fear of group extinction, while Albanians did not fear group extinction. Another positive factor was that neither side's mythology was focused primarily against the other. Most importantly, however, elites on both sides wanted to avoid violence, so they were willing to make modest efforts to restrain their nationalist symbolism in order to prevent the conflict from escalating. Most of all, led by the liberal communist President Kiro Gligorov and Albanian community leader Nezvat Halili, they prevented politics from turning into an all-out struggle for dominance in Macedonia's first years of independence. In the constitution, for example, the Macedonians labeled their country "the civil state of the Macedonian people," a rather ethnocentric formulation, but they also guaranteed "full equality as citizens" to Albanians. Similarly, each Macedonian government included some Albanians and an Albanian party in the governing coalition: though the Albanians were frequently ignored on substantive issues, Macedonian leaders did commit to addressing some of their concerns. Albanian politicians, for their part, did not abjure brinkmanship, occasionally speaking about all Albanians "living in one state" and frequently boycotting parliamentary votes they disliked. But they stopped short of forcibly establishing a politically autonomous region, concentrating their efforts on pursuing more modest concessions on cultural and economic issues.

Given this modicum of mutual goodwill, the two sides managed to crawl slowly toward resolution of substantive issues, such as provision of Albanian-language education, while avoiding serious violence. The United Nations chipped in with a small peacekeeping force meant primarily to reassure the peoples of Macedonia of the good will of the international community and also to discourage any potential foreign intervention. During the 1999 Kosovo conflict, the government managed to walk a fine line, caring for the Albanian refugees from Kosovo but keeping them near the border—assuaging Macedonian fears about demographic "tipping" by not letting them into the interior of the country—and transporting as many as possible to other states. And when, in the heat of the late-1999 political campaign, the ruling ex-communists turned to national extremist rhetoric, the opposition nationalist party, symbolically named IMRO, countered by allying with the Albanian party and campaigning successfully on an economic rather than an ethnic platform. As in the rest of the former Yugoslavia, Macedonia's population voted against confrontational policies; but unlike elsewhere, its leaders heeded the voters. Macedonia thus illustrated how other Yugoslav republics might have avoided war, though it remained vulnerable to extremist incitement by leaders on either side.

The Failure of Western Conflict Management Efforts

Western Policy

Western policy toward the Yugoslav crisis, while not entirely coherent, was aimed in the right direction for discouraging violence. Theoretically, the most promising answer to a case of government jingoism, which Milosevic represented, is inducement to the extremist leader. Along these lines, EC policy as of December 1990 was to hold out the promise of closer association for Yugoslavia if Yugoslavia could meet several key conditions: democracy, free market reforms, human rights, and unity.[126] Later EC declarations repeated the same stance, reinforced by appeals for dialogue and against the use of force, in late March and in early May 1991.[127] The idea was sensible, offering the Yugoslavs economic benefits if they avoided conflict while attempting to deter unilateral secession, which would of course be the trigger for war. As noted above, however, it asked more than the Yugoslavs could deliver, especially regarding human rights in Kosovo.

When the United States finally took an explicit position on Yugoslavia, on May 24, 1991, it essentially followed this European line.[128] The parties in Yugoslavia, however, took from this stance only what they wanted to hear. Thus the Serbs noted western opposition to unilateral secession and concluded that the West would quietly support forcible suppression of the Croats. The Croats and Slovenes, in contrast, picked up on western sympathy for their opposition to Milosevic's centralism and on the West's opposition to the use of force, and concluded that the EC would quickly recognize and support them if they declared independence.

The main reason Yugoslavia's wars broke out, though, was because by the summer of 1991, Kucan, Tudjman, and Milosevic all preferred war to compromise. Western efforts to broker a compromise therefore faced an almost insurmountable barrier. The demonstrated bad faith of the three leaders in negotiations further complicated matters by discrediting the bargaining process. The attempt to create a new, credible process involving EC mediation in 1991 failed because Milosevic did not trust the would-be mediators and so refused to take part. Indeed, by then, the leaders may not have been able to reverse their positions even if they had wanted to. As then-Montenegrin President Momir Bulatovic put it, the republics' presidents were already "captives" of their own policies.[129]

Given these fundamental obstacles, it is clear that the western policy of verbal encouragement and economic incentives could not have helped. The only other idea actually suggested by some European diplomats—a peacekeeping force for Yugoslavia—would, equally obviously, have been ineffective. Peacekeeping troops are only effective when the parties to a dispute wish for the peace to be kept. With such basic issues unsettled, the parties in Yugoslavia were not ready for peace. In that context, any peacekeeping force would have been reduced to impotence, as UNPROFOR was in Bosnia in 1992–95; or else turned into a combatant, as the U.S. Marines in Lebanon were in 1983.[130]

Thus the first counterfactual about any successful western effort to prevent the Yugoslav civil war is this: the policy would have had to be different from anything suggested at the time.

THE BEST THE WEST COULD HAVE DONE

If it was to have prevented the outbreak of Yugoslavia's wars, the West's first task would have been to deter the Slovenian and Croatian declarations of independence, the immediate *casi belli*. The actual U.S. policy of June 1991—threatening to leave Croatia and Slovenia to the tender mercies of the YPA by withholding recognition—was about the best that could have been done, if it had been explicitly applied earlier and by all western powers. Simultaneously, though, the YPA and the Serbs had to be deterred from using force as long as there was no secession. Here, very strong measures would have been required: the YPA could have been deterred by nothing less than western threats to recognize Croatian independence and to arm Croatia—and possibly also provide air support—if the YPA attacked. Serbian military aid for Krajina separatists would have been more difficult to deter, but also less significant in the absence of YPA intervention.[131]

Deterrence alone would not have been enough, however. The Croats and (to a lesser extent) the Slovenes knew they risked YPA attack if they declared independence; they went ahead because the alternatives seemed worse. Thus the deterrence policy would have had to have been supplemented by reassurance. The Slovenes and Croats needed to be reassured that the alternative to secession was tolerable, in that Milosevic could be defeated in his bid to dominate Yugoslavia. The Serbs of Croatia, on the other hand, needed reassurance that their interests would be safeguarded in a sovereign Croatia: their fears of Tudjman were as well founded as the Croats' fear of Milosevic. In short, if the parties were to change their preferences, they needed reason to expect that an acceptable modification of Yugoslavia's federal structure could be negotiated and implemented.

This was one of the elements most conspicuously missing from actual western policy. Reassurance of the Croats and Slovenes would have required coercing Milosevic into good-faith negotiations toward a new Yugoslav order with outside (perhaps NATO) mediation. In the negotiations, the mediators would have had to give Milosevic a choice between compromise or facing his worst-case outcome—western assistance and recognition for Croatia and Slovenia to secede with their territorial integrity intact. Throughout the negotiations, the mediators would have had to wield the threat of siding against whichever party was recalcitrant.

OBSTACLES TO EFFECTIVE WESTERN ACTION

A key problem for outside intervention was that there was no auspicious time: after the December 1990 Slovenian referendum, it was probably too late for compromise; but before the elections in Serbia, Bosnia, and Macedonia the same month, half of the key representatives to any negotiations would have been lame ducks. Another issue is that the kind of intervention outlined above would have been dubious under international law and roundly denounced by many as interference in Yugoslavia's internal affairs—as indeed was western intervention in Kosovo in 1999 on just those grounds. Worst of all, policy was not agreed, even in the West: the British and the French at first tilted toward the Serbian side, while Germany was consistently pro-Croatian, and the United States was at first reluctant to lead.

Even if the West had managed to formulate an energetic, coordinated policy such as this, it probably would have failed.[132] The Slovenes, in particular, would have been difficult to coerce since they expected to win, while Tudjman did not believe the Serbs would really fight. On the other side, the YPA, deeply suspicious of the West and determined to suppress autonomous republican military forces, might have been provoked rather than deterred by western threats. And the Soviet Union's sympathy for the Serbs would have bolstered Milosevic in his intransigence.

Assuming these problems could have been overcome, the negotiations would still have had to reassure not only the republican leaders but other key groups such as Serb minorities outside Serbia—especially in Croatia. Croatia's Serbs were the victims of serious discrimination, and outside mediators would have had to extract substantial changes in Croatian policy to assure the Serbs that their interests would be protected. The Tudjman government eventually did concede the principle of autonomy for Croatia's Serbs, but it is not clear that it would have done so in the absence of military pressure from the YPA.

The most complicated issues would have concerned Bosnia-Herzegovina and Kosovo. Both the Serb and Croat communities in Bosnia-Herzegovina were demanding autonomy, and in any negotiations the obvious solution would have been some form of cantonization. But as the experience of the Bosnian war shows, drawing canton borders would have been a contentious process, and the Muslim plurality opposed the idea entirely. The Kosovo problem was even more intractable: more than in the other conflicts, the enmity in Kosovo—the symbolic heart of Serbia with an overwhelmingly Albanian population—was probably between the Serb and Albanian peoples, not just the leaders. Compromise may well have been impossible, and the differences simply too wide to bridge. This is why the Kosovo crisis finally exploded into war in 1999, in spite of determined international efforts to head it off. A similar effort in 1990–91 would probably have met a similar fate.

Conclusions

Yugoslavia's ethnic wars were a case of elite-led violence, primarily government jingoism promoted by Milosevic's Serbia, but less clearly so than some have suggested. The start of Serbian mobilization, as exemplified by the 1986 protest rallies in Kosovo and the Academy "Memorandum" later that year, came before Milosevic lent his support to the nationalist cause. Nationalist political pressures in Serbia were real, and a chauvinist nationalist mythology was deeply rooted, making ethnic violence possible even if there had been no Milosevic. Perfectly free Serbian elections in the late 1980s could well have brought to power a nationalist politician who would have followed a course similar to Milosevic's—the one outlined in the 1986 "Memorandum," which was an open call for Serb dominance of Yugoslavia. In that case, the conflict would have been mass-led.

But that is not what happened in Yugoslavia. Most of the nationalist hysteria in Serbia was the result of symbol manipulation by Milosevic, his proxies, and the media he controlled. After 1986, virtually all of the violence in Serbia was either organized by Milosevic's machine or aimed against his chauvinist policies: the leader of the March 1991 protest, Vuk Draskovic, was a more sincere nationalist than was Milosevic, but he was opposed to violence. In Croatia and Slovenia, the backlash against Milosevic's policies brought to power highly defensive nationalists who caused the conflict to escalate further by seeking dominance within their republics. All three of those leaders, Kucan, Tudjman, and Milosevic, chose to pursue policies so unyielding that the inevitable result was confrontation; they bargained in such bad faith that they seemed intent on discrediting the very notion of negotiation. At the same time, they manipulated nationalist symbols to raise their followers' expectations, thereby "burning their bridges" that might have allowed compromise and retreat. Finally, Milosevic turned confrontation into war by organizing and arming the frightened Serbs of the Krajina, sending fanatics like Seselj to provoke violence, and then sending the YPA to support the Serb side. The fact that all of the different conflicts were interlocking made the conflict even more severe, since a single intractable problem could make all other potential bargains unworkable.

This case vividly illustrates the value of the symbolic politics approach to explaining ethnic war. Yugoslav politics makes sense only in the context of the nationalist myths and symbols that the peoples of Yugoslavia found so moving. The power of Milosevic had everything to do with his ability to appropriate and manipulate the symbol of Kosovo—using the themes of martyrdom, betrayal, and moral worth to turn the battle story into a metaphor not only for the plight of Kosovo's contemporary Serbs, but all contemporary Serbs, while appropriating for himself the mantle of the sainted Lazar. He also used the symbolism of the Ustasha to promote conflict in Croatia and Bosnia; and he tapped the nearly two-century-old strain of Great Serbian chauvinism (tracing back to his predecessors Garasanin and Pasic) to tie these themes into the program that he nearly managed to accomplish. In the end, however, the Kosovo myth was also Milosevic's undoing, as his authority did not long survive his 1999 defeat and Serbia's loss of control in that region.

Symbolism—and the contradictory messages embodied in the same symbols—were equally important for the other Yugoslav peoples. For Slovenes, the symbol was "Europe," which separated themselves from their Balkan neighbors' squabbles and aligned them, in their own minds, with the prosperity of the West. For the Croats, the national symbols (especially the *sahovnica* flag) represented their long-repressed, millennium-old claim to statehood, while for the Serbs it instead represented the horrors of the Ustasha terror. And the Croats, like the Serbs, have their own claim to national sanctity symbolized by the ambiguous martyrdom of Stepinac, which made it possible for them to vote in 1990 for a man who in his campaign rhetoric compared himself to God and Jesus.

The result of these nationalist mythologies was to create a series of interlocked and intractable security dilemmas resulting from competing demands for dominance. Serbs in Kosovo, feeling threatened, demanded a degree of repression of the Albanians that not only threatened the Albanians but also threatened the Eurocentric goals of the Croats and Slovenes. Milosevic's grab for power based on Serbian chauvinism was inherently threatening to the other peoples of Yugoslavia, but the backlash that produced Tudjman and Bosnian president Izetbegovic was threatening to Serbian minorities outside Serbia, while aggrieved Serbs in Serbia felt put-upon if their demands for dominance were not met. What is notable about these security dilemmas is how much they were the product of demands conditioned by nationalist mythology rather than anything an outside observer would see as security requirements. In principle, the Serbs and Croats could easily have negotiated a *modus vivendi* either in Yugoslavia or in an independent Croatia, but the familiar nationalist myths and symbols caused both sides to turn to chauvinism, so each side became a threat to the other. In sum, the path to war in Yugoslavia was top-down nationalist mobilization which fanned ethnic hostility and created a security dilemma.

Macedonia's experience illustrates what might have happened. In Macedonia, leaders found ways to be nationalist without going to the extremes of chauvinism. Ethnic Macedonian leaders instituted tough policies that assuaged their group's fear of extinction, for example by limiting the inflow of Albanian refugees from Kosovo, but stopped short of provoking fears of extinction among Albanians. The Albanians, for their part, quickly backed off from early demands for secession, which threatened to inflame the Macedonians' existential fears. Equally importantly, even the "extreme nationalist" IMRO found a way to maintain their nationalist credentials without inflaming national hostilities, allowing a safe transfer of power in 1999.

Northern Yugoslavia's intransigent leaders, in contrast, made conciliation impossible. Given these leaders' attitudes, western policy faced a probably impossible task in trying to prevent war. Aside from the barriers of international law and international disagreements, and the lack of appropriate institutions, the Yugoslav leaders were probably too intent on their goals, too trapped by their own constituencies, or simply too stubborn to change their demands.

In the end, perhaps the most important point about the Yugoslav conflict is how very many things had to go wrong before ethnic war came. There was indeed centuries-old ethnic hostility in the Krajina and in Bosnia, but in 1980 it was still quiescent. There was a recent history of savage violence, but that was a byproduct of World War II: without the Nazis, there never would have been an Ustasha terror. Serbian and Croatian nationalist myths and symbols did justify hostility and chauvinism, but that was largely because Tito stamped out the attempts of liberal Serbs and Croats to devise more moderate alternatives in the early 1970s. Simmering resentments simmered even more because of Yugoslavia's economic downturn, which was reasonably traceable to some aspects of the country's nationality policy and less reasonably but more easily blamed on others. And all of these other problems might still have been managed if the pivotal Serbs had been able to keep less chauvinistic or at least more cautious politicians in charge while a new Yugoslav structure was built—if, in short, there had been no Milosevic. All four of the stories about ethnic war introduced in chapter 1 are right in Yugoslavia, but they are only right together.

[7]

The Power of Symbols

This book did not turn out as planned. Intending to write a book about the short- and medium-term causes of ethnic war, I found as I wrote that the sections on histories and myths were growing ever-larger in proportion to the parts about more recent events. This happened partly because the participants in these dramas themselves referred over and over again to such historical myths, churning out massive quantities of "scholarship" and propaganda aimed at proving one or another historical point. But that was not the primary reason for the shift in focus: the fact that participants are obsessed with historical myths need not be the main reason why they fight. In fact, most contemporary theories of ethnic war assume they are not, directing attention instead to manipulative leaders, conflicts of tangible interests, or "structural" factors.

Conditions for Ethnic War

What I learned in writing this book is that these other explanations only make sense if one first understands the attitudes about ethnicity of the people involved, and a key source of those attitudes is the historical mythology that sets the context for conflict. The symbolic politics approach is useful because it offers not only a way to take attitudes and myths seriously, but also a way of thinking about the interaction between elites and masses that is at the core of so much political behavior—in ethnic conflict and otherwise. Why do leaders lead as they do—what is the point, for example, of the ill-defined blather that fills their speeches? On what basis do masses choose to follow the leaders? The proposition that they are, respectively, manipulating and responding to symbols provides an answer.

The symbolic approach is elegant theoretically because it explains the origins and nature of ethnicity in the same way that it explains ethnic war. If ethnic groups are, as Anthony Smith argues, defined by their "myth-symbol complexes," then it stands to reason that those myths and symbols would be at the heart of ethnic politics, and at the heart of any explanation of ethnic war. The symbolic approach also explains how other, competing models of ethnic war work. What is it that manipulative leaders manipulate? Emotive symbols rooted in historical mythologies about events such as the Armenian genocide, the *Mohajirstvo*, Kosovo Field, or the Ustasha terror. How do those involved frame the tangible interests at stake in ethnic conflict? Mostly as group interests understood as the nation's historical rights—which are again rooted in historical myths. What defines the structure of the situation? According to game theory, it is primarily the preferences of the actors, which of course are rooted in their attitudes, which derive largely from the historical myths.

With a few exceptions, however, the symbolic politics approach has been overlooked in recent years because it is seen as vague and unscientific.[1] I have tried to show in this book that in need not be either: the variables it identifies for explaining ethnic war are quite specific. Are there widely believed myths that justify ethnic hostility? Are fears cast in terms of a threat of group extinction? Are hostile attitudes widespread, and do they take the form of a drive for political dominance? These questions can be answered by rigorous research. The use by politicians of symbols referring to those myths is even easier to detect, catalogue, and measure. This book has taken a few steps in this direction, showing that hostile myths were present in the cases examined and that fears of group extinction, ethnic hostility, and a drive for political dominance were motivating factors. I have also shown that successful politicians do refer to the myths and fears, with the explicit purpose of stirring their followers emotionally.

Another reason for the unpopularity of the symbolic approach is that it seems more complicated than alternative rational-choice explanations. Again, I have tried to show that these objections are not valid. The simplest rational choice explanations—asserting that anarchy leads to security dilemmas, or that ethnic war is explicable by assuming a few universal motives—are not logically coherent, and they fail to explain why war breaks out in some cases but not others. "Softer" rational choice explanations are more successful but require a lot more information about participants' actual preferences. As I have tried to show, those preferences change sometimes, in ways shaped by widely believed ethnic myths. In other words, you cannot conduct solid rational-choice analysis without knowing something about the myths that shape people's preferences.

Examining historical myths also provides a more satisfactory understanding of ethnic war because it offers a different kind of understanding.

Historical myths help give meaning to people's lives. "This is who we are," the myths say: "the victims of the Turks (or the Georgians or World War II fascists) who refuse to be victimized again"; or, "the heirs to an ancient statehood who are determined to take our rightful place among the nations." Since the outside observer is also searching for meaning—asking, "how can we understand what makes people do this?"—the best answer is to try to understand what the participants think they are doing, what meaning they attach to their actions.

My fundamental explanation of ethnic war lies in the meanings the participants see. What makes the Karabagh conflict explicable is that it is a clash between an Armenian nation obsessed with its history of genocide and an Azerbaijani nation easily mobilized by such slogans as, "Freedom for the heroes of Sumgait!" What explains the Abkhazia conflict is the confrontation between the obtuse self-satisfaction of Georgian chauvinists who, like Gamsakhurdia, will tolerate minorities only so long as they do not threaten Georgian political dominance and territorial integrity; and the myopic inflexibility of Abkhaz nationalists determined to revive a centuries-old Abkhazian "statehood" on every inch of its traditional land, even where virtually no Abkhaz live. In mass-led conflicts such as these—clashes of self-proclaimed victims—the widespread acceptance of historical myths justifying hostility and the reality of long-standing popular hostility essentially is the explanation for ethnic war. The rest is details.

In the more elite-led conflicts in Yugoslavia and Moldova, the picture seems muddier. Many blame the wars in Yugoslavia on the obvious villains—Milosevic and his tools and henchmen; Tudjman and his thugs—and would extend the logic to Moldova, where the cynical Smirnov outmaneuvered the blundering Snegur. Security dilemma dynamics seem to explain the rest. But that argument by itself does not fully answer the question. Why was it so easy for Druc to mobilize thousands to march against Transnistrian or Gagauz separatists? Why were Milosevic and Tudjman able so easily to gain support for their national chauvinist platforms even before they controlled the media? Or why, to put it differently, did so many people so enthusiastically support men like Milosevic, who was pretending to be Prince Lazar, or Tudjman, who seemed to believe he was Jesus Christ?

The answer, again, is historical myth. Before the rise of Tudjman, the Croats had already taken as their national hero Cardinal Stepinac, who could never bring himself entirely to disown the Ustasha regime any more than Tudjman could. Similarly, knowing that the 1979 anniversary of Croatia's conversion to Catholicism turned into a national celebration does not completely explain why Croatia voted for a man who compared himself to Jesus, but it is a necessary part of the explanation. On the Serb side, the Kosovo mythology Milosevic evoked was based on an oral tradition many centuries old and which was first written down by Vuk Karadzic almost two centuries ago. The Ustasha atrocities in Croatia and Bosnia, of course, occurred within living memory, so Milosevic's tools there—Milan Babic in Croatia, Radovan Karadzic in Bosnia—found extremist appeals quite easy to make. Yugoslavia's wars were elite-led, but they were possible because long-standing myths made people willing to follow their leaders to war.

It is worth emphasizing that these myths were already prominent when extremist leaders came on the scene. Even Milosevic did not create the Serbian nationalist mood—let alone the myths on which that mood was based. Rather, it was the novels of Dobrica Cosic, the infamous "Memorandum" written by Serbian academics, and the sensationalism of Serbian nationalist journalists *before* Milosevic's rise to power that created that nationalist mood. Milosevic discovered and harnessed its power, and then fed it, but he could not have become an instant hero by defending Kosovo's Serbs unless Serbs were already disposed to heroize someone who did so. The same was true in other cases—it was cultural rather than political figures who shaped the milieu over the years or decades before the rise to power of nationalist leaders. In Armenia, the nationalist novels of Khanzatian played an important role; in all three Transcaucasian republics, the works of nationalist historians and pseudohistorians were influential.

Historical myths explain ethnic conflict most of all by explaining how ethnic groups understand their interests. On the surface, for example, it seems that the Armenians and Azerbaijanis should easily have been able to devise a mutually acceptable autonomy scheme for Mountainous Karabagh. But the Armenians, with their historical myths about genocide and lost territories, felt that only the outright transfer of the territory to Armenia would suffice. The Azerbaijanis, in contrast, with their identity focused on the state's integrity and with their prejudices about Armenians, felt driven to reject not only such transfer, but any substantial autonomy for Karabagh at all. What made the situation so fiendishly hard to manage was not the existence of ethnic minorities, or even the tragic history of the two groups, but the way historical myths and hostile attitudes led them to insist on mutually exclusive political goals.

Indeed, the key cause of war in every case examined in this book, mass-led or elite-led, was that both sides insisted on political dominance in the territory under dispute: Karabagh, Abkhazia, Transnistria, the Krajina. Other issues at stake may have been, in principle, negotiable; wars happened because the drive for dominance in these areas was nonnegotiable. This means that analyzing "the structure of the situation" is not very useful: there were no opportunities for peace tragically missed simply due to lack of trust or misunderstanding. War happened because both sides, or in elite-led conflicts the leaders of both sides, were determined to have victory and dominance, ruling out compromise.

The insistence on group dominance that motivated these wars stemmed from two main sources. One is simple chauvinism rooted in national mythology. The Serbs, for example, have a strong theme in their national mythology about the unique worth of their people—heroes and martyrs of the struggle against the Turks, heirs to the imperial glory of Byzantium and Stefan Dusan, a people chosen by God—which to some Serbs gives them the right to rule others. Georgian mythology, similarly, promotes the view that Georgians have the right to rule over all "Georgian lands," a right they see exemplified by the glories of David the Builder and Queen Tamar but originating even earlier.

More universal across the cases is fear of group extinction: not all groups were so openly chauvinistic, but all the ones that fought felt fears of national extinction based on their national mythologies. The Armenians' mythology placed fear of a repetition of the 1915 genocide at the center of their concerns, while Azerbaijanis feared the destruction of their state, on which their identity depended. The Georgians feared the machinations of Russia, the demographic growth of "Tatardom," and the dismemberment of their state, while the Abkhaz feared assimilation or a renewed *Mohajirstvo.* Moldovans, a nation defined linguistically, feared Russification; while Russophones in Moldova feared renewal of the savageries of the Iron Guard if Moldova were to reunite with Romania. The Croats feared Serbian chauvinism while the Serbs of Croatia and Bosnia feared a revival of the Ustasha terror. In some cases, these fears of extinction were exaggerated or fanciful—mythical in the more common sense of the word—but they do seem to have been a necessary cause of ethnic war.

The result of these historical myths, chauvinist desires, and ethnic fears was hostility—that is, both negative feelings and the attitude that the other group was an enemy. Among the Georgians, hostility was measured in a poll: 38 percent disliked Abkhaz, and 32 percent disliked Ossetians; the Abkhaz attitude is nicely summed up by Fazil Iskander's report of feared genocidal Georgian intentions. The proportion of hostile Georgians—only about one-third—points out another fact: it is not necessary, even in cases of mass-led violence, for strong hostility to be universal or even prevalent among the majority; it is enough if the fanatics are a substantial minority and if the rest do not reign them in. One of the features of symbolic politics is that political outcomes may be driven by the actions of highly motivated minorities, not by majority preference.

In cases of elite-led violence, the initial degree of hostility can be even lower: as long as leaders have myths to work with, they can create hostility and fear by provoking conflict and violence. In Croatia, for example, majorities of Serbs and Croats polled resisted the temptation to claim they were disadvantaged, but substantial minorities succumbed to that temptation.

These minorities provided Tudjman and Babic with their bases of support. Those determined to fight then provoked enough violence to evoke fear and hostility, making increasingly aggressive forms of "self-defense" seem necessary. Even then, the desire to fight was hardly universal: draft-dodging in Serbia, for example, was a significant problem throughout the war. In Moldova, mass hostility was lower still: only tiny minorities opposed mixed marriages, for example, even in postwar polls. This overwhelmingly moderate opinion made war difficult to sustain; as a result, the Transnistrian conflict was the least bloody by far of the conflicts examined in this book. Still, the actions of several thousand true believers on each side was enough to provoke a small war.

A striking similarity about all of the myths and fears which led to ethnic war is that in all the cases in this book, they are rooted in real twentieth-century histories of violent conflict, and the degree of violence in the latest round of conflict is roughly correlated with the previous degree of violence. The two most violent conflicts, in Yugoslavia and Karabagh, came after episodes of comparable savagery earlier in the century—the Armenian genocide and the Ustasha terror. Georgians fought Abkhazians and Ossetians in 1918–21, but the massacres were fewer and smaller: that pattern repeated itself in the 1990s. The Moldovans and Transnistrians, finally, had only an indirect history of conflict, as it was Romania (which included Moldova only briefly) and the Soviet Union (which included Transnistria except briefly) which had done the World War II–era fighting, and neither side had aimed massacres against the other; the result was a conflict which barely qualifies as a war by statistical measures. Logically, of course, a history of warfare cannot be a requirement for ethnic war, since every conflict has its first episode. Such a history does not ensure ethnic war, either: Russians fought Ukrainians in the Russian civil war of 1918–21 but not in the 1990s, for example. Still, the pattern is undeniable.

Given that ethnic war is explained mostly by historical myth and experience, chauvinism, fear, and hostility; specific current conflicts of interest are of little importance for explaining ethnic war. In some cases, as in Yugoslavia and the Karabagh conflict, competing arguments about economic inequities may be used to justify both sides' demands for dominance, but they are the language of the dispute, not the substance of it: the Karabagh Armenians, after all, rejected as irrelevant Moscow's economic package. The sides wanted political dominance, not money. In other cases, as in Abkhazia, economic issues play essentially no role at all: the Abkhazians' economic complaints had been settled in 1978; their ethnonationalist ones had not been, so they mobilized again. Even in Transnistria, where economic factors played a substantial role, the ultimate issue was not money, but who would be in control.

The three core preconditions for war are historical myths that justify hostility; fear; and opportunity. But what is striking about these cases is the variation in how much opportunity was needed. In Karabagh, the first petition drives came with the first hint of *glasnost*, and the first incidents of violence there did not so much come in response to a weakening of repression as reveal that weakening for the first time. In Georgia and Abkhazia, there was a long-standing tradition of mass nationalist mobilization; what the April 1989 Tbilisi tragedy showed was that the communist regime was no longer able to justify even to itself the sustained use of the force needed to suppress mobilization. When ethnic hostility is strong enough to drive mass-led nationalist mobilization, the only opportunity required is the absence of an army willing to impose peace by force.

In cases of elite-led violence—government-led in all the cases in this book—opportunity has a similar meaning: the absence of a superior level of government willing and able forcibly to restrain nationalist mobilization. In Transnistria, the Moldovan government wanted to suppress Russophone mobilization but lacked the capability, while the Soviet government connived with the Transnistrians rather than restraining them. In Croatia, the YPA may have had the capability to impose martial law to replace Tudjman's government but was unable to extract the authorization to do so; while the Croatian government lacked the capability to suppress the Krajina militia. In these conditions, elite conspiracy is not too difficult: municipal leaders like Smirnov in Transnistria or Babic in Krajina need only demonstrate to leaders of other cities their personal stake in joining the conspiracy (using force, when necessary, to make the point). Government jingoism is even easier: once the Yugoslav central government was rendered harmless, nothing prevented a Milosevic or a Tudjman from mobilizing for and provoking war.

Processes of Ethnic War

On the other hand, nothing guaranteed the success of Milosevic and Tudjman. In a situation like Yugoslavia's, in which there are both deep currents of hostile mythology and deep reserves of mutual tolerance, war is not inevitable. Indeed, if in three out of the four cases in this book (excepting only Moldova), war was preceded by substantial mutual ethnic hostility, it is also true that in three out of four cases (excepting only Karabagh) national leaders' actions were critically important in making war happen. Mutual hostility, or the mythology on which to base it, is a necessary condition for ethnic war; but skillfully belligerent leaders are usually necessary as well.

Even the Georgia-Abkhazia conflict, which was essentially mass-led, resulted in war due primarily to leaders' actions. If Kitovani had not insisted on invading Abkhazia, there probably would have been no war; if Ardzinba had not tauntingly proclaimed Abkhazian "statehood," Kitovani might not have been provoked; and if Shevardnaze had been more responsive to them, the Abkhaz might have been more restrained. The Yugoslav conflict, similarly, was largely the result of deadlocks manufactured by Milosevic, Tudjman, the Slovenes, and the YPA. And the Transnistrian violence was the creation of Smirnov and his cronies, with the aid of conservatives in Russia, the Fourteenth Army, and the blunders of Snegur and Druc.

If the "why" of ethnic war is basically myths justifying hostility, the essential "how" is symbolic politics: leaders manipulating symbols that tap into nationalist myths to mobilize people for war. In the Karabagh conflict, this happened at the local level: hostility was so high that mobs were easily mobilized, even if national leaders tried to restrain them. But in all four conflicts, the story of ethnic mobilization is essentially the story of nationalist leaders appealing to nationalist symbols. The mechanism was emotional: supportive of the emotions or not, nationalist leaders agreed that the emotions of the crowds they addressed, often unpredictable, were the barometer of the success of their efforts. The function of myths and symbols was to harness those emotions and use them to formulate political demands. Appeals to reason, and the incumbent leaders who made them, were simply swept aside by the tidal wave of emotional nationalism channeled against them by the symbolic appeals.

In the South Caucasus cases, the symbolic issues were specific, longstanding political demands: Karabagh and Abkhazia had been subjects of territorial dispute at least since 1918, with irredentists in each case challenging borders imposed by (and blamed on) Stalin. The trick for orators was to appeal to any emotional symbols that might engage the sympathies of the crowd. Often this led to provocative actions and violence, as in the attempts by Georgian demonstrators to display the Menshevik flag in South Ossetia's capital or the attempts by Moldovan demonstrators to raise their flag by force in the Russophone city of Bendery. These flag conflicts were, of course, attempts to play out real political conflicts symbolically: the acquiescence of Bendery citizens in an attempt by ethnic Moldovan demonstrators to raise the Moldovan flag (which Russophones associated with fascist wartime Romania) in their city would have been understood as abandonment of their drive for autonomy. The interpretation would have been right: determined autonomists or secessionists would have, and indeed did, find it emotionally impossible to chose a more low-key tactic, such as ignoring the Moldovans' rally and then hauling down the flag after they left.

References to recent violence also played a powerful role—the Sumgait rioters, for example, were rallied by claims of Armenian atrocities against Azerbaijanis, while Armenian leaders thereafter used Sumgait as a symbol for the justice of their demands (and the fruitlessness of any pursuit of compromise). Somewhat less directly, Georgian nationalists used popular revulsion against the Soviet attack on the April 1989 demonstrators to justify not only demands for independence but also their view that the Abkhazian and Ossetian demands were really part of a Soviet plot to weaken Georgia—hence the Abkhaz were in a sense to blame for the April tragedy.

In these mass-led disputes, leaders' room for maneuver is limited: if they try to take too moderate a line, they are likely to be displaced by more extreme, or "truer," nationalists. In the Karabagh conflict, leaders of Armenia and Azerbaijan did not directly control the course of the conflict at all, as most of the fighting was done by more or less autonomous militia groups: this is the pure case of mass-led violence. The outbreak of Georgia's South Ossetia conflict was similar—it began even before Gamsakhurdia's election as Georgian leader and was facilitated rather than intentionally escalated by Gamsakhurdia. Moldova's early ethnic clashes, in October–November 1990, had the same character, with Druc playing the role of recently installed nationalist leader facilitating unofficial action.

On the other hand, in situations of elite-led violence, leaders provoke war in the absence of mass pressures to do so. In the Krajina, the key steps in escalating to war were manipulative efforts by the governments of Milosevic and Tudjman. While the Serbian people worried about their economy, Milosevic organized and armed Babic, Martic, and Seselj, encouraging them first to defy Zagreb and then to start fighting. The Croats made their success possible by a combination of clumsy heavy-handedness and open provocations. Political conflicts were severe anyway, but the actions of extremists in or supported by governments were needed to build up the will to fight. Once violence started, and the perpetrators remained unpunished, myths and stereotypes justifying hostility became all too believable among relative moderates; but had those sparks been stamped out, war might have been avoided.

The Moldovan war had the same dynamic. While the initial confrontation was mass-led, at least on the Moldovan side, the war itself was the result of decisions by belligerent leaders. I count Smirnov and the Transnistrians as the aggressors, because they repeatedly launched attacks on villages and police stations in their area controlled by pro-Chisinau forces. Chisinau, however, repeatedly responded with counterattacks that led to escalation on both sides, climaxing in the battle at Bendery and the open intervention of Russia's Fourteenth Army. Both sides were able to find plenty of soldiers willing to fight, but the reasons for the fights were leadership decisions, not popular insistence.

Putting the Pieces Together

I have argued that the necessary preconditions for ethnic war boil down to three: myths justifying ethnic hostility, fear of ethnic extinction, and the opportunity to mobilize around these themes. These preconditions lead to war when they produce genuine mass hostility, a politics of extreme nationalist symbolism, and a security dilemma. What is complicated about ethnic war is that these factors interact in different proportions in different cases, reinforcing each other in intricate feedback loops.

In pure cases of mass-led conflict, as in the Karabagh and Abkhazia cases, the myths, fears, and mass hostility are all of long standing and present in large doses on both sides. In other words, a relatively large proportion of both populations consists of fanatics, strongly chauvinistic and hostile to competing groups. In such cases, only the tiniest of political opportunities—typically, a modest easing of political repression—is enough to produce a mass-led politics of nationalist extremism, which immediately produces a security dilemma because the opposing sides define their needs in mutually exclusive ways. If the conflict is mass-led only on one side, as in South Ossetia (where mass hostility among Ossetians was initially low), the process works a bit differently: extremist politics on one side produces a security dilemma for both, evoking hostility and extremist politics on the initially moderate side. Either way, violence results because at least one party rules out compromise—not because the parties want compromise but tragically miss the opportunity.

In elite-led conflicts, the initial mix of ingredients is different. While myths justifying hostility must already exist, fear and hostility on the mass level may not. In those cases, the politics of extreme nationalist symbolism is what creates fear and hostility by manipulating the myths and provoking violence. This is what was done by Milosevic in Serbia, Tudjman in Croatia, Babic in the Krajina, and Smirnov in Transnistria. The rising hostility, fear, and violence creates a backlash on the other side, resulting in a security dilemma and the escalation to war. In these cases, only a few fanatics are necessary to initiate the violence, since they can be organized by the government and need not fear government interference. Their ranks may be reinforced by common criminals, such as "Arkan" in the Yugoslav case.

The implication for identifying possible future ethnic wars is clear: the main thing we need to find out is what people are saying about each other. Popular culture is perhaps the most important indicator. If news media or popular films and books promote chauvinist myths or negative stereotypes of certain groups in the society, then there is some danger of ethnic violence against the targeted groups. If a group's political demands include ethnic dominance for themselves, the threat of war is more serious. The more pervasive those themes, the greater the danger of violence. For the purposes of diagnosis, it matters little whether the media are leading or following public opinion, because they are surely doing one or the other, and probably some of both in the sort of feedback loop always encountered in ethnic politics. Opinion polls or focus groups can reflect the degree of popularity of these themes; politicians' speeches will show the role of the political elite.

Other indicators sometimes used matter little. Population statistics, for example, may not help: the 70 percent majority of Georgians in Georgia felt a fear of extinction, while the 2 percent minority of Abkhaz (only 17.3 percent in Abkhazia itself) were enough to fight and win, with outside help, a secessionist war in their region. Economic variables also matter little: any economic system not wholly one-sided will advantage some groups in some ways and other groups in other ways. This means that both sides will typically have some issues to complain about—rich Slovenia felt overtaxed, for example, while poor Kosovo needed investment. The issue is whether economic gripes are cast in ethnic terms—a function of attitude, not finances. Even the substance of policies on ethnic issues matters less than attitudes toward them: for a group fearing extinction, like the Abkhaz, equality is not enough; they are likely to demand preferential treatment. Where popular opinion is hard to measure, analysis of dissident speech can be revealing: Georgian and Armenian dissident writings in the 1970s, for example, gave a fairly accurate preview of the policies that would be followed when politics in their countries became more open.

WARS AVOIDED, WARS THREATENING

The wars that did not happen, though examined only briefly in this study, provide additional suggestive evidence for the symbolic politics approach. In two cases—Moldova's Gagauz and Georgia's Azerbaijanis—it is the weakness or irrelevance of nationalist mythology that helps explain the absence of war. The Gagauz people, a small and culturally deprived group, is surely threatened with group extinction, which might have motivated its members to react violently. There was no war, however—in spite of the provocation of violence by Moldovans—in large part because the Gagauz lacked a body of myth to which leaders could appeal to unite them in a fight. Their historiography at the time offered them not a "father of their nation" but a dozen possibilities. The Azerbaijanis had a more coherent national mythology, but its themes of territorial integrity and opposition to Armenians did not provide a basis on which they could mobilize against Georgians. Instead, they focused on their quarrel with the Armenians.

Equally interestingly, all four cases in which war did not erupt—Kazakhstan's Russians, the Azerbaijanis of Georgia, Moldova's Gagauz, Macedonia's Albanians—were cases in which fears were not usually cast as fears of extinction but merely as fears of repression or discrimination.

In Kazakhstan, this was in part because the Russians perceived a relative balance of power in which the Kazakhs could not so threaten them. In Georgia, it was because the focus of Azeri fears was elsewhere. In Moldova, it was mostly because the Moldovans quickly showed themselves responsive to Gagauz concerns for cultural and later political autonomy. And in Macedonia, it was because leaders on both sides were careful not to threaten the other side's vital security needs. If fears of extinction are a common cause of ethnic war, the methods for avoiding them are as diverse as the cases examined.

These considerations suggest that some of these cases pose a greater threat of future violence than others. The Gagauz case is most likely to remain peaceful, as the Gagauz have been given political and cultural autonomy and their national identity remains embryonic. The Georgian-Azerbaijani relationship is also relatively stable, mostly because both parties perceive larger threats elsewhere. The cooperative relationship between the governments of Georgia and Azerbaijan and the chastening experience of both nations' lost ethnic wars presumably also help.

Kazakhstan and Macedonia remain more volatile. Nationalist myths are strong in both places, and they do justify ethnic hostility. Hostile attitudes and ethnic fears are also present, especially in Macedonia. Indeed, in both places, political leaders openly worry about the possibility of an ethnic explosion. But that fact, paradoxically, is the main reason explosions have not come: leaders are sensitive to the danger and intent on avoiding it, so they have steered away from actions that opposing groups might see as a mortal threat. International factors also help: Russia has avoided provoking trouble in Kazakhstan, while the UN and later NATO worked to stabilize Macedonia. Macedonia's Albanians were perhaps also sobered by their people's catastrophe in Kosovo in 1999, though some may be emboldened by their final victory.

Identifying other locations for future possible explosions should be a task for further research, but it is not difficult to compile a list of places worthy of study. Ukraine could theoretically be volatile, but its population of chauvinist Ukrainian nationalists is confined mostly to the far west of the country, and is heavily outnumbered by the Russified eastern and southern Ukrainians who, far from being hostile to Russians, scarcely distinguish themselves from Russians. Iran's Azerbaijan region has readily available to it Baku's nationalist ideology, but Azerbaijanis in Iran have persistently refused to adopt it.[2] Unless these conditions change, both countries seem unlikely to face ethnic war.

More likely sites for explosions are Pakistan and Indonesia. In Pakistan, the dominant Punjabis face potential unrest from the Pathans, exemplars of a warrior culture *par excellence* with potential support from co-ethnics in nearby Afghanistan; and among Sindhis, claimants to an autonomous identity thousands of years older than Pakistan's[3] and hosts to the exceptional violence of multiethnic Karachi. The Baluchis, another minority group, also have a well-developed nationalist mythology, and indeed the Baluchis fought a separatist war in the 1970s. Symbolic politics is clearly at work: former Pakistani President Zia once complained about the "emotional ethnic appeals" by successful ethnic leaders among Baluchis and Pathans.[4] Either a breakdown of the Pakistani state or an overly heavy-handed attempt to stabilize the country by force could easily send Pakistan spinning into a multisided ethnic war.

Finally, the vast archipelago of Indonesia remains an incubator of ethnic conflict.[5] The province of Aceh, at the northern end of Sumatra, closely fits the symbolic model: with a history as an autonomous Sultanate going back over four centuries, there is a clear Acehnese historical mythology of struggle against the "imperialist" Dutch and ethnic Javanese who dominate Indonesia; indeed, a deeply rooted secessionist insurgency has been active there since the 1970s.[6] Violence in the Molucca Islands, formerly called the Spice Islands, took the form of religiously defined clashes between Muslim and Christian street gangs in 1999–2000, but the Moluccas do have a distinct history (including a violent separatist bid in the 1940s), and since the Christians are mostly indigenous to the area and the Muslims are largely immigrants from other parts of Indonesia, the possibility of extremist symbolic ethnic politics exists: there is already a security dilemma.[7] A third trouble spot is Papua (formerly Irian Jaya), comprising the western half of New Guinea, which although extremely diverse linguistically is united by religion (it is 60 percent Protestant in predominantly Muslim Indonesia) and a history of suffering from the Indonesian Army's long-term, brutal campaign against a ragtag group of insurgents. A common Papuan identity may be in the process of forming. All three could be considered guerrilla wars (over 1000 casualties in each case), whose escalation is restrained primarily by limited opportunity—the overwhelming superiority of the Indonesian army.

How to Prevent Ethnic War

If the central causes of ethnic war are myths justifying hostility, opportunity to mobilize, and ethnic fears, which together lead to hostile attitudes, a politics of extremist symbolism, and a security dilemma, then preventing war means preventing extremist politics by limiting opportunity in the short run and changing the hostile myths and attitudes in the long run. In the medium run, economic growth and aid can also help by offering gainful employment to potential paramilitary recruits and by ameliorating economic conflicts that might become ethnic flash points.

All of these conclusions are commonsensical, but the first two run counter to oft-expressed liberal principles. In the short run, for example, the liberal inclination is to leave political competition unconstrained and let the most popular politician win.[8] The trouble with this prescription is illustrated by the Croatian case: a national chauvinist came to power by winning 43 percent of the vote on the strength of a better-funded and better-organized campaign team. The opening of Croatian politics to relatively free competition came in the worst possible conditions: chauvinist myths were strong, there was a real ethnic threat (from a Milosevic-led Serbia), and economic issues were already defined along ethnic lines. In this context, the most skillful manipulator of nationalist symbolism was predictably the winner, and he promptly led his people into a war they would have preferred to avoid.

Banning ethnic politics is, of course, difficult. By the 1980s, hostile myths were so entrenched in Yugoslavia and the South Caucasus that the decay of the Yugoslav and Soviet empires could only lead to a politics of ethnic symbolism. In that context, avoiding war in Yugoslavia and Georgia would have required the emergence of leaders with the charisma and the moral greatness of South Africa's Nelson Mandela among the pivotal Serbs, Croats, and Georgians; and of leaders who had at least the solid decency of Mandela's counterpart, F. W. De Klerk, among Slovenes, Bosnian Muslims, and Abkhaz. In the case of the Karabagh conflict, it is doubtful that any leaders could have averted war after Gorbachev's 1988 fumbles, and perhaps not even before then. Repressive or consociational rule over mutually hostile populations is only possible as a stopgap measure, which can work for some decades but not indefinitely. When it has run its course, what matters is whether the populations are still mutually hostile.

This means that the most important measures for avoiding ethnic war must be those taken to recast nationalist myths and erode the bases of ethnic hostility over the long run. If promoted by leaders of the group itself, this process is likely to be controversial but workable. The main, though not only, rule must be: no justifying murder or murderers in popular culture or historical teaching. The archetypal example of what to ban from the classroom is *The Mountain Wreath,* the Montenegrin epic poem justifying massacre of Muslims that was taught in Yugoslav classrooms. As Tim Judah puts it, "It is in this way that, for generations, literature that elsewhere would have long been banned from schools is still...shaping the worldview of Serbian children."[9] Croats' defense of the Ustasha, Georgians' absence of remorse over Menshevik massacres of Ossetians and Abkhaz, and Turkish failure even to admit that the Armenian genocide occurred belong in the same category. The common element is absence of a simple admission: "We, too, are sometimes wrong." The great failure of Soviet and Yugoslav nationality policy was this error of omission: the failure to promote credible literatures of national apology.

There are other themes, of course, some more or less difficult to manage. Clearly worthy of discouragement is literature denying other groups' nationhood—e.g., historical assertions that Croats or Bosnian Muslims are "really" Serbs, or that Muslims or Serbs are "really" Croats, or that Abkhaz are relatively recent migrants to Abkhazia. More difficult to control is the pervasive literature of national victimhood, which underlies every ethnic war. These are more difficult to discourage because they usually express legitimate grievances, though in an exaggerated way. When the question is tone rather than substance, influencing a debate is difficult even for a government imposing censorship.

Censorship seems even worse, of course, if it comes from outside—then it is labeled "interference in internal affairs." Nevertheless, foreign criticism of media bias, historiography, and school curricula is not only appropriate, but potentially the most effective long-term policy tool available for discouraging ethnic war. Most of the countries in this study have in common a desire to emulate and eventually "join" the West, not only economically but also, to a degree, culturally. In that context, it is entirely appropriate for western governments and nongovernmental organizations (NGOs) to point out that history textbooks justifying ethnic violence or media outlets promoting prejudiced views of other groups represent barriers to the political and cultural integration of their countries into the western system—and represent reasons to divert scarce foreign assistance resources to countries with less chauvinistic values. Systematic programs of studying schoolchildren's history textbooks, in particular, would be useful for monitoring core national policies on ethnic issues and could be routinely reported the way human rights records are by the U.S. State Department or the Organization for Security and Cooperation in Europe (OSCE). More positively, governments and NGOs might try to promote the creation of new cultural outlets promoting interethnic reconciliation and nonchauvinistic national mythologies.

Peacebuilding is designed to be a way for the parties to a potential conflict to work together, with or without outside intervention, to change hostile myths and attitudes, but it is not a panacea either. The deeply personal nature of the peacebuilding process means that participants are likely to benefit most from intense engagement in relatively small groups. But participants in small-scale efforts face the reentry problem: their chauvinist coethnics tend not to be receptive to their new, tolerant insights. Yet expanding such efforts to ameliorate the reentry problem by including larger numbers of people may strain the capacity of the peacebuilders: spiritual or moral conversion is hard to mass-produce. Misdirected peacebuilding efforts may also be wasted: one study found that multiple peacebuilding initiatives keep a small group of Abkhazian and Georgian NGOs busy every summer, but the initiatives do not expand their efforts to other elite groups or to the grass-roots level, keeping their impact minimal.[10] Much, in short, remains to be done to develop and spread knowledge of effective peacebuilding techniques, especially including how to coordinate them.

The more usual list of foreign policy tools—deterrence, reassurance, inducement, and isolation—is appropriate for trying to head off ethnic violence in the short run, as discussed in chapter 2. By the time such tools become needed, however, conflict is already in progress, so the prospects for heading off violence have already deteriorated.

Other Uses for the Symbolic Politics Approach

The symbolic politics approach is useful for analyzing any political dynamic involving elite-mass interaction. Sticking to more or less international issues, consider Jeremy Rosner's argument about the politics of American foreign policy, entitled "The Know-Nothings Know Something." Rosner asserts, "The pollster may ask about an issue's popularity, but the politician is interested in its power"—in particular, the ability of an issue to symbolize for key constituent groups the idea that one's opponent does not identify with "us" (the constituents) or does not represent community values.

Rosner cites a Congressional campaign manager on his campaign's opposition to placing U.S. troops under United Nations command: "We were looking for symbolic issues that might hint at larger differences. It's like abortion. Maybe only 2 or 3 percent of the public lists it as their most important issue. But if you hear that someone is pro-life, you may also assume—rightly or wrongly—other things about what they believe, that they are anti-gun control and other things. This issue did that.... Sometimes little things can raise the specter that maybe this guy is squishy on some things that would make me uncomfortable." Specifically, the issue allowed the candidate to paint his opponent in campaign literature as "out of touch with basic Oklahoma values." As Rosner puts it regarding another election race, such attacks are "part of a debate about... what it means to be a patriotic American."[11] Since the campaign manager quoted above helped his candidate to win, it seems sensible to assume that he knows what he is talking about. Only a symbolic politics approach allows one to analyze his thinking, which is the thinking of successful politicians everywhere.

This conclusion seems obvious, but many contemporary scholars start from the opposite assumption—that voters are rational—and suggest that symbols are just "cheap talk," a shorthand form of political communication which is useful for people who are "cognitive misers." This argument assumes that voters think as follow: if this candidate knows how to eat a tamale, he knows about Mexican-American culture and can be expected to be sensitive to the needs of Mexican-Americans; therefore if I am a Mexican-

American, that is the candidate I should vote for, and I need not bother studying position papers.

Such rationalist arguments are logically consistent, but they fly in the face of the common wisdom among political practitioners—and are, indeed, the reason political scientists are so often despised by practitioners and journalists. Instead of arguing that it is "rational" to be swayed by a slogan instead of finding accurate information, it is simpler and more accurate to assume that many voters and campaign workers are swayed by emotion rather than interest, and that those emotions are most easily accessible through symbols. Why, for example, do American politicians find it so hard to compromise on abortion-related issues? Because, as the campaign manager quoted above hints, it tends to be more in their interest to be extreme—that is, unambiguous and clear—so the issue will work as a symbol. It also attracts pro-life or pro-choice activists to work for their campaigns: activists are emotionally motivated, and therefore tend to be extremist. The infamous Willie Horton television ad in the 1988 presidential campaign was successful because it appealed emotionally to racial prejudice and to myths about crime. Such examples are not exceptional but the everyday stuff of politics, and theories about politics should place them at the center of analysis. A symbolic politics approach would allow theorists to do this, resulting in theories not only closer to the truth but more practically useful as well.

A second illustration of the value of the symbolic politics approach is its answer to the question: Why do extremists tend to win power in revolutions? They repeatedly did so in the rebellious republics I study here: Elchibey in Azerbaijan, Gamsakhurdia in Georgia, Ardzinba in Abkhazia, Druc in Moldova, Tudjman in Croatia, Babic in the Krajina, all against more moderate rivals. Then there are the famous cases, such as Robespierre in France or Lenin in Russia. A basic explanation is the nature of symbolic politics: since the motive force of symbolic politics is emotional, there is little distinction between the intensity of feeling and the extremism of goals. As a result, the people who are most easily mobilized in nationalist (or ideological) campaigns—the ones, by definition, who most strongly support the cause—will also tend to be the ones least willing to make concessions to other groups.

As a revolution begins to age, therefore, and as the moderate participants begin to go home, the crowd on the street will come to be dominated by extremists, in a situation in which the new institutions of government are weak. This vanguard will tend to respond to extremist politicians and is likely to follow them to overthrow the moderates who may initially have taken power. In some cases, this will happen very early: one moderate in the Abkhazian nationalist movement, for example, reported being marginalized from the very beginning. The Abkhazian crowd wanted independence from Georgia, not something so ambiguous-sounding as "sovereignty," which had a less radical connotation in the Soviet context. Hence the Abkhazian nationalist movement was from the beginning heading determinedly toward confrontation with Georgia.

The symbolic politics approach also suggests a useful way to rethink the concept of the security dilemma in international relations. The usual model of the security dilemma is a situation in which both sides prefer cooperation to confrontation, but lack of trust and the inability to enforce agreements cause serious conflicts to erupt anyway. In the cases I examine in this book, this concept of the security dilemma does not apply. War erupted because one or both sides preferred confrontation to cooperation. The dilemma in preventing war is not in finding a way to enforce a desirable compromise but in finding a way to convince the sides that compromise would be a good idea: insecurity comes from hostility and fear, not uncertainty. And underpinning the hostility among Karabagh Armenians, Abkhaz, Cossacks in Transnistria, and Krajina Serbs was a martial tradition equating self-defense with military action.

Without the fear, hostility, and the norm favoring war, ethnic war is unlikely. This is one of the common threads among the briefly discussed cases that did not lead to war: Kazakhstan's Russians, Georgia's Azerbaijanis, Moldova's Gagauz, and Macedonia's Albanians. None of these minority groups has a mythology defining the majority as the national enemy—the Azerbaijanis focus their enmity on the Armenians, and the Albanians' quarrels are primarily with Serbs and Greeks. A similar pattern occurs in other relatively peaceful parts of the former Soviet Union. Russians in Estonia and Latvia, for example, do not feel hostile to Estonians and Latvians; while Estonians and Latvians lack a martial ethic. Russians fought a war in Chechnya largely because of strong mutual hostility and the violent Chechen culture; the almost equally secessionist Tatarstan avoided war with Russia because the two groups are not mutually hostile and neither glorifies war any longer.

I suspect that the same insight applies to international war. Historically, international hostility was the rule: countries were always ready to fight each other when their rulers decided it accorded with the national interest—or the rulers' own interest, if the two were distinguished at all. This was true almost throughout recorded history: attempts at conquest were accepted as the normal goal of international politics, and the myth of the glory of conquest was already ancient when the Assyrians conquered and exiled the Ten Lost Tribes of Israel in the eighth century B.C.E. Throughout early modern times, similarly, war was the sport of kings, and until World War I it was the accepted measure of nations. There was a security dilemma, therefore, because mutual hostility between countries was axiomatic: it could never be safely assumed that a potential rival would pass up a favorable opportunity to fight.

What this means is that wars before World War I were the result of a security dilemma defined by hostile attitudes and an acceptance of war. Even World War I, often held up as the ultimate example of undesired war brought about by a security dilemma, is better explained by hostility and militarism.[12] Soldiers in every major country marched gladly off to war, not reluctantly, and each country fought with aggressive aims against the others—the Germans and Austrians wanted to dominate Europe, while the Entente powers wanted to divide the Ottoman Empire and conquer Germany's colonies. The soldiers were sent to fight with the rhetoric of hostile national mythologies ringing in their ears. The best of the more recent examples of a security dilemma leading to war—the 1967 Arab-Israeli war—is also better explained by hostility and militarism. While the evidence suggests that Egypt's Nasser was not planning to start a war, his regime was explicit about its desire to annihilate the state of Israel: the security dilemma Israel faced was the result of this intense and open hostility, not merely its strategic position.

In sum, security dilemmas that lead to war are not the result of international anarchy. Where there is mutual hostility and a militarist tradition, as in Karabagh, a security dilemma can emerge even if there is a previously unquestioned common authority. Conversely, where there is no mutual hostility and militarism is weak, as in contemporary Europe and North America, there is no security dilemma in spite of the absence of any common authority. Security dilemmas result from hostility and militarism, not from anarchy.[13]

What these arguments are meant to show is the broad value and applicability of the symbolic politics approach. Using the symbolic approach requires a focus on different factors than are usually studied—we need to know less about people's "objective" interests and more about their attitudes and the myths and symbols that influence those attitudes. The case studies in this book have shown that the symbolic politics approach is the most useful for explaining at least these four cases of ethnic civil wars, and the approach can be applied to all ethnic wars. I have tried to suggest in these concluding thoughts that the symbolic approach can also explain other kinds of politics—the politics of American political campaigns, the politics of revolutions, and the politics of international war and peace. Such a useful and common-sense approach deserves more attention.

Notes

Chapter 1. Stories about Ethnic War

1. Laura Silber and Allan Little, *Yugoslavia: Death of a Nation,* rev. ed. (New York: Penguin Books, 1997), p. 245.
2. Rezak Hukanovic, "The Evil at Omarska," *The New Republic,* February 12, 1996, p. 29.
3. Robert D. Kaplan, *Balkan Ghosts: A Journey through History* (New York: Random House, 1993), p. xxi.
4. Ibid., p. 22.
5. Andrej Gustincic, quoted in Misha Glenny, *The Fall of Yugoslavia: The Third Balkan War,* 3d rev. ed. (London: Penguin, 1996), p. 170.
6. Ibid., pp. 172–73.
7. Bogdan Denitch, *Ethnic Nationalism: The Tragic Death of Yugoslavia* (Minneapolis: University of Minnesota Press, 1994), p. 62.
8. V. P. Gagnon, "Ethnic Nationalism and International Conflict: The Case of Serbia," *International Security* 19, no. 3 (1994/95): 132.
9. Denitch, *Ethnic Nationalism,* p. 62.
10. Susan Woodward, *Balkan Tragedy* (Washington, D.C.: Brookings Institution, 1995).
11. Barry R. Posen, "The Security Dilemma and Ethnic Conflict," *Survival* 35, no. 1 (1993): 27–47.
12. Two such attempts are Lenard Cohen, *Broken Bonds: Yugoslavia's Disintegration and Balkan Politics in Transition,* 2d ed. (Boulder: Westview Press, 1995); and Sabrina Petra Ramet, *Balkan Babel: The Disintegration of Yugoslavia from the Death of Tito to Ethnic War,* 2d ed. (Boulder: Westview Press, 1996).
13. The term is borrowed from David O. Sears, Carl P. Hensler, and Leslie K. Speer, "Whites' Opposition to 'Busing': Self-Interest or Symbolic Politics?" *American Political Science Review* 73, no. 2 (1979): 369–84; and Murray Edelman, *Politics as Symbolic Action: Mass Arousal and Quiescence* (New York: Academic Press, 1971).
14. Susanne Hoeber Rudolph and Lloyd I. Rudolph, "Modern Hate," *The New Republic,* March 22, 1993, pp. 24–29.

Chapter 2. The Symbolic Politics of Ethnic War

1. Anthony Smith, *The Ethnic Origins of Nations* (Oxford: Basil Blackwell, 1986), pp. 22–28.
2. Ernst Haas, "What Is Nationalism and Why Should We Study It?" *International Organization* 40, no. 3 (1986): 726.
3. The usual definition of nationalism is from Ernest Gellner, *Nations and Nationalism* (Ithaca: Cornell University Press, 1983), p. 1. On nationalism versus chauvinism, see Alexander Motyl, *Sovietology, Rationality, Nationality* (New York: Columbia University Press, 1990), p. 51.
4. Edelman, *Politics as Symbolic Action: Mass Arousal and Quiescence* (New York: Academic Press, 1971), p. 14.
5. Smith, *Ethnic Origins of Nations,* discusses myth-symbol complexes. On the use of symbols, see Zdzislaw Mach, *Symbols, Conflict, and Identity: Essays in Political Anthropology* (Albany, N.Y.: State University of New York Press, 1993), p. 37.
6. Robert Bates, "Modernization, Ethnic Competition, and the Rationality of Politics in Contemporary Africa," in *State vs. Ethnic Claims: African Policy Dilemmas,* ed. Donald Rothchild and Victor A. Olorunsola (Boulder: Westview, 1983), p. 152.
7. Donald Rothchild, "Collective Demands for Improved Distribution," in *State vs. Ethnic Claims,* ed. Rothchild and Olorunsola, p. 173.
8. E. J. Hobsbawm, *Nations and Nationalism since 1780: Programme, Myth, Reality* (Cambridge: Cambridge University Press, 1990), p. 53.
9. Gellner, *Nations and Nationalism,* p. 34.
10. Walker Connor, "Eco- or Ethno-Nationalism?" *Ethnic and Racial Studies* 7, no. 3 (1984): 342–59.
11. Ted Robert Gurr, *Minorities at Risk: A Global View of Ethnopolitical Conflicts* (Washington, D.C.: United States Institute of Peace, 1993), pp. 81, 124.
12. The classic study is Ted Robert Gurr, *Why Men Rebel* (Princeton: Princeton University Press, 1970).
13. One measure suggests that the Soviet economy grew 0.6 percent per year in the early 1980s, 3 percent in 1986, 1 percent in 1987, and not at all in 1988, before descending into recession starting in 1989. Calculations of Grigori Khanin, quoted in Anders Aslund, *Gorbachev's Struggle for Economic Reform,* updated and expanded edition (Ithaca: Cornell University Press, 1991), p. 200.
14. See especially Russell Hardin, *One for All: The Logic of Group Conflict* (Princeton: Princeton University Press, 1995); and David Lake and Donald Rothchild, eds., *The International Spread of Ethnic Conflict: Fear, Diffusion, and Escalation* (Princeton: Princeton University Press, 1998).
15. Hardin, *One for All,* pp. 143, 148.
16. Timur Kuran, "Ethnic Dissimilation and Its International Diffusion," in *International Spread of Ethnic Conflict,* ed. Lake and Rothchild, pp. 35–60.
17. For a different account of the role of criminals, see John Mueller, "The Banality of 'Ethnic War'," *International Security* 25, no. 1 (2000): 42–70.
18. David Lake and Donald Rothchild, "Spreading Fear: The Genesis of Transnational Ethnic Conflict," in ibid., pp. 3–32. Cf. Stephen Saideman, "Is Pandora's Box Half Empty or Half Full? The Limited Virulence of Secessionism and the Domestic Sources of Disintegration," in ibid., pp. 127–50.
19. For the standard neorealist understanding of the security dilemma on which this argument draws, see Robert Jervis, "Cooperation under the Security Dilemma," *World Politics* 30, no. 2 (1978): 167–214; and Jervis, *Perception and Misperception in International Politics* (Princeton: Princeton University Press, 1976).

20. Jack Snyder, "Nationalism and the Crisis of the Post-Soviet State," *Survival* 35, no. 1 (1993): 5–26.
21. I am indebted to Robert Jervis for suggesting this point.
22. See, for example, Edward N. Muller, Henry A. Dietz, and Steven E. Finkel, "Discontent and the Expected Utility of Rebellion: The Case of Peru," *American Political Science Review* 85, no. 4 (1991): 1261–82.
23. Alvin Rabushka and Kenneth A. Shepsle, *Politics in Plural Societies* (Columbus, Ohio: Charles E. Merrill, 1972).
24. Alexander Motyl, *Sovietology, Rationality, Nationality,* especially pp. 37–39.
25. Harold R. Isaacs, *The Idols of the Tribe* (New York: Harper and Row, 1975), pp. 26, 38.
26. Walker Connor, *Ethnonationalism: The Quest for Understanding* (Princeton: Princeton University Press, 1994).
27. Ibid., pp. 220–21.
28. Crawford Young suggests the "constructivist" label in "The Dialectics of Cultural Pluralism," in *The Rising Tide of Cultural Pluralism,* ed. Crawford Young (Madison: University of Wisconsin Press, 1993), p. 21. On invented history, see Leroy Vail, Preface to *The Creation of Tribalism in Southern Africa,* ed. Vail (Berkeley: University of California Press, 1989).
29. Clifford Geertz, quoted in Charles F. Keyes, "The Dialectics of Ethnic Change," in *Ethnic Change,* ed. Keyes (Seattle: University of Washington Press, 1981), p. 5.
30. Smith, *Ethnic Origins of Nations,* pp. 210–13.
31. William McGowan, "Mythconceptions," *The New Republic,* June 7, 1993, pp. 14–15. Cf. Gannath Obeyesekere, "On Buddhist Identity in Sri Lanka," in *Ethnic Identity: Creation, Conflict, and Accommodation,* ed. Lola Romanucci-Ross, 3d ed. (Walnut Creek, Calif.: Alta Mira Press, 1995), pp. 237–39.
32. Crawford Young, *The Politics of Cultural Pluralism* (Madison: University of Wisconsin Press, 1976). A statement of the synthesis is Anthony D. Smith, *Nationalism and Modernism* (London: Routledge, 1998).
33. Johan M. G. van der Dennen makes the argument about protection of kin groups in "Ethnocentrism and In-group/Out-group Differentiation: A Review and Interpretation of the Literature," in *The Sociobiology of Ethnocentrism: Evolutionary Dimensions of Xenophobia, Discrimination, Racism, and Nationalism,* ed. Vernon Reynolds, Vincent Falger, and Ian Vine (London: Croom Helm, 1987), pp. 1–47; Ralph B. Taylor, *Human Territorial Functioning* (Cambridge: Cambridge University Press, 1988), documents human tendencies toward territoriality.
34. Gary R. Johnson et al., "The Evocative Significance of Kin Terms in Patriotic Speech," in *The Sociobiology of Ethnocentrism,* ed. Reynolds et al., pp. 157–74.
35. Smith, *Ethnic Origins of Nations,* pp. 15–16 and passim.
36. Carleton J. H. Hayes, *Essays on Nationalism* (New York: Macmillan, 1941), pp. 104–10.
37. On ancient ethnic groups, see Smith, *Ethnic Origins of Nations.*
38. Benedict Anderson attributes the rise of ethno-nationalism to the emergence of modern "print-capitalism." See Anderson, *Imagined Communities: Reflections on the Origin and Spread of Nationalism* (Norfolk: Thetford, 1983).
39. Donald Horowitz, *Ethnic Groups in Conflict* (Berkeley: University of California Press, 1985), especially pp. 185, 226–27. Young makes a similar case in *The Politics of Cultural Pluralism.*
40. Horowitz, *Ethnic Groups in Conflict,* pp. 145–47. Anthony Smith makes a similar argument in *The Ethnic Revival* (Cambridge: Cambridge University Press, 1981), p. 28.

41. Charles Stangor, Linda A. Sullivan, and Thomas E. Ford, "Affective and Cognitive Determinants of Prejudice," *Social Cognition* 9, no. 4 (1991): 359–80.
42. Donald Horowitz, "Making Moderation Pay: The Comparative Politics of Ethnic Conflict Management," in *Conflict and Peacemaking in Multiethnic Societies*, ed. Joseph V. Montville (Lexington, Mass.: Lexington Books, 1990), p. 455.
43. Young, *Politics of Cultural Pluralism*, pp. 161–62.
44. Irving L. Janis and Leon Mann, *Decision Making: A Psychological Analysis of Conflict, Choice, and Commitment* (New York: Free Press, 1977), pp. 7–17 and passim.
45. *Edelman,* Politics as Symbolic Action, *p. 5.*
46. A discussion of framing is in Samuel L. Popkin, *The Reasoning Voter: Communication and Persuasion in Presidential Campaigns*, 2d ed. (Chicago: University of Chicago Press, 1994), p. 81ff. Applications of the concept to social movements are in Doug McAdam, John D. McCarthy, and Mayer N. Zald, eds., *Comparative Perspectives on Social Movements* (Cambridge: Cambridge University Press, 1996).
47. Susan T. Fiske and Shelley E. Taylor, *Social Cognition*, 2d. ed. (New York: McGraw Hill, 1991), p. 456.
48. Robert B. Zajonc, "Feeling and Thinking: Preferences Need No Inferences," *American Psychologist* 35, no. 2 (1980): 151–75. An application of the "hot cognition" concept to politics is in William A. Gamson, *Talking Politics* (Cambridge: Cambridge University Press, 1992), p. 7 and passim.
49. Fiske and Taylor, *Social Cognition*, p. 433.
50. Donald R. Kinder, "Reason and Emotion in American Political Life," in *Beliefs, Reasoning, and Decision Making: Psycho-Logic in Honor of Bob Abelson*, ed. Roger C. Schank and Ellen Langer (Mahwah, N.J.: Lawrence Erlbaum Associates, 1994), p. 307.
51. Popkin, *The Reasoning Voter*, p. 16.
52. Zajonc, "Feeling and Thinking."
53. Kari Edwards, "The Interplay of Affect and Cognition in Attitude Formation and Change," *Journal of Personality and Social Psychology* 59, no. 2 (1990):. 202–16; and Kari Edwards and William von Hippel, "Hearts and Minds: The Priority of Affective Versus Cognitive Factors in Person Perception," *Personality and Social Psychology Bulletin* 21, no. 10 (1995): 996–1011.
54. Edelman, *Politics as Symbolic Action*, pp. 14–15, 69.
55. Mach, *Symbols, Conflict, and Identity*, p. 37.
56. A creative application of the idea of symbolic politics to American politics is E. J. Dionne, *Why Americans Hate Politics* (New York: Simon and Schuster, 1991).
57. Charles D. Elder and Roger W. Cobb, *The Political Uses of Symbols* (New York: Longman, 1983), pp. 37–46, 58–62.
58. Edelman, *Politics as Symbolic Action*, p. 19 and passim.
59. Leonard Berkowitz, "On the Formation and Regulation of Anger and Aggression: A Cognitive-Neoassociationistic Analysis," *American Psychologist* 45, no. 4 (1990): 494–503.
60. On the Chechen myth-symbol complex, see Anatol Lieven, *Chechnya: Tombstone of Russian Power* (New Haven: Yale University Press, 1998), pp. 303–10, 324–35.
61. Jack Snyder, *From Voting to Violence: Democratization and Nationalist Conflict* (New York: Norton, 2000).
62. Horowitz, *Ethnic Groups in Conflict*, pp. 175–80.
63. Stephen Van Evera, "Hypotheses on Nationalism and War," *International Security* 18, no. 4 (1994).
64. Horowitz, "Making Moderation Pay."
65. Ibid.

66. Posen, "The Security Dilemma and Ethnic Conflict," *Survival* 35, no. 1 (1993): 27–47.
67. *New York Times,* February 4, 1993, p. 1.
68. Paul C. Stern, "Why Do People Sacrifice for Their Nations?" in *Perspectives on Nationalism and War,* ed. John L. Comaroff and Paul C. Stern (Luxembourg: Gordon and Breach, 1995), p. 117.
69. Daniel Jonah Goldhagen, *Hitler's Willing Executioners* (New York: Vintage Books, 1997).
70. Among those making this point are Charles Tilly, *From Mobilization to Revolution* (Reading, Mass.: Addison Wesley, 1978), and Milton J. Esman, *Ethnic Politics* (Ithaca: Cornell University Press, 1984), p. 31. A thoughtful discussion is Mark R. Beissinger, "How Nationalisms Spread: Eastern Europe Adrift the Tides and Cycles of Nationalist Contention," *Social Research* 43, no. 1 (1996): 97–146.
71. Michael Brown, "International Dimensions of Internal Conflict," in *International Dimensions of Internal Conflict,* ed. Brown (Cambridge: MIT Press, 1996), p. 580.
72. Snyder, *From Voting to Violence,* p. 72.
73. Jack L. Snyder, "Perceptions of the Security Dilemma in 1914," in *Psychology and Deterrence,* ed. Robert Jervis, Richard Ned Lebow, and Janice Gross Stein (Baltimore: Johns Hopkins University Press, 1985), pp. 153–79; Robert Jervis, "Was the Cold War a Security Dilemma?" *Journal of Cold War Studies* 3, no. 1 (2001): 36–60. Cf. Jack Snyder and Robert Jervis, "Civil War and the Security Dilemma," in *Civil Wars, Insecurity, and Intervention,* ed. Barbara Walter and Jack Snyder (New York: Columbia University Press, 1999). Robert Jervis's standard formulation is in Jervis, *Perception and Misperception in International Politics,* especially chapter 3; and Jervis, "Cooperation under the Security Dilemma."
74. On processes of positive feedback, see Robert Jervis, *System Effects* (Princeton: Princeton University Press, 1997), pp. 146 ff.
75. Among those who make the case for such a process operating in mass-led ethnic conflict are Horowitz, "Making Moderation Pay"; and Rabushka and Shepsle, *Politics in Plural Societies.*
76. Goldhagen, *Hitler's Willing Executioners.*
77. Mueller, "The Banality of 'Ethnic War'."
78. A seminal discussion of consociationalism is Arend Lijphart, *Democracy in Plural Societies: A Comparative Exploration* (New Haven: Yale University Press, 1977).
79. Stephen Ryan, *Ethnic Conflict and International Relations* (Aldershot, England: Dartmouth, 1990), p. 51.
80. I am indebted to Robert Jervis for emphasizing this point, which is supported by a number of my interviews.
81. Richard N. Haass, *Conflicts Unending: The United States and Regional Disputes* (New Haven: Yale University Press, 1990), pp. 27–29; cf. I. William Zartman, *Ripe for Resolution: Conflict and Intervention in Africa* (New York: Oxford University Press, 1985).
82. John Paul Lederach, *Building Peace: Sustainable Reconciliation in Divided Societies* (Washington, D.C.: United States Institute of Peace, 1997), pp. 68–69; Jacob Bercovitch, "Mediation in International Conflict: An Overview of Theory, A Review of Practice," in *Peacemaking in International Conflict: Methods and Techniques,* ed. I. William Zartman and J. Lewis Rasmussen (Washington, D.C.: United States Institute of Peace, 1997), pp. 137–38; Kumar Rupesinghe, *Civil Wars, Civil Peace* (London: Pluto, 1998), p. 105.
83. On the importance of a good formula and of implementation, see Fen Osler Hampson, *Nurturing Peace: Why Peace Settlements Succeed or Fail* (Washington, D.C.: United States Institute of Peace, 1996); and Timothy D. Sisk, *Power Sharing*

and International Mediation in Ethnic Conflicts (Washington, D.C.: United States Institute of Peace, 1996).

84. Roy Licklider, "The Consequences of Negotiated Settlements in Civil Wars, 1945–93," *American Political Science Review* 89, no. 3 (1995): p. 686.
85. On reassurance, see Janice Gross Stein, "Deterrence and Reassurance," in *Behavior, Society, and Nuclear War,* vol. II, ed. Philip E. Tetlock et al. (New York: Oxford University Press, pp. 8–72. Graduated reciprocation in tension-reduction, or GRIT, was proposed by Charles E. Osgood, *An Alternative to War or Surrender* (Urbana: University of Illinois Press, 1962).
86. See, e.g., Paul F. Diehl, *International Peacekeeping* (Baltimore: Johns Hopkins University Press, 1993); Alan James, *Peacekeeping in International Politics* (New York, St. Martins, 1990); and *The Blue Helmets: A Review of United Nations Peace-keeping,* 2d. ed. (United Nations, 1990).
87. Stuart Kaufman, "Preventing Ethnic Violence: Conditions for the Success of Peacekeeping," in *Peace in the Midst of Wars: Preventing and Managing International Ethnic Conflicts,* ed. David Carment and Patrick James (Columbia: University of South Carolina Press, 1998), pp. 194–229.
88. Two of the best works on the subject are Lederach, *Building Peace;* and Harold H. Saunders, *A Public Peace Process: Sustained Dialogue to Transform Racial and Ethnic Conflicts* (New York: St. Martin's, 1999). Cf. Herbert C. Kelman, "Negotiation as Interactive Problem Solving," *International Negotiation* 1 (1996): 99–123.
89. The experience with Israeli and Arab teenagers is described in John Wallach, *The Enemy Has a Face: The Seeds of Peace Experience* (Washington, D.C.: United States Institute of Peace, 2000).
90. Most of these examples are from Lederach, *Building Peace,* pp. 46–54 and passim.
91. Stephen Van Evera, "Primed for Peace: Europe After the Cold War," *International Security* 15, no. 3 (1990/91); and Van Evera, "Hypotheses on Nationalism and War."
92. Francis Deng, *War of Visions: Conflict of Identities in the Sudan* (Washington, D.C.: Brookings, 1995).

Chapter 3. Karabagh and the Fears of Minorities

1. Suzanne Goldenberg, *Pride of Small Nations: The Caucasus and Post-Soviet Disorder* (London: Zed Books, 1994), p. 155.
2. Ibid., p. 157.
3. John P. LeDonne, *The Russian Empire and the World, 1700–1917: The Geopolitics of Expansion and Containment* (New York: Oxford, 1997), p. 116.
4. Goldenberg, *Pride of Small Nations,* pp. 157–58.
5. Christopher J. Walker, ed., *Armenia and Karabagh: The Struggle for Unity* (London: Minority Rights Publications, 1991), p. 24.
6. Ibid., pp. 86–87; and Tadeusz Swietochowski, "National Consciousness and Political Orientations in Azerbaijan, 1905–1920," in *Transcaucasia, Nationalism and Social Change: Essays in the History of Armenia, Azerbaijan, and Georgia,* rev. ed., ed. Ronald Grigor Suny (Ann Arbor: University of Michigan Press, 1996), p. 215.
7. Walker, *Armenia and Karabagh,* p. 91; Goldenberg, *Pride of Small Nations,* p. 159.
8. Mark Malkasian, *Gha-ra-bagh! The Emergence of the National Democratic Movement in Armenia* (Detroit: Wayne State University Press, 1996), p. 25.
9. Walker, *Armenia and Karabagh,* pp. 117–19; Ronald Grigor Suny, *Looking toward Ararat: Armenia in Modern History* (Bloomington: Indiana University Press, 1993), p. 195.

10. Gerard J. Libaridian, *The Karabagh File: Documents and Facts on the Region of Mountainous Karabagh, 1918–1988* (Cambridge, Mass.: Zoryan Institute, 1988), pp. 42–48.
11. Ronald Grigor Suny, quoted in Ben Fowkes, *The Disintegration of the Soviet Union: A Study in the Rise and Triumph of Nationalism* (New York: St. Martin's, 1997), p. 133.
12. Constantine Khandoyan, *Soviet Armenia* (Yerevan, 1976), p. 7.
13. Stephan H. Astourian, "In Search of Their Forefathers: National Identity and the Historiography and Politics of Armenian and Azerbaijani Ethnogeneses," in *Nationalism and History: The Politics of Nation Building in Post-Soviet Armenia, Azerbaijan, and Georgia*, ed. Donald V. Schwartz and Razmik Panossian (Toronto: University of Toronto Centre for Russian and East European Studies, 1994), p. 47.
14. Fowkes, *Disintegration of the Soviet Union*, p. 116.
15. "Armenian SSR," in *Great Soviet Encyclopedia*, 3d ed. [1970], translated edition (New York: Macmillan, 1973), vol. 2, p. 322.
16. See, e.g., Gevorg Emin, *Seven Songs of Armenia* (Yerevan: Armenian Society for Friendship and Cultural Relations with Foreign Countries, 1970).
17. Suny, *Looking toward Ararat*, pp. 5–9.
18. "Armenian SSR," in *Great Soviet Encyclopedia*, vol. 2, p. 325.
19. Rafael Ishkhanian, "The Law of Excluding the Third Force," in *Armenia at the Crossroads: Democracy and Nationhood in the Post-Soviet Era*, ed. Gerard J. Libaridian (Watertown, Mass: Blue Crane Books, 1991), p. 10.
20. Zori Balayan, "The Threat of Pan-Turanism," in *Armenia at the Crossroads*, ed. Libaridian, pp. 151–54.
21. Libaridian, ed., *The Karabagh File*, pp. 44–48.
22. Shireen Hunter, "Azerbaijan: Search for Identity and New Partners," in *Nations and Politics in the Soviet Successor States*, ed. Ian Bremmer and Ray Taras (New York: Cambridge University Press, 1993), p. 247.
23. Malkasian, *Gha-ra-bagh!* pp. 19–26.
24. Quoted in ibid., p. 23.
25. Richard G. Hovannisian, "Historical Memory and Foreign Relations: The Armenian Perspective," in *The Legacy of History in Russian and the New States of Eurasia*, ed. S. Frederick Starr (Armonk, N.Y.: M. E. Sharpe, 1994), pp. 244–45.
26. Balayan, "The Threat of Pan-Turanism."
27. Libaridian, *Armenia at the Crossroads*, p. 158.
28. Sero Khanzadian, "Letter by Sero Khanzadian to Leonid E. Brezhnev," in *The Karabagh File*, ed. Libaridian, p. 50.
29. "Armenians Petition Gorbachev on Karabagh and Nakhichevan," in *The Karabagh File*, ed. Libaridian, p. 87.
30. Walker, *Armenia and Karabagh*, p. 121.
31. Mark Saroyan, *Minorities, Mullahs, and Modernity: Reshaping Community in the Former Soviet Union* (Berkeley: International and Area Studies, University of California, 1997), pp. 177–78; Swietochowski, "National Consciousness and Political Orientations," p. 213.
32. A. N. Guliev, ed., *Ocherki po drevnei istorii Azerbaidzhana* (Baku: Izdatel'stvo Akademii Nauk Azerbaidzhanskoi SSR, 1956), pp. 36–37, 45, 68.
33. "Azerbaijan SSR," in *Great Soviet Encyclopedia*, 3d ed., vol. 1, p. 550.
34. Dzh. B. Guliev, ed., *Istoriia Azerbaidzhana* (Baku: Elm, 1979), pp. 49–52.
35. On ancient Azerbaijanis' martial prowess, see Zul'fali Ibragimov and E. Tokarzhevskii, *Pisateli i istoriki o muzhestvo i doblesti azerbaidzhantsev* (Baku: Azerneshr, 1943), p. 5.
36. "Azerbaijan SSR," *Great Soviet Encyclopedia*, vol. 1, p. 551.

37. Audrey L. Alstadt, *The Azerbaijani Turks* (Stanford, Calif.: Hoover Institution, 1992), p. 7.
38. Guliev, *Istoriia Azerbaidzhana,* pp. 51–52.
39. The debate is briefly discussed in Alstadt, *The Azerbaijani Turks,* p. 7.
40. Ziya Buniatov, *Istoricheskaia geografia Azerbaidzhana* (Baku: Elm, 1987), cited in Alstadt, *The Azerbaijani Turks,* p. 9. Alstadt notes that the manuscript was completed in 1986, before the reemergence of the Karabagh conflict.
41. Suleiman Alijarly, "The Republic of Azerbaijan: Note on the State Borders in the Past and Present," in *Transcaucasian Boundaries,* ed. John F. R. Wright, Suzanne Goldenberg, and Richard Schofield, (New York: St. Martin's Press, 1996), p. 129.
42. Swietochowski, "National Consciousness and Political Orientations," pp. 212–16.
43. Ibid., p. 214.
44. The importance of the "backward" vs. "advanced" stereotypes is suggested in Donald Horowitz, *Ethnic Groups in Conflict* (Berkeley: University of California Press, 1985). Azerbaijani stereotypes are described in Tadeusz Swietochowski, "Azerbaijan: Between Ethnic Conflict and Irredentism," *Armenian Review,* 43, no. 2–3 (1990): 36.
45. Quoted in Ronald Grigor Suny, "Nationalism and Democracy in Gorbachev's Soviet Union: The Case of Karabagh," in *The Soviet Nationality Reader: The Disintegration in Context,* ed. Rachel Denber (Boulder: Westview Press, 1992), pp. 492–93.
46. Quoted in *Sumgait Tragedy: Pogroms against Armenians in Soviet Azerbaijan,* ed. Samuel Shahmuratian, trans. Steven Jones (New Rochelle, N.Y.: Aristide D. Caratzas, 1990), p. 165. While the woman in question was interviewed after the Sumgait pogroms of February 1988, she specified that she had heard such statements "not just in the past year."
47. Fowkes, *Disintegration of the Soviet Union,* p. 117.
48. Mark Saroyan, "The 'Karabagh Syndrome' and Azerbaijani Politics," *Problems of Communism* 39, no. 5 (1990): 14–29.
49. *Komsomolskaya Pravda,* March 26, 1988, trans. in *Current Digest of the Soviet Press* (hereafter *CDSP*) 40, no. 14 (May 4, 1988): 13.
50. *Izvestia,* March 15, 1988, trans. in *CDSP* 40, no. 13 (April 27, 1988): 8.
51. *Pravda,* March 21, 1988, trans. in *CDSP* 40, no. 12 (April 20, 1988): 9.
52. Malkasian, *Gha-ra-bagh!* p. 27.
53. Tamara Dragadze, "Azerbaijanis," in *The Nationalities Question in the Soviet Union,* ed. Graham Smith (London: Longman, 1990), p. 169.
54. Suny, *Looking toward Ararat,* p. 189.
55. Elizabeth Fuller, "Moscow Rejects Armenian Demands for Return of Nagorno-Karabakh," *Radio Liberty Research Bulletin* (hereafter *RL*) 91/88 (February 29, 1988): 2; Malkasian, *Gha-ra-bagh!* p. 28.
56. Walker, *Armenia and Karabakh,* p. 119.
57. *Izvestia,* March 24, 1988, trans. in *CDSP* 40, no. 13 (April 27, 1988): 7; Mark R. Beissinger, "How Nationalisms Spread: Eastern Europe Adrift the Tides and Cycles of Nationalist Contention," *Social Research* 63, no. 1 (1996): 109.
58. Fuller, "Moscow Rejects Armenian Demands."
59. Malkasian, *Gha-ra-bagh!* p. 29.
60. Vera Tolz, "USSR This Week," *RL* 90/88 (February 26, 1988).
61. *Izvestia,* March 24, 1988, trans. in *CDSP* 40, no. 13 (April 27, 1988): 7.
62. Suny, *Looking toward Ararat,* p. 196.
63. Elizabeth Fuller, "Mass Demonstration in Armenia against Environmental Pollution," *RL* 421/87 (October 20, 1987): 1.

64. Elizabeth Fuller, "Armenians Demonstrate for Return of Territories from Azerbaijan," *RL* 441/87 (October 20, 1987): 1.
65. Libaridian, ed., *The Karabagh File*, pp. 69–73.
66. Elizabeth Fuller, "Mass Demonstrations in Armenia," *RL* 79/88 (February 22, 1988).
67. Vera Tolz, "USSR This Week," *RL* 90/88 (February 26, 1988).
68. Elizabeth Fuller, "A Preliminary Chronology of Recent Events in Armenia and Azerbaijan," *RL* 101/88 (March 15, 1988).
69. Elizabeth Fuller, "Moscow Rejects Armenian Demands."
70. For an example of Demirchyan's rhetoric, see, *Kommunist* (Erevan), February 23, 1988, trans. in *CDSP* 40, no. 8 (March 23, 1988): 4.
71. *Pravda*, March 21, 1988, trans. in *CDSP* 40, no. 12 (April 20, 1988): 8.
72. Nora Dudwick, "Armenia: The Nation Awakens," in *Nations and Politics in the Soviet Successor States*, ed. Bremmer and Taras, p. 276.
73. Malkasian, *Gha-ra-bagh!* p. 38.
74. Quoted in ibid.
75. Quoted in ibid., p. 47.
76. Claire Mouradian, "The Mountainous Karabakh Question: Inter-Ethnic Conflict or Decolonization Crisis?" *Armenian Review* 43, no. 2–3/170–71 (1990): 15.
77. *Komsomolskaya Pravda*, March 25 1988, trans. in *CDSP* 40, no. 14 (May 4, 1988): 14.
78. Elizabeth Fuller, "Nagorno-Karabakh: The Death and Casualty Toll to Date," *RL* 531/88 (Dec. 14, 1988): 1–2.
79. Shahmuratian, *Sumgait Tragedy*.
80. Malkasian, *Gha-ra-bagh!* pp. 52.
81. *Moskovskie novosti*, April 17, 1988, trans. in *CDSP* 40, no. 17 (May 25, 1988): 12–13.
82. *Moskovskie novosti*, May 22, 1988, trans. in *CDSP* 40, no. 23 (July 6, 1988): 10.
83. Malkasian, *Gha-ra-bagh!* pp. 51–53.
84. *Moskovskie novosti* no 21, May 22, 1988, trans. in *CDSP* 40, no. 23 (July 6, 1988): 10.
85. Shahmuratian, *Sumgait Tragedy*, pp. 13, 99.
86. Ibid., pp. 77–82, 149, 173, 199.
87. Fuller, "Nagorno-Karabakh: The Death and Casualty Toll to Date," 1–2.
88. Fuller, "A Preliminary Chronology."
89. In late March, reports suggested there were only about 1,000 Azerbaijani and 2,000 Armenian refugees (*Kommunist*, March 23, 1988, trans. in *CDSP* 40, no. 12 [April 20, 1988]: 11). By mid-July, an Azerbaijani official reported over 20,000 Azeri refugees (*Pravda*, July 20, 1988, trans. in *CDSP* 40, no. 29 (August 17, 1988): 3).
90. Elizabeth Fuller, "Whither the Nagorno-Karabakh Campaign?," *RL* 133/88 (March 29, 1988).
91. Malkasian, *Gha-ra-bagh!* p. 68.
92. Elizabeth Fuller, "New Demonstrations in Armenia and Azerbaijan Exemplify Polarization of Views over Nagorno-Karabagh," *RL* 220/88 (May 20, 1988).
93. Malkasian, *Gha-ra-bagh!* p. 71.
94. *Pravda*, June 10, 1988, trans. in *CDSP* 40, no. 23 (July 6, 1988): 11.
95. Edmund M. Herzig, "Armenians," in *The Nationalities Question in the Soviet Union*, ed. Smith, p. 156.
96. Elizabeth Fuller, "Recent Developments in the Nagorno-Karabagh Dispute," *RL* 312/88 (July 11, 1988).
97. *Pravda*, July 20, 1988, trans. in *CDSP* 40, no. 29 (August 17, 1988): 1.
98. Edmund M. Herzig, "Armenia and the Armenians," in *The Nationalities Question in the Post-Soviet States*, ed. Smith, pp. 257–58.
99. Fuller, "New Demonstrations in Armenia and Azerbaijan."

100. *Bakinskii Rabochii,* March 19, 1988, trans. in *CDSP* 40, no. 11 (April 13, 1988): 8.
101. *Bakinskii Rabochii,* March 24, 1988, trans. in *CDSP* 40, no. 12 (April 20, 1988): 7.
102. *Bakinskii Rabochii,* March 26, 1988, trans. in *CDSP* 40, no. 13 (April 27, 1988): 9; and *Bakinskii Rabochii,* April 2, 1988, trans. in *CDSP* 40, no. 16 (May 8, 1988): 12.
103. Elizabeth Fuller, "Further Fatality Reported as New Violence Flares Up in Nagorno-Karabakh," *RL* 428/88 (October 15, 1988).
104. Elizabeth Fuller, "Nagorno-Karabakh: An Ulster in the Caucasus?" *RL* 534/88 (December 14, 1988); Saroyan, *Minorities, Mullahs, and Modernity,* p. 185.
105. William Reese, "The Role of the Religious Revival and Nationalism in Transcaucasia," *RL* 535/88 (December 14, 1988); Mirza Michaeli and William Reese, "Azerbaijani Dissident Reveals Arrest of Nemat Panakhov," *Radio Liberty Report on the USSR* (hereafter *Report on the USSR)* 1, no. 2 (January 13, 1989): 14; and Elizabeth Fuller, "The Nemat Panakhov Phenomenon—As Reflected in the Azerbaijani Press," *Report on the USSR* 1, no. 7 (February 17, 1989): 4.
106. *Komsomolskaia pravda,* November 27, 1988, trans. in *Foreign Broadcast Information Service Daily Report: Soviet Union* (hereafter *FBIS-SOV*), *FBIS-SOV-88-230* (November 30, 1988): 58.
107. Fuller, "Nagorno-Karabagh: An Ulster in the Caucasus?"
108. Saroyan, *Minorities, Mullahs, and Modernity,* p. 185.
109. Fuller, "Nagorno-Karabagh: The Death and Casualty Toll to Date."
110. Goldenberg, *Pride of Small Nations,* p. 163; Walker, *Armenia and Karabagh,* p. 128.
111. Mirza Michaeli, "Formation of Popular Front in Azerbaijan," *RL* 558/88 (December 28, 1988).
112. Saroyan, *Minorities, Mullahs, and Modernity,* p. 189.
113. Fuller, "Nagorno-Karabagh: An Ulster in the Caucasus?"
114. Reese, "The Role of the Religious Revival."
115. Baku domestic service in Azerbaijani, November 22, 1988, trans. *FBIS-SOV-88-227* (November 25, 1988): 42.
116. Quoted in Fuller, "Nagorno-Karabagh: An Ulster in the Caucasus?"
117. Malkasian, *Gha-ra-bagh!* chapter 11.
118. Dudwick, "Armenia: The Nation Awakens," pp. 276–77.
119. TASS, February 7, 1989, trans. *FBIS-SOV-89-024* (February 7, 1989): 56; and *Izvestia* February 16, 1989, p. 2, trans. *FBIS-SOV-89-034* (February 22, 1989): 63.
120. *Bakinskii rabochii,* January 19, 1989, trans. *FBIS-SOV-89-024* (February 7, 1989): 57.
121. Elizabeth Fuller, "Nagorno-Karabagh and the Rail Blockade," *Report on the USSR* 1, no. 41 (October 13, 1989): 23.
122. Alstadt, *The Azerbaijani Turks,* p. 206.
123. Mirza Michaeli and William Reese, "The Popular Front in Azerbaijan and Its Program," *Report on the USSR* 1, no. 34 (August 25, 1989): 31.
124. *Pravda,* August 23, 1989, trans. *CDSP* 41, no. 34 (September 20, 1989): 30.
125. Saroyan, *Minorities, Mullahs, and Modernity,* p. 194–96.
126. Erevan radio, August 21, 1998, trans. *FBIS-SOV-89-167* (August 30, 1989): 32.
127. Armenpress, August 22, 1998, trans. *FBIS-SOV-89-167* (August 30, 1989): 29.
128. Herzig, "Armenia and the Armenians," p. 259.
129. Vera Tolz and Melanie Newton, "USSR This Week," in *Report on the USSR* 2, no. 3 (January 19, 1990): 31–35.
130. Tamara Dragadze, "Azerbaijan and the Azerbaijanis," in *The Nationalities Question in the Post-Soviet States,* ed. Smith, p. 281.
131. Elizabeth Fuller and Mark Deich, "Interview with Gary Kasparov," *Report on the USSR* 2, no. 5 (February 2, 1990): 19.

132. Fowkes, *Disintegration of the Soviet Union*, p. 160.
133. Shireen Hunter, "Azerbaijan: Search for Identity and New Partners," in *Nations and Politics in the Soviet Successor States*, ed. Bremmer and Taras, p. 253.
134. Walker, *Armenia and Karabagh*, p. 130.
135. *Kommunist*, June 5, 1990, trans. in *CDSP* 42, no. 22 (July 4, 1990): 10; *Pravda*, April 13, 1990, trans. in *CDSP* 42, no. 15 (May 16, 1990): 27.
136. Edgar O'Ballance, *Wars in the Caucasus, 1990–95* (Basingstoke: Macmillan, 1997), p. 46.
137. For reports of two small massacres of Armenians, see *Komsomolskaia pravda*, February 17, 1990, p. 1, trans. in *FBIS-SOV-90-034* (February 20, 1990): 88.
138. See, for example, Yerevan Radio, February 11, 1990, trans. *FBIS-SOV-90-029* (Feb. 12, 1990): 120–21; and Yerevan Radio, February 14, 1990, trans. *FBIS-SOV-90-043* (Feb. 20, 1990): 90.
139. *Izvestia*, May 22, 1990, trans. *CDSP* 42, no. 22 (July 4, 1990): 10.
140. See Baku Radio reports in *FBIS-SOV-90-063* (April 2, 1990): 112–14.
141. See, for example, *Izvestia* August 22 and 23, 1990, trans. in *CDSP* 42, no. 34 (September 26, 1990): 14; and O'Ballance, *Wars in the Caucasus*, p. 54.
142. *Izvestia*, July 26, 1990, trans. in *CDSP* 42, no. 30 (August 29, 1990): 19; and *Izvestia* August 28 and 29, 1990, trans. in *CDSP* 42, no. 35 (October 3, 1990): 14–15.
143. This point is made in Michael P. Croissant, *The Armenia-Azerbaijan Conflict: Causes and Implications* (Westport, Conn.: Praeger, 1998), p. 40.
144. Levon Chorbajian, Introduction to the English language edition of Levon Chorbajian, Patrick Donabedian, and Claude Mutafian, *The Caucasian Knot: The History and Geo-Politics of Nagorno-Karabagh* (London: Zed Books, 1994), pp. 37–38.
145. U.S. Committee for Refugees, *Faultlines of Nationality Conflict: Refugees and Displaced Persons from Armenia and Azerbaijan* (Immigration and Refugee Services of America, 1994), pp. 14–15.
146. *Moskovskie novosti*, April 12, 1992, trans. *CDSP* 44, no. 14 (May 6, 1992): 25.
147. Radio Yerevan, July 30 and 31, 1990, trans. *FBIS-SOV-91-148* (August 1, 1991): 69.
148. Croissant, *The Armenia-Azerbaijan Conflict*, pp. 45–46.
149. Goldenberg, *Pride of Small Nations*, pp. 164–65.
150. *Izvestia*, October 18, 1992, trans. *CDSP* 44, no. 43 (November 25, 1992): 14–15.
151. Croissant, *The Armenia-Azerbaijan Conflict*, p. 46.
152. Ibid., pp. 165–67.
153. A startling account of the Khodzhaly massacre is in Thomas Goltz, *Requiem for a Would-Be Republic: The Rise and Demise of the Former Soviet Republic of Azerbaijan; A Personal Account of the Years 1991–1993* (Istanbul: Isis Press, 1994), pp. 173–84.
154. *Izvestia*, February 24, 1992, p. 1, trans. *CDSP* 44, no. 8 (March 25, 1992): 11.
155. Widely cited accounts of Russian involvement are Thomas Goltz, "Letter from Eurasia: The Hidden Russian Hand," *Foreign Policy* 92 (Fall 1993): 92–116; and Fiona Hill and Pamela Jewitt, *Back in the USSR: Russia's Intervention in the Internal Affairs of the Former Soviet Republics and the Implications for United States Policy toward Russia* (Cambridge, Mass.: Strengthening Democratic Institutions Project, John F. Kennedy School of Government, Harvard University, January 1994).
156. *Izvestia*, March 25, 1988, p. 3, trans. *FBIS-SOV-88-058* (March 25, 1988): 38–40.
157. Malkasian, *Gha-ra-bagh!* pp. 62–63.
158. Quoted in Malkasian, *Gha-ra-bagh!* p. 115.
159. Croissant, *The Armenia-Azerbaijan Conflict*, discusses these and other mediation efforts.
160. Malkasian, *Gha-ra-bagh!* pp. 90–91.

161. Erik Melander, "The Escalation of the Nagorno-Karabakh Conflict," unpublished manuscript, 2000; cf. V. B. Arutiunyan, *Sobytiia v Nagornom Karabakhe: Khronika,* part 4, January 1991–January 1993, pp. 19–20, 52–63.
162. See "Kazakh Soviet Socialist Republic," in *Great Soviet Encyclopedia,* 3d ed., vol. 11, pp. 507–9; cf. *Uchebnoe posobie po istorii Kazakhstana c drevneishikh vremen do nashikh dnei* (Alma-Ata, Ministry of Education of the Republic of Kazakhstan, 1992).
163. Nancy Lubin, "Leadership in Uzbekistan and Kazakhstan: The Views of the Led," in *Patterns in Post-Soviet Leadership,* ed. Timothy J. Colton and Robert C. Tucker (Boulder: Westview Press, 1995), p. 232.
164. Ann Sheehy, "Conference on Internationalist Education in Alma-Ata," *Radio Liberty Research Bulletin* 172/87 (April 30, 1987).
165. Bhavna Dave, "National Revival in Kazakhstan: Language Shift and Identity Change," *Post-Soviet Affairs* 12, no. 1 (1996): 53.
166. Vladimir Barsamov, "Kazakhstan: How Long Can Ethnic Harmony Last?" in *Managing Conflict in the Former Soviet Union: Russian and American Perspectives,* ed. Alexei Arbatov et al. (Cambridge, Mass.: MIT Press, 1997), p. 279.
167. Robert Kaiser and Jeff Chinn, "Russian-Kazakh Relations in Kazakhstan," *Post-Soviet Geography* 36, no. 5 (1995): 261.
168. See M. K. Kozybaev and I. M. Kozybaev, *Istoriia Kazakhstana* (Alma-Ata: Atamura-Kazakhstan, 1992).
169. Lubin, "Leadership in Uzbekistan and Kazakhstan," p. 232.
170. Quoted in Ian Bremmer, "Nazarbaev and the North: State-Building and Ethnic Relations in Kazakhstan," *Ethnic and Racial Studies* 17, no. 4 (1994): 626.
171. Martha Brill Olcott, "Nursultan Nazarbaev and the Balancing Act of State Building in Kazakhstan," in *Patterns in Post-Soviet Leadership,* ed. Colton and Tucker, p. 183.
172. Neil Melvin, *Russians beyond Russia: The Politics of National Identity* (Chatham House Papers, Royal Institute of International Affairs, 1995), p. 111; Paul Kolstoe, *Russians in the Former Soviet Republics* (Bloomington: Indiana University Press, 1995), pp. 248–49.
173. Pal Kolsto, "Anticipating Demographic Superiority: Kazakh Thinking on Integration and Nation Building," *Europe-Asia Studies* 50, no. 1 (1998): 57–69.
174. Quoted in Olcott, "Nursultan Nazarbaev and the Balancing Act," p. 187.

Chapter 4. Georgia and the Fears of Majorities

1. Ronald Wixman, *The Peoples of the USSR: An Ethnographic Handbook* (Armonk, N.Y.: M. E. Sharpe, 1984).
2. Ibid., pp. 151–52.
3. Julian Birch, "The Georgian/South Ossetian Territorial and Boundary Dispute," in *Transcaucasian Boundaries,* ed. John F. R. Wright, Suzanne Goldenberg, and Richard Schofield (New York: St. Martin's Press, 1996), pp. 151–60.
4. Ronald Grigor Suny, *The Making of the Georgian Nation* (Bloomington: Indiana University Press, 1988), pp. 42–48.
5. A pro-Georgian treatment of this period is Avtandil Menteshashvili, *Some National and Ethnic Problems in Georgia, 1918–1922* (Tbilisi: Samshoblo, 1992), p. 12 and passim.
6. Stephen F. Jones, "Georgia: A Failed Democratic Transition," in *Nations and Politics in the Soviet Successor States,* ed. Ian Bremmer and Ray Taras (New York: Cambridge University Press, 1993), p. 291.

7. David Marshall Lang, *A Modern History of Georgia* (New York: Grove Press, 1962), p. 265. According to Lang (p. 255), by 1926 Abkhaz accounted for only one-third of the total population in their autonomous region.
8. Suny, *The Making of the Georgian Nation*, p. 290.
9. See Igor Marykhuba, ed., *Abkhazskie pis'ma, 1947–1989: Abkhaziia v Sovetskuiu epokhu: Sbornik dokumentov [Abkhazian letters, 1947–1989: Abkhazia in the Soviet epoch: Collection of documents]*, vol. 1 (Sukhumi, 1994), pp. 7–11; and Darrell Slider, "Crisis and Response in Soviet Nationality Policy: The Case of Abkhazia," *Central Asian Survey* 4, no. 4 (1985): 60. Cf. Elizabeth Fuller, "Abkhaz-Georgian Relations Strained," Radio Liberty *Report on the USSR* (hereafter *Report on the USSR*) 1, no. 10 (March 10, 1989): 26.
10. Nodar Natadze, interview by author, Tbilisi, June 1998.
11. Interview by author, Sukhumi, June 1998.
12. Vazha Adamia, interview by author, Tbilisi, June 1998.
13. One claim of GRU support for arming the Abkhazians is published as Lyuluy Chkhenkeli, *Dvukh istin ne byvaet (Pokazaniia rezidenta GRU v Avtonomnoi Respublike Abkhaziia) [There are no two truths: Revelations of a GRU resident in the Autonomous Republic of Abkhazia]* (Tbilisi: Soiuz Grazhdan Gruzii, 1996).
14. This version is summarized in Mariam Lordkipanidze, *Essays on Georgian History* (Tbilisi: Metsniereba, 1994), pp. 191–92.
15. Suny, *Making of the Georgian Nation*, p. 11.
16. Shireen T. Hunter, *The Transcaucasus in Transition: Nation Building and Conflict* (Washington, D.C.: The Center for Strategic and International Studies, 1994), p. 111.
17. N. A. Berdzenishvili et al., *Istoriia Gruzii, t. 1, s drevneishikh dnei do 60-x godov XIX veka* (Tbilisi, 1962), p. 122.
18. Ibid., pp. 163, 189.
19. A journalist's account of how some Georgians react to seeing the cross is in Peter Nasmyth, *Georgia: A Rebel in the Caucasus* (London: Cassell, 1992), pp. 107–8.
20. Lynn D. Nelson and Paata Amonashvili, "Voting and Political Attitudes in Soviet Georgia," *Soviet Studies* 44, no. 4 (1992): 691.
21. Berdzenishvili, *Istoriia Gruzii*, p. 406.
22. "Abkhazian Autonomous Soviet Socialist Republic," *Great Soviet Encyclopedia*, 3d ed. (1970; trans. and republished New York: Macmillan, 1975), vol. 1, p. 19.
23. Georgian Academy of Sciences, Research Centre for Relations between Nations, *Historic, Political, and Legal Aspects of the Conflict in Abkhazia* (Tbilisi: Metsniereba, 1995), p. 9.
24. This theory is outlined, and debunked, in B. G. Hewitt, "Abkhazia: A Problem of Identity and Ownership," in *Transcaucasian Boundaries*, ed. Wright et al., pp. 197–99.
25. This is the main point of Avtandil Menteshashvili, *Some National and Ethnic Problems in Georgia* (Tbilisi: Samshablo, 1992).
26. Georgian Academy of Sciences, *Historical, Political, and Legal Aspects*, pp. 37–41.
27. See Akakii Bakradze and Liana Tatishvili, eds., *Osetinskii vopros* (Tbilisi: Kera-21, 1994).
28. Quoted in Ronald Grigor Suny, "Transcaucasia: Cultural Cohesion and Ethnic Revival in a Multinational Society," in *The Nationalities Factor in Soviet Politics and Society*, ed. Ljubomyr Hajda and Mark R. Beissinger (Boulder: Westview Press, 1990), p. 241.
29. Elizabeth Fuller, "Georgia," *Report on the USSR* 1, no. 51 (December 29, 1989): 19.
30. Stephen Jones, "Georgia: A Failed Democratic Transition," in *Nations and Politics in the Soviet Successor States*, ed. Bremmer and Taras, p. 289.
31. Quoted by Suny, in *The Nationalities Factor*, ed. Hajda and Beissinger, p. 235.

32. This quote from a nineteenth-century Russian viceroy was repeated by Natadze, interview, June 1998. Other interviews, including with Alexander Rondeli (May 1998) elicited similar points.
33. Reported in *Izvestia,* June 14, 1990, p. 3, trans. in *Current Digest of the Soviet Press (CDSP)* 42, no. 24 (July 18, 1990): 25.
34. Robert Sturua, interview reported in Nasmyth, *Georgia: A Rebel in the Caucasus,* p. 102.
35. The quotation is from Natadze, interview, June 1998. The rest of the paragraph is my own reconstruction of Georgian attitudes.
36. "Fairy tale" was the phrase of a Tbilisi restaurant manager, interview by author, May 1998. "Speculation" was the term of Archil Gegeshidze, advisor to President Shevardnadze, interview by author, Tbilisi, June 1998.
37. Calculated from data in Nelson and Amonashvili, "Voting and Political Attitudes in Soviet Georgia," p. 692.
38. Interview by author with Abkhazian intellectual, Sukhumi, June 1992. The quotation about "sucking the juices" was attributed to a 1989 edition of *Literaturuli Sakartvelo,* and the other from conversations with pro-Gamsakhurdia activists in the fall of 1988.
39. Z. V. Anchabadze, *Istoriia i kul'tura drevnei Abkhazii* (Moscow: Nauka, 1964), p. 120.
40. Z. V. Anchabadze, *Iz istorii srednovekovoi Abkhazii (VI–XVII vv.)* (Sukhumi: Abkhazian State Press, 1959), pp. 66, 81.
41. "Abkhazian ASSR," *Great Soviet Encyclopedia,* vol. 1, p. 19; cf. Anchabadze, *Iz istorii srednovekovoi Abkhazii,* p. 69.
42. Sh. D. Inal-Ipa, *Abkhazy: Istoriko-etnograficheskie ocherki,* 2d ed. (Alashara, 1965), pp. 130–35.
43. "Abkhazian ASSR," *Great Soviet Encyclopedia,* vol. 1, p. 19.
44. Inal-Ipa, *Abkhazy,* pp. 150–55.
45. Ibid., pp. 171–72.
46. Lykhny Appeal, reprinted in *Sovetskaia Abkhaziia,* March 24, 1989, p. 2.
47. Reprinted in *Abkhazskie pis'ma,* p. 176.
48. The fate of the Ubykhs is highlighted in Liana Kvarchelia, "Visions from Abkhazia," unpublished manuscript, November 6, 1996, but is frequently mentioned even by relatively uneducated Abkhazians as a cautionary tale.
49. Ordjonikidze is quoted in the dissident letter, reprinted in *Abkhazskie pis'ma,* p. 160.
50. Fazil Iskander, *Sandro of Chegem,* trans. Susan Brownsberger (London: Jonathan Cape, 1983), pp. 309–10.
51. *Abkhazskie pis'ma,* p. 159.
52. Slider, "Crisis and Response in Soviet Nationality Policy," p. 60.
53. Paata Zakareishvili, interview by author, Tbilisi, May 1998.
54. Interview by author with Kosta Kochiev, advisor to South Ossetian president, Tskhinvali, June 1998.
55. Robert H. Hewsen, "Ossetians," in *Modern Encyclopedia of Russian and Soviet History,* vol. 26 (Gulf Breeze, Fla.: Academic International Press, 1982), p. 136.
56. Yu. C. Gogluyti, *Iuzhnaia Osetiia* (Tskhinvali, 1993), esp. p. 25.
57. Yu. C. Gogluyti et al., *Iz istorii osetino-gruzinskikh vzaimootnoshenii* (Tskhinvali, 1995), pp. 22–30.
58. Gogluyti, *Iuzhnaia Osetiia;* and Kochiev, interview, June 1998.
59. Birch, "The Georgian/South Ossetian Territorial and Boundary Dispute," p. 155.
60. Kochiev, interview, June 1998.

61. Adamia, interview, Tbilisi, June 1998. Ronald Wixman goes further, stating that Ossetians were being assimilated by Georgians. Wixman, *The Peoples of the USSR.*
62. On the availability of foodstuffs, see Nasymth, *Georgia: A Rebel in the Caucasus.*
63. Slider, "Crisis and Response in Soviet Nationality Policy," pp. 57–58.
64. These economic-political issues are detailed in "Abkhazskoe pis'mo 'shestidesiati' 1988 goda," reprinted in *Abkhazskie pis'ma,* pp. 428–33.
65. See Eduard Shevardnadze's statement quoted in Bohdan Nahaylo and Victor Swoboda, *Soviet Disunion: A History of the Nationalities Problem in the USSR* (New York: The Free Press, 1990), p. 191. The statistics are from Darrell Slider, "The Politics of Georgia's Independence," *Problems of Communism* 40, no. 6 (1991): 75.
66. Fuller, "Abkhaz-Georgian Relations Strained."
67. Elizabeth Fuller, "Georgian Parliament Votes to Abolish Ossetian Autonomy," *Report on the USSR* 2, no. 51 (December 21, 1990): 9.
68. *Komsomolskaia pravda,* April 26, 1998, p. 4, trans. in *Foreign Broadcast Information Service Daily Report: Soviet Union* (hereafter *FBIS*), April 27, 1988, pp. 45–47.
69. Ludmilla Alexeyeva, *Soviet Dissent: Contemporary Movements for National, Religious, and Human Rights* (Middletown, Conn.: Wesleyan University Press, 1987), pp. 106–9.
70. Suny, *The Making of the Georgian Nation,* p. 320.
71. Robert Parsons, "Georgians," in *The Nationalities Question in the Soviet Union,* ed. Graham Smith (London: Longman, 1990), pp. 188–89.
72. "Nationalists Stage Demonstrations in Georgia," AFP report, September 23, 1988, reprinted in *FBIS,* September 26, 1988, p. 63.
73. Natadze, interview, Tbilisi, June 1998. Natadze claimed the November 12 protest attracted 80,000 demonstrators.
74. Parsons, "Georgians," in *The Nationalities Question,* ed. Smith, pp. 189–90.
75. *Sovetskaya Kultura,* December 3, 1988, trans. in *FBIS,SOV-88-234* (December 6, 1988), p. 51; and Toomas Ilves, "Estonian Press on Georgian Events," *Report on the USSR* 1, no. 19 (May 12, 1989): 22.
76. Nodar Natadze, personal interview, Tbilisi, June 1998.
77. Nasmyth, *Georgia,* p. 86.
78. Nodar Natadze and Tengiz Sigua, interviews by author, Tbilisi, June 1998.
79. *Pravda,* April 9, 1989, p. 3, trans. in *CDSP* 41, no. 15 (May 10, 1989): 1.
80. Nodar Natadze, interview by author, Tbilisi, June 1998.
81. For the differing versions of the events of the Tbilisi massacre see Elizabeth Fuller and Goulnara Ouratadze, "Georgian Leadership Changes in the Aftermath of Demonstrators' Deaths," *Report on the USSR* 1, no. 16 (April 21, 1989): 30.
82. Interview by author with Abkhazian intellectual, Sukhumi, June 1998.
83. Reprinted in *Abkhazskie pis'ma,* p. 435.
84. Interviews by author with Abkhazian intellectual, Sukhumi, June 1998; and with Kochiev, Tskhinvali, June 1998.
85. Information on the organization is from Sergei Shamba, interview by author, Sukhumi, June 1998. The assessment of Gogua is my own.
86. Interview by author with Abkhazian intellectual, former *Aidgylara* leader, Sukhumi, June 1998.
87. Elizabeth Fuller, "Georgia, Abkhazia, and Chechno-Ingushetia," *RFE/RL Research Report* 1, no. 6 (February 7, 1992): 5.
88. Lykhny Appeal, p. 2.
89. Konstantin Ozgan, interview by author, Sukhumi, June 1998.
90. Interview by author with Abkhazian intellectual, former *Aidgylara* leader, Sukhumi, June 1998.

91. *Izvestia,* April 1, 1989, p. 2, trans. in *FBIS,* April 3, 1989, p. 71.
92. *Edinenie* (first issue of *Aidgylara* newspaper), October 25, 1989, p. 2.
93. AFP, April 8, 1989, trans. in *FBIS,* April 10, 1989, p. 39.
94. Elizabeth Fuller, "New Abkhaz Campaign for Secession from Georgia," *Report on the USSR* 1, no. 14 (April 7, 1989): 28.
95. Spartak Zhidkov, *Brosok maloi imperii* (Maikop: Adygeya, 1996), pp. 58, 63.
96. Darrell Slider, "The Politics of Georgia's Independence," pp. 66–67.
97. Interview by author with scholar, Tbilisi, May 1998.
98. Elizabeth Fuller, "Georgian Prosecutor Accused of Inciting Interethnic Hatred," *Report on the USSR* 2, no. 17 (April 27, 1990): 13; and Zhidkov, *Brosok maloi imperii,* p. 63.
99. Natella Akaba, interview by author, Sukhumi, June 1998.
100. Zhidkov, *Brosok maloi imperii,* p. 63–64.
101. For differing versions of the events of July 15, 1989, see Elizabeth Fuller, "Georgian Prosecutor Accused of Inciting Interethnic Hatred," p. 13; and Zhidkov, *Brosok maloi imperii,* p. 65. An account of the Mingrelian march was given by Adamia, leader of Merab Kostava Society, interview by author, Tbilisi, June 1998.
102. *Izvestia,* July 26, 1989, p. 6, trans. in *FBIS,* July 26, 1989, p. 74.
103. Zhidkov, *Brosok maloi imperii,* p. 72.
104. *Kommunisti,* July 25, 1989, trans. and summarized by Khatuna Chkheidze.
105. *Kommunisti,* August 5, 1998, trans. Khatuna Chkheidze.
106. *Kommunisti,* August 20, 1998, trans. and summarized by Khatuna Chkheidze.
107. Birch, "Georgian/South Ossetian Territorial and Boundary Dispute," p. 168.
108. Elizabeth Fuller, "The South Ossetian Campaign for Unification," *Report on the USSR* 1, no. 49 (December 8, 1989): 17–18.
109. Ibid., p. 18.
110. Natadze, interview, Tbilisi, June 1998.
111. Fuller, "The South Ossetian Campaign for Unification," p. 18. *Report on the USSR* 1, no. 30 (July 28, 1989), reported that Georgians were disproportionately among those killed (two-thirds of 22) and wounded (302 of 448).
112. Fuller, "The South Ossetian Campaign for Unification," p. 18.
113. Elizabeth Fuller, "Georgian Writers' Union Issues Secession Ultimatum," *Report on the USSR* 1, no. 29 (July 21, 1989): 28.
114. Moscow radio report, August 19, 1989, trans. in *FBIS-SOV-89-160* (August 21, 1989), p. 85.
115. *Izvestia,* October 29, 1989, p. 4, trans. in *FBIS-SOV-89-208* (October 30, 1989), p. 78.
116. Fuller, "The South Ossetian Campaign for Unification," p. 19.
117. Protests were reported in *Report on the USSR* 1, no. 45 (November 10, 1989): 30, and 1, no. 46 (November 17, 1989), p. 28. On the parliament's actions, see Elizabeth Fuller, "Georgia," *Report on the USSR* 1, no. 52 (December 29, 1989): 19.
118. The slogan of "head through the tunnel" was reported by Kochiev, interview, Tskhinvali, June 1998. The Georgian leader claiming the aim of "brotherhood" is Vazha Adamia, interview, Tbilisi, June 1998.
119. The charge of Georgian atrocities is reported in Elizabeth Fuller, "Georgian Parliament Votes to Abolish Ossetian Autonomy," *Report on the USSR* 2, no. 51 (December 21, 1990): 8. The charge of infanticide is alluded to by Fuller, and specified by Natadze, interview, Tbilisi, June 1998.
120. Fuller, "The South Ossetian Campaign for Unification," and "Georgian Parliament Votes to Abolish Ossetian Autonomy," pp. 8–9.
121. *Report on the USSR* 2, no. 41 (October 12, 1990): 29–30.

122. Elizabeth Fuller, "Democratization Threatened by Interethnic Violence," *Report on the USSR* 3, no. 1 (January 18, 1991): 43.
123. *TASS*, June 20, 1990, reported in *Report on the USSR* 2, no. 26 (June 29, 1990): 33.
124. Kochiev, interview, Tskhinvali, June 1998.
125. Elizabeth Fuller, "Round Table Coalition Wins Resounding Victory in Georgian Supreme Soviet Elections," *Report on the USSR* 2, no. 46 (November 16, 1990): 16.
126. Interview by author, Tbilisi, May 1998.
127. Nodar Tsuleiskiri, as quoted in *Izvestia*, May 21, 1991, trans. in *CDSP* 43, no. 20 (June 19, 1991): 25.
128. Slider, "Politics of Georgia's Independence," p. 70.
129. Hunter, *The Transcaucasus in Transition*, p. 120. Cf. *Report on the USSR* 3, no. 9 (March 1, 1991): 38.
130. Quoted in Valery Vyzhutovich, "Deadly Arguments," *Izvestia*, November 10, 1990, trans. in *CDSP* 42, no. 45 (December 12, 1990): 9.
131. Birch, "Georgian/South Ossetian Territorial and Boundary Dispute," p. 166.
132. Fuller, "Georgian Parliament Votes to Abolish Ossetian Autonomy," p. 9.
133. Quoted in Birch, "Georgian/South Ossetian Territorial and Boundary Dispute," p. 166.
134. Adamia, interview, Tbilisi, June 1998.
135. Quoted in Ronald Suny, "Elite Transformation in Late-Soviet and Post-Soviet Transcaucasia," in *Patterns in Post-Soviet Leadership*, ed. Timothy J. Colton and Robert C. Tucker (Boulder: Westview Press, 1995), p. 158.
136. The sequence of events is from *Izvestia*, December 12, 1990, p. 3; *Izvestia* December 13, 1990, p. 2; and *Izvestia* December 15, 1990, p. 1; all trans. in *CDSP* 42, no. 50 (January 16, 1991): 25–26. The inference of a causal connection is the author's.
137. *Pravda*, February 9, 1991, p. 1, trans. in *CDSP* 43, no. 6 (March 13, 1991): 25.
138. *Vestnik Gruzii*, March 22, 1991, p. 1, trans. in *FBIS-SOV-91-064* (April 4, 1991), p. 73.
139. Quoted in Birch, "Georgian/South Ossetian Territorial and Boundary Dispute," p. 166.
140. Natadze, interview, Tbilisi, June 1998.
141. Birch, "Georgian/South Ossetian Territorial and Boundary Dispute," p. 175.
142. *Report on the USSR* 3, no. 5 (February 1, 1991): 49; and Adamia, interview, Tbilisi, June 1998.
143. *Vestnik Gruzii*, March 27, 1991, p. 1, trans. in *FBIS-SOV-91-064* (April 3, 1991): 72.
144. *Report on the USSR* 3, no. 17 (April 13, 1991): 30; and 3, no. 24 (June 7, 1991): 39.
145. *Report on the USSR* 3, no. 7 (February 15, 1991): 44.
146. Gamsakhurdia's charge is in *Der Spiegel*, March 11, 1991, trans. in *FBIS* (March 12, 1991): 83–84. Evidence on Gorbachev's using the Dniestrian separatists to pressure the Moldovan government into signing the Union Treaty is discussed in chapter 5.
147. *Report on the USSR* 3, no. 16 (April 6, 1991): 23.
148. Elizabeth Fuller, "How Wholehearted Is Support in Georgia for Independence?" *Report on the USSR* 3, no. 15 (April 12, 1991): 19–20.
149. Details of the Georgian presidential race may be found in Elizabeth Fuller, "The Georgian Presidential Elections," *Report on the USSR* 3, no. 23 (June 7, 1991): 20–23.
150. Sigua, interview, June 1998.
151. *Report on the USSR* 3, no. 36 (September 6, 1991): 76.
152. Suzanne Goldenberg, *Pride of Small Nations: The Caucasus and Post-Soviet Disorder* (London: Zed Books, 1994), p. 83.
153. Ibid., p. 81. Goldenberg makes the point about personalism in ibid., p. 82.

154. Interview by author with Georgian intellectual, Tbilisi, July 1998.
155. Zhidkov, *Brosok maloi imperii,* pp. 146–49.
156. Suny, *The Making of the Georgian Nation,* p. 328.
157. *RFE/RL Research Report* 1, no. 22 (May 29, 1992): 66.
158. *RFE/RL Research Report* 1, no. 30 (July 24, 1992): 74.
159. Edward Ozhiganov, "The Republic of Georgia: Conflict in Abkhazia and South Ossetia," in *Managing Conflict in the Former Soviet Union: Russian and American Perspectives,* ed. Alexei Arbatov et al. (Cambridge, Mass.: MIT Press, 1997), p. 375.
160. Zhidkov, *Brosok maloi imperii,* p. 90.
161. Elizabeth Fuller, "Abkhazia on the Brink of Civil War?" *RFE/RL Research Report* 1, no. 35 (September 4, 1992): 2.
162. Zhidkov, *Brosok maloi imperii,* p. 100.
163. Georgian officials would allege tampering with the results, which cast serious doubt on the claimed Abkhazian support for Georgian independence in the state referendum two weeks later.
164. Quoted in Hewitt, "Abkhazia: A Problem of Identity and Ownership," pp. 207, 215.
165. Alexidze's authorship of the plan was mentioned in numerous interviews; the quote about Gamsakhurdia's flexibility is from Jonathan Aves, "The Georgian Crisis," in *Brassey's Defence Yearbook* (London: Brassey's, 1993), p. 98.
166. For details of the relations between Georgians and Abkhazians in early 1991, see Fuller, "Abkhazia on the Brink of Civil War?" pp. 2–3.
167. Svetlana Chervonnaya, *Conflict in the Caucasus,* p. 91.
168. Ibid., p. 92.
169. A shrill example is Tamaz Nadareishvili, *Genocide in Abkhazia* (Tbilisi: 1994).
170. Eteri Astemirova, interview by author, Tbilisi, June 1998.
171. Interview by author with Natella Akaba, former member of Abkhazian Supreme Soviet, Sukhumi, June 1998.
172. *RFE/RL Research Report* 1, no. 21 (May 22, 1992): 70.
173. Chervonnaya, *Conflict in the Caucasus,* p. 106.
174. Zhidkov, *Brosok maloi imperii,* pp. 153–55.
175. Sigua, interview, Tbilisi, June 1998.
176. Zhidkov, *Brosok maloi imperii,* pp. 164–65.
177. Gueorgui Otyrba, "War in Abkhazia: The Regional Significance of the Georgian-Abkhazian Conflict," in *National Identity and Ethnicity in Russia and the New States of Eurasia,* ed. Roman Szporluk (Armonk, N.Y.: M. E. Sharpe, 1994), p. 287.
178. Ibid.
179. *Komsomolskaia pravda,* August 7, 1992, p. 2, trans. in *FBIS-SOV-92-153* (August 7, 1992): p. 83.
180. *Izvestia,* July 27, 1992, p. 1, trans. in *CDSP* 44, no. 30 (August 26, 1992): 25.
181. Chervonnaya, *Conflict in the Caucasus,* p. 114.
182. George Khutsishvili, "The OSCE and Conflict in Georgia," in *Balancing Hegemony: The OSCE in the CIS,* ed. S. Neil MacFarlane and Oliver Thranert (Kingston, Ontario: Queen's University Press, 1997), p. 106. Khutsishvili here is describing Georgian attitudes measured after the war, but the attitudes quoted seem to have been current before it as well.
183. Ghia Nodia, "Georgia's Identity Crisis," *Journal of Democracy* 6, no. 1 (January 1995): 108.
184. Sigua, interview, Tbilisi, June 1998.
185. See, for example, the comments of Jaba Ioseliani in *Smena* (Bratislava), August 3, 1992, p. 11, trans. in *FBIS-SOV-92-151* (August 5, 1992): 82.

186. Elizabeth Fuller, "Transcaucasia: Ethnic Strife Threatens Democratization," *RFE/RL Research Report* 2, no. 1 (January 1, 1993): 23.
187. Zhidkov, *Brosok maloi imperii*, p. 206.
188. Ibid., pp. 207–8.
189. The story about the envoys is from Shamba, interview, Sukhumi, June 1998.
190. Natella Akaba, interview by author, Sukhumi, June 1998; Sergei Shamba, who was soon to be named defense chief, corroborates the surprise of the Abkhazian side. Shamba, interview, Sukhumi, June 1998.
191. Chervonnaya, *Conflict in the Caucasus*, p. 118.
192. Ozhiganov, "The Republic of Georgia," p. 379.
193. B. G. Hewitt, "Abkhazia: A Problem of Identity and Ownership," p. 217.
194. Catherine Dale, "Turmoil in Abkhazia: Russian Responses," *RFE/RL Research Report* 2, no. 34 (August 27, 1993): 50.
195. *New York Times*, September 29, 1993, p. 6.
196. Dale, "Turmoil in Abkhazia," p. 53.
197. Ibid., p. 55.
198. Elizabeth Fuller, "Russia's Diplomatic Offensive in the Transcaucasus," *RFE/RL Research Report* 2, no. 39 (October 1, 1993): 31.
199. Elizabeth Fuller, "The Transcaucasus: War, Turmoil, Economic Collapse," *RFE/RL Research Report* 3, no. 1 (January 7, 1994): 57.
200. Chervonnaya, *Conflict in the Caucasus*, p. 136.
201. Nadareishvili, *Genocide in Abkhazia*, 127.
202. Vitalii Shariia, *Abkhazskaia tragediia: Sbornik* (Sochi, 1993), pp. 84–90.
203. Ibid., p. 119.
204. Ruth Seifert, "War and Rape: A Preliminary Analysis," in *Mass Rape: The War against Women in Bosnia-Herzegovina*, ed. Alexandra Stiglmayer, trans. Marion Faber (Lincoln: University of Nebraska Press, 1984), p. 55.
205. Revaz Gachechiladze, *The New Georgia: Space, Society, Politics* (College Station: Texas A & M University Press, 1994), pp. 74, 92, 174–75.
206. Elizabeth Fuller, "Azerbaijani Exodus from Georgia Imminent?" *Report on the USSR* 3, no. 7 (February 15, 1991): 17.
207. Ibid.; Gachechiladze, *The New Georgia*, p. 92; and Nelson and Amonashvili, "Voting and Political Attitudes in Soviet Georgia," p. 692.
208. Georgi Derluguian, unpublished paper, n.d.
209. Adamia, interview, Tbilisi, June 1998.

Chapter 5. Elite Conspiracy in Moldova's Civil War

1. On the Gagauz, see Jeff Chinn and Steve D. Roper, "Territorial Autonomy in Gagauzia," *Nationalities Papers* 26, no. 1 (1998): 87–101.
2. See Pal Kolsto and Andrei Malgin, "The Transnistrian Republic: A Case of Politicized Regionalism," *Nationalities Papers* 26, no. 1 (1998): 103–28.
3. Crawford Young, *The Politics of Cultural Pluralism* (Madison: University of Wisconsin Press, 1976).
4. Pal Kolsto and Andrei Edemsky with Natalya Kalashnikova, "The Dniestr Conflict: Between Irredentism and Separatism," *Europe-Asia Studies* 45, no. 6 (1993): 977.
5. Michael F. Hamm, "Kishinev: The Character and Development of a Tsarist Frontier Town," *Nationalities Papers* 26, no. 1 (1998): 25, 28.

6. Wim van Meurs, "Carving a Moldavian Identity out of History," *Nationalities Papers* 26, no. 1 (1998): 41–43; and Charles King, "Moldovan Identity and the Politics of Pan-Romanianism," *Slavic Review* 53, no. 2 (1994): 348.
7. Irina Livezeanu, "Moldavia, 1917–1990: Nationalism and Internationalism Then and Now," *Armenian Review* 43, no. 2–3 (1990): 166–69.
8. Oazu Nantoi, former Popular Front leader, interview by author, July 1998, Chisinau.
9. Iurie Rosca, interview by author, July 1998.
10. Nicholas Dima, *From Moldavia to Moldova,* 2d ed. (Boulder, Colo.: East European Monographs, 1991), pp. 1–2.
11. "Moldavians" and "Moldavian Soviet Socialist Republic," *Great Soviet Encyclopedia,* vol. 16 (1974), pp. 423–27.
12. Ibid., p. 426.
13. Dima, *From Moldavia to Moldova,* p. 11.
14. Archimandrite Felix Dubneac, "Christian Creative Values in the Thought of Mihai Eminescu," in *Eminescu: The Evening Star of Romanian Poetry,* ed. Jean Carduner, Lucian Rosu, and Karl Natanson, The First Mihai Eminescu Symposium at the University of Michigan, Ann Arbor, and at the International Institute in Detroit (Ann Arbor: University of Michigan Department of Romance Languages, 1986), p. 14.
15. Dima, *From Moldavia to Moldova,* pp. 17–18.
16. Livezeanu, "Moldavia, 1917–1990," p. 163.
17. Quoted in ibid., p. 171.
18. King, "Moldovan Identity," p. 348.
19. "Resolution of the Committee of the Supreme Soviet of the S.S.R. of Moldova on the Political and Legal Evaluation of the Soviet-German Non-Aggression Pact and the Supplementary Secret Protocol from August 23rd 1939 and on Their consequences for Bessarabia and Northern Bucovina," reprinted in *The Pact: Molotov-Ribbentrop and its Consequences for Bessarabia,* ed. Ion Shishcanu and Vitaliu Varatec (Chisinau: Universitas, 1991).
20. Dima, *From Moldavia to Moldova,* pp. 94–98.
21. Ibid., p. 71.
22. William Crowther, "The Politics of Mobilization: Nationalism and Reform in Soviet Moldavia," *Russian Review* 50, no. 2 (1991): 186–87.
23. Jonathan Eyal, "Moldavians," in *The Nationalities Question in the Soviet Union,* ed. Graham Smith (New York: Longman, 1990), p. 127.
24. "Moldavian Soviet Socialist Republic," in *Great Soviet Encyclopedia,* vol. 16 (1974).
25. Ibid.
26. Ibid.
27. Ibid.
28. Vladimir Socor, "The Moldavian Democratic Movement: Structure, Program, and Initial Impact," *Report on the USSR* 1, no. 8 (February 24, 1989): 32.
29. Irina Livezeanu, "Urbanization in a Low Key and Linguistic Change in Soviet Moldavia, Part I," *Soviet Studies* 43, no. 3 (1981): 574.
30. See Stuart Kaufman, Leokadia Drobizheva, and Airat Aklaev, "Nationalist Mobilization in Estonia and Moldova" (paper prepared for delivery at the 1994 Annual Meeting of the American Political Science Association, September 1994).
31. Crowther, "The Politics of Mobilization," p. 186.
32. Valeriu Motei, member of Parliament of Moldova, interview by author, March 1995, Chisinau.
33. On the situation in education, see Kathleen Mihalisko, "*Komsomolskaia Pravda* Defends Special Historical Issue of Moldavian Student Newspaper," *RFE/RL*

Research Bulletin, RL 182/88 (April 27, 1988); on workers' complaints, see Crowther, "The Politics of Mobilization." On the state of the language, see *Izvestia,* June 2, 1989, trans. in *CDSP* 41, no. 27 (August 2, 1989): 9–10.

34. An example of the tone just before the leadership change is *Sovetskaia Moldavia,* November 8, 1989, trans. in *CDSP* 41, no. 46 (December 13, 1989): 21.
35. *Sovetskaia Moldavia* (Kishinev), 16 July 1989, p. 1.
36. *Sovetskaia Moldavia,* July 15, 1989 p. 1.
37. *Sovetskaia Moldavia,* July 9, 1989, p. 2.
38. Livezeanu, "Moldavia, 1917–1990," p. 176.
39. Vladimir Socor, in *Report on the USSR* 1 (September 8, 1989): 35. The estimate of 100,000 is from an interview with one of the organizers: interview by author with Oazu Nantoi, July 1998, Chisinau.
40. Quoted in Vladimir Socor, "The Moldavian Democratic Movement," *Report on the USSR* 1, no. 8 (February 24, 1989): 32.
41. Christian Democratic Popular Front, *Identity Act* (Chisinau: Tara, 1995), p. 4.
42. The rally's demands are listed in ibid., p. 5.
43. Nantoi, interview, July 1998.
44. Ibid.
45. Crowther, "The Politics of Mobilization," pp. 192–96.
46. Vladimir Solonari, member of Parliament of Moldova, interview by author, March 1995.
47. Vladimir Rylyakov, former member of Parliament of Moldova, interview by author, March 1995, Tiraspol.
48. *Sovetskaia Moldavia,* May 27, 1990; and *Izvestia* June 6, 1990, trans. in *CDSP* 42, no. 23 (June 27, 1990): 21.
49. *Sovetskaia Moldavia,* May 24, 1989, summarized in *CDSP* 42, no. 21 (June 13, 1990): 15, n. 3.
50. For an example, see ibid.
51. William Crowther, "Exploring Political Culture: A Comparative Analysis of Romania and Moldova," report to the National Council for Soviet and East European Research, n.d., Tables 4 and 5
52. Zinaida Nikolaevna Ocunsky, Department of National Minorities, interview by author, March 1995.
53. *Sovetskaia Moldavia,* June 8, 1990, pp. 1–2, trans. in *FBIS-SOV-90-126* (June 29, 1990): 116.
54. Christian Democratic Popular Front, *Identity Act,* pp. 6–7, 24.
55. *Izvestia,* May 23, 1991, trans. in *CDSP* 43, no. 21 (June 26, 1991): 23.
56. Nantoi, interview, July 1998.
57. *Dniestrovskaia Pravda* (hereafter *DP*), May 4, 1990, p. 3.
58. *Pravda,* June 27, 1990, trans. in *CDSP* 42, no. 21 (June 13, 1990): 15–16. One Russian-speaking deputy noted that Snegur had little motivation to protect the deputies from the Dniestr region: Snegur himself had been abused during a visit to that region not long before. Solonari, interview, March 1995.
59. Rylyakov, interview, March 1995.
60. *Sovetskaia Moldavia,* September 4, 1990.
61. Nantoi, interview, July 1998, Chisinau.
62. Mircea Snegur, interview by author, July 1998, Chisinau.
63. Vasile Nedelciuc, member of Parliament of Moldova, former Popular Front leader, interview by author, March 1995, Chisinau.
64. Valeriu Muravschi, interview by author, March 1995, Chisinau.
65. *Sovetskaia Moldavia,* November 4, 1990; *Dialog,* no. 19, 1990.

66. Interviews by author with Nicolae Chirtoaca, former national security aide to President Snegur, and Viktor Grebenschikov, former aide to Prime Minister Druc, March 1995, Chisinau.
67. Andrei Safonov, former member of Parliament of Moldova, interview by author, March 1995, Tiraspol.
68. Interview by author with former Popular Front leader, March 1995, Chisinau.
69. Nantoi, interview, July 1998, Chisinau.
70. Interview by author with official of the Christian Democratic Popular Front, March 1995.
71. Interview by author with official of the Liberal Democratic Party, March 1995.
72. *DP,* September 7, 1989.
73. *DP,* September 9, 1989, p. 1.
74. *DP,* September 14, 1989, p. 2.
75. *Sovetskaia Moldavia,* August 25, 1989, p. 3.
76. Socor, in *Report on the* USSR 1 (September 8, 1989): 33–34.
77. Alexandru Mosanu, former chairman, Parliament of Moldova, interview by author, March 1995, Chisinau.
78. *DP,* September 12, 1989, p. 3.
79. *DP,* September 2, 1989, p. 1.
80. *DP,* September 2, September 5, and September 23, 1989.
81. *DP,* September 23, 1989, p. 3.
82. *DP,* September 9, 1989.
83. *Sovetskaia Moldavia,* January 30, 1990.
84. *Sovetskaia Moldavia,* May 25, 1990, trans. in *CDSP* 42, no. 21 (June 27, 1990): 15.
85. *Sovetskaia Moldavia,* September 4, 1990.
86. *DP,* May 8, 1990; May 9, 1990, p. 1; June 13, 1990.
87. *DP,* May 1, 1990, p. 3; cf. *DP,* May 13, 1990, p. 1.
88. *DP,* June 7, 1990, p. 3.
89. *DP,* May 1, 1990, p. 1.
90. See, for example, *DP,* June 5 and June 7, 1990.
91. See, for example, *DP,* September 5, 1991.
92. *FBIS,* March 18, 1992, p. 55.
93. *DP,* September 2, 1991 and September 6, 1991, p. 1.
94. *Pravda,* November 16, 1991, trans. in *CDSP* 43, no. 46 (December 18, 1991): 12; and *Nezavisimaia gazeta,* December 17, 1991, trans. in *CDSP* 43, no. 50 (January 15, 1992): 29.
95. On flaws in the balloting process, see Kolsto et al., "The Dniestr Conflict," pp. 985–86.
96. Interview by author with dissident from Tiraspol, March 1995, Chisinau.
97. "Moldova and the Case of Ilie Ilascu," unpublished manuscript circulated by Nicholas Dima.
98. Col. Mikhail Bergman, Fourteenth Russian Army, interview by author, March 1995, Tiraspol.
99. Solonari, interview, March 1995, Chisinau.
100. See, for example, the account of a battle in December 1991, *Nezavisimaia gazeta,* December 17, 1999, trans. in *CDSP* 43, no. 50 (January 15, 1993): 29–30.
101. See, for example, Radio Bucharest, May 7, 1992, trans. in *FBIS-SOV-92-090* (May 8, 1990): 51.
102. See *Izvestia,* March 6, 1992, trans. in *FBIS,* March 11, 1992, p. 55; and *Izvestia,* March 11, 1992, trans. in *FBIS,* March 12, 1992, p. 29.
103. *Nezavisimaia gazeta,* March 31, 1992, trans. in *CDSP* 44, no. 13 (April 29, 1992): 11.

104. Pavel Creanga, *Ia khochu rasskazat'* (Kishinev, 1998), p. 135.
105. G. P. Volovoi, *Krovavoe leto v Benderakh: Khronika pridnestrovskoi tragedii [Bloody summer in Bendery: Chronicles of the Transnistrian tragedy]* (Bendery: Poligrafist, 1993), p. 5.
106. Former presidential national security advisor Nicolae Chirtoaca, for example, suspects that a "third force" was launching mines at both sides. Interview by author, March 1995, Chisinau.
107. Creanga, *Ia khochu rasskazat'*, p. 136.
108. Ibid.; and Chirtoaca, interview, March 1995.
109. Socor, "Gorbachev and Moldavia," *Report on the USSR* 2, no. 51 (December 21, 1990): 11–14.
110. TASS, September 14, 1989, trans. in *FBIS*, September 14, 1989, p. 37.
111. *Pravda* September 11, 1989, trans. in *FBIS*, September 11, 1989, p. 61.
112. *Pravda*, September 3, 1989, trans. in *CDSP* 41, no. 35 (September 27, 1989): 7.
113. *Pravda*, August 28, 1989, trans. in *CDSP* 41, no. 35 (September 27, 1989), pp. 5–8; *Moskovskie Novosti*, November 10, 1989, trans. in *CDSP* 41, no. 46 (December 13, 1989): 21–23.
114. *Izvestia*, September 3, 1990, trans. in *CDSP* 42, no. 35 (October 10, 1990): 27–28; *Izvestia*, November 1, 1990, trans. in *CDSP* 42, no. 43 (November 28, 1990): 5–6.
115. *Krasnaia Zvezda*, September 8, 1990, p. 5, trans. in *FBIS*, Sept. 12, 1990, p. 98.
116. "Vremya" television broadcast, September 6, 1990, trans. in *FBIS*, September 6, 1990, p. 94.
117. Snegur, interview, July 1998.
118. Motei, interview, March 1995, Chisinau. Motei, a member of the Moldovan delegation, was present at the time.
119. Interview by author with dissident from Tiraspol, March 1995, Chisinau.
120. Besides the habit of the military press referring to the Dniester Republic as if it were legal, leading military officers repeatedly complained of Chisinau's antimilitary policies. An early example of the latter is in *Krasnaia zvezda*, April 5, 1990, trans. in *FBIS* April 23, 1990, p. 135.
121. According to Nicholas Dima, three Soviet officers in civilian clothing were arrested for such activity in November 1990. See Dima, *From Moldavia to Moldova*, p. 152.
122. Moscow television news broadcast, September 8, 1990, trans. in *FBIS*, September 11, 1990, p. 90.
123. *Sovetskaia Moldavia*, July 24, 1990, trans. in *FBIS*, August 13, 1990, p. 95.
124. See Vladimir Socor, "Gorbachev and Moldavia."
125. TASS, November 20, trans. in *FBIS*, November 20, 1990, p. 68; and TASS, November 22, 1990, trans. in *FBIS*, November 23, 1990, p. 46.
126. In May, Snegur openly advocated a "renewed federation"; see *Sovetskaia Moldavia*, May 1, 1990; a later hint in the same direction is in *Izvestia*, June 25, 1990, trans. in *CDSP* 42, no. 25 (July 25, 1990): 24.
127. *Izvestia*, November 5, 1990, trans. in *CDSP* 42, no. 43 (November 28, 1990): 7; and *Izvestia*, November 15, 1990, trans. in *CDSP* 42, no. 46 (December 19, 1990): 24.
128. A similar but not identical interpretation is in Socor, "Gorbachev and Moldavia."
129. TASS, April 26, 1991, reprinted in *FBIS*, April 29, 1991, p. 55.
130. *Izvestia*, June 12, 1992, trans. in *CDSP* 44, no. 24 (July 15, 1992): 13.
131. TASS, September 23, 1991, trans. in *FBIS*, September 24, 1991, p. 77.
132. Brian D. Taylor, "Commentary on Moldova," in *Managing Conflict in the Former Soviet Union: Russian and American Perspectives*, ed. Alexei Arbatov, Abram Chayes, Antonia Handler Chayes, and Lara Olson (Cambridge, Mass.: MIT Press,

1997), p. 214. Cf. Edward Ozhiganov, "The Republic of Moldova: Transdniester and the 14th Army," in ibid., pp. 178–79.

133. The story of the white Mercedes is from Chirtoaca, interview, March 1995, Chisinau. That the Fourteenth Army provided the Transnistrians with weapons was confirmed by Col. Mikhail Bergman, Tiraspol garrison commandant, Fourteenth Russian Army, interview by author, March 1995, Tiraspol.
134. Muravschi, interview, March 1995, Chisinau.
135. TASS, September 23, 1991, trans. in *FBIS*, September 24, 1991, p. 77.
136. The superior was Lt. Gen. Kuznetsov, first deputy commander of the Odessa Military District, to which the Fourteenth Army was subordinated. TASS, December 7, 1991, trans. in *FBIS*, December 9, 1991, p. 57.
137. On Moscow's reaction, see Interfax, December 9, 1991, reprinted in *FBIS*, December 10, 1991, pp. 59–60; Yakovlev's reappearance as commander was noted on Chisinau radio, January 9, 1992, trans. in *FBIS*, January 10, 1992, p. 46.
138. TASS, January 10, 1992, trans. in *FBIS*, January 10, 1992, p. 45.
139. Kishinev Radio, January 21, 1992, trans. in *FBIS*, January 22, 1992, p. 80.
140. *Izvestia*, June 1, 1992, trans. in *CDSP* 44, no. 22 (July 1, 1992).
141. TASS, March 27, 1992, trans. in *FBIS*, March 26, 1992, p. 15.
142. Snegur, interview, July 1998.
143. Socor, "Moldova's 'Dniestr' Ulcer," *RFE/RL Research Report* 2, no. 1 (January 1, 1993): 14. Cf. Neil V. Lamont, "Territorial Dimensions of Ethnic Conflict: The Moldovan Case, 1991–March 1993," *Journal of Slavic Military Studies* 6, no. 4 (December 1993): 583.
144. See Vladimir Socor, "Russia's Army in Moldova: There to Stay?" *RFE/RL Research Report* 2, no. 25 (June 18, 1993): 42–49.
145. Radio Romania, March 12, 1992, trans. in *FBIS*, March 16, 1992, p. 85; *Rossiiskaia gazeta*, March 31, 1992, trans. in *FBIS*, April 1, 1992, p. 56.
146. *Izvestia*, June 12, 1992, trans. in *CDSP* 44, no. 24 (July 15, 1992): 13; *Nezavismaia gazeta*, May 27, 1992, trans. in *CDSP* 44, no. 21 (June 24, 1992).
147. Interviews by author with NGO leader, March 1995, Chisinau; and with Oazu Nantoi, July 1998, Chisinau.
148. Taylor, "Commentary on Moldova."
149. Radio Odin, March 26, 1992, trans. in *FBIS*, March 26, 1992, p. 66.
150. Kolsto et al., "The Transnistrian Republic," p. 988; Chirtoaca, interview, March 1995.
151. Charles King, "Eurasia Letter: Moldova with a Russian Face," *Foreign Policy* 97 (Winter 1994): 111.
152. *Izvestia*, July 7, 1992, trans. in *CDSP* 44, no. 27 (August 5, 1992): 13; *Nezasisimaia gazeta*, July 30, 1992, trans. in *CDSP* 44, no. 30 (August 26, 1992): 20.
153. Socor, "Moldova's 'Dniestr' Ulcer," p. 15.
154. *Izvestia*, July 16, 1992, trans. in *CDSP* 44, no. 28 (August 12, 1992): 19.
155. *Nezavisimaia gazeta*, August 11, 1992, trans. in *CDSP* 44, no. 32 (September 9, 1992): 21.
156. *Nezavisimaia gazeta*, October 22, 1992, trans. in *CDSP* 44, no. 42 (November 18, 1992): 21; and *Isvestia*, December 8, 1992, trans. in *CDSP* 44, no. 49 (January 6, 1993): 24.
157. *ITAR-TASS*, April 3, 1992, trans. in *FBIS*, April 3, 1992, p. 59.
158. Compare Radio Romania, March 30, 1992, trans. in *FBIS*, March 31, 1992, p. 55, with *Izvestia*, February 25, 1994.
159. Creanga, *Ia khochu rasskazat'*, pp. 131–32.

160. Chinn and Roper, "Territorial Autonomy in Gagauzia," pp. 87–90; S. S. Kuroglo and M. V. Marunevich, *Sotsiologicheskie preobrazovaniia v bytu i kul'ture gagauzskogo naseleniia MSSR* (Kishinev: Shtiintsa, 1983), pp. 86–93.
161. I. I. Meshcheriuk, *Antikreposticheskaia bor'ba Gagauzov i Bolgar Bessarabii* (Kishinev: State Press of Moldova, 1957).
162. Charles King, "Minorities Policy in the Post-Soviet Republics: The Case of the Gagauzi," *Ethnic and Racial Studies* 20, no. 4 (1997): 742.
163. Chinn and Roper, "Territorial Autonomy in Gagauzia."

Chapter 6. Government Jingoism and the Fall of Yugoslavia

1. Census data are reported in Vojislav Stanovcic, "Problems and Options in Institutionalizing Ethnic Relations," *International Political Science Review* 13, no. 4 (1992): 369.
2. Paul Lendvai, "Yugoslavia without Yugoslavs: The Roots of the Crisis," *International Affairs* 67, no. 2 (1991): 253.
3. These numbers are reported in James Gow, "Deconstructing Yugoslavia," *Survival* 33, no. 4 (1991): 293.
4. Lenard J. Cohen, *Broken Bonds: Yugoslavia's Disintegration and Balkan Politics in Transition* (Boulder: Westview Press, 1995), p. 241.
5. These kingdoms are discussed, *inter alia,* in Ivo Banac, *The National Question in Yugoslavia* (Ithaca: Cornell University Press, 1984); and Barbara Jelavich, *History of the Balkans,* vol. 1 (Cambridge: Cambridge University Press, 1983).
6. Marcus Tanner, *Croatia: A Nation Forged in War* (New Haven: Yale University Press, 1997), pp. 9–15.
7. Sources include Jelavich, *History of the Balkans;* Sir Charles Eliot, *Turkey in Europe* (New York: Barnes and Noble, 1900/1965); Harold W. V. Temperley, *History of Serbia* (London: G. Bell and Sons, 1919); and H. G. Koenigsberger and George L. Mosse, *Europe in the Sixteenth Century* (London: Longman, 1968).
8. Quoted in Tanner, *Croatia,* p. 48.
9. L. S. Stavrianos, *Balkans since 1453* (New York: Rinehart and Company, 1958), pp. 462–64, 590; Tim Judah, *The Serbs: History, Myth, and the Destruction of Yugoslavia* (New Haven: Yale University Press, 1997), pp. 87–89.
10. Stavrianos, *Balkans since 1453,* pp. 624–32.
11. Judah, *The Serbs,* p. 115.
12. Milovan Zanic, quoted in Tanner, *Croatia,* p. 150.
13. The casualty estimates are those of Vladimir Zerjavic, cited in Sabrina Petra Ramet, *Nationalism and Federalism in Yugoslavia, 1962–1991,* 2d ed. (Bloomington: Indiana University Press, 1992), p. 255.
14. Tanner, *Croatia,* p. 169; Judah, *The Serbs,* p. 130.
15. Ramet, *Nationalism and Federalism in Yugoslavia,* p. 255.
16. Ibid., chap. 7.
17. On Yugoslavia's chauvinist myths, see Svijeto Job, "Yugoslavia's Ethnic Furies," *Foreign Policy* 92 (Fall 1993): 52–74.
18. Judah, *The Serbs,* pp. 20–21.
19. Serbian folk song, reprinted and translated in *Marko the Prince: Serbo-Croat Heroic Songs,* trans. Anne Pennington and Peter Levi (New York: St. Martin's, 1984), pp. 17–18.

20. Quoted in Laura Silber and Allen Little, *Yugoslavia: Death of a Nation,* rev. ed. (New York, Penguin Books, 1997), p. 72.
21. Judah, *The Serbs,* pp. 35–36.
22. Jack Snyder, *Voting for Violence: Democratization and Nationalist Conflict* (New York: Norton, 2000), notes the importance of state propaganda in this effort.
23. Ilia Garasanin, "Nacertanije," reprinted and trans. in Ante Beljo et al., eds., *Greater Serbia: From Ideology to Aggression* (Zagreb: Croatian Information Centre, 1993), pp. 10–12.
24. Vuk Karadzic, "Serbs All and Everywhere," in *Greater Serbia,* ed. Beljo et al., pp. 18–22.
25. Quoted in Tanner, *Croatia,* p. 103.
26. Judah, *The Serbs,* pp. 76–77.
27. Quoted in ibid., p. 103.
28. Ibid., pp. 133, 128.
29. Quoted in Cohen, *Broken Bonds,* p. 29.
30. Tanner, *Croatia,* pp. 6–9.
31. Ramet, *Nationalism and Federalism in Yugoslavia,* p. 205.
32. Judah, *The Serbs,* p. 13.
33. Banac, *The National Question in Yugoslavia,* pp. 71–75.
34. Quoted in Tanner, *Croatia,* p. 75.
35. Banac, *The National Question in Yugoslavia,* pp. 76–77.
36. Ibid., pp. 85–90.
37. Ibid., pp. 147–51.
38. A summary of this history is in Cohen, *Broken Bonds,* 8–21. Cf. Alex Dragnich, *Serbia, Nikola Pasic, and Yugoslavia* (New Brunswick, N.J.: Rutgers University Press, 1974).
39. Quoted in Tanner, *Croatia,* p. 223.
40. Kaplan, *Balkan Ghosts,* pp. 11–18.
41. Banac, *The National Question in Yugoslavia,* pp. 111–15.
42. Ramet, *Nationalism and Federalism in Yugoslavia,* pp. 117, 207–9.
43. Florence Hamlish Levinsohn, *Belgrade: Among the Serbs* (Chicago: Ivan R. Dee, 1994), p. 15.
44. The discussion here is based on Susan Woodward, *Balkan Tragedy* (Washington, D.C.: Brookings Institution, 1995), pp. 52–55.
45. See Elez Biberaj, "Albanian-Yugoslav Relations and the Question of Kosove," *East European Quarterly* 16, no. 4 (1983): 485–509.
46. Silber and Little, *Yugoslavia: Death of a Nation,* p. 38.
47. Tanner, *Croatia,* p. 212.
48. Silber and Little, *Yugoslavia: Death of a Nation,* pp. 37–45.
49. Judah, *The Serbs,* p. 160.
50. For a similar interpretation of Milosevic's rise, see Aleksa Djilas, "A Profile of Slobodan Milosevic," *Foreign Affairs* 72, no. 3 (1993): 81–96.
51. Ivo Banac, "The Fearful Asymmetry of War: The Causes and Consequences of Yugoslavia's Demise," *Daedalus* 121, no. 2 (1992): 155.
52. Milan Andrejevich, "Milosevic and the Socialist Party of Serbia," *Radio Free Europe Report on Eastern Europe* (hereafter *RFE*) 1, no. 31 (August 3, 1990): 44.
53. Milan Andrejevich, "Yugoslavia's Lingering Crisis," *RFE* 1, no. 1 (January 5, 1990): 34.
54. Quoted in Silber and Little, *Yugoslavia: Death of a Nation,* p. 72.
55. Dennison Rusinow, "Yugoslavia: Balkan Breakup?" *Foreign Policy* 83 (Summer 1991): 150–51.

56. Ramet, *Nationalism and Federalism in Yugoslavia*, p. 242.
57. Ibid., chap. 1.
58. Ibid., p. 209.
59. Gow, *Legitimacy and the Military*, pp. 79–88.
60. Ramet, *Nationalism and Federalism in Yugoslavia*, p. 211.
61. Silber and Little, *Yugoslavia: Death of a Nation*, pp. 79–80.
62. Milan Andrejevich, "Slovenia Heading toward Independence," *RFE* 1, no. 13 (March 30, 1990): 37; and Andrejevich, "Communist Wins Presidential Run-off in Slovenia," *RFE* 1, no. 18 (May 4, 1990): 34.
63. Cohen, *Broken Bonds*, pp. 90, 173–74.
64. Ivan Grdesic et al., *Hrvatska u izborima '90* (Zagreb: Naprijed, 1991), p. 108, table trans. by William Zimmerman.
65. Glenny, *The Fall of Yugoslavia*, p. 63.
66. U.S. Congress. Hearing of the Senate Committee on Foreign Relations, Subcommittee on European Affairs, *Civil Strife in Yugoslavia: The United States Response*, Prepared Statement of Veljko Miljus, 102d Congress, 1st Sess., February 21, 1991 (S. Hrg. 102–12), p. 55.
67. Tanner, *Croatia*, pp. 223–29.
68. Kaplan, *Balkan Ghosts*, p. 13.
69. BBC, *Yugoslavia: Death of a Nation*, video series, part 2.
70. Tanner, *Croatia*, pp. 226–28.
71. Institut drustvenih nauka, *Jugoslavija na krizsnoj prekretnici* (Beograd, 1991), p. 211, table trans. William Zimmerman; and Cohen, *Broken Bonds*, p. 173.
72. Grdesic et al., *Hrvatska u izborima '90* p. 111. Table trans. William Zimmerman.
73. Milan Andrejevich, "Crisis in Croatia and Slovenia: Proposal for a Confederal Yugoslavia," *RFE* 1, no. 44 (November 2, 1990): 31.
74. Milan Andrejevich, "Croatia between Stability and Civil War (part 1)," *RFE* 1, no. 37 (September 14, 1990): 40.
75. Milan Andrejevich, "The Yugoslavia Crisis: No Solution in Sight," *RFE* 2, no. 8 (February 22, 1991): 40.
76. Milan Andrejevich, "Political Crisis in Serbia," *RFE* 1, no. 29 (July 20, 1990): 42.
77. "Weekly Record of Events," *RFE* 2, no. 30 (July 26, 1991): 45.
78. Belgrade domestic [radio] service, November 13, 1990, trans. in *Foreign Broadcast Information Service Daily Report: Eastern Europe* (hereafter *FBIS-EEU*), November 15, 1990, p. 70.
79. Milan Andrejevich, "Serbia on the Eve of the Elections," *RFE* 1, p. 51 (December 21, 1990): 35.
80. Tanjug domestic [radio] service, December 5, 1990, trans. in *FBIS-EEU*, December 7, 1990, p. 67.
81. Ljubljana domestic [radio] service, December 26, 1990, trans. in *FBIS-EEU*, December 27, 1990, p. 37.
82. Milan Andrejevich, "Vojvodina Hungarian Group to Seek Cultural Autonomy," *RFE* 1, no. 41 (October 12, 1990): 43.
83. Andrejevich, "Serbia on the Eve of the Elections," *p.* 33.
84. The same case is made in Denitch, *Ethnic Nationalism*.
85. Grdesic et al., *Hrvatska u izborima*, p. 108.
86. Andrejevich, "Croatia between Stability and Civil War (part 2)," *RFE* 1, no. 39 (September 28, 1990): 41.
87. Silber and Little, *Yugoslavia: Death of a Nation*, p. 95.
88. The quote is from Jovan Raskovic's daughter, quoted in ibid., p. 96.
89. Rusinow, "Yugoslavia: Balkan Breakup?" p. 155.

90. Robert D. Kaplan, "Croatianism," *New Republic* (November 25, 1991), p. 16–18.
91. Andrejevich, "Croatia between Stability and Civil War (part 1)," p. 41.
92. Glenny, *The Fall of Yugoslavia*, pp. 3, 13; U.S. Congress, Hearing of the Senate Committee on Foreign Relations, Subcommittee on European Affairs, *Civil Strife in Yugoslavia: The United States Response*, Prepared Statement of Nikola J. Dragash, and Prepared Statement of Veljko Miljus, 102d Congress, 1st Sess., February 21, 1991 (S. Hrg. 102–12), pp. 54–60.
93. Andrejevich, "Croatia between Stability and Civil War (part 2)," pp. 38–43.
94. Andrejevich, "Croatia between Stability and Civil War (part 1)," p. 41.
95. Milan Andrejevich, "A Week of Great Political Importance," *RFE* 2, no. 3 (January 18, 1991): 26.
96. Robert M. Hayden, "Constitutional Nationalism in the Formerly Yugoslav Republics," *Slavic Review* 51, no. 4 (1992): 657–58.
97. Denitch, *Ethnic Nationalism*, p. 106.
98. Silber and Little, *Yugoslavia: Death of a Nation*, pp. 92–100.
99. Andrejevich, "Croatia between Stability and Civil War (part 2)," p. 39.
100. Milan Andrejevich, "State Presidency Agrees on Measures to Prevent Further Ethnic Violence," *RFE* 2, no. 23 (June 7, 1991): 19.
101. Andrejevich, "The Yugoslavia Crisis: No Solution in Sight," p. 38.
102. Aleksa Djilas, "The Nation That Wasn't," *The New Republic*, September 21, 1992, 25–31.
103. Quoted in *Facts on File*, October 14, 1988.
104. Viktor Zakelj, quoted in David Olive, *Political Babble: The 1,000 Dumbest Things Ever Said by Politicians* (New York: Wiley, 1992), p. 161.
105. Former U.S. Ambassador to Yugoslavia Warren Zimmermann called Milosevic "the slickest con man in the Balkans." Warren Zimmermann, quoted in Djilas, "A Profile of Slobodan Milosevic," p. 95. See also Glenny, *The Fall of Yugoslavia*, p. 36.
106. Andrejevich, "A Week of Great Political Importance," p. 26–19.
107. Andrejevich, "The Yugoslavia Crisis: No Solution in Sight," p. 34.
108. Andrejevich, "Croatia and Slovenia Propose Separation of Yugoslav Republics," *RFE* 2, no. 11 (March 15, 1991): 25–26.
109. Quoted in Silber and Little, *Yugoslavia: Death of a Nation*, p. 113.
110. Ibid., pp. 112–16.
111. "Weekly Record of Events," *RFE* 2, no. 11 (March 15, 1991): 26.
112. Silber and Little, *Yugoslavia: Death of a Nation*, pp. 119–21.
113. Andrejevich, "Retreating from the Brink of Collapse," *RFE* 2, no. 15 (April 12, 1991): 25–30.
114. "Yugoslav Crisis Eases; Republic Leaders in Talks," *Facts On File*, April 4, 1991, p. 245.
115. Silber and Little, *Yugoslavia: Death of a Nation*, pp. 141–42.
116. Glenny, *The Fall of Yugoslavia*, p. 38.
117. Norman Cigar, "The Serbo-Croatian War, 1991: Political and Military Dimensions," *Journal of Strategic Studies* 16, no. 3 (1993): 311.
118. Silber and Little, *Yugoslavia: Death of a Nation*, pp. 136–37, 140–44.
119. Judah, *The Serbs*, pp. 185–88.
120. BBC, *Yugoslavia: Death of a Nation*, videotape, part 3.
121. H. N. Brailsford, *Macedonia: Its Races and Their Future* (London: Methuen, 1906), pp. 101–3.
122. Hugh Poulton, *Who Are the Macedonians?* (Bloomington: Indiana University Press, 1995), pp. 101–2.

123. Stoyan Pribichevich, *Macedonia: Its People and History* (University Park: Pennsylvania State University Press, 1982), pp. 70–71.
124. See, e.g., Kyril Drezov, "Macedonian Identity: An Overview of the Major Claims," in *The New Macedonian Question*, ed. James Pettifer (New York: St. Martin's, 1999), pp. 47–59.
125. See Stavro Skendi, *The Albanian National Awakening, 1878–1912* (Princeton: Princeton University Press, 1967).
126. Predrag Simic, "The West and the Yugoslav Crisis," *Review of International Affairs* (Belgrade) 42, no. 985 (April 20, 1991): 5.
127. European Communities, "Declaration on Yugoslavia," March 26, 1991; and "Statement on Yugoslavia," Brussels, May 8, 1991, reprinted in *Review of International Affairs* (Belgrade) 42, no. 995–97: 19.
128. "U.S. Policy toward Yugoslavia," Statement Released by Margaret Tutwiler, May 24, 1991, *U.S. Department of State Dispatch*, June 3, 1991, p. 395.
129. Cohen, *Broken Bonds*, p. 218.
130. Rosalyn Higgins, "The New United Nations and the Former Yugoslavia," *International Affairs* 69, no. 3 (1993), 465–84, makes a similar argument concerning UN peacekeepers in Bosnia. Stephen Ryan, *Ethnic Conflict and International Relations* (Aldershot, England: Dartmouth, 1990), provides a general assessment of the value of peacekeepers in ethnic conflicts.
131. As Norman Cigar shows in "The Serbo-Croatian War," Croatian troops were able to defeat the Serb militias; the unofficial Serb groups were effective primarily at terrorizing and "cleansing" Croat civilians.
132. Myron Weiner, "The Macedonia Syndrome: An Historical Model of International Relations and Political Development," *World Politics* 23, no. 4 (1971): 665–83, argues that nothing less than regional hegemony by a major power can stop nationalist extremism of this kind. While this may not always be true, his insight does accurately reflect the degree of external effort required in such cases.

Chapter 7. The Power of Symbols

1. Exceptions include the journal *Political Communication* and the work of David O. Sears. See, e.g., David O. Sears, "Symbolic Politics: A Socio-Psychological Theory," in *Explorations in Political Psychology*, ed. Shanto Iyengar and William J. McGuire (Durham, N.C.: Duke University Press, 1993).
2. See, e.g., Touraj Atabaki, *Azerbaijan: Ethnicity and Autonomy in Twentieth Century Iran* (London: British Academic Press, 1993), p. 184; and David B. Nissman, *The Soviet Union and Iranian Azerbaijan: The Use of Nationalism for Political Penetration* (Boulder: Westview, 1987), p. 3.
3. A statement of the official Sindhi historical mythology is "Historical, Cultural Background and Geography of Sindh," Government of Sindh official website, http://Sindh.gov.pk.
4. See, e.g., Selig S. Harrison, "Ethnicity and the Political Stalemate in Pakistan," in *The State, Religion, and Ethnic Politics: Afghanistan, Iran, Pakistan*, ed. Ali Banuazizi and Myron Weiner (Syracuse: Syracuse University Press, 1986), pp. 267–95.
5. Lee Khoon Choy, *A Fragile Nation: The Indonesian Crisis* (Singapore: World Scientific, 1999).
6. See Donald Emmerson, "Will Indonesia Survive?" *Foreign Affairs* 79, no. 3 (2000): 95–106.

7. *Newsweek*, on-line version, January 17, 2000, p. 36.
8. The best treatment of this problem is Jack Snyder, *From Voting to Violence: Democratization and Nationalist Conflict* (New York: Norton, 2000).
9. Tim Judah, *The Serbs: History, Myth, and the Destruction of Yugoslavia* (New Haven: Yale University Press, 1997), p. 78.
10. Susan Allen Nan, "Complementarity and Coordination of Conflict Resolution Efforts in the Conflicts over Abkhazia, South Ossetia and Trandniestria," Ph.D. diss., George Mason University, 1999.
11. Jeremy D. Rosner, "The Know-Nothings Know Something," *Foreign Policy* 101 (Winter 1995–96): 119–28.
12. Stephen Van Evera, "Primed for Peace: Europe after the Cold War," *International Security* 15, no. 3 (1990/91).
13. A different version of this argument is put forward by constructivist theorists of international relations. See, e.g., Alexander Wendt, "Anarchy Is What States Make of It: The Social Construction of Power Politics," *International Organization* 46, no. 3 (1992): 391–425.

Index